Silvia Marino • Łucja Biel • Martina Bajčić • Vilelmini Sosoni
Editors

Language and Law

The Role of Language and Translation in EU Competition Law

Springer

Editors
Silvia Marino
Department of Law, Economics and Culture
University of Insubria
Como, Italy

Łucja Biel
Institute of Applied Linguistics
University of Warsaw
Warsaw, Poland

Martina Bajčić
Faculty of Law, Department of Foreign Languages
University of Rijeka
Rijeka, Croatia

Vilelmini Sosoni
Department of Foreign Languages, Translation & Interpretation
Ionian University
Corfu, Greece

The Project is co-financed by the Commission of the European Union, DG Competition (Ref.: HT: 4983, Call for proposals 2015: Training of National Judges in EU Competition Law and Judicial Cooperation between National Competition Law Judges).

ISBN 978-3-030-08128-7 ISBN 978-3-319-90905-9 (eBook)
https://doi.org/10.1007/978-3-319-90905-9

This Springer imprint is published by the registered company Springer Nature Switzerland AG
The registered company address is: Gewerbestrasse 11, 6330 Cham, Switzerland

Language and Law

Contents

Introduction: The Role of the Language in EU Law

Silvia Marino

1 Multilingualism in the EU as a Tool to strengthen Democracy

The European Union's (EU) legal system raises many challenges for the lawyer. One of those is multilingualism. All the legal acts and measures must be drafted in all the 24 official languages of the EU.[1] It is not the first example of a multilingual system, but it is surely the most prominent.

The idea behind this choice—i.e. the use of all the national official languages as EU official languages—is the promotion of the democratic principle within the EU. The possibility to use every official national language is a necessary tool in order to put EU citizens and institutions into contact. Furthermore, it makes some of the rights granted by the EU Treaties effective.

Article 24 of the Treaty on the Functioning of the European Union (TFEU) grants every EU citizen the right to address the EU institutions in any EU official language, and to receive an answer in the same language. This right is an integral part of the democratic principle, since it aims at creating a stable link between the citizens and the EU. Still, it would be a rather theoretical right, if the citizens were obliged to use a foreign language. The opportunity to use native languages makes it easier to contact the EU institutions effectively.

The same is true if we think of the rights to file a complaint with the European ombudsman (Article 228 TFEU), and to address a petition to the European Parliament (Article 227 TFEU).

[1] Regulation No 1, determining the languages to be used by the European Economic Community, as amended (OJ L 17, 6.10.1958, p. 385).

S. Marino (✉)
Department of Law, Economics and Culture, University of Insubria, Como, Italy
e-mail: silvia.marino@uninsubria.it

S. Marino et al. (eds.), *Language and Law*,
https://doi.org/10.1007/978-3-319-90905-9_1

Furthermore, all the legal binding acts addressed to the general public must be drafted in all the official languages. This rule safeguards the citizens' right to be able to understand the law: everyone can have a direct and effective access to the law. The Court of Justice of the European Union (CJEU) has already made it clear that an EU binding measure does not produce any effect against the citizens of a Member State, until it is published in the Official Journal in the official language of that Member State.[2]

EU citizens might have an active role within the EU, too. Under Article 2 of Protocol No 2 on the Application of the Principles of Subsidiarity and Proportionality, the Commission shall consult widely before proposing legislative acts. According to the general praxis, the Commission publishes a Green Paper, a non-binding document wherein the institution assesses the problem to be tackled, suggests possible solutions and submits questions to the civil society. Everyone is invited to give their view on the topic, following the guidelines and the queries presented by the Commission. The right to take part to consultations would prove, once more, highly ineffective if the Green Papers were written—and if the answers were acceptable—only in selected languages.

In this framework, the European ombudsman has already made it clear that EU citizens must be granted an effective right to take part to consultations.[3] Indeed, it is not reasonable to expect participation without understanding: if the consultations kick-off documents are drafted only in English, all the non-English speaking citizens are excluded, thus preventing from reaching the target of a *large* consultation. If there is no obligation to publish everything in every official language, restrictions must be objectively justified. Limited financial resources and time constraints do not amount to insurmountable difficulties in order to translate the consultation documents into all the official languages. The institutions must at least grant full or partial translations upon request, or give the basic information on the consultation in all the EU official languages.

2 Interpretation of Multilingual Treaties

Promoting the democratic principle through the use of native languages creates practical and economical difficulties related to the translation and the interpretation of all the EU legal binding and general measures. Indeed, the institutions use a selected group of working languages (usually English, French, German, to a more limited extent Spanish and Italian, and in the next future Polish), and the first draft of legal acts is submitted in one of those languages. Nevertheless, the transposition of

---

[2]Case C-161/06 *Skoma Lux* [2007] ECR I-10841, ECLI:EU:C:2007:773.

[3]Decision of the European Ombudsman closing his inquiry into complaint 640/2011/AN against the European Commission, 4 October 2012. Available via EUROPEAN OMBUDSMAN. https://www.ombudsman.europa.eu/en/cases/decision.faces/el/12009/html.bookmark. Accessed 15 Apr 2018.

legal concepts into many languages is not an automatic operation. Every legal concept has a precise meaning that could even not exist altogether in another legal system. The translation must be as accurate as possible: the output is legally not a *translation*, but an official version of the act. The existence of a number of official versions might bring interpretative concerns for the jurist.

According to the 1969 Vienna Convention on the Law of the Treaties, all the official languages have the same relevance. Therefore, the interpretation of a rule in an international Convention must take all the linguistic versions into due consideration, and look for a meaning that is acceptable in all of them (Article 33 of the Convention). Usually, international Conventions are written in no more than three languages. The United Nations Organisation has six official languages (English, French, Spanish, Russian, Arab, and Chinese). The challenge within the EU, with its 24 official languages, is apparently bigger.

The interpretation of EU Law does not disregard this fundamental general rule of international law. Many examples demonstrate that the CJEU analyses different linguistic versions in order to interpret the same rule, in all the fields within the EU competence. One of the most recent and meaningful examples is the *JZ* case.[4] The primary concern related to the meaning of the word 'detention' for the purpose of Article 26(1) of the framework Decision 2002/584 on the European arrest warrant. The Court scrutinised six different linguistic versions (German, Greek, French, English, Polish, and Dutch), dividing them into three groups, in order to demonstrate that the literal interpretation was not enough in order to reach a unique meaning of the word. Indeed, it gave rise to three possible different interpretations of the word.[5]

3 The Procedure for Preliminary Ruling in the EU

In this framework, the relevance of the procedure for preliminary ruling in the EU should be immediately clear. Only a central judicial body can have the necessary competence to duly scrutinise a multilingual text and to analyse its legal meaning and impact. An open oriented and comparative perspective can be more easily granted within a European body: the CJEU's judges come from all the Member States, and each of them can take advantage of the cooperation of other jurists—as the Advocates general and their collaborators.

This is one of the reasons for the extremely high success of the procedure for preliminary ruling. It is rather impossible for national Courts to face 24 different languages and 28 jurisdictions, given that the meaning of technical words and

[4]Case C-294/16 *JZ* [2016] ECLI:EU:C:2016:610.

[5]The first known case where the Court adopted a wide-linguistic approach expressly is the judgment issued on Case 29/69 *Stauder* [1969] ECR 419, ECLI:EU:C:1969:57. At the time, the EU counted only four official languages, but all of them were analysed in order to understand the exact meaning of the expression: *bon individualisé, buono individualizzato, auf ihren Namen ausgestellten Gitschein, op naam gestelde bon* (see Bajčić and Martinović in of this book).

expressions depends on national legal traditions. At the same time, one national legal and linguistic tradition cannot prevail over the others: such a solution would be discriminatory and might jeopardise the uniform interpretation and application of EU Law. Therefore, the CJEU has opted for an autonomous interpretation of EU Law. Since the EU is an own legal system autonomous from national jurisdictions, with special and original nature,[6] its law cannot be subject to national traditions and legal categories and cannot be interpreted according to national law. EU Law has its meaning, which might depend both on the comparison of the various linguistic versions and a legal comparative approach to the meaning of the words and expressions used in such linguistic versions. Furthermore, the judgment is binding *erga omnes*, i.e. not only on the requesting Court, but on all the bodies that will need to interpret and apply the rule in the future.

National judges are well aware of the impact of the procedure for preliminary ruling, as demonstrated by the statistics. In 2017, 533 requests for preliminary rulings were brought, which represents about 30% of all the cases filed with the CJEU (including the General Court).

This task is so important that national courts of last instance are under a duty to refer a preliminary question to the CJEU (Article 267 TFEU). The rule aims at granting the correct application of EU Law in last-instance cases, since no ordinary remedy against it is possible, and 'wrong' precedents issued by a generally highly distinguished national court might nevertheless influence the future case law.

4 The *Acte Claire* Principle

These duties are not without exception. According to the *CILFIT* judgment,[7] in three cases the duty becomes a faculty: the last instance Court has a full margin of appreciation in order to evaluate the opportunity to refer. One of these exceptions is a paramount example of the role of multilingualism in EU Law. There is no duty to refer to the CJEU if the rule to be interpreted and applied is *clear*. But what does *clear* mean in this framework, with 24 official languages and the scattered application of EU Law? In para. 16 the CJEU stated that:

> the correct application of Community law may be so obvious as to leave no scope for any reasonable doubt as to the manner in which the question raised is to be resolved. Before it comes to the conclusion that such is the case, the national court or tribunal must be convinced that the matter is equally obvious to the courts of the other Member States and to the Court of Justice.

The national court deciding the case must be convinced that the courts seating in other Member States would reach the same interpretative conclusion. It is not enough to refer to the legal categories of each legal system. The judge must also

[6]Case 6/64 *Costa c. ENEL* [1964] ECR 1141, ECLI:EU:C:1964:66.

[7]Case 283/81 *CILFIT* [1982] 3415, ECLI:EU:C:1982:335.

handle foreign linguistic versions and adopt a comparative approach. If this exception was read in a restrictive manner, finally it would have no scope of application: it would be rather impossible to reach the high level of certainty required by the CJEU. Nevertheless, the national court must be well aware of the fact that a purely national focus in not enough. We only need to remind that the incorrect application of EU Law by the last instance court might engage the civil responsibility of the State.[8] Still, the judge must make an effort to give justice to the parties while applying EU Law.

5 English as a *Lingua Franca*: The Perspective of a Jurist Within EU Competition Law

A common *lingua franca* can be extremely useful in that respect. English is a natural choice, because it is the language of economics, it is increasingly relevant in international relationships and it is the most commonly used language when national law (legislation, case law, praxis) is translated into another language.

In very technical subject matters such as Competition Law, where legal, economical and complicated factual issues are at stake, the understanding of more than one language can help Courts in carrying out their tasks. Regulation No 1/2003[9] and Directive 2014/104/UE[10] long for a cooperation among different authorities. National courts might need to work with the EU Commission, to read foreign National Competition Authorities decisions and to take into consideration proceedings pending before foreign courts. All these players must therefore have a linguistic tool in order to cooperate, but must be aware, too, of the dangers of its use. A mere literal translation from the national language into English might be misleading, when cooperating with foreign authorities/judges (whose native language might not be English).

Moreover, English is a language of a common law system. However, within the EU, it is used among predominantly civil law systems of the Member States. This brings to a development of the English language, when used by non-native speakers and within the EU. The path is towards simplification, where originally technical terms of the British—English language lose their original meaning, and new meanings are associated to traditional technical words and expression.

[8]Case C-224/01 *Köbler* [2003] ECR I-10239, ECLI:EU:C:2003:513; Case C-168/15 *Tomášová* [2016] ECLI:EU:C:2016:602.

[9]Council Regulation (EC) No 1/2003 of 16 December 2002 on the implementation of the rules on competition laid down in Articles 81 and 82 of the Treaty (OJ L 1, 4.1.2001, p. 1).

[10]Directive 2014/104/EU of the European Parliament and of the Council of 26 November 2014 on certain rules governing actions for damages under national law for infringements of the competition law provisions of the Member States and of the European Union (OJ L 349, 5.12.2014, p. 1).

In this framework, the knowledge of the language could not be enough. Rather, we need to scrutinise what lies behind interpretation, translation and the development of the language(s).

The studies collected here are part of the biennial projet *Training action for legal practitioners: Linguistic skills and translation in EU Competition Law*, funded by the European Commission and developed in two seminaries in Como, Italy, and Warsaw, Poland, with the participation of Università degli Studi dell'Insubria, Uniwersytet Warszawski, Ionian University, University of Rijeka-Jean Monnet Inter-University Centre of Excellence Opatija and Universidad de Burgos. The Editors wish to thank the Italian and the Greek Antitrust Authority and all the experts, for their partecipations in the seminars, and for the contribution given in this book.

The first part collects studies on current legal issues in EU Competition Law; the second focuses on the key linguistic problems, with special regard to the use of English as a "common" language in international and intra-EU relationships.

Silvia Marino is Professor of European Union Law at the University of Insubria, Varese and Como, Italy, and Coordinator of the Project "Training Action for Legal Practitioners: Linguistic Skills and Translation in EU Competition Law".

Part I
Public and Private Enforcement of EU Law in a Cooperative Perspective

On Economic Rationale of Competition Policy

Flavia Cortelezzi

Abstract The aim of this contribution is to briefly explore the economic foundation of competition policy and its main goals established in the European Union. The economic rationale of competition policy lies in teleological and deontological theories and its main objectives are consumer welfare, society welfare and an efficient allocation of resources. Another type of efficiency goal regards a pluralistic market or a free market, on which everyone can compete. We conclude discussing the non-efficiency goals, which are nowadays at the heart of the debate.

1 Introduction

Competition Law plays a prominent role in the business environment of many nations. Indeed, if one is a newspaper reader, the chances are good of seeing in any given week at least one article devoted to some aspect of antitrust policy, whether about a recently announced merger of two large companies, a case alleging that an important software company has violated the antitrust laws by suppressing competition, or the disclosure that a group of international firms producing an important food additive have conspired to fix prices. A significant statement why competition and, thus, competition policy is important for everyone was provided by the European Competition Commissioner Joaquín Almunia in a speech in February 2011[1]:

> Ladies and Gentlemen: Competition is an instrument, not an end in itself. But it is indeed a vital instrument in very many respects. Without fair, robust, and effective competition policy and enforcement, I don't see how we Europeans can overcome the crisis rapidly and shape up to compete with the other, dynamic players that are increasingly present on the world

[1]European Commission (2011) The European Commission Press Release Database. http://europa.eu/rapid/pressReleasesAction.do?reference=SPEECH/11/96&format=HTML&aged=0&language=EN&guiLanguage=en. Accessed 15 Apr 2018.

F. Cortelezzi (✉)
University of Insubria, Como, Italy
e-mail: flavia.cortelezzi@uninsubria.it

S. Marino et al. (eds.), *Language and Law*,
https://doi.org/10.1007/978-3-319-90905-9_2

> scene. Of course, competition is not the only tool we should use to pursue this goal. But we need a vibrant and competitive environment in the single market if we are serious about leading in the information age. We need competition to be equal partners with the US, China, and the other leading global players; we need competition to grow; we need competition to preserve our social model for the benefit of our citizens and of the future generations. Considering our demographic trends and the imperative task of building sustainable and green economic and social models, Europe needs all its resources and resourcefulness. The EU competition system is one of the best, if not the best in the world. My commitment is to use it to the full extent of the law, because I am convinced that this is what I must do within my area of responsibility to contribute to a better future for Europe. Thank you.

Thus, economics lies at the heart of Competition, or Antitrust, Law. This section is intended to serve as an introduction to the economics behind antitrust policies. While in the early days the application of antitrust rules was almost entirely left to experts with only a legal background, it is now widely accepted that the proper interpretation of these rules requires an understanding of how markets work and of how firms can alter their efficient functioning. This knowledge is the realm of economic science.[2] As the awareness of the central role of economics in antitrust has progressed, so has the research. An industrial economist would probably say that the growth in the demand for economic knowledge coming from administrative bodies, courts, companies, and lawyers (in short, the antitrust community) has led to a reorganization of the industry, with a sharp increase in the supply of new theoretical models and more reliable empirical methods. This reorganization has taken place mostly over the last 30 years or so, and has significantly changed the landscape.

Firms might restrict competition in a way which is not detrimental.[3] Let us consider the case of an industry with no barriers to entry. One might think that market forces, and in particular the threat of new entrants, will eliminate monopolies or dominant positions and reduce prices. Yet, firms might resort to anti-competitive actions that create a dominant (or monopolistic) position and, more generally, to actions that increase their profits, but reduce welfare: collusive agreements (e.g. the lysine cartel was formed by ADM and several large Asian rivals), anti-competitive mergers (e.g. Coke with Dr Pepper) and exclusionary behaviour (e.g. US vs Microsoft) are cases in point. Collusive agreements can take different forms: firms might agree on sales prices, allocate quotas among themselves, divide markets so that some firms decide not to be present in certain markets in exchange for being the sole seller in others, or coordinate their behaviour along some other dimensions. Collusive practice allows firms to exert market power they would otherwise have, and artificially restricts competition to increase prices, thereby reducing welfare. Mergers—in particular mergers between competitors—might allow both the merged firm to unilaterally exercise market power and raise prices, and favours collusion in the industry. In this last case, the merging firm would not be able to unilaterally raise

[2]The role of economists in European Competition Law enforcement (the so-called more economic approach) has been described by the former chief economist at DG-Comp, Lars-Hendrik Röller. He makes it clear that the "question for effective enforcement is not one of "more" or "less" economics, but rather what kind of economics and especially how economic analysis is used [...]." (2005), p. 11.

[3]For a more detailed discussion, see Motta (2004).

prices in a significant way, but the merger could generate new industry conditions which enhance the scope for collusion. Prices could than increase as firms are more likely to attain a (tacitly or explicitly) collusive outcome. Still, in most markets, producers do not sell their goods directly, but reach final customers through intermediaries, wholesalers and retailers. Further, in many cases production of the final good is made up of several stages, from the raw material, to the intermediate good, to the final product. At the various stages of the vertical process, firms do not simply rely on spot market transactions, but engage in contracts of various types that are signed in order to reduce transaction costs, guarantee stability of supplies, and better coordinated actions. These agreements are called vertical restraints, i.e. a party can try to use contracts and clauses so as to limit the choice of the other and induce an outcome which is more favourable to this party. Finally, Monti (2007) presents the Staples-case from the 1990s as an early example of empirical fact-finding:

> Increased empirical attention to the specific circumstances in an industry had an impact on the Federal Trade Commission v. Staples merger decision. The nub of the dispute was market definition: the parties to the merger (Staples and Office Depot, the two largest office superstore chains in the US) claimed that the relevant market was the sale of consumable office products through all retail outlets, where the firms held a combined market share of 5.5 per cent, which posed no anticompetitive risks. However, the FTC (Federal Trade Commission) defined the market as one for consumable office supplies sold through office superstores. From a Chicago School approach, this narrow market makes little sense: a pen is a pen wherever it is purchased, and as consumers shop around for the cheapest deal, any attempt by office superstores to raise prices will lead to a loss of sales to other retail outlets. This intuition about the consumer's shopping skills was however denied by the facts: there were three main office superstores in the US and in the geographical areas where Staples faced no competition prices were 13 per cent higher than in markets where Staples competed with Office Depot and Office Max; similarly Office Depot's prices were well over 5 per cent higher in areas where it faced no competition. Moreover, the FTC constructed econometric models that demonstrated how little impact other retail outlets have on the pricing decisions of office superstores, and that if all three office superstores were to merge, prices would increase by 8.49 per cent. This econometric evidence led the FTC to conclude that the prices of goods in office superstores are affected primarily by the other office superstores, and that non-superstore competition is not a significant check on prices. Thus, before the merger, the three superstores already enjoyed a degree of market power, which the merger would enhance by eliminating a particularly aggressive competitor. The decision is significant for its use of econometric studies to identify a competition risk which on a cursory analysis, biased by presumptions about consumer reactions to higher prices, appeared unrealistic.

For all these reasons, Competition Law and competition authorities that enforce these laws are necessary.[4]

This section does not strive to be comprehensive in its coverage. Rather, I focus selectively on three main elements. The first regards philosophical and economical theories behind Competition policy. The second is related to the objectives that Competition policies should pursue. Finally, I turn my attention to some 'non efficiency' considerations that have, at different, times influenced the enforcement of competition policy.

---

[4]Baker (2003) provides more evidence of the necessity and success of antitrust enforcement.

2 Economic and Philosophical Theories Behind Competition Policy

When analysing Competition Law from an economic point of view, we need the classical distinction between two types of ethical theories, i.e. teleological theories on the one hand, and deontological theories on the other.[5] This distinction is usually understood in terms of the two concepts that are perhaps most basic to ethical reasoning at large, i.e. right and good. In teleological theories, the good has conceptual priority over the right. Typically, they define what it means for a thing or a state of affairs to be good, and then what it means for an act or a life to be morally high. A crucial point is that "the good is defined independently of the right". Consequently, non-teleological theories are exactly those which either dispute that there can be an ethically relevant independent definition of the good. Non-teleological ethical doctrines are commonly referred to as deontological. Both approaches are therefore based on strong theoretical foundation. In what follows, we explain why they are so relevant in competition policy.

2.1 *Utilitarianism and Teleological Theories*

Teleological ethics is best represented by utilitarianism. Roughly speaking, classic utilitarianism is associated to the views that:

(i) pleasure is the relevant concept of the individual's good
(ii) the right action is that which maximises the total sum of individual amounts of good.

As is generally known, utilitarianism *à la* Bentham allows individual agents to have moral preferences and to act in the interest of others, when action toward others generates a net utility gain for the individual.[6] However, the original Benthamite utilitarian principle of comparing individual utility is rejected in welfare economics and replaced by the Paretian principle,[7] which states that we can only identify situations where no one can be better off without making someone else worse off. Whenever a situation is Pareto optimal, it means that the utility is distributed in the most economical efficient way.

For welfare economics, the Pareto optimality can be achieved in the economy only if the choices of individuals are based on the "self-interest behaviour". Thus, it is strictly related to the results of a market operating under perfect competition. When there are no external influencing factors to the market, a competitive market is

[5]For an extended discussion on this topic see, e.g., Mongin and D'Aspremont (1998).

[6]Baker (1996).

[7]See, e.g. Carlton and Perloff (2004) and Mankiw (2003) for a detailed discussion on Pareto principle.

always Pareto optimal. The balance is the opposite, i.e. a Pareto optimal market is equal to perfect Competition, when there are especially “no economics of large scale” and “for some initial distribution of endowments”. By using the theory of Pareto optimality, ethical statements of what is a ‘good’ life, is directly connected with efficiency.

According to the proponents of utilitarianism, when there is an efficient allocation of resources,[8] the market reflects an ideal state of market structure and competition platform.

The aim of perfect competition is to create efficient results and the meaning of such results is that it creates efficient positions, i.e. positions in which everyone is the best as they can be without lowering the benefits of anyone else.

Applied to Competition Law, the utilitarian approach means that the most benefits should be given to the consumers and as such, the society as a whole. Competition as an object in itself is not important as long as the welfare in a society is maximised. Thus, Competition is not an independent economic value. Competition is perceived, as a way to achieve something which *ipso facto* has a higher value than competition itself, i.e. welfare. The importance of the utilitarian perception of Competition is beyond dispute. However, the question remains ‘the importance’ for ‘what’? An instrumentalised Competition policy can indeed be beneficial for welfare, innovation, industrial growth and market integration. But should it constitute the core of antitrust analysis? Does it fill in the whole value spectrum of competition? Does not competition itself constitute an important societal interest that could be seen independently from its welfare-maximising effects? Is it not for consumer policy to deal with the interests of consumers? Should industrial, innovation and market integration policies not deal with their respective goals by themselves? The utilitarian vision of competition is therefore contestable.

If utilitarian goals, such as consumer welfare or efficiency, are considered to be the only reason for antitrust policy to exist, then antitrust policy becomes consequentialist (“the ends justify the means” type of reasoning). In this case the very principle of a free market with undistorted competition is under threat. Whenever greater efficiency can be achieved through dirigistic regulatory practices (understood in this context as the practices that go against the free market), competition standards would be considered as an obstacle for generating efficiency, thereby losing any economic justification, legitimacy and, eventually, legality.

It should also be noted that the Paretian principle rejects redistributions, thus removing the moral basis of utilitarianism from welfare economics. Critics of the utilitarian approach hold that even though the overall utilitarian objective is good, the lack of an overall aim of equal distribution makes the theory morally blind and therefore wrong.

---

[8]The efficient allocation of resources, which is one of the main objectives of Article 101 of the Treaty on the Functioning of the European Union (TFEU) according to the Commission’s guidelines.

A major alternative to utilitarianism, which has attracted the attention of many economists, is deontology.

2.2 Deontological Theories

The deontological approach to ethics regards morality as a duty, or a moral rule that ought to be followed. Deontological ethics is about following universal norms that prescribe what people ought to do, how they should behave, and what is right or wrong.[9] It is a morality of principles,[10] not of consequences. Deontology resides in reason, not in utility providing feelings.

At a first sight, deontology and economics do not seem to be compatible. Whereas economics is concerned with behaviours characterised by choices and ends, deontology is concerned with behaviour characterised by duties and limitations. While economics is about markets and allocation problems, deontology implies a rule setting authority and distribution problems. As it is widely acknowledged among economists, an economy can function only when certain normative requirements are fulfilled. Rights such as property rights and contractual rights, and norms, i.e. formal and informal institutions, have been widely understood to influence the economic behaviour of individual agents, firms, and the State, as constraints on choice. Moral rules limit choices, but these limits are necessary to ensure that people are free to trade and that they will not reduce other people's freedom to trade. Such constraints are often concerned with ensuring free markets; they range from protecting property rights to rules for free competition, such as antitrust laws, prohibitions on insider trading, and anti dumping regulations. These are all examples of deontological ethics, and express the Kantian idea of equality applied to markets, thereby ensuring fair competition.

In this sense, competition should be protected and fostered with no direct subordination to its eventual outcomes, but as an important element of freedom.

Deontological competition theories have raised concerns with the instrumentalisation of competition by utilitarian antitrust theories. In fact, according to these theories competition is an end in itself and not something used to justify other objectives. Consequently, deontological proponents do not care about the end result of a conduct, only that the market is regulated in such a way that it generates the most freedom for individuals. This is preserved in a liberal democracy, where State interference is minimised.

---

[9]Moral judgment derives from the correct understanding of the rightness/wrongness distinction.

[10]The maxim of an action is a moral principle only if it is universalisable. This condition is contained in the so-called Categorical Imperative: "Act only on the maxim through which you can at the same time will that it be a universal law".

Most of the supporters of the deontological view on competition developed their ideas within the tradition of the Austrian and Ordoliberal Schools.[11]

They are both considering the main objective of Competition Law to be the establishment of a pluralistic market structure with a free competition as an end in itself. The differences between them relate to their perspective on the authority and the measures best used to "establish, maintain, protect and promote competition" as well as the concepts of individual and collective rights. It may also be called disciplined pluralism, i.e. all individuals should allow all individuals to participate unhampered by the economic power of the others (pluralism) while the risk of monopolies or cartels necessitates laws to sustain economic freedom (discipline).

> In [the light of ordoliberalism] the discipline of the market is as fundamental as contract law or property rights. [. . .] liberal discourse is based on the values of personal liberty and equality; in contrast, the neo-classical definition of competition is embedded in utilitarian and laissez-faire economic philosophy, where intervention is called for as a second best, when the market fails to deliver economic efficiency [. . .]. [In contrast], ordoliberalism necessitates rules that safeguard economic freedom in the marketplace by imposing obligations of fair conduct and suppressing economic power.[12]

However, in many cases the design practice of competition policy is the same in the neoclassical and Ordoliberal view of competition.

These two schools are substantially divided in their perception of the role of competition in economic life and even more explicitly on the mechanisms applied by States in order to establish, maintain, protect and promote competition. Leaving aside the discrepancies, their conceptual similarities are more important for our aim. Methodologically, both perceive the phenomenon of competition separately from the outcomes which competition can eventually generate. Both submit that in some cases competition should be protected as an independent economic value.

This implies the conceptual recognition of situations where competition can be protected even though it does not generate any measurable economic benefits and sometimes even if such benefits are diminished or sacrificed. Competition is protected therefore as a matter of evolutionary choice and an important societal value.

---

[11]The ideas developed by the Austrian school are based upon the deep ideological roots of *laissez-faire* individualism. Unlike mainstream neo-classical schools, Austrians see competition as a process of the spontaneous interaction, inspired by the entrepreneurial endeavours of individuals. The dynamism and unpredictability of this conception of Competition distinguish it from most of the other antitrust schools. The Austrians are known to be strong advocates of the minimalist State, claiming that the invisibility of the market's hand cannot be replaced or even improved by the rational actions of policy-makers. The Ordoliberal thought is much more sceptical in its assessment of the capacity of the unregulated economy to be self-sufficient or even sustainable. According to them, Competition cannot exist without strong regulatory interventions by the State, which should prevent any abuse of this delicate model.

[12]Monti (2007), pp. 23–24.

3 Competition Policy and Regulation

It is worth noticing that we talk about competition (or antitrust) policy, and not about regulation. In general, competition policy tends to apply quite broadly, and focuses on maintaining certain basic rules of competition that enable the competitive interaction among firms in the marketplace to produce good outcomes. Competition policy applies to sectors where structural conditions are compatible with a normal functioning of competition (whether the market functions well in practice or not is another matter).

Instead, regulation applies to special sectors, whose structure is such that one would not expect competitive forces to operate without problems. Regulation tends to be industry-specific and to involve the direct setting of prices, product characteristics, and entry, usually after regular and elaborate hearings. Regulation would usually concern markets where fixed costs are so high that no more than one firm would profitably operate (natural monopoly): examples might be electricity and railways (networks).

3.1 Scope and Definition of Competition Policy

> Principally, the need for competition law intervention arises when there is a market failure – so long as markets remain competitive, consumers benefit from low prices and innovative products because firms are driven by the desire to maximise profits and sell as many goods as is economically feasible at the lowest price. The market system is perceived to be the ideal mechanism through which the fundamental economic questions are answered: what goods to produce, how many to produce, and how to distribute them.[13]

Thus, the aim of Competition policy is to promote the competitiveness of markets and prevent distortions of market outcomes. In Europe, this is specified in Articles 3 and 119 of the Treaty on the Functioning of the European Union (TFEU):

> The Union shall have exclusive competence in [. . .] the establishing of the competition rules necessary for the functioning of the internal market

according to "the principle of an open market economy with free competition".

The role of Competition policy is controversially debated. According to Monti (2007)

> it is impossible to identify the 'soul' of competition law; the most that can be done is to show that there are different, equally legitimate opinions of what competition policy should achieve. Moreover, within each country, the purposes of competition law can change over time, even without an amendment to the legislative texts. [. . .] Understanding competition law thus is not only about dissecting legislative texts [. . .] but is also about understanding the particular forces that have influenced the direction of competition policy at particular times.

[13]Monti (2007), p. 55.

Competition policy basically covers two elements:

1. The first involves putting in place a set of policies that promote competition in local and national markets, such as introducing an enhanced trade policy, eliminating restrictive trade practices, favouring market entry and exit, reducing unnecessary governmental interventions and putting greater reliance on market forces.
2. The second, known as Competition Law, comprises legislation, judicial decisions and regulations specifically aimed at preventing anti-competitive business practices, abuse of market power and anti-competitive mergers. It generally focuses on the control of restrictive trade (business) practices (such as anti-competitive agreements and abuse of a dominant position) and anti-competitive mergers and may also include provisions on unfair trade practices.

Therefore, it can be broadly defined as a governmental policy that promotes or maintains the level of competition in markets, and includes governmental measures that directly affect the behaviour of enterprises and the structure of industry and markets.

3.2 *The Benefits of Competition Policy*

The introduction of a Competition Law will provide the market with a set of "rules of the game" that protects the competition process itself, rather than competitors in the market.

In this way, the pursuit of fair or effective competition can contribute to improvements in

(i) economic efficiency
(ii) economic growth and development
(iii) consumer welfare.

Economic efficiency refers to the effective use and allocation of the economy's resources. Competition tends to bring about enhanced efficiency, in both a static and a dynamic sense, by disciplining firms to produce at the lowest possible cost and pass these cost savings on to consumers, besides motivating firms to undertake research and development to meet customer needs. Competition policy contributes to economic growth to the ultimate benefit of consumers, i.e. welfare, in terms of better choice (new products), better quality and lower prices. Consumer welfare protection may be required in order to redress a perceived imbalance between the market power of consumers and producers. The imbalance between consumers and producers may stem from market failures such as information asymmetries, the lack of bargaining position towards producers and high transaction costs. Competition policy may serve as a complement to consumer protection policies to address such market failures. Finally, as far as economic growth and development are concerned, the increase in the value of goods and services produced by an economy is a key indicator of economic development. Economic development refers to a broader definition of an economy's well being, including employment growth, literacy and mortality rates and other measures of quality of life. Competition may bring about greater economic growth and development through improvements in economic efficiency and the reduction of wastage in the production of goods and services. The market is therefore able to reallocate resources more rapidly, improve productivity and attain a higher level of economic growth. Over time, sustained economic growth tends to lead to an enhanced quality of life and greater economic development. In addition, competition policy is also beneficial to developing countries. Due to worldwide deregulation, privatisation and liberalisation of markets, developing countries need a competition policy, in order to monitor and control the growing role of the private sector in the economy so as to ensure that public monopolies are not simply replaced by private monopolies.

Competition policy complements trade policy, industrial policy and regulatory reform. Competition policy targets business conduct that limits market access and reduces actual and potential competition, while trade and industrial policies encourage adjustment to the trade and industrial structures in order to promote productivity-based growth and regulatory reform eliminates domestic regulation that restricts entry and exit in the markets. Effective competition policy can also increase investor confidence and prevent the benefits of trade from being lost through anticompetitive practices. In this way, competition policy can be an important factor in enhancing the attractiveness of an economy to foreign direct investment, and in maximising the benefits of foreign investment.

4 Efficiency and Non-Efficiency Objectives of Competition Policy

The debate about the desirable objectives of EU Competition Law is complex. Monti (2007) considers it

> helpful to think about the factors that influence competition law and the decisions that stem from those rules on the basis of the interactions of three components: a political decision about the aims of competition law; an economic theory about how markets behave, how and when they fail, and how market failures may be remedied; and the institution in charge of enforcing competition law.

Based on this classification, three questions arise.

1. A Political question: Should competition policy (only) be concerned with economic welfare, i.e. maximising productive, allocative, and dynamic efficiency, or should it be used to pursue a variety of other goals, for example to maximise economic freedom, preserve employment, promote national champions, facilitate restructuring, protect small firms, safeguard cultural values, conserve the environment, and so on
2. An Economic questions: Should Competition policy be concerned with creating industry structures that make adverse effects to welfare unlikely, e.g. promoting the number of

firms in an industry? Which welfare measures should be used, i.e. should competition policy be concerned with maximising total welfare or consumer surplus?
3. An Institutional question: It should be decided whether the enforcement should be done by independent (judicative and/or administrative) bodies or by legislative/governmental bodies. In the former case, one has to decide whether competition authorities may decide cases (in the first instance) or whether the decision must be made by a court. The latter case is most relevant when competition policy is designed to achieve goals beyond maximising economic welfare.[14]

In this section, we concentrate on the economic questions and the political and institutional questions are addressed only briefly. On an economic ground we distinguish efficiency and non-efficiency goals. The efficiency goals can be summarised into two different fields. On one hand we have the approach supporting consumer welfare and efficiency. This includes consumer welfare, society welfare and an effective allocation of resources. The other type of efficiency goal is a pluralistic market or a free market, on which everyone can compete. We should also consider other types of objectives that have been discussed in relation to EU Competition Law, the so-called non-efficiency objectives. According to Townley,[15] these objectives should be considered part of the consumer welfare test and if so, they are not an objective in itself. The debate about non-efficiency goals has been seen as an important contribution to the debate about the objectives of EU Competition Law. In what follows, we first discuss the efficiency objectives and then the non-efficiency objectives.

4.1 *The Efficiency Objectives in Competition Policy*

We first focus on the efficiency goals supporting welfare. Economic welfare is the standard concept used in economics to measure how well an industry performs. It aggregates the welfare of different groups in the economy. In general, welfare is given by total surplus, i.e. the sum of consumer and producer surplus. The surplus of an individual is given by the difference between his or her willingness to pay for the good considered and the price he or she has to pay for it. Consumer surplus (or welfare) is the aggregate measure of the surplus of all consumers. Producer surplus (or welfare) is the sum of all profits of all producers in the same industry. From this definition, it follows that an increase of the price at which goods are sold reduces consumer surplus and increases producer surplus. It turns out that welfare is the lowest when the market price equals the monopoly price, and the highest when it

[14]Monti (2007), p. 4.

[15]Townley (2008, 2011).

equals the marginal cost of production (it is the case of perfect competition). It is worth noticing that it overlooks the issue of income distribution among consumers and producers. Thus, economic welfare is a measure of how efficient is a given industry as a whole.[16]

In most circumstances a decrease in total welfare brings about a decrease of consumer welfare and *vice versa*. However, this is not always the case. For example, perfect price discrimination maximises welfare to the detriment of consumers; a merger that allows merging firms to decrease their fixed costs might increase total welfare while increasing prices and thus decreasing consumer welfare.

Consumer welfare as a short-term goal has long been criticised in that it does not value dynamic efficiency, i.e. if the focus is on maximising consumer surplus and there are no incentives to invest for the producers. Of course, there are clearly some industries (e.g. medicines and cures for deadly illnesses) where innovations are essential for the society to develop. Everyone in the society benefits from these investments but the initial costs are extremely high for the companies and, thus, the incentives to innovate cannot be totally unprotected. Consumer welfare as a long-term goal considers producer surplus insofar as it ultimately creates benefits for the consumers. Consumer welfare as a long-term goal has been criticised for three main reasons.

It is difficult to say whether competition authorities and courts favour in practice consumer welfare or total welfare objectives. Different jurisdictions seem to have different objectives. In the EU, Article 81(3) TFEU allows agreement, decision or concerned practice

> which contributes to improving the production or distribution of goods [. . .], *while allowing consumers a fair share of the resulting benefit.* (emphasis added)

Furthermore, Article 2(1) of the Merger Regulation accepts in principle an efficiency defence "provided that it is to consumers' advantage".[17] This provision may indicate that consumer welfare is the ultimate objective of Competition Law. In the US, both the courts and the antitrust agencies seem to tend for a consumer

---

[16]'Economic welfare [emphasis added] is one of the anticipated benefits of membership of the EC, and the Commission noted the contribution of competition policy to economic efficiency early on. In the First Report on Competition Policy we find this passage: Competition is the best stimulant of economic activity since it guarantees the widest possible freedom of action to all. An active competition policy pursued in accordance with the provisions of the Treaties establishing the Communities makes it easier for the supply and demand structures continually to adjust to technological development. Through the interplay of the decentralised decision-making machinery, competition enables enterprises to improve their efficiency continuously, which is the sine qua non for the steady improvement in living standards and employment prospects of the Community' (Monti (2007), p. 44).

[17]Council Regulation (EC) No 139/2004 of 20 January 2004 on the control of concentrations between undertakings (the EC Merger Regulation) (OJ L 24, 29.1.2004, p. 1).

welfare standard. In other jurisdictions, e.g. Canada, Australia and New Zealand, competition authorities seem instead to lean toward a total welfare standard.

The main difference between consumer welfare and social welfare is related to the view on the redistribution of wealth. Consumer welfare is considered to be a regressive form of redistribution with the aim of transferring "the wealth from individuals with a lower marginal utility of income to individuals with a higher marginal utility of income". Social welfare is, on the other hand, a more natural way of redistributing the wealth in a society.

Besides contributing to trade and investment policies, competition policy can accommodate other policy objectives (both economic and social) such as the integration of national markets and promotion of regional integration, the promotion or protection of small businesses, the promotion of technological advancement, the promotion of product and process innovation, the promotion of industrial diversification, environment protection, fighting inflation, job creation, equal treatment of workers according to race and gender or the promotion of welfare of particular consumer groups.

Let us focus on the following general objectives, which have been indicated in different circumstances and in different jurisdictions as the ones competition policy should pursue:

(i) Defence of smaller firms
(ii) Promoting market integration
(iii) Economic freedom
(iv) Fighting inflation
(v) Fairness and equity.

The objective of maintaining a pluralistic market structure (iii) or a free market (i) means that small firms should be protected, barriers to enter should not exist and there should be a the possibility for everyone to compete on the market since they are the essence of competition itself. The Ordoliberal theory believes that competition is necessary in order to ensure economic development and the creation of a free market economy. Protection of the freedom to compete may help to weaken the economic power of dominant undertakings and achieved deconcentrated markets. Ordoliberal theories should be viewed as an attempt to preserve political democracy. Thus, the favourable treatment of small firms is not necessarily in contrast with the objective of economic welfare if it is limited to protecting such firms from the abuse of larger enterprises, or giving them a small advantage to balance the financial and economic power of larger rivals. On the contrary, helping small firms to survive when they are not operating at an efficient scale of production is in contrast with economic welfare objectives. This would encourage inefficient allocation of resources and would contribute to keep high prices in the economies. The European Commission seems to have taken the view that small or medium-sized enterprises (SMEs) are dynamic, more likely to create employment than large firms, and more likely to create innovation (empirical arguments are quite ambiguous on this topic). Thus, competition authorities do not use their scarce resources to monitor agreements and mergers that involve SME(s).

Promoting market integration (ii) is one of the key objectives of EU Competition Law as stated by the Treaty. It is a political objective, not necessarily consistent with economic welfare. Precisely, EU Competition Law forbids price discrimination across national borders since there is no economic rationale for such a different treatment. Motta suggests the following example.[18] Let us consider two countries, e.g. Germany and Portugal, characterised by different income and willingness to pay (Germany is a high income country with a higher willingness to pay). If the firms were able to set different prices in the two countries, they would increase their profits. If the firms were obliged to set identical prices, Germans would be better off. In this case, the welfare effect is ambiguous. By setting the highest price, the firms would loose the Portuguese market. If this second strategy prevails, the prohibition of price discrimination increases the differences in market conditions between Germany and Portugal.

EU Competition Law includes one objective that is not present in, e.g., US-American or German Competition Law, i.e. the goal of establishing a single market. Article 26 TFEU specifies that the

> Union shall adopt measures with the aim of establishing or ensuring the functioning of the internal market [. . . that comprises] an area without internal frontiers in which the free movement of goods, persons, services and capital is ensured [. . .].
>
> Some eminent scholars and the Commission have gone so far as to say that market integration is the 'first principle' of EC competition policy.[19]

In the light of this objective, Article 101 TFEU (see European Commission 2011) prohibits anticompetitive agreements between firms which may affect trade between Member States while Article 102 prohibits any "abuse [. . .] of a dominant position [. . .] in so far as it may affect trade between Member States". The main concern is that firms may create market divisions, e.g., agreements on the allocation of exclusive territories, the prevention of parallel trade between Member States, or price discrimination across Member States.[20]

Thus, a *per se* rule which forbids firms from price discriminating across countries is not justified on economic welfare grounds, and might work against the objective of market integration and in some circumstances might even work against the objective of market integration.

Competition Laws might incorporate objectives such as (iv) fighting inflation, (v) fairness and equity. Fighting inflation has been indicated as a reason for introducing control over cartels in Germany. However, it is not clear if Competition policy can be used to attain such objective. As for fairness, Competition Law can be used to prevent dominant firms from charging excessive prices (Article 82 TFEU, see European Commission 2009). As for equity, firms should have the same initial opportunities in the marketplace. This objective is compatible with Competition

[18]Motta (2004).

[19]Monti (2007), p. 39.

[20]See, for further details, Jones and Sufrin (2014).

policy, which should guarantee a level playing field for all the firms. *Ex-post* equity, i.e. equal outcomes of market competition, does not necessarily coincide with competition policy.

4.2 Non-Efficiency Goals

A number of public policy considerations often affect Competition Laws and their enforcement. It is easy to verify that competition authorities and courts often adopt weaker stances[21] on competition issues than economic considerations alone would have suggested, due to social, political or strategic reasons. The debate today concerns *inter alia* the question whether non-efficiency goals should be a part of the objectives of EU Competition Law. However, there is no clear definition of what would count as a non-efficiency goal if non-efficiency goals were to be applied in EU Competition Law matters. The OCED defines non-efficiency goals, in relation to Competition Law, as broader social or industrial policy goals that could be linked to economic efficiency. These broader goals are "public goals and public interests other than competition and economic efficiency". This definition includes e.g. benefits from creating new employments, protection of the environment, health and safety of individuals and promoting ethical behaviour. Such goals have in some cases been considered by the EU Courts in Competition Law cases but there is no consistency in the Courts' precedents. However, the question of whether and when public policies should be relevant to EU Competition Law is a hard one to answer and it has been argued that a consideration of non-efficiency goals requires a more systematic and theological approach to the overall objectives of the Treaty than is usually undertaken by the courts.

In a past decision, the Commission, for example, approved an agreement among producers and importers of washing machines that together account for more that 95% of European sales. The agreement aims at discontinuing production and imports

[21]Part of the ongoing debate relating to what the objectives of EU competition law should be is the question of what weight should be given to non-efficiency goals. It has been argued that the Commission's views of using non-efficiency goals as a defense for an anti-competitive behaviour "have hardened over time", giving more weight to non-efficiency goals. The statement is focusing on the Commission's ruling in CECED (2000), in which it held that environmental protection benefiting society at large could be accepted under Article 101(3) TFEU. This approach has however not been consistent. According to the Commission's guidelines since 2004, non-efficiency goals seem to have had a minor role, in that they are considered but never required in determining an anti-competitive behaviour. Later guidelines (2011) contain a similar viewpoint of non-efficiency goals as secondary to primary objectives such as efficiency gains, consumer welfare and economic interests. Overall the guidelines on Article 101 TFEU do not give much help in determining what weight, if any, should be given to non-efficiency goals. The same is true for cases brought under Article 102 TEFU. In these cases, the Commission focuses on the specific circumstances in each case and decides the most reasonable and appropriate outcome on a case-by-case basis.

of the least energy efficient machines. The agreement removes one of the dimensions along which sellers compete, and as such it might negatively affect competition and increase prices. However, the Commission considered that the agreement will benefit society in environmental terms, allowing the reduction of energy consumption, and that such an objective would not have been attained without the agreement. This is because consumers do not properly take into account all the externalities involved in their purchase and consumption decisions, and firms would not give up a tool of market competition unless bound by an agreement. Kieran argues that since the Treaty is part of the primary law of the EU, these general objectives of the Treaty should be implemented in all areas of EU law, including Competition policies.

It has been argued that it is the pyramidal structure of the Treaty that has caused the debate about non-efficiency goals. The structure causes objectives of different Articles to interfere with each other and the methods of reaching a goal may be by referring to and using other provisions. For example, may an improvement of health in the EU require a stronger support of environmental protection, since health may be improved by a reduction of pollution? It is unclear which objective is superior and which is subordinated and it is still a matter of discussion.

5 Conclusions

This section has provided some insight on the economic foundation of competition policy and its main goals. We first focused on the classical distinction between two types of ethical theories, i.e. teleological theories which are best represented by utilitarianism, and deontological theories. We then focused on the main objective of competition policy as established in the Treaty. Competition Law is often influenced by historical and social reasons and might respond to quite different objectives (e.g. economical, political and institutional), which can be broadly distinguished into two different fields. On one hand we have identified the approach supporting consumer welfare and efficiency. This includes consumer welfare, society welfare and an effective allocation of resources. The other type of efficiency goal is a pluralistic market or a free market, on which everyone can compete. Finally, we briefly discussed the non-efficiency goals, which are nowadays at the heart of the debate.

References

Baker JB (1996) Vertical restraints with horizontal consequences: competitive effects of 'Most-favored-customer' clauses. Anti-trust Law J 64:517

Baker JB (2003) The case for antitrust enforcement. J Econ Perspect 17(4):27–50

Carlton DW, Perloff JM (2004) Modern industrial organization. Pearson, Addison-Wesley

European Commission (2009) Communication from the Commission – Guidance on the Commission's enforcement priorities in applying Article 82 of the EC Treaty to abusive exclusionary conduct by dominant undertakings. Official Journal of the European Union
European Commission (2011) Guidelines on the applicability of Article 101 of the Treaty on the Functioning of the European Union to horizontal co-operation agreements. Official Journal of the European Union. C11/1
Jones A, Sufrin BE (2014) EU competition law. Oxford University Press, New York
Mankiw GN (2003) Principles of microeconomics. South-Western College Publishing, Meson
Mongin P, d'Aspremont C (1998) Utility theory and ethics. In: Barberá S, Hammond PJ, Seidl C (eds) Handbook of utility theory, vol 1. Kluwer Academic, Boston, pp 371–481
Monti G (2007) EC competition law. Cambridge University Press, Cambridge
Motta M (2004) Competition policy: theory and practice. Cambridge University Press, Cambridge
Röller LH (2005) Economic analysis and competition policy enforcement in Europe. Mimeo
Townley C (2008) Is anything more important than consumer welfare (in Article 81 EC)? Reflections of a community lawyer. Camb Yearb Eur Legal Stud 10(12):345–381
Townley C (2011) Which goals count in article 101 TFEU? Public policy and its discontents. Eur Competition Law Rev 9:441–448

Flavia Cortelezzi is Associate Professor in Political Economy at University of Insubria, Varese and Como, Italy.

An Overview of the Recent Application of EU and National Competition Law by the Italian Competition Authority

Paolo Caprile

Abstract This chapter provides a general survey of the antitrust public enforcement in Italy during recent years. It emerges that efforts have been put to ascertain abuses that have been very rarely scrutinised in the past, such as abuses of dominant position through excessive prices. Moreover strict antitrust enforcement was necessary to avoid the possibility that cartels would undermine the positive implications of the more centralised approach in public purchasing which Italy has adopted. Alongside these lines of antitrust intervention, the Italian Competition Authority has often used its advocacy powers to ensure the role of competition in promoting dynamic markets and economic growth especially in the fields of the new digital and sharing economy.

1 Introduction

During the last years the Italian Competition Authority (ICA or the Authority) has been deeply committed to increase antitrust deterrence, by strengthening its enforcement activity and adopting a rigorous sanctioning policy, complemented by extensive advocacy activity.[1]

Through its enforcement activity the ICA addressed both traditional issues and new matters related to disruptive innovation.

[1]Taking into account the period between January 2016 to April 2017, 13 cases of anticompetitive agreements and 9 cases of abuse of dominance have been scrutinised. The mergers reviewed by the ICA were 73. Considering the outcomes of the appeals of the ICA's decisions before the administrative Courts, the sanctions imposed in 2016 for anticompetitive conducts amount to € 112,296,064.73.

P. Caprile (✉)
Italian Competition Authority, Rome, Italy
e-mail: paolo.caprile@agcm.it

S. Marino et al. (eds.), *Language and Law*,
https://doi.org/10.1007/978-3-319-90905-9_3

One of the Authority's priorities has been to combat bid rigging in public procurement tenders. Moreover the ICA rediscovered a form of abuse—abuse through excessive prices—which has been very rarely ascertained in the past.[2]

Alongside these lines of antitrust intervention, the ICA has applied its advocacy and enforcement activity to ensure efficiency and openness to competition with particular attention to the sector of digital and sharing economy.

2 The Rediscovery of Abuses of Dominant Position Through Excessive Prices

Abuse through excessive prices has been fined by the ICA in the market for life-saving drugs (the so-called *Aspen* case).[3]

The case at issue involved a group of anti-cancer/life-saving medicinal products (Alkeran, Leukeran, Purnethol and Tioguanina, altogether known as "Cosmos drugs"), the costs of which were reimbursed by the Italian National Health System.

After acquiring the rights to market these drugs from their original owner (GlaxoSmithKline), Aspen started negotiations with the Italian Medicines Agency (Italian initials AIFA), in order to obtain an extremely significant increase of the prices of these medicines.

In January 2014, AIFA accepted the requests of Aspen, so that these products registered a steep increase in their prices, between 300 and 1500%.

Thus, the ICA affirmed that there was an excessive disproportion between the costs that were incurred by Aspen and the prices that were requested to AIFA.[4]

In this case the relevant market was defined according to the traditional criteria of the therapeutical classes of the drugs. The dominant position of Aspen has been established considering the absence of substitute products or potential alternatives as well as the fact that Aspen was the only undertaking authorised to commerce these drugs based on the relevant molecules at stake. As a consequence it was deemed that the pricing power of this pharmaceutical company was effectively constrained only by the capacity to pay of the patient or health provider.

As for the possible efficiencies related to this conduct, the ICA put particular emphasis on the fact that Aspen did not face any research costs for the Cosmos drugs, since it merely acquired the right to sell these drugs from GlaxoSmithKline.

[2]It is important to underline that in September 2017 the Court of Justice of the European Union clarified a number of extremely relevant issues regarding excessive pricing (Case C-177/16 *Biedrība "Autortiesību un komunicēšanās konsultāciju aģentūra - Latvijas Autoru apvienība" Konkurences padome* [2017] ECLI:EU:C:2017:689). More recently is it interesting to have a look at the conclusions which were drawn on these issues at the Rome Antitrust Forum. See Sokol (2018).

[3]ICA Case A480, Decision No 26185, 29 September 2016. As for abuses of dominant position in the pharmaceutical sector, see Pitruzzella and Muscolo (2016) and Oecd (2012).

[4]The ICA did not establish which was exactly the price that Aspen could have requested to AIFA.

Moreover it was considered the fact that Aspen did not contribute to any increase in the quality of the Cosmos drugs.

Therefore, in September 2016, the ICA imposed a fine to Aspen equal to Euro 5.2 million for breach of Article 102(a), of the Treaty on the Functioning of the European Union (TFEU).[5]

It seems important to highlight that later on the Italian administrative Court of first instance of the Lazio Region[6] (TAR Lazio) rejected the appeal brought by Aspen against this decision. Moreover other antitrust Authorities, such as the European Commission, the Spanish *Comisión Nacional de los Mercados y la Competencia* (CNMC) as well as the South African Competition Commission (SACC) announced the opening of similar investigations against Aspen.[7]

Abuse through excessive prices also featured in another recent case which concerned the electricity market and was opened after a report from the Regulatory Authority for Electricity Gas and Water (Italian initials ARERA).

In this case it was pointed out that the high costs incurred in 2016 by Terna S.p.A.[8] (Terna) for dispatching services required to ensure the safe operation of the electricity grid in the geographic area of Brindisi, and so the high economic burden borne by consumers (domestic and business), possibly stemmed from abusive conducts by the dominant operator Enel S.p.A. (Enel) in its supply offering for its production plant in Brindisi. In early May 2017 the Authority accepted the commitments submitted by Enel, which will prevent any repetition of unjustified energy costs for the coming years.[9] More specifically, Enel undertook to ensure that, for each of the years 2017, 2018 and 2019, the net annual revenue from its Brindisi plant will not exceed a certain level.[10] This will generate savings of over 500 million euro for consumers over the 3 years.[11]

---

[5]The ICA recently opened a proceeding in order to verify whether Aspen is complying with this decision. ICA Case A480B, Decision No 26432, 1 March 2017.

[6]The Italian Code of Administrative Procedure (Legislative Decree 2 July 2010, No 104) reserves exclusive jurisdiction on the decisions issued by the Italian Competition Authority to administrative courts, and concentrates all litigation at the first instance into the functional competence of the TAR Lazio (Articles 133 and 135 of the Code of Administrative Procedure). The judgments issued by the TAR Lazio can be further appealed before the Consiglio di Stato (Council of State) acting as a Court of last instance.

[7]In the USA, where the Supreme Court has not generally endorsed excessive pricing doctrine, several scholars have recently argued that there is no reason in principle why in "Aspen-like cases" the Sherman Act should not address excessive pricing "as such". See Abbott (2016), p. 289.

[8]Terna is the national electricity grid operator.

[9]ICA Case A498A, Decision No 26562, 4 May 2017.

[10]That is much lower than the amount that the current criteria for the quantification of the plant's costs would have produced.

[11]In addition, and more generally, through further commitments regarding its conducts as to offers on the wholesale market, Enel has considerably limited the possibility that Terna should be required to purchase dispatching services, possibly at high prices, even from other operators in the Brindisi area, such as Sorgenia, whose investigation was closed at the same time, having established that there were insufficient legal grounds to proceed against them.

3 Bid Rigging in the Scenario of a More Centralised Approach in Public Procurements

Another of the Authority's priorities in recent years has been to combat bid rigging in public procurement tenders. Notably, in this respect, strict competition enforcement was necessary to avoid the possibility that cartels would undermine the positive implications of the more centralised approach in public purchasing which Italy has adopted.

The ICA has thus initiated many proceedings in order to ascertain and fine illicit cartels aimed at rigging tender competition procedures issued by Consip S.p.A. (Consip), which is the Italian central purchasing body for the public administration. In all these cases it was ascertained that the members of the cartel concerted their participation with the aim to allocate the different lots of the tender *ex-ante*, influencing the relevant awarding dynamics.

As examples of these decisions, it is possible to mention the ascertainment of the cartel related to the tender for cleaning services in schools, which was worth about 1.63 billion euro overall,[12] as well as the fines worth about 23 millions euro to the so-called big-four accountants for having illegally concerted their participation in the Consip tender for assistance to public administration in the field of auditing of EU funds.[13]

Other investigations into possible cartels set up to take part in public tenders are also currently on-going. These cases are related to the Consip tender for "facility management services" for buildings belonging to the public administration, universities and other research institutes,[14] and to the various public tenders in the market for forest fire-fighting and helicopter rescue services.[15]

Nowadays, from a deterrence point of view, what seems important to underline is that these kinds of sanctions, once they become *res judicata*, could lead to the potential exclusion of the undertakings concerned from future public tender procedures related to the same market.[16]

[12]ICA case I785, Decision No 25802, 22 October 2015. The fines which were originally imposed amounted to more than 110 million of euro. In its decision dated 26 January 2017, the Italian Council of State confirmed the ICA's decision to fine such cartel. However the Council of State also confirmed the Lazio TAR's decision that the fines to the members of the cartel should have been lowered.

[13]ICA Case I796, Decision No 26816, 18 October 2017.

[14]ICA Case I808, Decision No 26454, 21 March 2017 and Decision No 26868, 22 November 2017.

[15]ICA Case I806, Decision No 26445, 14 March 2017 and Decision No 26688, 19 July 2017.

[16]Article 80(5)(c) of Legislative Decree No 50, 18 April 2016 (so-called Italian Public Procurement Code) and point No 2.2.3.1 of the Italian Anti-Corruption Authority Guidelines No 6, as recently modified by the Italian Anti-Corruption Authority Decision No 1008/2017.

4 Safeguarding Competition in the Era of Growth of Ultra-Broadband Network and Digital Markets

Alongside these lines of antitrust intervention, the ICA also applied its enforcement and advocacy activity to ensure efficiency and openness to competition. In this respect particular attention has been deserved to the development in Italy of the ultra-broadband network and to oversee all the recent trends in the "Big Data" as well as in the digital and sharing economy.

4.1 The Telecom Italia Case

With respect to the first line of intervention, the ICA started a proceeding in 2017, which is still on-going, against Telecom Italia S.p.A. (TI) to investigate the possible infringements of Article 102 TFEU. According to the preliminary information obtained by the Authority, TI is suspected to have instituted multiple behaviour aimed at pursuing two objectives that are harmful to the competition:

(i) impeding the carrying out of tenders for the development of ultrabroadband infrastructures (FTTH) in the areas of market failure in Italy, in order to preserve the monopoly they have held historically in these territories and prevent the entry of new competing operators;
(ii) exclude customers of the new retail ultrabroadband (UBB) telecommunication services segment through anticompetitive commercial policies (predatory prices and lock-in clauses). In this way, the suspicion is that TI would achieve a double purpose: on the retail market, make its customer base less contestable to other competitors; on the wholesale market, discourage investments in the new networks and make them less profitable.

In particular, the hypothesis is that TI has allegedly organised a complex strategy to slow down the holding of the tenders announced by Infratel Italia S.p.A. (Infratel). Notably, while the competitions announced by Infratel were in progress, TI announced modifications to the investment plan that was previously communicated to Infratel during the public consultation aimed at defining the areas that would not be covered by any private investment in UBB infrastructure (market failure or white areas). The supposition is that, in this way, TI has tried to bring back into question the market failure areas that resulted from the public consultation, by declaring its intention to invest in white areas anyway. The revision of the investment plan was said to have been announced even though the tender process had already started and after the approval Decision of the European Commission.[17]

[17]Commission Decision SA.41647 Italy—Strategia Banda Ultra Larga (OJ C 256, 15.7.2016, p. 1).

TI's strategy to slowdown the progress of the competitors was also alleged to have been conducted through a sham litigation strategy. By slowing down the procedure for the selection of the parties charged with implementing the ultrabroad networks in white areas, TI could have impeded the development of infrastructural competition and the entrance of new competitors. As for the commercial offer of ultrabroadband telecommunication services, it should be assessed whether the technical and economic conditions contained in these offers are such as to lock-in the customer to TI for a long period and with prices that cannot be replicated by alternative operators. This conduct could result in unduly shrinking the contestable market and limiting competition in the market for ultrabroadband retail telecommunication service, when UBB penetration is starting to increase among customers.

4.2 The Big Data Enquiry

With regard to the second line of action, on 30 May 2017 the ICA, the Communications Authority and the Italian Data Protection Authority opened a joint sector inquiry into the so-called Big data. Big data, as it is well known, are characterised by the quantity of information they contain (size); the continuous updating of that information and the possibility of instant analysis through the use of complex algorithms (speed); the differentiation of content and formats (variety).

This sector inquiry aims at identifying potential competition concerns and defining a regulatory framework able to foster competition in the markets of the digital economy, to protect privacy and consumers, and to promote pluralism within the digital ecosystem.

From an antitrust and regulatory perspective it will be crucial to assess whether, and under which circumstances, access to Big Data might constitute an entry barrier, or in any case facilitate anticompetitive practices that could possibly hinder technological progress.

The other focus will be to ascertain whether their use creates specific risks for the preservation of users' privacy given that new technologies and new forms of data analysis in many cases allow to re-identify an individual through apparently anonymous data.

Finally the ever growing role exercised by "Big data" on information pluralism will be analyzed. Indeed, online news access increasingly occurs through digital intermediaries such as social networks and search engines, that employ users' information as a strategic asset following the logic of multisided markets and through forms of profiling and the definition of algorithms able to affect both the preservation of the net neutrality principle, and the plurality of the representations of facts and opinions.

All this work will be carried out considering, on the other hand, that this type of data has become essential for stimulating economic growth, the provision of innovative services, employment generation and overall social progress.

4.3 Removing Obstacles to the Digital and Sharing Economy

Finally the ICA's third line of action involved the digital and sharing economy, which is generally considered to have the potential to benefit consumers, since it allows the offer of innovative services.

Thus, the ICA tried to promote the elimination of regulatory obstacles to the digital and sharing economy, which, as stated by the European Commission, refers to business models where activities are facilitated by collaborative platforms that create an open marketplace for the temporary usage of goods or services often provided by private individuals (for profit or not-for-profit).[18]

4.3.1 The Urban Transport Sector

In September 2015,[19] the ICA asked that rules should be laid down as soon as possible to regulate urban transport operations by non-professional drivers through digital platforms for smartphones and tablets. In its response to a question by the Ministry of the Interior at the request of the Council of the State, the ICA hoped that the legislator would intervene in the least intrusive way possible to allow an expansion of these systems for the offer of transport services.

With regard to digital platforms covering private non-scheduled transport services such as those provided for by UberBlack and UberVan, the ICA affirmed the legitimacy of these platforms in the absence of any legal framework. Indeed, the ICA considered as "effectively inapplicable" the obligations established by the legislation in force (Law No 21/92), maintaining that

> a digital platform that connects a demand via smartphone with an offer for services provided by car rental operators with driver cannot in fact by definition observe a regulation that requires drivers to provide a service from a garage and to return to the garage at the end of the trip.

With reference to digital platforms dealing with the offer of transport service by non-professional drivers such as UberPop, the ICA only asked the legislator to adopt "a basic set of rules for this type of service". According to the ICA this kind of services could have many benefits: greater ease in the implementation of mobility services; a wider coverage of a demand that is frequently not met; a consequent

[18]Communication from the Commission to the European Parliament, the Council, the European Economic and Social Committee and the Committee of the Regions: a European agenda for the collaborative economy (COM(2016) 356 final). Available at eur-lex. https://eur-lex.europa.eu/legal-content/IT/TXT/?qid=1523874166793&uri=CELEX:52016DC0356. Accessed 16 Apr 2018.

[19]ICA Case AS1222, 29 September 2015.

reduction of costs for users; and, to the extent that it discourages the use of private vehicles, a relief of congestion in urban traffic.[20]

Later on, with the opinion sent in March 2017 to the Italian Parliament and to the Government, the ICA recommended a reform of the sector of non-scheduled public transport services.[21]

According to the ICA, since the sector of non-scheduled public transport services is still regulated by Law No 21/1992, a reform of this legislation is indeed a clear priority for it to be in line with the development of the market.

The ICA advocated that several regulatory burdens should be eliminated. For instance, particular attention has been put on the fact that, as already mentioned, the current regulation forces non-taxi professional drivers (so-called car-and-driver hire operators) to return to their garage before offering a new ride to customers.

Moreover it was highlighted that a greater operational flexibility should be guaranteed for the drivers having a taxi license, and at the same time, provisions limiting the non-taxi professional drivers activity on a territorial basis should be eliminated.

This reform, according to the ICA, should also cover the services that connect non-professional drivers and end users via digital platforms.

At the same time, in ICA's opinion, the current taxi drivers, until the entry into force of the reform, should be entitled to receive a compensation related to the possible diminishment of the value of their license to be financed by new operators and by new revenues from the modification of tax scheme.

4.3.2 Accommodation Facilities in the Hotels Sector

As it is well known, restrictions on hotel pricing were scrutinised by several European Competition authorities, including in France, Italy, Sweden, Germany and the UK. On 21 April 2015, the ICA decided to render the commitments offered by Priceline Group's companies Booking.com BV and Booking.com (Italy) legally binding and closed the investigation opened in May 2014 with respect to these companies. In this case the ICA, as stated in its opening decision, was concerned that

[20]The Case C-434/15 *Asociación Profesional Elite Taxi* [2017] ECLI:EU:C:2017:981 clarified that an intermediation service such as that at issue, the purpose of which is to connect, by means of a smartphone application and for remuneration, non-professional drivers using their own vehicle with persons who wish to make urban journeys, must be regarded as being inherently linked to a transport service and, accordingly, must be classified as 'a service in the field of transport' within the meaning of EU Law. Consequently, such a service must be excluded from the scope of the freedom to provide services in general as well as the Directive on services in the internal market and the Directive on electronic commerce. It follows that, as EU Law currently stands, it is for the Member States to regulate the conditions under which such services are to be provided in conformity with the general rules of the TFEU.

[21]ICA Opinion S2782, 10 March 2017 available at AGCM. http://www.agcm.it/component/joomdoc/allegati-news/S2782Segnalazione.pdf/download.html. Accessed 20 Feb 2018.

the so-called 'parity clauses'[22] might significantly restrict competition on the fees required by online travel agencies (OTA) to hotels, affecting final prices for hotel rooms, to the detriment, ultimately, of final consumers. During the investigation, conducted in collaboration with the National Competition Authorities of France and Sweden, with the coordination of the European Commission, Booking.com—the market leader in Italy—submitted commitments consisting in a significant reduction of the scope of the said clauses. The revised clauses would apply to prices and other conditions publicly offered by the hotels through their own direct online sales channels, leaving them free to set prices and conditions on other OTAs and on their direct offline channels, as well as in the context of their loyalty programs.

In order to complement this line of action, in 2017 the ICA together with the European Commission and nine other national Competition authorities (the NCAs of Belgium, Czech Republic, France, Germany, Hungary, Ireland, Netherlands, Sweden and UK), published a report on the monitoring activity, conducted during 2016, in the online hotel-booking sector.[23] The purpose of the monitoring activity covered various aspects of the way hotels sell their rooms, focusing on room price and room availability differentiation by hotels between sales channels and online travel agent commission rates.

The participating authorities sent questionnaires to a sample of 16,000 hotels in the ten Member States, 20 online travel agents, 11 metasearch websites and 19 large hotel chains.

The results of the exercise suggest that measures applied to the parity clauses, namely

(a) allowing large online travel agents to use narrow parity clauses, and
(b) prohibiting online travel agents from using them altogether, have generally improved conditions for Competition and led to more choice for consumers.[24]

4.3.3 Non-Hotel Accommodation Facilities

An example of the ICA intervention in the sharing economy has been in the field of accommodation facilities other than in the hotels sector.

In August 2015 the Lazio Region issued a new Regulation concerning non-hotel accommodation facilities (Regulation No 8/2015). Such Regulation established

---

[22]According to these clauses the supplier of accommodation facilities undertakes to guarantee the best price conditions to the intermediary concerned as compared with any other dealer.

[23]Available via European Commission. http://ec.europa.eu/competition/ecn/hotel_monitoring_report_en.pdf. Accessed 20 Feb 2018.

[24]In August 2017, following the ban of parity clauses from online booking platforms in Germany, France and Austria, also Italy altogether prohibited such clauses in contracts with hotel partners. The new passage in Article 1, para. 166 of Law No 124, 4 August 2017, reads as follows: "any agreement by which the hotel is obliged not to offer to the final clients, by any means or any instruments, prices, terms and any other conditions better than those offered by the same hotel through intermediaries, regardless of the law applicable to the contract, is void".

closure periods for these accommodation facilities, as well as several conditions for opening them. These provisions had an impact also on the accommodation facilities offered through platforms like Airbnb or Booking.

In particular, the Regulation established the obligation for non-professional accommodation services providers to stop their activity for 100 days per year. In addition, such Regulation established a minimum duration for rents (i.e. 3 days).[25]

Therefore, in December 2015 the ICA decided to challenge the Lazio Regulation before the Administrative Court (TAR Lazio). According to the ICA, the closure periods imposed by this Regulation contrasted with the principle of free competition, since the establishment of opening and closing hours for economic activities generally hinders the free determination of offer conditions and their adaptation to the demand. The 100 days closure period, as well as the rules on the minimum duration of rents, were deemed to limit the output without any justification, thus producing damages to economic operators and to consumers.

In June 2016, the Administrative Court granted the appeal lodged by the Authority and repealed the Lazio Region corresponding provisions.[26]

Afterwards, the ICA decided once again to intervene in this field. The occasion was given by Article 4 of Legislative Decree No 50/2017, through which the Italian Government introduced a tax on the vacation rentals in order to re-organise the rental market and contain tax evasion; the new fiscal measure for the short term rental aims to collect money from the agency/web platform that takes the holiday booking. To solve this problem the Italian Government has stated that the agency or web-portal directly withholds 21% of the payment on short term holiday rentals which must then be paid to the State. The measure entered into force on 1 June 2017. It is important to notice that this measure did not introduce a new tax but rather a different (new) option to pay tax on the rental inferior to 30 days stay; previously, in fact, home owners were obliged to declare by themselves the income coming from this kind of rentals and add it on top of their year income.

In its opinion dated 24 November 2017, the ICA affirmed that this kind of tax scheme appears to be potentially suitable to alter the competitive dynamics between the various operators, with possible negative effects on end-users of short lease services.

The Authority is said to be

> fully aware that the intervention of the legislator aims to achieve a public interest of a fiscal nature and to counteract the phenomenon of evasion.

The ICA, while also observing that this kind of provision would represent an *unicum* in the European landscape, affirmed that the introduction of those obligations was not proportionate to the pursuit of these aims, since they could be pursued

[25]On 30 September 2015 the Lazio Region modified the afore-said Regulation; in particular, pursuant to such modification, the provisions concerning closure periods will not be applied before 2017.

[26]See TAR Lazio, 13 June 2016, Decision No 6755/2016.

equally effectively by means which do not at the same time give rise to possible distortions of competition in this sector.

For instance, according to the ICA, the duty to transmit all the relevant information on the transactions concluded to the competent fiscal agencies could be considered sufficient.

Moreover, it was observed that the system that has been envisaged could discourage the offer by online matching platforms of digital payment methods for their clients, since this would provide them with additional administrative burdens.

Thus, according to the ICA, this system could give an advantage to those platforms which act as "pure intermediaries", without also receiving the money directly by the guests.

In these respects, the ICA underlined that this could not benefit consumers since the payment of the accommodation directly to the platform is usually accompanied by the fact that the latter offers additional services to the clients (such as its guarantee to refund if the guest is not satisfied with the services offered by the host etc.).

In turn this mechanism was deemed capable of altering the commercial conditions on the various (traditional and not) markets for the offer of accommodation facilities.

Finally the ICA also stressed the (negative) impact that this kind of measure could have vis-à-vis other sectors of the digital economy that have been not affected by the provision at issue.

5 Conclusion

During recent years the ICA has been intensively committed to combat bid rigging in public procurement tenders.

At the same time efforts have been put to ascertain abuses that have been very rarely scrutinised in the past, such as abuses of dominant position through excessive prices charged to the national health system. Besides these examples of exploitative conducts, the Authority dealt with many other traditional antitrust cases but also with new matters related to disruptive innovation.

Notably, the ICA has very often used its advocacy powers to ensure the role of competition in promoting dynamic markets and economic growth especially in the fields of the new digital and sharing economy.

However, the ICA horizons were clearly not limited to the enforcement of Competition Law, consumer protection and advocacy, but also on promoting the culture of competition and compliance. In these respects, the provision of relevant reductions in the size of the fines for companies that have adopted compliance programs as well the on-going initiative of offering guidelines on compliance programs show the clear intention of bringing Competition Law easier to access especially for small businesses.

References

Abbott F (2016) Excessive pharmaceutical prices and competition law: doctrinal development to protect public health. UC Irvine Law Rev 6:289–295

OECD (2012) Excessive prices. http://www.oecd.org/competition/abuse/49604207.pdf. Accessed 27 Feb 2018

Pitruzzella G, Muscolo G (eds) (2016) Competition and Patent Law in the pharmaceutical sector, an international perspective. Wolters Kluwer, The Netherlands

Sokol D (2018) Rome Antitrust Forum - Summary of the fourth annual meeting. http://lawprofessors.typepad.com/antitrustprof_blog. Accessed 15 Feb 2018

Paolo Caprile is Commissioner's Muscolo Legal Advisor at the Italian Competition Authority. The views and opinions expressed in this chapter are those of the author and do not reflect the official policy or position of any Authority or Agency of the Italian government.

The CJEU Case Law After Preliminary Ruling on Behalf of Private Enforcement of EU Competition Law

Mar Jimeno-Bulnes

Abstract The Court of Justice of the European Union case law on private enforcement of EU Competition Law will be examined in order to explain the developments on the topic until the enactment of specific legislative instruments such as Directive 2014/104/EU. In this context, some leading cases are analysed, with particular regard to those that have led to further elaboration of jurisprudence or doctrine, as the decisive judgments *Courage Ltd v. Crehan*, *Masterfoods Ltd. v. HB Ice Cream, Ltd.* and *Vincenzo Manfredi v. Lloyd Adriatico Assicurazioni* SpA, consolidating the previous case law. In all the case law compliance with the characteristics of the European legal order shall be specified too. The relevance of the direct effect will be highlighted, since it might be problematic in the case of the Directive. Most of this case law has been the result of questions referred for a preliminary ruling directly to the Court of Justice from the courts of the Member States. These courts are responsible for complying with the EU measures to settle disputes at a national level between natural or legal persons in mainly civil or commercial matters.

The financial support of the Spanish Ministry of Economy and the European Commission is gratefully acknowledged (Research Projects A step forward in the consolidation of the European judicial area and its practical application in Spain: from the perspective of civil and criminal procedures, DER2015-71418-P and JUST-2015-JCOO-AG, 723198, and Training action for legal practitioners: linguistic skills and translation in EU Competition Law, HT.4582-6). Also my special thanks to Professor Luis Velasco San Pedro, Professor of Commercial Law at the University of Valladolid, for his bibliographical recommendation.

M. Jimeno-Bulnes (✉)
University of Burgos, Burgos, Spain
e-mail: Mjimeno@ubu.es

S. Marino et al. (eds.), *Language and Law*,
https://doi.org/10.1007/978-3-319-90905-9_4

1 Introduction

It is widely known that Directive 2014/104/EU[1] establishes the so-called "private enforcement" of EU Competition Law, referring to national courts the observance of European rules on the topic, essentially Articles 101 and 102 of the Treaty on the Functioning of the European Union (TFEU) (former Articles 81 and 82 of the Treaty on European Communities (TEC)). The new measure represents a step forward in relation to the Regulation No 1/2003,[2] which just provided the "public enforcement" under the role carried out by the Commission and National Competition Authorities (NCAs). This private enforcement is contemplated as the possibility by particulars to claim compensation before national courts due to the damages caused by infringement of Competition Law.[3]

Nevertheless such private enforcement of EU Competition Law was indeed anticipated by the Court of Justice of the European Union (CJEU) with relevant case law,[4] recognising first the direct effect of primary EU Law and second the right to individuals to promote an action for recovering damages from the other party in national jurisdiction. It must be remembered that

> the last word on the legal interpretation of the EU Competition rules lies with the ECJ[5]

which case law must be strictly followed by national courts in general; not only such one, who requests the question under preliminary ruling proceeding *ex* Article 267 TFEU but all of them in application of same interpreted rules.[6] In fact the CJEU acts as "an engine" of the European integration and dynamic vehicle of the EU itself[7] under the special instrument, as it is the preliminary ruling contemplated in Article

---

[1]Directive 2014/104/EU of the European Parliament and of the Council of 26 November 2014 on certain rules governing actions for damages under national law for infringements of the competition law provisions of the Member States and of the European Union (OJ L 349, 5.12.2014, p. 1), also known as "damages directive" or Directive on damages actions. See Ioannidou (2015), p. 182. See specifically at the time Editorial comments (2014), pp. 1333–1342. For Spanish comments, see: Ordoñez Solís (2015), available via http://www.elderecho.com/ and extensively Ruiz Peris (2016).

[2]Council Regulation (EC) No 1/2003 of 16 December 2002 on the implementation of the rules on competition laid down in Articles 81 and 82 of the Treaty (OJ L 1, 4.1.2001, p. 1), giving place to so-called "modernisation of Community procedural rules". See, eg, Liu (2009). In Spain basic references by Fernández Torres and Fuentes Navarro (2013), pp. 289–317 arguing for the application of an "uncentralized model on application of competition rules" (p. 289).

[3]See generally in Spain Velasco San Pedro et al. (2011), pp. 143–187; Dune (2014).

[4]On the role of the CJEU case law in relation to the construction of the private enforcement theory of EU Competition Law see in Spain Torres Sustaeta (2014), p. 129 ff.

[5]Slot and Farley (2017), p. 194.

[6]On the effect *erga omnes* of preliminary ruling judgments see Jimeno-Bulnes (2013a), p. 205; *in extenso*, Jimeno Bulnes (1996), p. 455 ff. In CJEU case law see: Case 28/62-30/62 *Da Costa en Schaake* [1963] ECR 31, ECLI:EU:C:1963:6; Case 283/81 *CILFIT* [1982] ECR 3415, ECLI:EU:C:1982:335.

[7]See Horsely (2013), pp. 931–964 reproducing the debate existing in the literature between judicial activism and judicial restraint defenders. Also analysis providing examples by Rosas et al. (2013).

267 TFEU, which represents the so-called "dialogue between judges",[8] i.e. between CJEU and national courts, "both keeping their respective jurisdiction",[9] but ensuring the imperative application of EU Law at national level "if need be by disapplying the provisions of national Law".[10]

This chapter addresses the analysis of such CJEU case law within the private enforcement of EU Competition Law in order to interpret the above-mentioned legislative instruments. First, I shall begin with the examination of the leading cases, with special regard to those that have led to further elaboration of legislation as it was at the time the Regulation No 1/2003. These are initial judgments *SA Brasserie de Haecht*,[11] explicitly recognising the direct application of European Competition Law and the further and decisive judgment *Courage Ltd v. Crehan*.[12] Besides the mentioned case law, some other resolutions can be quoted as the *Masterfoods Ltd*.[13]

Second, further case law shall be analysed as giving the occasion to the adoption of the Directive 2014/104/EU. These are the famous *Manfredi* judgment,[14] which consolidated the case law of the *Courage* case and cases as *Pfleiderer*,[15] *Otis*,[16] *Donau Chemie*,[17] or, even later, *Kone AG*.[18] All these judgments stem from requests for preliminary rulings before the CJEU by national courts[19] asking for interpretation of Articles 101 and 102 TFEU as EU primary Law or Regulation No 1/2003 as EU secondary Law. The CJEU declares in all cases the direct effect of requested legislation providing right for compensation to individuals due to infringement of EU Competition Law by participating countries.

Other recent jurisprudence on the topic shall be analised too, because it consolidates previous case law or establishes new principles in this matter. In this context,

---

Final critical comments on judicial activism by Cappelletti (2015), pp. 311–322. In Spain Fidalgo Gallardo (2016).

[8]Cosimo (2011). First CJEU case mentioning such need of dialogue between judges on behalf of judicial cooperation between CJCE and national courts Case 16/65 *Schwarze* [1965] ECR 877, ECLI:EU:C:1965:117. See in the literature Von Danwitz (2010), pp. 143–147.

[9]*Schwarze* judgment, cit., para. 3.

[10]Case C-105/12, *Taricco* [2015] ECLI:EU:C:2015:555. See criticism by Perlo (2017), pp. 739–768.

[11]Case 23/67, *SA Brasserie de Haecht* [1967] 407,ECLI:EU:C:1967:54.

[12]Case C-453/99, *Courage and Crehan* [2001] ECR I-6297, ECLI:EU:C:2001:465.

[13]Case C-344/98, *Masterfoods Ltd v. HB Ice Cream, Ltd.* [2000] ECR I-11369, ECLI:EU:C:2000:689.

[14]Joined Cases C-295/04 to C-298/04, *Manfredi and others* [2006] ECR I-6619, ECLI:EU:C:2006:461.

[15]Case C-360/09, *Pfleiderer AG v Bundeskartellamt* [2011] ECR I-5161, ECLI:EU:C:2011:389.

[16]Case C-199/11, *Otis and others* [2012] ECLI:EU:C:2012:684.

[17]Case C-536/11, *Donau Chemie* [2013] ECLI:EU:C:2013:366.

[18]Case C-557/12, *Kone AG and Others v ÖBB-Infrastruktur AG* [2014] ECLI:EU:C:2014:1327.

[19]In fact the preliminary ruling procedure is known as 'the jewel in the Crown of the jurisdiction of the Court of Justice'; see Smulders and Eisele (2012), pp. 112–127.

the newest and most important CJEU case law in the use of the preliminary ruling procedure by national courts shall be here scrutinised. Due to the occasion of this contribution, if there are specific rulings on the topic as a result of preliminary rulings promoted by Croatian, Greek, Italian, Polish and Spanish Courts, these shall be quoted. Other CJEU proceedings shall be envisaged, as they are appeals under Article 56 of the Statute of the CJEU or actions for annulment delivered by General Court *ex* Article 263 TFEU.[20]

In all the case law analysed we will examine compliance with the characteristics of the European legal order. The relevance of the direct effect will be highlighted,[21] which, despite it beign explicit in the Regulation No 1/2003, may be more problematic in the case of the Directive. Thus, CJEU's doctrine from the well-known *Van Gend en Loos* judgment (1963)[22] is applicable. National courts are responsible for complying with the Regulation and Directive in order to settle disputes at a national level between natural or legal persons in mainly civil or commercial matters. In the case of Directive 2014/104/EU the term for transposition expired on 27 December 2016 implementing Member States its content in national Law.[23]

Finally we shall draw some provisional conclusions.

2 Early CJEU Case Law: Leading Cases on Direct Effect of EU Competition Law

The present paragraph aims at commenting initial CJEU judgments in relation to recognition of direct effect of EU Competition rules contained in the Treaties, specifically current Articles 101, 102 and 106 TFEU. As the CJEU declared in prior *Van Gend en Loos* judgment

[20]The most important judgments are: Case C-510/11P, *Kone Oyj* [2013] ECLI:EU:C:2013:696; Case T-342/11, *Confederación Española de Empresarios de Estaciones de Servicio (CEEES) and Asociación de Gestores de Estaciones de Servicio v European Commission* [2014] ECLI:EU:T:2014:60; Case C-365/12P, *EnBW Energie* [2014] ECLI:EU:C:2014:112; Case T-341/12, *Evonik Degussa* [2015] ECLI:EU:T:2015:51; Case T-677/13, *Axa Versicherung* [2015] ECLI:EU:T:2015:473; Joined Cases C-164/15P and 165/15P, *Aer Lingus* [2016] ECLI:EU:C:2016:990; Case T-480/15, *Agria Polska* [2017] ECLI:EU:T:2017:339; Case C-517/15P, *AGC Glass Europe* [2017] ECLI:EU:C:2017:598.

[21]See on the topic, eg, Robin-Olivier (2014), pp. 165–188; also generally Prinssen and Schrauwen (2002) and Pescatore (2015).

[22]Case 26/62, *van Gend & Loos* [1963] ECR 1, ECLI:EU:C:1963:1. On its impact see, eg, Chalters and Barroso (2014), pp. 105–134 and Rasmussen (2014), pp. 136–163; more critical Weiler (2014), pp. 94–103. In opposition Derlén and Lindholm (2014), pp. 667–687.

[23]It is the case of Spain by Royal Decree Law 9/2017 of 26 May 2017, available via Spanish Official Journal. https://www.boe.es/diario_boe/txt.php?id=BOE-A-2017-5855. (Accessed 16 Jan 2018).

> the Community constitutes a new legal order of international law for the benefit of which the states have limited their sovereign rights, albeit within limited fields, and the subjects of which comprise not only Member States but also their nationals.[24]

As a consequence

> Community Law therefore not only imposes obligation on individuals but is also intended to confer upon them rights which become part of their legal heritage. These rights arise not only where they are expressly granted by the Treaty, but also by reason of obligations which the Treaty imposes in a clearly defined way upon individuals as well as upon the Member States and he institutions of the Community.[25]

Such rights, as part of Community Law at the time

> can be invoked by their nationals before... Courts and tribunals.[26]

In this context the *SA Brasserie de Haecht* case is considered to be first precedent of CJEU doctrine related to direct effect of EU Competition Law.[27] The judgment was delivered on 12 December 1967, after a request for preliminary ruling by the *Tribunal de Commerce (Liège)* on the basis of, at the time, Article 177 of the Treaty establishing the European Economic Community (TEEC). Here the interpretation of prior Article 85(1) TEEC, currently Article 101(1) TFEU, is required in order to determine if the agreements whereby a dealer undertakes for a certain period the right to be the exclusive supplier with the exclusion of all others are or not prohibited. Facts were related to the nature of "exclusive dealing" of three loan contracts signed between Brasserie de Haecht and Oscar & Marie Wilkin, owners of a coffee shop at Esnaux, in order for the first one to be the exclusive supplier of beer, liquors and soft drinks for the purpose of their business and for their personal needs. Brasserie de Haecht brought an action before the *Tribunal de Commerce* of Liège against Mr and Mrs Wilking because of the non-fulfilment of their exclusive purchase obligations contained in the contracts claiming the repayment of the loans, the return of the furniture and the payment of damages. Defendants opposed that the agreements of the dispute were void under Article 85(1) TEEC. This is the

[24](Ground B) 5. On the autonomy of EU Law introduced by prior *Van Gend en Loos* case see criticism by Klamert (2017), p. 815.

[25](Ground B) 5 again. This is the so-called vertical direct effect by contrast to the horizontal direct effect recognised by the CJEU in later case law such as *Defrenne*, where the invocation of the rights recognised by the Treaties before national jurisdictions takes place not only in the relations between the State and the individuals, but also between individuals themselves (Case 43/75, *Defrenne* [1976] ECR 455 ECLI:EU:1976:56). For a basic explanation on such difference see information provided by Eur-Lex database at http://eur-lex.europa.eu/legal-content/EN/TXT/?uri=LEGISSUM%3Al14547 (Accessed 23 Jan 2018). Nevertheless, see recent criticism related to this comparison between effect direct and subjective rights for individuals by Pfeiffer (2017), pp. 665–695, especially at pp. 689 ff. proposing a parallel theory to the effect direct opposite to *Van Gend en Loos* case law.

[26]Ground B) 4. See in relation to Spanish jurisdiction specifically Benavides Velasco (2005), p. 282 regarding the application of Articles 81 and 82 TEC at the time.

[27]See in Spain Berenguer Fuster (2011), p. 52, also considering such judgment as first case where the CJEU at the time declared the direct effect of EU Competition Law rules.

reason of the request of a preliminary ruling by national judge according to former Article 177 TEEC.

The Court of Justice ruled in general terms that

> agreements whereby an undertaking agrees to obtain its supplies from one undertaking to the exclusion of all others do not by their very nature necessarily include all the elements constituting incompatibility with the Common Market as referred to the Article 85 (1) of the Treaty

but

> they may affect trade between Member States and. . . they have either as their object or effect the prevention, restriction or distortion of Competition.

As suggested by the opinion of Advocate General Roemer in this process of evaluation of agreements as anticompetitive practices

> must be taken into consideration, in particular, the number of such agreements, their duration, the volume of goods affected, how they compare with 'free' trade, and opportunities for opening new trade outlets.

As established, the restriction of competition must be examined not only by object but also by effect, taking into account "both actual and potential effects" as well as "such negative effects must be appreciable".[28] In sum, direct effect of Article 85(1) TEEC was recognised as far as private individuals pleaded before national court the annulment of disputed agreements because of infringement of EU Competition Law; specifically, such contract loans alter competition and hamper the economic interpenetration sought by the Treaty.

Further clarification regarding the enforcement of the explicit direct effect doctrine by the CJEU took place in *BRT/SABAM* case, judgment pronounced on 27 March 1974,[29] a Belgian case, too. Here reference for preliminary ruling *ex* Article 177 TEEC was made by *Tribunal de Premiere Instance* at Brussels asking for interpretation of former Articles 86 (current Article 102 TFEU) and 90(2) TEEC (current Article 106(2) TFEU) in order to decide about the validity of several contracts concluded in 1963 and 1967 between parties in national proceedings between the Belgian Association of Authors, Composers and Publishers (SABAM) and two authors, in which the latter assigned some of their rights to SABAM. In this case, the national Court promoted several questions related to the significance of "abuse of dominant position in the market", but a last one was added specifically addressed to the question of direct effect, i.e., if

> the provisions of Article 90 (2) of the Treaty (can) create rights in respect of private parties which national courts must safeguard.

Concerning the first group of questions, the Court of Justice declared that

> the undertaking in question in fact exercised a quasi-monopoly within Belgian territory and consequently occupied a dominant position in a substantial part of the common market

[28]Ezrach (2016), p. 96.

[29]Case 127/73 *BRT* [1974] ECR 313, ECLI:EU:C:1974:6.

considering it necessary

> to ascertain whether SABAM was abusing its dominant position through its statutes and contracts with its members.[30]

Finally, the CJEU ruled that SABAM abused of dominant position as far as it

> imposes on its members obligations which are not absolutely necessary for the attainment of its object and which thus encroach unfairly upon a member's freedom to exercise his copyright.

This allowed national courts

> to decide whether and to what extent they (such abusive practices) affect the interests of authors or third parties concerned, with a view to deciding the consequences with regard to the validity and effect of the contracts in dispute or certain of their provisions.

According to the last sentence, the answer is implicit in favour of such direct effect by the argued Treaty provisions in benefit of individuals, contrary to the opinion of Mr. Advocate General Mayras in the *BRT* case considering that those provisions

> cannot, at the present time, create individual rights which national courts must safeguard.[31]

Another interesting case is *Masterfoods*, judgment of 14 December 2000,[32] as a result of a preliminary reference *ex* former Article 177 TEC by the Irish Supreme Court, requesting the interpretation of former Articles 85 and 86 TEC in relation again to the "exclusivity clause" contained in agreements signed by defendant HB Ice Cream and national ice-cream companies for the supply of freezer cabinets. The plaintiff in national proceeding, the US company Masterfoods, alleged in national proceeding that such exclusivity clause is null and void according to domestic and Community Law (*ex* former Articles 85 and 86 TEC). But here the special issue concerns that, during the contentious procedure, Masterfoods lodged a complaint against HB Ice Cream before the Commission, which concluded in infringement of Article 85(1) TEC[33]; subsequently, further action for annulment under Article 173 TEC was initiated by HB Ice Cream, now acting as Van der Bergh Foods Ltd,

[30]Ground 5. Regarding the relation between Competition and dominant position see classic literature such as Waelbroeck (1989), pp. 481–490. We recall the definition of dominant position provided for by the CJEU case in *Hoffman-La Roche* as "position of economic strength enjoyed by an undertaking which enables it to prevent effective competition being maintained on the relevant market by affording it the power to behave to an appreciable extent independently of its competitors, its customers and ultimately of the consumers" (Case 85/76 *Hoffman-La Roche* [1979] ECR 461, ECI:EU:C:1979:36, para. 38).

[31]P. 328.

[32]See, eg, comments by Kjolbey (2002), p. 175.

[33]Commission Decision 98/531/EC of 11 March 1998 (OJ L 246, 4.9.1998, p. 1). The administrative proceeding is taken under Article 3 of the Council Regulation No 17 of 6 February 1962 (first Regulation implementing Articles 85 and 86 of the Treaty) (OJ L 13, 21.2.1962, p. 204).

but the application was dismissed as unfounded by the former Court of First Instance.[34]

In fact, one of the questions referred to the CJEU by the judge *a quo* was related to procedural issues concerning the notion of *lis pendens* itself. The national judicial authority asked if the national proceeding giving place to the present preliminary reference had to stay until the resolution of the contentious "appeal"—in fact, action for annulment—against the Commission Decision before the former Court of First Instance (currently, General Court). The Court of Justice established how this cooperation between the Commission and national courts operates in order to make the administrative procedure for the public enforcement compatible with the judicial review aimed at the private enforcement of the same EU Competition rules at national level, precisely due to the recognised direct effect of Articles 85 and 86 TEC.[35] In sum, the Court of Justice ruled that

> it is for the national court to decide whether to stay proceedings pending final judgment in that action for annulment or in order to refer a question to the court for a preliminary ruling.

This approach is consistent with the conferral of competences between national jurisdiction and CJEU in preliminary ruling procedure as far as it is among the first decisions on the relevance to promote the preliminary reference (*Prüfungsrecht*).[36]

The most decisive CJEU doctrine on private enforcement of EU Competition Law is doubtlessly the *Courage* case, issued on 20 September 2001.[37] Here the Court of Justice first stated the admissibility of damages actions before national jurisdiction. The occasion was given by a preliminary reference promoted by the English Court of Appeal under former Article 234 TEC, on the interpretation of former Article 85 TEC. Facts concerned again to unpaid supplies of beer by the defendant, Mr. Crehan, who opposed the unlawfulness of the agreement concluded between the plaintiff, Courage, a brewery holding, and the company Intrepreneur Estates Ltd. (IEL), which represented all tenants of public houses (pubs) in UK imposing an obligation to purchase from Courage. In addition Mr. Crehan proposed a counterclaim for damages against Courage arguing that Courage sold its beers to independent tenants of pubs at substantially lower prices than those fixed to tenants attached to IEL and subject to a beer tie; he contended that this price difference reduced the profitability of its business. English Law at the time did not contemplate

---

[34]Case T-65/98 *Van der Bergh Foods* [2003] ECR II-4653, ECLI:EU:T:2003:281.

[35]See in Spain, Castillo de la Torre (2001), pp. 29–44; also specifically Calvo Caravaca, Suderow (2015), p. 117, where the authors explain the functioning of "two different proceedings and diverse normative sets".

[36]*Schwarze* judgment, para. 3. Also in *Van Gend en Loos* the Court of Justice declared that "the considerations which may have led a national Court or tribunal to its choice of questions as well as the relevance which it attributes to such questions in the context of a case before it are excluded from review by the Court of Justice" (ground A) 4.

[37]Among different comments: Fernández Vicién and Moreno-Tapia (2002); critical Reich (2005), pp. 35–66.

the possibility to claim damages between parties before national courts because of an illegal agreement, even when the incompatibility with Article 85 TEC is declared.

In fact, the four preliminary questions queried whether provision of the recovery of damages between parties because of the violation of EU Competition Law, now prohibited in English Law, as a consequence of the direct effect of former Article 85 TEC (private enforcement). The Court of Justice comes into prior *BRT/SABAM* case law recalling that Article 85 TEC

> produces direct effects in relations between individuals and creates rights for the individuals concerned which the national courts must safeguard,

reason for which

> any individual can rely on a breach of Article 85 (1) of the Treaty before a national court even where he is party to a contract that is liable to restrict or distort Competition within the meaning of that provision.

Otherwise,

> the full effectiveness of Article 85 of the Treaty... would be put at risk if it were not open to any individual to claim damages for loss caused to him by a contract or by conduct liable to restrict or distort Competition.

As a consequence, the Court of Justice declares that it is the duty of national law to provide the appropriate action in order to make effective rights provided by EU Law (principle of effectiveness), action not less favourable

> than those governing similar domestic actions (principle of equivalence).[38]

Here the Court of Justice follows, as most of the times, the opinion of Mr. Advocate General Mischo also establishing the "significant responsibility" that can involve a party in relation to the distortion of competition; in this case the denial of the right to obtain damages from the other contracting party by national law is not precluded by EU Law. Moreover, the standing to act before national jurisdiction in order to claim for damages derived from infringement of EU Competition rules belongs not only to direct purchasers but also to indirect ones, i.e., consumers. This means the admissibility of the so-called 'passing on defence',[39] which is now

[38]Ground 23, 24, 26 and 29, respectively. As a consequence the Court of Justice entails that national Court must impede "unjust enrichment of those benefited for such private actions" (para. 30). Both principles of equivalence and effectiveness were enounced in prior CJEU case law such as Case C-261/95, *Palmisani* [1997] ECR I-4025, ECLI:EU:C:1997:351: "the conditions, in particular time-limits, for reparation of loss or damage laid down by national law must not be less favourable than those relating to similar domestic claims (principle of equivalence) and must not be framed so as to make it virtually impossible or excessively difficult to obtain reparation (principle of effectiveness)" (para. 27). In the Spanish literature in relation to Directive 2014/104 EU see Iglesias Buhigues (2016), pp. 99–108.

[39]Also known as "indirect purchaser rule", its origin is placed in the US Antitrust Law; see specifically Velasco San Pedro and Herrero Suárez (2011), pp. 595 ff. in relation to the American origin of offensive passing-on actions, and pp. 584 f. in relation to the standing of indirect purchasers. Also interesting on the topic Commission documents such as Ashurst Report—Study

expressly contemplated under the above mentioned Article 14 of the Directive 2014/104/EU. In this context, the burden of proof shall rest on the claimant, according to the classical principle *actoris incumbat probatio*[40] in order to prove that he

> found himself in a markedly weaker position than the other party, so serious as to compromise or even eliminate his freedom to negotiate the terms of the contract and his capacity to avoid the loss or reduce its extent, in particular by availing himself in good time of all legal remedies available to him.

This fact shall be appreciated by the national court taking into account "the economic and legal context in which the parties find themselves" and "the respective bargaining power and conduct of the parties to the contract".[41]

3 Towards the Adoption of Directive 2014/104/EU on Behalf of the Private Enforcement of EU Competition Law

If the prior *Courage* case represents the acceptance of the passing on defense doctrine, the *Manfredi* case, of 13 July 2006,[42] is the symbol of the recognition of the so-called *follow-on actions* in EU Competition Law. These are claims for damages derived of prior declaration of infringement of EU Competition rules by European or national administrative authorities. These are opposed to *stand-alone actions*, where this prior declaration of infringement due to administrative proceeding does not take place.[43] In effect, the preliminary reference takes place as a result of action for damages claimed by Vicenzo Manfredi and others against respective insurance companies, started once the agreement between the last ones, signed for the purpose of exchanging information on the insurance sector, was declared unlawful by the Italian Competition Authority (ICA). ICA's decision, issued on 28 July 2000, had been also challenged by the insurance companies before the

on the conditions of claims for damages in case of infringement of EC competition (2004), available at http://ec.europa.eu/competition/antitrust/actionsdamages/study.html (Accessed 30 Jan 2018), Green Paper—Damages actions for breach of the EC antitrust rules, COM (2005) 672 final and White paper on damages actions for reach of the EC antitrust rules, COM (2008) 165 final; see comments by Torres Sustaeta (2014), pp. 28 ff.

[40]See Castillo de la Torre and Gippini Fournier (2017), p. 22 in relation to different standards of proof applied in actions for annulment against the Commission Decision related to infringements of Articles 101 and 102 TFEU.

[41]Paras. 33 and 32, respectively. It means that the evaluation by national Court not only must include economic parameters but also the "rule of reason" as it was established by the US Supreme Court; see Torres Sustaeta (2014), p. 142.

[42]See comments in Spain by Carpagnano (2007).

[43]Castellanos Ruiz (2011), p. 622, stressing the differences on evidence for both actions. In Spain as a result of Directive 2014/104/EU see Casado Navarro (2016), pp. 427–450; in relation to both actions Olmedo Peralta (2015), pp. 171–188.

Administrative Court (*Tribunale amministrativo regionale per il Lazio*) and further before the Council of the State (*Consiglio di Stato*), both judicial reviews confirming the administrative decision.

According to ICA the average price of civil liability car insurance premiums charged by the insurance companies was 20% higher than it would have been without the illegal agreement between them, which resulted in harm to final consumers as far as such excessive repayment had taken place. National judicial authority considered that not only violation of national EU Competition rules took place but also former Article 81 TEC; it was also declared that there was causal link between the harm suffered by the consumer as the end user of a service and the prohibited agreement recognising the right of third parties to claim compensation for damages when prior conditions are fulfilled. The CJEU stated that "Community Competition Law and national Competition Law applied in parallel" and

> Article 81 (1) EC produces direct effect in relations between individuals and creates rights for the individuals concerned which the national courts must safeguard

according to prior CJEU case law.[44] The most significant pronouncement of the present case is to be found in para. 61

> any individual can claim compensation for the harm suffered where there is a causal relationship between the harm and an agreement or practice prohibited under Article 81 EC

in accordance with the judge's *a quo* criterion as well as the opinion of Advocate General Geelhoed.

Nevertheless, the Court of Justice, after the recognition of availability of punitive damages in Competition cases[45] and the extension of the right of compensation for damages to third parties as a consequence of infringement of EU Competition rules, defers to domestic procedural law and judicial practice the establishment of legal remedies in order to make such rights effective. The only condition is the accomplishment with of the principles of equivalence and effectiveness, taking into account that the last one implies the recognition

> not only for actual loss (*dammum emergens*) but also for loss of profit (*lucrum cessans*) plus interest[46]

---

[44]Mention to *BRT* and *Courage* cases among others is done in para. 39. Here paras. 38 and 58 are replicated.

[45]See on the topic in Spain Vaquero López (2011), pp. 683–691.

[46]Para. 97. As ruled, "in the absence of Community rules governing that field, it is for the domestic legal system of each Member State to set the criteria for determining the system of damages for harm caused by an agreement or practice prohibited under Article 81 EC, provided that the principles of equivalence and effectiveness are observed. Therefore..., if it is possible to award particular damages, such as exemplary or punitive damages in domestic actions similar to actions founded on the Community competition rules, it must also be possible to award such damages in actions founded on Competition rules. However Community law does not prevent national courts from taking steps to ensure that the protection of the rights guaranteed by Community law does not entail the unjust enrichment of those who enjoy them" (ruling 5).

avoiding unjust enrichment. Therefore the Court of Justice imposes limits as these ones for further regulation of national law on the topic, which is in charge of making the protection of individuals recognised by EU Law effective. In conclusion, it is a competence conferred to national law to provide for the appropriate procedural rules, where the issue of evidence becomes essential in case-by-case basis at national level at the time of quantifying the damages and prejudices derived from the violation of Competition rules.[47] Undoubtedly the *Manfredi* case greatly influenced the further legislative policy of EU institutions and Directive 2014/104/EU.[48]

CJEU's case law continues providing for the right for compensation to individuals due to the infringement of EU Competition Law at the time of recognising the direct effect of Articles 101 and 102 TFEU as EU primary Law or to Regulation No 1/2003 as EU secondary Law.[49] It is also interesting to note the fact that, under the basis of the compliance with both principles of equivalence and effectiveness, the procedural autonomy of Member States[50] is admitted, too, as far as national legislation must regulate access to individuals to exercise their right to obtain compensation due to violation of EU Competition rules. This principle is stressed *Pfleiderer*,[51] where the *Amstgericht* (Local Court) Bonn asked for interpretation of Articles 11 and 12 of the Regulation No 1/2003. In this case, the request for full access to the file relating to the imposition of a fine in the décor paper sector by the *Bundeskartellamt* (the German Competition Authority)[52] requested by the applicant in a national proceeding was challenged for the first time at European level before the Court of Justice.[53] The scope was again to file a civil action for damages by Pfleiderer as a third party, a final customer of the fined undertakings, who claimed to have purchased goods of a value in excess of 60 million euro over the previous 3 years since the sanction.

Once more the CJEU affirms the principle of procedural autonomy of the Member States by recognising that

> neither the provisions of the EC Treaty nor Regulation No 1/2003 lay down common rules on leniency or common rules on the right of access to documents relating to a leniency

[47]See specifically Cristina Tudor (2011), pp. 567–578, exposing several models such as the mentioned Ashurst Report and others.

[48]See De Smijter and O'Sullivan (2006), pp. 23–26 in relation to Commission Green Paper on damages actions for breach of antitrust rules prior enounced.

[49]Also known at the time just as EU legislation by comparison to the Treaties, which represent the EU Constitution; see Robinson (2017), pp. 229–256. In Spain Gutiérrez Zarza (2002), pp. 1626–1633.

[50]See conclusion by Couronne (2010), p. 308, although no uniform national procedural rules have been reached between Member States.

[51]See comments by Völcker (2012), pp. 695–720.

[52]See official website http://www.bundeskartellamt.de/EN/. See specifically Fiebig (2014), pp. 373–408.

[53]See Martínez Moriel (2013), pp. 61–74. Also interesting on the topic Pérez Carrillo (2011), pp. 433–444 and Süderow (2011), pp. 535–550.

> procedure which have been voluntarily submitted to a national Competition authority pursuant to a national leniency programme.

As a consequence, due to

> the absence of binding regulation under European Union Law on the subject, (it is) for Member States to establish and apply national rules on the right of access, by persons adversely affected by a cartel, to documents relating to leniency procedures.[54]

As the Advocate General Mazák pointed out, the denial of such access to self-incriminating statements voluntarily provided by leniency applicants in recognition of infringement of Article 101 TFEU

> may create obstacles to or hinder to some extent an allegedly injured party's fundamental right to an effective remedy and to a fair trial guaranteed by Article 47... of the Charter of Fundamental Rights of the European Union (CFREU).[55]

In sum, the Court of Justice considers such leniency programmes "useful tools" for protecting the right of individuals to claim damages for loss caused by conducts restricting or distorting EU Competition rules as stated in the above mentioned cases *Courage* and *Manfredi*. It also worries about jeopardising the effective application of Article 101 TFEU by national competition authorities; in fact the last ones manage with the Commission these leniency programmes where the use of confidential information becomes essential. For this reason the Court of Justice pronounces a Solomonic decision ruling that

> it is... for the Courts and tribunals of the Member States, on the basis of their national Law, to determine the conditions under which such access must be permitted or refused by weighing the interests protected by European Union Law.

That means the conferral to national courts of a margin of appreciation with regard to the disclosure of such confidential information related to leniency in a case-by-case basis.

Precisely, the interpretation of Article 47 of the CFREU is requested by a Belgian Court, the *Rechtbank van koophandel te Brussel*, in combination with other dispositions of the Treaties and EU legislation in *Otis* case, of 6 November 2012.[56] Again the issue affects the disclosure of information but the most relevant discussion takes place with regard to the application of the fundamental right contained in Article 47 of the CFREU within the European Union in general and the European Commission in particular. The institution aims at consolidating its standing in national jurisdictions in order to bring civil actions of damages due to the loss caused to the European Union by agreements or practices violating EU Competition Law (Articles

[54]Paras. 20 and 23. See enthusiastic approach on such leniency procedures by Blake and Schnichels (2004), pp. 7–13; more critical Marvao (2016), pp. 1–27. About European and national policy in Spain Cantero Gamito (2011), pp. 695–707 as well as Jeleztcheva Jeleztecheva and Ruiz Muñoz (2011), pp. 719–734.

[55]Para. 48. See in the literature on the topic of fair trial *ex* Article 47 of the CFREU, eg, Galera Rodrigo (2015), pp. 7–29 and in Spain Faggiani (2014); also recently Milione (2017), pp. 659–674.

[56]See comments by Botta (2013), pp. 1105–1117; also Canapa and Hager (2013), pp. 113–119.

101 and 102 TFEU). In fact the European Union as a legal entity brought an application before the referring Court seeking the compensation by the defendants to pay to € 7,061,688 plus interest and costs derived from the loss caused as result of their anti-competitive practices established in prior Commission Decision of 21 February 2007.

Here the CJEU ruled that the European Union enjoys the same right recognised to individuals in the *Manfredi* case in order to

> claim compensation for the harm suffered where there is a causal relationship between the harm and an agreement or practice prohibited under Article 81 (1) EC (para. 43)

and the European Commission represents the European Union before the national jurisdiction. Again the Court of Justice strictly follows the opinion delivered by Advocate General Cruz-Villalón, who adds that this right to effective judicial protection attributed to the European Commission on behalf of the European Union in order to claim for damages before national courts is not precluded

> even though it was the Commission itself which previously conducted an infringement procedure which culminated in the decision that has formed the basis for the claim (para. 72).

As it shall be later concluded, public and private enforcement of EU Competition Law comes hand in hand and no obstacle to private enforcement can be derived because of prior public enforcement of the same anti-competitive behaviour although the principle of equality or arms apparently can be distorted due to the privilege of information that has the European Commission over the defendants as it is argued here.[57]

The *Donau Chemie* case, of 6 June 2013,[58] confirms the previous judgments such as *Pfleiderer*. Accordingly, the national court must decide on a case-by-case basis on the access to the file by third parties in order to facilitate their bringing actions for damages before national courts. Here the request for preliminary ruling made by the *Oberlandesgericht Wien* under Article 267 TFEU makes use of such precedent, asking for interpretation of both principles of effectiveness and equivalence in the light of the rules applicable in the Austrian legal system to actions for damages in respect of breach of EU Competition Law. In fact, the Austrian High Regional Court acting here as Cartel Court deals with the application lodged by an association of undertakings (*Verbrand Druck & Medientechnik,* VDMT) seeking access to the file related to a prior judicial proceeding brought by the Austrian Federal Competition Authority (*Bundeswettbewerbsbehörde*)[59] against Donau Chemie and other

---

[57] As here the Court of Justice justifies, the information to which the defendants in the main proceedings refer have not been provided to the national Court by the Commission, the latter having also explained that it has relied only on the information available in the non-confidential version of the decision finding an infringement of Article 81 EC (para. 73); for this reason it is concluded that no breach of the principle of equality of arms takes place.

[58] See for example comments by Dworschak and Maritzen (2013), pp. 829–844.

[59] See basic references in Fürlinger (2017), also comments about other national competition authorities are here included.

enterprises, which final judgment condemned the latter to pay a fine of € 1.5 million due to anti-competitive practices in violation of Article 101 TFEU. Specifically, VDMT wants to gather evidence in order to determine the amount of the potential loss suffered by its members and, if it is the case, to file an action for damages against Donau Chemie and others; such access, according to the Austrian Law, requires the consent of parties at the procedure in order to provide access to the files.[60]

CJEU confirm previous case law:

1. Article 101(1) of the TFEU produces direct effects in relations between individuals and creates rights for the individuals (*Manfredi* case)
2. The practical effect of the prohibition laid down in that provision would be put at risk if it were not open to any individual to claim damages for loss caused to him by a contract or by conduct liable to restrict or distort Competition (*Courage* case)[61]
3. The national courts whose task is to apply the provisions of EU Law in areas within their jurisdiction must ensure that those rules take full effect and must protect the rights which they confer on individuals (*Manfredi* and *Courage* cases among others)[62]
4. That right... allows persons who have suffered harm due to that infringement (of Article 101 (1) TFEU) to seek full compensation not only for actual loss (*dammum emergens*) but also for loss of profit (*lucrum cessums*) plus interest[63] (*Manfredi* case)
5. It is for the Member States to establish and apply national rules on the right of access, by persons believing themselves to be adversely affected by a cartel, to documents relating to national proceedings concerning the cartel (*Pfleiderer* case)[64]
6. The national courts must weigh up the respective interests in favour of disclosure of the information and in favour of the protection of that information', which should be done 'only on a case-by-case basis (*Pfleiderer* case)[65]

[60] Para. 39 (2) *Kartellgesetz* (2005) available via https://www.jusline.at/gesetz/kartg/paragraf/39 and para. 219 *Zivilprozeßordnung* available via https://www.jusline.at/gesetz/zpo/paragraf/219 (Accessed 29 Jan 2018), both regulations are still in force.

[61] Para. 21 quoting paras. 39 in *Manfredi* case and 26 in *Courage* case.

[62] Case 106/77 *Simmenthal* [1978] ECR 629, ECLI:EU:C:1978:49, para. 16 and Case C-213/89 *Factortame Ltd and others* [1990] ECR 2433, ECLI:EU:C:1990:257, para. 19.

[63] Para. 24 referring to para. 95 in *Manfredi* case.

[64] Para. 26 quoting para. 23 in *Pfleiderer* case. In previous para. 25 it has been stated that "in the absence of EU rules governing the matter, it is for the domestic legal system of each Member State to lay down the detailed procedural rules governing actions for safeguarding rights which individuals derive from EU law".

[65] Paras. 30 and 34 quoting paras. 30 and 31 in *Pfleiderer* case.

Last, after defining the principles of equivalence and effectiveness according to the *Courage* and *Manfredi* cases,[66] the Court of Justice rules only on the basis of the latter declaring that the

> European Union Law, in particular the principle of effectiveness, precludes a provision of national Law under which access to documents forming part of the file relating to national proceedings concerning the application of Article 101 TFEU, including access to documents made available under a leniency programme, by third parties who are not party to those proceedings with a view to bringing an action for damages against participants in an agreement or concerted practice is made subject solely to the consent of all parties to those proceedings, without leaving any possibility for the national courts of weighing up the interests involved.

By contrast, the Court of Justice does not use the grounding argument in the opinion of the Advocate General Jäaskinen related to the principle of equivalence, which provided for a totally opposite solution.[67]

The final decision to be exposed here is *Kone AG,* judgment of 5 June 2014,[68] where request for interpretation of Article 101 TFEU takes place. The preliminary reference is requested by *Oberster Gerichtshof* (Austria). The Court of Justice grounds its decision on the examined previous case law in order to deal with the issue of the so-called "umbrella pricing" effects.[69] Specifically, the defendant in national proceeding, ÖOB-Infrastruktur, a subsidiary of Austrian Federal Railways, claimed that

> part of the loss it suffered was caused by the fined cartel, which made it possible to maintain a market price at such a high level that even competitors not party to the cartel were able to benefit from a market price that was higher than it would otherwise have been but for the existence of that cartel (para. 27)

The issue was disputed because the Austrian Civil Code at the time required a direct casual link according to prior contract between parties in order to seek

---

[66] "The rules applicable to actions for safeguarding rights which individuals derive from the direct effect of EU law must not be less favourable than those governing similar domestic actions (principle of equivalence) and must not make it in practice impossible or excessively difficult to exercise rights conferred by EU law (principle of effectiveness)" in para. 27 according to *Courage* case, para. 29, and *Manfredi* case, para. 62.

[67] "The principle of equivalence under European Union law does not preclude a national provision that makes grant of access to documents before a national Court, and which have been gathered within competition law proceedings involving the application of European Union competition law to third persons who are not parties to those competition law proceedings, subject, without exception, to the condition that all the parties to the competition law proceedings must give their consent thereto, when the rule applies in the same way to purely national competition law proceedings but differs from national provisions applicable to third party access to judicial documents in the context of other types of proceedings, in particular contentious and non-contentious civil proceedings and criminal proceedings" (para. 71 (2)).

[68] See comments by Monti (2014), pp. 464–475.

[69] See on the topic Svetlicinil and Botta (2016), pp. 399–411, comparing both legal systems also in relation to the *Kone* case. In Spain Olmedo Peralta (2014), pp. 107–130 arguing in favour of the non-contractual liability in private enforcement of competition rules after the *Kone* case.

compensation for injuries.[70] According to the CJEU, the rule risks at jeopardising the full effectiveness of Article 101 TFEU. For this reason the CJEU rules according to the opinion by Advocate General Kokott[71] that Article 101 TFEU must be interpreted as contrary of such national legislation with acceptance of the possible causal link between cartel activity and umbrella pricing; this ruling means as said that

> the Union's interest in promoting effective Competition supersedes Member State Law on this matter.[72]

4 Recent CJEU Case Law on Private Enforcement of EU Competition Law After Preliminary Rulings and Other CJEU Proceedings

One of the most relevant issues in this chapter is the relevance of other CJEU proceedings dealing with the issue of private enforcement of EU Competition Law. Those are proceedings by nature contentious[73]; in particular, actions for annulment delivered by General Court *ex* Article 263 TFEU and subsequent appeals under Article 56 of the CJEU Statute must be scrutinised. It is the case of *Kone Oyj*, delivered on 24 October 2013, on appeal introduced by the Finnish corporation Kone Oyj and its European group against the judgment of the General Court,[74] which dismissed their prior action for annulment of the Commission Decision under proceeding of infringement *ex* former Article 81 TEC.[75] In this context the General Court operates as the first instance Commercial Court at European level as far as it deals with Competition rules solving questions of fact, too, under action for annulment *ex* Article 263 TFEU[76] and not only *de iure* as the Court of Justice does after preliminary ruling proceedings *ex* Article 267 TFEU.

[70]At the time Article 1295 *Allgemeines Bürgerliches Gesetzbuch* (ABGB), today amended, available at: https://www.jusline.at/gesetz/abgb/paragraf/1295 (Accessed 29 Jan 2018).

[71]The Advocate General concludes that Article 101 TFEU "preclude(s) the interpretation and application of domestic legislation enacted by a Member State which categorically excludes, for legal reasons, any civil liability of undertakings belonging to a cartel for loss resulting from the fact that an undertaking not party to the cartel, benefiting from the protection of the cartel's practices, set its prices higher than would otherwise have been expected under competitive conditions" (para. 90 textually reproduced by CJEU ruling).

[72]Ezrach (2016), p. 606.

[73]See extensively on the topic of the preliminary ruling's non contentious nature Jimeno Bulnes (1996), pp. 145 ff.

[74]Case T-171/07 *Kone Oyj* [2011] ECR II-5313, ECLI:EU:T:2011:365.

[75]Commission Decision of 21 February 2007 (OJ C 75, 26.3.2008, p. 19).

[76]See on the topic, eg, Albors Llorens (2002), p. 135 in relation to action for annulment. In Spain specifically Soldevilla Fragoso (2014), pp. 385–404.

The Court of Justice here, after preliminary considerations on behalf of the principle of effective judicial protection according to Articles 47 of CFREU and 6 (1) of the European Convention of Human Rights (ECHR),[77] declares that EU Courts have

> unlimited jurisdiction… to substitute its own appraisal for the Commission's and, consequently, to cancel, reduce or increase the fine or periodic penalty payment imposed[78]

clarifying the distribution of competences between European Commission and EU Courts. As specified

> an action for annulment has neither the object nor the effect of replacing a full investigation of the case in the context of an administrative procedure

but it has to deal not only on the matter

> whether the evidence relied on is factually accurate, reliable and consistent but also ascertain whether that evidence contains all the information which must be taken into account in order to assess a complex situation and whether it is capable of substantiating the conclusions drawn from it.[79]

In fact, after the review of legality carried out by the Court of Justice, all the grounds of appeal are rejected and the appeal dismissed as a whole.

In the case of action for annulments under current Article 263 TFEU, which is the usual EU contentious proceeding dealing with Competition Law by the CJEU, the case *CEES Madrid,* judgment of 6 February 2014, is one of the landmark Spanish cases related to EU Competition Law. In fact, both associations of undertakings holding license to operate service stations promoted an action for annulment *ex* Article 263 TFEU against a Commission Decision,[80] which rejected their prior complaint concerning infringement of EU Competition rules by Repsol, a Spanish oil company. Grounds of annulment proposed by the applicants were the infringement by the Commission of Articles 9(2), 23(2)(c) and 24(1)(c) of the Regulation No 1/2003 claiming the reopening of the administrative proceeding against Repsol by the Commission. At the same time a national administrative proceeding was carried out by the Spanish National Competition Commission (*Comisión Nacional de la Competencia,* CNC)[81] against Repsol.

---

[77]See on the topic related to Competition Law Piroddi (2011), pp. 447–462.

[78]Para. 23, ruled on the basis of Articles 31 of the Regulation No 1/2003 and 261 TFEU. The latter provides that "Regulations adopted jointly by the European Parliament and the Council, and by the Council, pursuant to the provisions of the Treaties may give the Court of Justice of the European Union unlimited jurisdiction with regard to the penalties provided for in such regulations".

[79]Paras. 26 and 28 respectively. On the topic of judicial review of EU Competition rules' infringement see Castillo de la Torre and Gippini Fournier (2017), p. 265.

[80]Commission Decision C(2011) 2994 final of 28 Apr 2011, not reported.

[81]Today appropriate title and acronym are *Comisión Nacional de los Mercados y la Competencia*, CNMC; more information available CNMC. https://www.cnmc.es/en (Accessed 29 Jan 2018). In relation to the new denomination see in the literature Carlón Ruiz (2014).

The General Court dismisses the action arguing that the Commission has discretion to act under Article 9(2) of the Regulation No 1/2003 in order to evaluate the concrete interests on Competition Law by the European Union;

> it is incumbent on the Commission to assign different priorities to Competition problems which are brought to its attention and to decide whether further investigation of a case is in the European Union interest.

In addition it is recalled that

> the person lodging a complaint concerning infringement of Article 101 TFEU or Article 102 TFEU does not have the right to require the Commission to adopt a final decision as regards the existence or otherwise of the alleged infringement.

Lastly, it is declared that

> decisions adopted by the Commission do not affect the power of the national Competition authorities to apply Articles 101 TFEU and 102 TFEU.[82]

What is even more interesting is the separation established by the General Court between public and private enforcement of Competition rules as an answer to the alleged CJEU case law such as the *Courage* and *Manfredi* cases; as expressly declared, they are independent procedures and here only the first one is dealt in the case at stake.[83]

Another interesting appeal under Article 56 of the CJEU Statute is the *EnBW Energie* case, issued on 27 February 2014, where the European Commission challenges the judgment of the General Court[84] by which its prior Decision was annulled refusing the request made by EnBW Energie Baden Württemberg (Germany) for access to the case-file derived from an administrative proceeding of infringement *ex* former Article 81 TCE.[85] In this case the special rule of "professional secrecy" envisaged by Article 28 of the Regulation No 1/2003 is applicable. The provision imposes the obligation not to disclose information related to administrative Competition proceedings addressed to Commission and national competition authorities of Member States as well as to their officials, servants or other persons attached to them. Nevertheless the General Court privileges the observance of the general rule

[82] Paras. 58, 59 and 66 respectively.

[83] "It is necessary to reject the applicants' argument based on the case law of the Court of Justice, according to which the full effectiveness of Articles 101 TFEU and 102 TFEU requires that each person may claim damages for the loss caused by an infringement of those rules (Case *Courage and Crehan*, para. 26, and Joined Cases *Manfredi and Others*, para. 60). Since that case law relates to the implementation of those provisions on the initiative of a person who has suffered the damage, it is not possible to infer from it that, in the context of the implementation of those provisions on the initiative of a competition authority, which has only limited resources, a penalty would be imposed in all cases in which an undertaking does not comply with a commitment made binding under Article 9(1) Regulation No 1/2003" (para. 92).

[84] Case T-344/08 *EnBW Energie Baden-Württemberg* [2012] ECLI:EU:T:2012:242. See comments by Maillo González-Orús (2014), pp. 287–290.

[85] Commission Decision SG.E.3/MV/psi D (2008) 4931 of 16 June 2008, not reported.

providing the right of access to EU documents contemplated within the Treaties as well as within Regulation No 1049/2001[86] as far as it is declared that

> the institution concerned must also provide explanations as to how access to that document could specifically and actually undermine the interest protected by an exception laid down[87]

in Article 4 of the Regulation.

At the same time the Court of Justice referes back to prior case law in order to highlight that

> any person is entitled to claim compensation for the loss caused to him by a breach of Article 81 EC

and how this

> right strengthens the working of the EU Competition rules, thereby making a significant contribution to the maintenance of effective Competition in the European Law.[88]

The Court recalls also that this right must be balanced with the public interest by the European Commission within the administrative proceedings under current Article 101 TFEU, in order to challenge anti-competitive practices "on a case-by-case basis".[89] In addition,

> it is highly unlikely that the action for damages will need to be based on all the evidence in the file related to that proceeding[90]

ex former Article 81 TEC. In conclusion and basically, the Court of Justice overrules the judgment issued by the General Court considering that the defendant EnBW, first, was not

> able to show specifically in what way certain individual documents were covered by the exception provided for in Article 4(2) and (3) of that regulation (No. 1049/2001)

second, had

> also failed to demonstrate that there is an overriding public interest in disclosure of those documents by virtue of Article 4(2) and (3) of Regulation No. 1049/2001.

By contrast, the defendant EnBW

[86]Regulation (EC) No 1049/2001 of the European Parliament and of the Council of 30 May 2001 regarding public access to European Parliament, Council and Commission documents (OJ L 145, 31.5.2001, p. 43).

[87]Para. 64 quoting prior CJEU case law on the topic.

[88]Para. 104 quoting *Courage*, *Manfredi*, *Pfleiderer* and *Donau Chemie* cases.

[89]Para. 107. As said, "the risk of facilitating access to the leniency file to third parties harmed by the cartel may lie in the fact that the cartelists no longer have sufficient incentives to request clemency" and "without these incentives, the cartel may not be detected or administratively sanctioned, which in turn would make any claim for damages much more difficult"; see Maillo González-Orús (2014), p. 289.

[90]Para. 106 quoting the *Donau Chemie* case (para. 33).

> simply stated that it was 'utterly dependant' on disclosure of documents in the file in question, without showing that such disclosure would have enabled it to obtain the evidence needed to establish its claim for damages as it had no other way of obtaining that evidence.[91]

Other cases related to actions for annulment *ex* Article 263 TFEU dealing as well with access to the file and disclosure of information are both German cases such as *Evonik Degussa,* a judgment of 28 February 2015,[92] and *Axa Versicherung,* a judgment of 7 July 2015. Concerning the first case, essentially the applicant complains for the lack of confidential treatment due to the publicity given to the Commission Decision delivered after proceeding on infringement of former Article 81 TEC.[93] The General Court dismisses the action declaring that

> the interest of a company which has participated in an infringement of Article 81 EC in avoiding such action is not an interest worthy of protection, particularly in the light of the right which any person has to claim damages for loss caused to him by conduct liable to restrict or distort Competition.[94]

Nevertheless, further appeal before the Court of Justice partially overrules the judgment of the General Court and annuls the contested Commission Decision in contrast with the Opinion of Advocate General.[95] The outcome seems not consonant with further CJEU judgments resolving as well appeals on same issue of confidential treatment requests. For example, in the case *AGC Glass Europe*, judgment of 26 July 2017, the Court of Justice dismisses the appeal introduced by several car glass manufacturers challenging prior General Court's judgment[96] denying professional secrecy and confirming the Commission Decision.[97]

Conversely, in the second case the General Court

> annuls Commission Decision 2012/817 and 2012/3021 Gestdem of 29 October 2013, refusing two requests for access to documents in the file of Case COMP/39.125 (Carglass) in so far as it refuses to grant Axa Versicherung AG access to references to the 'leniency documents' included in the table of contents of that file.

Indeed, the Court recalls how

> all persons are entitled to claim compensation for the loss caused to them by a breach of the EU rules on Competition[98]

[91]Paras. 129, 130 and 132, last one with reference to the *Donau Chemie* case (paras. 32 and 44).

[92]See e.g. Kantza and Picod (2015), pp. 159–165.

[93]Decision C(2006) 1766 final, case COMP/38.620, of 3 May 2006, known as *PHP* Decision (Hydrogen Peroxide and Perborate), not reported.

[94]Para. 110 quoting prior CJEU case law such as the *Courage*, *Manfredi* and *Otis* cases.

[95]Case C-162/15P *Evonik Degussa* [2017] ECLI:EU:T:2017:205. The Opinion of Advocate General Spuzner was delivered on 21 July 2016.

[96]Case T-465/12, *AGC Glass Europe and Others* [2015] ECLI:EU:T:2015:505.

[97]Commission Decision C(2012) 5179 final of 6 August 2012, not reported.

[98]Para. 66, quoting cases such as *Courage* (paras. 26 and 27) and *Commission v EnBW* (para. 104).

as well as declares that

> it is highly unlikely that the action will need to be based on all the evidence in the file relating to that proceeding.[99]

For all these reasons the Court confers to the Commission the task of

> weigh up, on a case-by-case basis, the respective interests in favour of disclosure or such documents and in favour of the protection of those documents, taking into account all the relevant factors in the case;[100]

moreover, it is

> still necessary for the Commission to substantiate its refusal to give access to the requisite factual and legal standard, on the basis of a reasonably foreseeable risk of specific and actual harm to one or more of the interests protected by the exceptions laid down in Article 4 (2) of Regulation No. 1049/2001.[101]

Another interesting case after an action of annulment is the *Aer Lingus* judgment, issued on 21 December 2016.[102] The CJEU delivers a first interpretations on Directive 2014/104, making clear difference between private and public enforcement of Competition rules at European and national level. In the context of the appeal promoted by the European Commission against prior GC judgments[103] annulling its Decision ordering the recovery of State aid by each affected passenger from the beneficiaries (Aer Lingus and Ryanair flight companies),[104] the Court of Justice states that

> the recovery of unlawful aid had a different purpose from that of Directive 2014/104.

In particular the Court points out that the

> directive, as is made clear in recitals 3 and 4 thereof, seeks to ensure that any person who considers that he has been adversely affected by an infringement of the Competition rules laid down in Articles 101 and 102 TFEU may effectively exercise his right to claim

---

[99]Para. 68, quoting again the case *Commission v EnBW* case (para. 106) as well as the *Donau Chemie* case (para. 33).

[100]Para. 69, with reference to the *Commission v EnBW* case (para. 107) as well as Case T-534/11 *Schenker AG* [2014] ECLI:EU:T:2014:854 (para. 95).

[101]Para. 101 quoting two judgments pronounced by the Court of Justice on appeal: Joined Cases C-39/05P and C-52/05P *Turco* [2008] ECR I-4713, ECLI:EU:C:2008:374; Case C-280/11P *Access Info Europe* [2013] ECLI:EU:C:2013:671. Article 4(2) of the Regulation No 1049/2001 expressly provides the exception to public access of European institutions' documents when "disclosure would undermine the protection of commercial interests of a natural or legal person, including intellectual property; Court proceedings and legal advice; and the purpose of inspections, investigations and audits, unless there is an overriding public interest in disclosure".

[102]See annotation by Skovgaard Olykke (2017), pp. 93–98.

[103]Case T-432/12 *Aer Lingus* [2015] ECLI:EU:T:2015:78; Case T-500/12 *Ryanair* [2015] ECLI:EU:T:2015:73.

[104]Commission Decision 2013/199/EU of 25 July 2012 on State aid Case SA.29064 (OJ L 119, 30.4.2013, p. 30).

> compensation for the harm which he believes he has suffered' by contrast with the purpose of aid recovery, which 'is not seek compensation for individual harm of any kind but to re-establish on the market in question the situation as it was before the aid was granted.[105]

This argument is used by the Court in order to set aside prior judgments by General Court in relation to the fixed amount to be recovered by passengers.

The last case to be mentioned is very significant in connection with the relationship maintained between public and private enforcement of EU Competition Law through proceedings provided for by Regulation No 1/2003 and Directive 2014/104. This is the *Agria Polska* case, judgment of 16 May 2017, as a result of an action for annulment before the General Court *ex* Article 263 TFEU promoted by two Polish undertakings with a German and Austrian ones against a Commission Decision.[106] The General Court rejected their complaint concerning infringements of Articles 101 and 102 TFEU allegedly committed, essentially, by 13 producers and distributors of plant protection products with the assistance or through four professional organisations and a law firm. Recently dismissed the appeal at the time of writing,[107] the General Court makes an interesting observation in order to differentiate public and private enforcement of Competition rules as far as it declares that the remedies independent, each other reaching different results. In particular, it is expressly declared that

> any refusal by a national Competition authority or the Commission to open an investigation, which may lead to an assessment by one of those administrative authorities as to the existence of an infringement of the Competition rules and, where appropriate, the imposition of a financial penalty on the undertaking concerned by that investigation, cannot have the effect of limiting the applicants' right to bring proceedings before the national courts for damages caused by infringement of Articles 101 and 102 TFEU (para 82).[108]

5 Final Conclusions

As it is foreseeable, the CJEU case law on the interpretation of the Directive 2014/104 has increased in recent years. As an example, at the time of writing, there was an interesting application under Article 267 TFEU promoted by a Portuguese Court.

---

[105]Para. 105. We recall that Recital 4 of the Directive 2014/104/EU provides that "the right in Union law to compensation for harm resulting from infringement of Union and national competition law requires each Member State to have procedural rules ensuring the effective exercise of that right" according to Articles 19(1) TFEU and 47 CFREU.

[106]Commission Decision C(2015) 4284 final, of 19 June 2015 (Case AT.39864 .BASF), available at http://ec.europa.eu/competition/antitrust/cases/dec.../39864_575_5.pdf (Accessed 31 Jan 2018); Case T-480/15 *Agria Polska* [2017] ECLI:EU:T:2017:339.

[107]Case C-373/17P *Agria Polska* [2018] ECLI:EU:C:2018:756.

[108]Moreover it is remembered that "actions for damages before national courts, in the same way as the action of the Commission and the national competition authorities, can make a significant contribution to the maintenance of effective competition in the EU" (para. 84) according to *Courage* case.

The national court casts doubts on the direct effect of the Directive on behalf of creating rights to private parties in order to seek compensation for alleged damages even when the deadline for its implementation on national law had not yet expired. This is the *Cogeco Communications* case, lodged by the *Tribunal Comercial da Comarca de Lisboa* on 15 November 2017, asking for interpretation of Articles 9 (1) and 10(2, 3, 4) of the Directive 2014/104.[109] Here the Court of Justice has a challenging task as far as the main issue is connected with the recognition of the direct effect to Directives before expiration of its implementation's deadline at a whole. Such question certainly is not yet clear in the panorama of CJEU case law[110] contrary to when such deadline has already expired, where the effect direct is unanimously recognised.

Concerning Spain,[111] the implementation of Directive 2014/104/EU has taken place after the deadline through Royal Decree Law 9/2017 of 26 May, amending both substantive and procedural Spanish rules and in particular the Law 15/2017, of 3 July 3, on Defence on Competition and Law 1/2000, of 7 January, on Civil Procedure (*Ley de Enjuiciamiento Civil,* LEC).[112] Especially interesting is this last amendment adding new Articles 283 *bis* (a) to 282 *bis* (k) LEC, providing for the requirements in order to ask for access to evidence by parties in civil compensation claims, if confidential information is involved. The rules are influenced by common law systems[113] and introduce a sort of discovery providing for a disclosure rule of documentary evidence unknown until know in Spanish civil procedure (and criminal one) as it is logical in a Civil Law model of procedure.[114]

In fact, this is a thorny issue, which makes a difference between the public and private enforcement of Competition Law as two different ways to ensure compliance with the Regulations governing Competition Law at European and national level and of the pre-eminence of the latter or the former.[115] Access to sources of evidence and, in general, compliance with procedural guarantees are more favourably contemplated in judicial proceedings taking place before national courts as it operates for private enforcement than in administrative proceedings promoted by European

[109]Case C-637/17, OJ C 32, 29.1.2018, p. 14.

[110]See Rassu (2017), p. 168, suggestion possible direct effects even before the transposition; on the opposite to Korkea-aho (2015), pp. 70–88. In Spain specifically Alonso García (2017), pp. 13–24, who also believes the question has not yet been solved by the CJEU case law.

[111]See San Martin Calvo in this book.

[112]See English version available at http://www.mjusticia.gob.es/cs/Satellite/Portal/es/servicios-ciudadano/documentacion-publicaciones/publicaciones/traducciones-derecho-espanol (Accessed 2 Feb 2018) under payment. See in Tobío Rivas (2013–2014), pp. 630–634 as well as Herrero Suárez (2016), pp. 150–183 in relation to the Spanish Bill at the time. In relation to the approved law see ie specific issue *La defensa (privada) de la competencia. El notario del siglo XXI,* (74), 2017.

[113]See Herrero Suárez (2016), p. 160; also specifically Ferrándiz (2017).

[114]See generally Jimeno-Bulnes (2013b), pp. 409–459.

[115]On the pre-eminence of public enforcement Herrero Suárez (2016), p. 151; Torres Sustaeta (2014), p. 80; on the pre-eminance of private enforcement: Tobío Rivas (2013–2014), p. 84.

Commission or national competition authorities protecting public enforcement of EU and, if it is the case, national rules on Competition. In this last context access to information is generally restricted for legal and individual persons in their disputes against European and national authorities.[116] This undermines the fairness of public enforcement of competition rules; moreover, such lack of defense rights can take place, not only in administrative proceedings but also in judicial ones, for example before the General Court when the annulment of Commission Decisions restricting anti-competitive practices is discussed.[117]

In this context, the private enforcement is presented as an adequate guarantee of protection and compliance of Competition rules at national level especially for individuals, who, according to prior CJEU case law, do not need any previous decision on public enforcement by a national or European authority in order to claim compensation for the harm caused due to anti-competitive behavior (*Agria Polska* case).[118] Indeed, the coexistence between public and private enforcement is presented as the best solution that can be given to the protection of Competition Law, even under the risk of the existence of contradictory solutions due to the independence of each remedy. On the contrary, a close cooperation is desirable between European Commission, national Competition authorities and national courts in order to promote a good and fair functioning of the market.[119] Once more the contribution of the CJEU case law has been decisive on the matter.

References

Albors Llorens A (2002) EC competition law and policy. William Publishing, Portland

Alonso García R (2017) La interpretación del Derecho nacional en función de la entrada en vigor de las Directivas y de su fecha límite de transposición. Revista Española de Derecho Europeo 64:13–24

Benavides Velasco P (2005) Aplicación de las normas de defensa de la competencia por la jurisdicción ordinaria. La competencia atribuida a los Juzgados de lo Mercantil. In: Font Galán J, Pino Abad M (eds) Estudios de Derecho de la Competencia. Marcial Pons, Madrid, pp 273–286

Berenguer Fuster L (2011) La aplicación privada del Derecho de la Competencia. In: Velasco San Pedro LA, Alonso Ledesma C et al (eds) La aplicación privada del derecho de la competencia. Lex Nova, Madrid, pp 51–60

Blake S, Schnichels D (2004) Leniency following modernisation: safeguarding Europe's leniency programmes. Competition Policy Newsl 2:7–13

Botta M (2013) Commission acting as plaintiff in cases of private enforcement of EU Competition Law: Otis – Case C-199/11, Europese Gemeenshap v Otis NV and others, Judgment of the

[116]See at a whole in relation to national administrative proceedings Tobío Rivas (2013–2014).

[117]See Nascimbene (2013), pp. 573–583, including several proposals *de lege ferenda*, such as the creation of specific agencies and even a specific European Court with the aim to separate investigative and decision-making tasks as well as to reduce the duration of proceedings.

[118]Remember prior *Agria Polska* case, above mentioned, at least till the appeal is solved by the Court of Justice and other opinion be delivered.

[119]See for example Slot and Farley (2017), pp. 196 ff.

Court of Justice (Grand Chamber) of 6 November 2012. Common Mark Law Rev 50 (4):1105–1117

Calvo Caravaca AL, Suderow J (2015) El efecto vinculante de las resoluciones de las autoridades nacionales de competencia en la aplicación privada del Derecho antitrust. Cuadernos de Derecho Transnacional 7(II):114–157

Canapa C, Hager P (2013) Right of European Union to claim compensation before a national court against the member of a cartel: Case C-199/11, Europese Gemeenshap v Otis NV and Others, Judgement of 6 November, not yet reported. Maastricht J Eur Comp Law 20(1):113–119

Cantero Gamito M (2011) Los programas de clemencia en la lucha antitrust. In: Velasco San Pedro LA, Alonso Ledesma C et al (eds) La aplicación privada del derecho de la competencia. Lex Nova, Madrid, pp 695–707

Cappelletti M (2015) Is the European Court of Justice ‘running wild’? Eur Law Rev 40:311–322

Carlón Ruiz M (ed) (2014) La Comisión Nacional de los Mercados y la Competencia. Aranzadi, Cizur Meno, Navarra

Carpagnano M (2007) El private enforcement del Derecho comunitario de la competencia en acción: análisis crítico de la decision del Tribunal de Justicia en los asuntos acumulados C-295/298/04. Available via InDret. http://www.indret.com. Accessed 5 May 2018

Casado Navarro A (2016) La Directiva 2014/104/UE sobre acciones por daños en materia de competencia; una apuesta por las follow-on actions. In: Ruiz Pérez JI (ed) La compensación de los daños por infracción de normas de competencia tras la directiva 2014/104/UE. Directiva y propuesta de transposición. Thomson Reuters Aranzadi Cizur Menor. Navarra, pp 427–450

Castellanos Ruiz E (2011) Competencia judicial internacional en las acciones de reparación de daños por infracción del Derecho antitrust. In: Velasco San Pedro LA, Alonso Ledesma C et al (eds) La aplicación privada del derecho de la competencia. Lex Nova, Madrid, pp 619–651

Castillo de la Torre F (2001) Decisiones de la Comisión en maeria de política de la competencia ante los tribunales nacionales: la sentencia Masterfoods. Gaceta jurídica de la Unión europea y de la competencia 213:29–44

Castillo de la Torre F, Gippini Fournier E (2017) Evidence, proof and judicial review in EU Competition Law. Edward Elgar, Cheltenham

Chalters D, Barroso L (2014) What Van Gend en Loos stands for. Int J Const Law 12(1):105–134

Cosimo ED (2011) Repetita. . . iuvant? Sulla priorità interpretativa nell’ ordinamento giuridico dell’ Unione. Il dialogo fra le corti e la question prioritaire de constitutionnalité al vaglio della Corte di Giustizia. Revista General de Derecho Público Comparado. Available via http://www.iustel.com. Accessed 5 May 2018

Couronne V (2010) L’autonomie procédurale des États members de l’Union européenne à l’épreuve du temps. Cahiers de droit europeen 46(3–4):273–309

Cristina Tudor E (2011) La cuantificación de daños y perjuicios en la aplicación privada del derecho europeo de la competencia. In: Velasco San Pedro LA, Alonso Ledesma C et al (eds) La aplicación privada del derecho de la competencia. Lex Nova, Madrid, pp 567–578

De Smijter E, O’Sullivan D (2006) The Manfredi judgment of the ECJ and how it relates to the Commission’s initiative on EC antitrust damages actions. Competition Policy Newsl 3:23–26

Derlén M, Lindholm J (2014) Goodbye van Gend en Loos, hello Bosman? Using network analysis to measure the importance of individual CJEU judgments. Eur Law J 20:667–687

Dune N (2014) The role of private enforcement within EU Competition Law. Camb Yearb Eur Legal Stud 16:143–187

Dworschak S, Maritzen L (2013) Einsicht - der ersten Schritt zur Besserung? Zur Akteneinsicht in kronzeugendokumente nach dem Donau Chemie-Urteil des EuGH. Wirtschaft und Wettbewerb 63:829–844

Editorial Comments (2014) One bird in the hand. . . The Directive on damages actions for breach of the competition rules. Common Mark Law Rev 51:1333–1342

Ezrach A (2016) EU Competition Law: an analytical guide to the leading case, 5th edn. Hart, Oxford

Faggiani V (2014) El derecho a la tutela judicial efectiva y a un proceso con todas las garantías en la Carta de los Derechos Fundamentales de la Unión Europea. Revista General de Derecho Constitucional- Available via Iustel. http://www.iustel.com. Accessed 5 May 2018

Fernández Torres I, Fuentes Naharro M (2013) La aplicación de los artículos 101 y 102 TFUE. El Reglamento No. 1/2003. In: Signes de Mesa JI, Fernándz Torres I, Fuentes Naharro M (eds) Derecho de la Competencia. Civitas & Thomson Reuters, Madrid, pp 289–317

Fernández Vicién C, Moreno-Tapia I (2002) A step forward in the enforcement of community competition law by Member State judges: the Courage case. Available via InDret. http://www.indret.com. Accessed 5 May 2018

Ferrándiz P (2017) Discovery en reclamaciones de daños por prácticas restrictivas de la competencia (el nuevo artículo 283 bis LEC). Diario La Ley 9052. Available via http://diariolaley.laley.es. Accessed 2 Oct 2017

Fidalgo Gallardo C (2016) El proceso de desplazamiento de la autoridad normativa en los ordenamientos europeos, desde los legislativos nacionales a las instituciones de la Unión Europea. El TJUE como estrella emergente en el firmamento de la Unión. Revista General de Derecho Procesal. Available via Iustel. http://www.iustel.com. Accessed 5 May 2018

Fiebig AR (2014) The German Federal Cartel Office and the application of competition law in reunified Germany. Univ Pa J Int Law 14:373–408

Fürlinger S (2017) Austria: the Federal Competition Authority. The European Middle Easter and African Antitrust Review. Available at https://globalcompetitionreview.com/insight/the-european-middle-eastern-and-african-antitrust-review-2018/1145609/austria-federal-competition-authority. Accessed 29 Jan 2018

Galera Rodrigo S (2015) The right to a fair trial in the European Union: lights and shadows. Revista de Investigaçoes Constitucionais 2(2):7–29

Gutiérrez Zarza MA (2002) Fuentes comunitarias del Derecho procesal español. La Ley: revista jurídica española de doctrina, jurisprudencia y bibliografía 3:1626–1633

Herrero Suárez C (2016) La transposición de la directiva de daños antitrust. Reflexiones a raíz de la publicación de la propuesta de ley de transposición de la directiva. Cuadernos de Derecho Transnacional 8(I):150–183

Horsely T (2013) Reflections on the role of the Court of Justice as the 'motor' of European integration: legal limits to judicial making. Common Mark Law Rev 50:931–964

Iglesias Buhigues JL (2016) Principios de efectividad y equivalencia en la Directiva 2014/104/UE. In: Ruiz Peris JI (ed) La compensación de los daños por infracción de normas de competencia tras la directiva 2014/104/UE. Directiva y propuesta de transposición. Thomson Reuters, Aranzadi, Cizur Menor, Navarra, pp 99–108

Ioannidou M (2015) Consumer involvement in private EU Competition Law enforcement. Oxford University Press, Oxford

Jeleztcheva Jeleztecheva M, Ruiz Muñoz M (2011) La política de clemencia en la UE y algunos aspectos ético-jurídicos sobre su aplicación. In: Velasco San Pedro LA, Alonso Ledesma C et al (eds) La aplicación privada del derecho de la competencia. Lex Nova, Madrid, pp 719–734

Jimeno Bulnes M (1996) La cuestión prejudicial del artículo 177 TCE. J.M.Bosch Editor, Barcelona

Jimeno-Bulnes M (2013a) La cuestión prejudicial. In: Pardo Iranzo V (ed) El sistema jurisdiccional de la Unión Europea. Thomson Reuters Aranzadi, Cizur Menor, Navarra, pp 173–210

Jimeno-Bulnes M (2013b) American criminal procedure in a European context. Cardozo J Int Comp Law 21:409–459

Kantza C, Picod F (2015) Concurrence - programme de clémence - publication des décisions constatant une infraction - droits des victimes de pratiques anticoncurrentielles Trib. UE, 28 janvier 2015, (2 arrêts) Evonik Degussa / Commission, aff. T-341/12 et AKZO e.a. / Commission, aff. T-345/12. Revue des affaires européennes 25:159–165

Kjolbey L (2002) Case C-344/98, Masterfoods v. HB Ice Cream. Common Mark Law Rev 391:175–184

Klamert M (2017) The autonomy of the EU (and of EU law): through the kaleidoscope. Eur Law Rev 42:815–830

Korkea-aho E (2015) Legal interpretation of EU framework directives: a soft law approach. Eur Law Rev 40:70–88

Liu H (2009) Liner conferences in competition law. Springer, Hamburg
Maillo González-Orús J (2014) Sentencia del Tribunal de Justicia de la Unión Europea, de 27 de febrero de 2014, asunto C-365/12P, Comisión Europea contra EnBW Energie Baden-Württemberg AG v European Commission. Acceso a información documental de instituciones en procedimientos de libre competencia. Ars Iuris Salmanticensis 22:287–290
Martínez Moriel I (2013) La protección de la información aportada en el contexto de una solicitud de clemencia ante las acciones civiles de daños y perjuicios. Gaceta jurídica de la Unión Europea y de la competencia 32:61–74
Marvao C (2016) The leniency programme and recidivism. Rev Ind Organ 48:1–27
Milione C (2017) La interpretación del artículo 47 CDFUE como expresión de la labor hermenéutica del Tribunal de Luxemburgo en la construcción de un estándar europeo de protección de los derechos. Teoría y realidad constitucional 39:655–674
Monti G (2014) Umbrella pricing as a sword. Case C-557/12, Kone AG and Others v ÖOB-InfrastrukturAG, Judgment of 5 June 2014. Maastricht J Eur Comp Law 213:464–475
Nascimbene B (2013) Fair trial and the rights of the defence in antitrust proceedings before the commission: a need for reform? Eur Law Rev 38:573–583
Olmedo Peralta E (2014) Daños derivados de la subida de precios bajo el paraguas de un cártel (umbrella pricing). Una lectura jurídica del nuevo paso en la aplicación privada del Derecho de la Competencia. Revista del Derecho de la Competencia y de la distribución 15:107–130
Olmedo Peralta E (2015) La reclamación de daños sufridos por los consumidores como conscuncia de un cartel (private enforcement): follow-on actions vs stand alone actions. In: Miranda Serrano LM, Pagador López J, Pino Abad M (eds) La protección de los consumidores en tiempos de cambio: ponencias y comunicaciones del XIII Congreso de la asociación Sainz de Andino. Iustel, Madrid, pp 171–188
Ordoñez Solís D (2015) La Directiva 2014/104/UE, la aplicación privada del derecho de la competencia y el contexto jurisprudencial de su transposición en España. El Derecho. Available via http://www.elderecho.com/ Accessed 1 May 2015
Pérez Carrillo EF (2011) Acceso a los documentos y transparencia: elementos para facilitar la reclamación de daños y perjuicios derivados de infracciones del derecho a la libre competencia en la Unión Europea. In: Velasco San Pedro LA, Alonso Ledesma C et al (eds) La aplicación privada del derecho de la competencia. Lex Nova, Madrid, pp 433–446
Perlo N (2017) L'affaire Taricco: la voie italienne pour preserver la collaboration des juges dans l'Union europénne. Revue trimestrielle de droit européen 534:739–768
Pescatore P (2015) The doctrine of 'direct effect': an infant disease by Community Law. Eur Law Rev 40:135–153
Pfeiffer O (2017) Un possible malentendu en droit de l'Union européenne: l 'droit subjectif' comme condition de l'effet direct. Revue trimestrielle de droit européen 53:665–695
Piroddi P (2011) Reparación de daños y perjuicios por el incumplimiento de las normas de competencia y el derecho a un juicio justo en virtud del artículo 6 (1) CEDH. In: Velasco San Pedro LA, Alonso Ledesma C et al (eds) La aplicación privada del derecho de la competencia. Lex Nova, Madrid, pp 447–462
Prinssen JM, Schrauwen A (eds) (2002) Direct effect. Rethinking a classic of EC legal doctrine. European Law Publishing, Groningen
Rasmussen M (2014) Revolutionizing European Law: a history of the Van Gend en Loos judgment. Int J Const Law 12:136–163
Rassu F (2017) L'invocabilité des directives européennes et son incidence sur l'ordre juridique italien. Revue du Droit de l'Union Européenne 26:167–193
Reich N (2005) The 'Courage' doctrine: encouraging or discouraging compensation for antitrust injuries. Common Mark Law Rev 42:35–66
Robin-Olivier S (2014) The evolution of direct effect in the EU: stocktaking, problems, projections. Int J Const Law 2:165–188
Robinson W (2017) EU legislation. In: Karpen U, Xanthaki H (eds) Legislation in Europe: a comprehensive guide for scholars and practitioners. Hart, Oxford, pp 229–256
Rosas A, Levits E, Bots Y (eds) (2013) The Court of Justice and the construction of Europe: analysis and perspectives on sixty years of case-law/ La Cour de Justice et la construction de la

Europe: analysis et perspectives de soixante ans de jurisprudence. T. M. C. Asser Press, The Hague
Ruiz Peris JI (ed) (2016) La compensación de los daños por infracción de normas de competencia tras la directiva 2014/104/UE; directiva y propuesta de transposición. Thomson Reuters Aranzadi, Cizur Menor, Navarra
Skovgaard Olykke G (2017) Commission v Aer Lingus and Commission v Ryanair - Joined Cases C-164/15 P and C-165/15 P. Eur State Aid Law Q 16:93–98
Slot JS, Farley M (2017) An introduction to competition law. Hart, Oxford
Smulders B, Eisele K (2012) Reflections on the institutional balance, the community method and the interplay between jurisdictions after Lisbon. Yearb Eur Law 31:112–127
Soldevilla Fragoso S (2014) El Tribunal General y el Derecho de la Competencia. In: Martinez Lage S, Pedraz Calvo M, Ordoñez Solís D (eds) El Derecho europeo de la competencia y su aplicación en España. Liber Amicorum en homenaje a Santiago. Wolters Kluwer & La Ley, Madrid, pp 385–404
Süderow J (2011) El acceso a las pruebas en expedientes de la Comisión Europea y los límites establecidos por su programa de clemencia. In: Velasco San Pedro LA, Alonso Ledesma C et al (eds) La aplicación privada del derecho de la competencia. Lex Nova, Madrid, pp 535–550
Svetlicinil A, Botta M (2016) 'Umbrella pricing' in private enforcement of EU Competition Law and US Antitrust Law: another transatlantic divergence? Eur Law Rev (41):399–411
Tobío Rivas AM (2013–2014) Reparación por daños derivados de un ilícito 'antitrust' y acceso a la documentación que forma parte de un procedimiento ante una autoridad nacional de competencia. Actas de Derecho Industrial y Derecho de Autor 34:630–634
Torres Sustaeta MV (2014) La aplicación del Derecho de la Competencia en Europa. Intereses en juego y vías de tutela. Thomson Reuters Aranzadi, Cizur Menor, Navarra
Vaquero López C (2011) Sobre la posibilidad de reconocimiento en España de 'daños punitivos'como consecuencia de la infracción de Derecho Comunitario de la Competencia. In: Velasco San Pedro LA, Alonso Ledesma C et al (eds) La aplicación privada del derecho de la competencia. Lex Nova, Madrid, pp 51–60
Velasco San Pedro L, Herrero Suárez C (2011) La 'passing-on defence', ¿un falso dilema. In: Velasco San Pedro LA, Alonso Ledesma C et al (eds) La aplicación privada del derecho de la competencia. Lex Nova, Madrid, pp 593–604
Velasco San Pedro LA, Alonso Ledesma C et al (eds) (2011) La aplicación privada del derecho de la competencia. Lex Nova, Madrid
Völcker SB (2012) Case C-360/09, Pfleiderer AG v Bundeskartellamt, Judgment of the Court of Justice (Grand Chamber) of 14 June 2011. Common Mark Law Rev 49:695–720
Von Danwitz T (2010) Kooperation der Gerichtsbarkeiten in Europa. Zeitschriftfür Rechtspolitik 43;143–147
VV.AA (2017) La defensa (privada) de la competencia. El notario del siglo XXI (74)
Waelbroeck M (1989) Meeting competition: is this a valid defence for a firm in a dominant position?. In: Starace et al (eds) Divenire sociale e adeguamento del diritto: studi in onore di Francesco Capotorti. Giuffrè, Milano, pp 481–490
Weiler JHH (2014) Van Gend en Loos: the individual as subject and object and the dilemma of European legitimacy. Int J Const Law 12:94–103

Mar Jimeno-Bulnes is Professor of Procedural Law at Universidad de Burgos, Spain.

The Direct Effect of EU Competition Law: From Regulation No 1/2003 to Directive 2014/104/EU

Marina San Martín-Calvo

Abstract This chapter addresses the study of the direct application of Competition Law at European level, as well as the problems that have arisen in practice. The importance of the principle of direct effect of Community legislation, the cornerstone on which European Competition Law is based, is of particular interest. We must not forget that the development of the protective rules of free Competition is at the origin of the European Union, since the Treaty of Rome of 1957. After a brief introduction on the Regulation and the background of private enforcement of Competition Law, the legislative context will be examined. This context will show how Community Law recognises the direct applicability of Competition rules to relations between individuals. These legal texts are mainly Council Regulation (EC) No 1/2003 of 16 December 2002 on the implementation of the rules on competition laid down in Articles 81 and 82 Treaty on the Functioning of the European Union and Directive 2014/104/EU of the European Parliament and of the Council of 26 November 2014 on certain rules governing actions for damages under national law for infringements of the Competition Law provisions of the Member States and of the European Union.

I would like to express my warm thanks to PhD Mar Jimeno Bulnes, Professor of Procedural Law at the University of Burgos and sponsor in this public institution of this research study, for inviting me to take part in this project; as well as Professor Luis Velasco San Pedro, Professor of Commercial Law at the University of Valladolid, for his bibliographical recommendation. The financial support of the Spanish Ministry of Economy and the European Commission is gratefully acknowledged (Research Projects *A step forward in the consolidation of the European judicial area and its practical application in Spain: from the perspective of civil and criminal procedures, DER2015-71418-P* and *JUST-2015-JCOO-AG, 723198, and Training action for legal practitioners: linguistic skills and translation in EU Competition Law, HT.4582-6*).

M. San Martín-Calvo (✉)
Faculty of Law, University of Burgos, Burgos, Spain
e-mail: mscalvo@ubu.es

S. Marino et al. (eds.), *Language and Law*,
https://doi.org/10.1007/978-3-319-90905-9_5

1 Introduction

There is no doubt that the prohibition of behaviour that affects competition has a central place in European Union Competition Law. Anti-competitive practices, such as collusive practices or abuses of positions of dominance can cause damage in two aspects. On the one hand, these infringements jeopardise general interest. Secondly, antitrust infringements can cause damage to individual assets, too, affecting the particular interests of consumers or companies.[1] As a consequence of the infringement of the antitrust rules, there is a possibility of declaring the nullity of the unlawful agreements, as well as the obligation to repair the damage caused.[2] Therefore, the performance of any non-competitive behaviour implies not only the right to request the full nullity of that conduct, preventing the contract from displaying its effects, but also the obligation to repair the damage that would have been caused by the illegal behaviour.[3]

Competition Law must include the appropriate sanctions that dissuade enterprises from carrying out restrictive agreements. So, it should incorporate enough incentives to stimulate the disappearance of existing cartels; but, at the same time, Competition Law must serve to a compensatory purpose, allowing the legal redress of the subjects affected by the anti-competitive practices.[4]

Therefore, according to Directive 2014/104/EU, repressive and sanctioned aims are mainly achieved through the public application of Competition Law; while the indemnification purpose is entrusted to the private application. As a result, the enforcement of EU Competition Law shall comprise the interplay between public enforcement, aimed at deterrence, and private enforcement, aimed at compensation, whose balance point is represented by the access to evidence held by Competition authorities.[5]

Competition Law public enforcement refers to the system where Article 101—prohibiting agreements, decisions by associations of undertakings and concerted practices that are restrictive of Competition—and Article 102—prohibiting abuses of dominant position—of the Treaty on the Functioning of the European Union (TFEU) are enforced by the European Commission, and by the National Competition Authorities (NCAs) of the Member States when the anti-competitive practices affect trade between Member States. In this regard, European legislation and national rules about Competition Law have been subject to public application, mainly, with

[1]Quijano González (2011), p. 479.

[2]The obligation to repair the damage is, from the Roman Law, an effect linked to the harmful event. It derives from the infringed contract, but also from the breach of the obligation expressed in the *alterum non laedere* principle, regardless of the legal relationship that binds the parties. However, while full nullity is a consequence expressly referred to in Article 101(2) TFEU, the right to be repaired for the damages suffered does not occur automatically Torre Sustaeta (2014), p. 124 ff.

[3]Ortíz Baquero (2011), p. 17.

[4]Olmedo Peralta (2016), p. 392.

[5]Migani (2014), p. 85.

administrative procedures directed to the imposition of sanctions. Meanwhile, private enforcement has been pushed into the background, in contrast to the existing situation in other jurisdictions, such as the US system, what is undoubtedly due to the particular American system, which favours the exercise of these actions.[6]

At this point, it is necessary to emphasise that, unlike in the case of US, where the success of the system derives from the deterrent effect of large fines imposed on infringing companies, as a result of practices, in Europe, the importance of the principle of prohibition of unjust enrichment slowed down the private application of Competition Law. However, at the European level several steps have been taken.

Lawsuits filed by private individuals have suffered non-competitiveness since the beginning of the century. The aim was to encourage the exercise of private actions for the infringement of EU Competition Law, as well as the role of civil judges in their application.[7] In fact, until very recently, the rights of individuals injured as a result of anti-competitive practices have been protected by civil law articulated under the figure of civil liability. In practice, the exercise of the rights was remitted to national courts, with very different solutions regarding the protection granted and the judicial procedures to make them effective in the different Member States.[8] But this has not meant that EU Law has been left out of the private application of Competition Law. Rather, European institutions have been the ones which, in view of the deficient implementation of the private application of competition rules in EU Member States, have taken the initiative to promote it, adopting different measures.[9]

Among the measures adopted, the work carried out by the jurisprudence of the Court of Justice of the European Union (CJEU) must be highlighted, which has issued important rulings in this area. The starting point of the European private enforcement is determined by the acknowledgement of the direct applicability of Competition rules between individuals, which was first recognised in cases as *SA Brasserie de Haecht,* of 12 December 1967,[10] as well as *BRT/SABAM Case,* of 21 March 1974.[11] However, the only sanction imposed on these infractions was the nullity of the agreement or decisions.[12]

---

[6]Herrero Suarez (2016), pp. 150–183. The author points out, among a wide access system to the evidence, the *treble damages mechanism*, which allows the plaintiff to demand three times the amount of damages suffered, plus the reimbursement of a reasonable legal fee. Furthermore, we should consider the importance, in the American system, of the class actions. See Hovenkamp (2011), p. 652.

[7]Casado Navarro (2016), pp. 428–429.

[8]So, while certain national jurisdictions, such as the UK, contains an equivalent requirement already exists under the rules governing civil procedure, for other Member States such an obligation represents a dramatic departure from the standard rules of civil litigation. See Slot and Farley (2017), p. 232.

[9]Tobío Rivas (2016–2017), pp. 84–85.

[10]Case 23/67, *SA Brasserie de Haecht* [1967] 407,ECLI:EU:C:1967:54.

[11]Case 127/73, *BRT* [1974] ECR 313, ECLI:EU:C:1974:25.

[12]On a more comprehensive analysis about the CJEU case law, see Jimeno Bulnes, in this book.

2 The Council Regulation (EC) No. 1/2003 of 16 December 2002: One More Step Further

The principle of direct applicability of Competition rules between individuals was clearly established by the Regulation No 1/2003[13] that recognises the direct effect of former Articles 81 and 82 Treaty on the European Communities (TEC) (current Articles 101 and 102 of the Treaty on the Functioning of the European Union—TFEU).[14] The main objective of the new Regulation was to establish a new system that would ensure that Competition Law would serve to face up the challenges of an integrated market and a future enlargement of the European Community involved.[15]

The importance of the Regulation No 1/2003 was undoubted. It brought fundamental changes in the application of European Competition Law. First, the previous system slowed down the application of European Competition rules by the Courts and the Competition authorities of Member States. Therefore, it was necessary to reconsider the system of application of the exception to the prohibition of agreements restricting Competition set out by the former Article 81(3) TEC. In order to achieve this aim, the new Regulation replaces the system of prior authorization by one of legal exception (Article 1).

Second, the new system reinforced the role of civil judges in the application of Competition rules, which until then was almost irrelevant. Article 81(3) TEC (currently Article 101 TFEU) becomes directly applicable, enabling National Competition Authorities and National Courts to apply Articles 81 and 82 TEC (now Articles 101 and 102 TFEU) in their entirety, including para. 3 of Article 81. In particular, Article 6 of the Regulation establishes the competence of National Courts to apply the rules on Competition Law and they have a direct effect.

Furthermore, the Regulation seeks to coordinate public and private application of Competition Law, through a mechanism of cooperation between the Commission and the Competition Authorities of Member States and National Courts, introduced by Article 15 of the Regulation. In this respect, the Regulation recommended that networks of public authorities be established between the Commission and the Competition Authorities of the Member States, applying the Community Competition rules in close cooperation. For that purpose it was necessary to set up arrangements for information and consultation. The Commission should establish other forms of cooperation within the network with the Member States.[16]

---

[13]Council Regulation (EC) No 1/2003 of 16 December 2002 on the implementation of the rules on competition laid down in Articles 81 and 82 of the Treaty (OJ 2003 (L1)1).

[14]The new Council Regulation, which came into effect on 1 May 2004, replaces Council Regulation No 17, which has been in force for more than 40 years without significant modification, and which was the key to enforcement in Community Competition law (Council Regulation No 17 of 6 February 1962 (OJ L 13, 21.2.1962, 204/62).

[15]Müller (2004), pp. 721–740.

[16]In this sense, and in relation to the networks of public authorities mentioned above, the Regulation No 1/2003 provided that, in spite of any national provision to the contrary, the exchange of

Nevertheless, the growing role of NCA's in the application of Articles 101 and 102 TFEU cannot prejudice the uniform application of EU Competition Law. In fact, the Regulation expressly affirms the principle of primacy of EU Law, adopting the necessary actions to avoid jeopardising that principle.[17]

It has been precisely through recognition of the direct effect of the Competition rules, that the Court of Justice has introduced the compensation action files by a company or consumer, as a consequence of an unlawful restriction of Competition in the common market. This right has been expressly defended in the extremely important *Courage Case* and consolidated in further case law.[18]

Indeed, the subsequent jurisprudence of the Court of Justice went a step further, establishing that any person has the right to bring an action for damages, whether the claimant is the Commission itself, as in *Otis Case*,[19] or a consumer, as in *Manfredi Case*.[20] Furthermore, the damage action aims to compensate any loss suffered by the affected party, as a result of these behaviours. Therefore, full compensation should include compensation not only for actual loss (*damnum emergens*), but also for loss of profit (*lucrum cessans*), plus interest. Thus, the injured party should be put into the same situation as he would have if the infringement had not been committed.[21]

During the years following the adoption of Regulation 1/2003, Community bodies continued to develop private enforcement through several documents. Thus, in 2005, the Commission presented the Green Paper entitled 'Reparation of damages for breach of the community rules of defense of competition',[22] devoted to the restoration of damages for infringement of the antitrust legislation. The Green Paper recognises the right of companies and individuals to claim damages for an infringement of the EU Competition rules,[23] because it is considered that the private

information and the use of such information in evidence should be allowed between the members of the network, even where the information was confidential. The information obtained through the networks could be used for the application of Articles 81 and 82 TEC (now Articles 101 and 102 TFEU), as well as for the parallel application of National Competition Law (Article 11).

[17]Martín Aresti (2014), pp. 21–60.

[18]Case C-453/99, *Courage and Crehan* [2001] ECR I-6297, ECLI:EU:C:2001:465. In the *Courage* case, the CJEU stated that the full effectiveness of the Treaty rules would not be achieved without the possibility that any affected party could claim compensation for damages caused by anti-competitive behaviour. See Ruiz Peris (2016), pp. 15–52.

[19]Case C-199/11, *Otis and others* [2012] ECLI:EU:C:2012:684.

[20]Joined Cases C-295/04 to C-298/04, *Manfredi and others* [2006] ECR I-6619, ECLI:EU:C:2006:461. This implies, as the judgment of the *Manfredi* case itself stated, that the compensation received should not casue an unjust enrichment for the damaged party Ruiz Peris (2016), p. 19.

[21]See, *inter alia*, Velasco San Pedro and Herrero Suarez (2011), pp. 600 ff.

[22]Green Paper of 19 December 2005, Damages actions for breach of the EC antitrust rules [COM (2005) 672 final].

[23]The Court of Justice explicitly recognised their right to do so in its judgment in the *Courage* case. The CJEU stated that the actual exercise of this right not only enables those who have suffered loss as a result of anti-competitive conduct to be compensated but also helps ensure that the Community Competition rules are fully effective and will deter anti-competitive conduct (paras. 26 and 27).

application of Competition Law is a useful tool to protect free competition as the public application.[24]

Later on, in 2008, the Commission presented the White Paper 'Actions for damages for breach of the community antitrust rules', which already includes specific measures and policies in the following matters: legal standing, access to evidence, binding effect of the resolutions of the National Competition Authorities; guilty behaviour requirement; damages; impact of excessive costs; limitation period; costs of claims for compensation for damages; and interaction between leniency programs and claims for compensation for damages.[25]

Nevertheless, some problems persisted and limited the access of individuals, especially consumers and small businesses, to compensation for damages. The need to revise antitrust regulations was highlighted, especially in relation to one of the main problems posed by the practical application of private enforcement. This problem was the difficulty of access to evidence for potential plaintiffs, which often depend on the infringing companies.

To date, Articles 101 and 102 TFEU have been almost exclusively enforced through administrative procedures carried out by the Commission and the NCA's, pursuant to the rules laid down in the TFEU, Regulation 1/2003, Commission Regulation 773/2004,[26] various Commission notices and guidelines, and the jurisprudence of the EU Courts. Public enforcement has been effective since the very first decades of the European Economic Community, being considered the principal form of enforcement of Competition Law.[27]

[24]Background and Objectives of Green Paper 1.1 Damages claims as part of the enforcement system of Community antitrust law. Antitrust rules in Articles 81 and 82 of the Treaty are enforced both by public and private enforcement. Both forms part of a common enforcement system and serve the same aims: to deter anti-competitive practices forbidden by antitrust law and to protect firms and consumers from these practices and any damages caused by them. Private as well as public enforcement of antitrust law is an important instrument to create and sustain a competitive economy.

[25]The White Paper already contains a series of measures aimed at the creation and development of an effective system for the private application of Competition rules in Europe Velasco San Pedro and Herrero Suarez (2011), pp. 593–604.

[26]Commission Regulation (EC) No 773/2004 of 7 April 2004 relating to the conduct of proceedings by the Commission pursuant to Articles 81 and 82 of the EC Treaty (OJ L 123, 27.4.2004, p. 18).

[27]Migani (2014), pp. 85 ff.

3 The Main Contributions of the Directive 2014/104/EU of the European Parliament and of the Council, of 26 November 2014

In this context, the Directive 2014/104 represents a significant step forward in the European process aimed to foster the private enforcement of Competition Law.[28] In fact, the innovations introduced affect crucial aspects of the actions for damages, especially the difficulties in exercising compensation actions, as well as the difference in legislation systems.

In this respect, the Directive introduces rules of a substantive and procedural nature aimed at harmonising the Competition Law of Member States in civil compensation proceedings brought before their competent National Courts for infringement of Articles 101 and 102 TFEU.

It is also very important to make clear that the Directive protects just private interests affected by collusive practices and abuses of dominant position, but does not include acts of unfair competition, although they affect the public interest. This is probably due to the fact that the Directive has content and purpose that is difficult to apply to cases of unfair Competition, such as the provisions on joint and solidarity obligations of infringers, or those related to the impact of extra costs.

The Directive seeks to harmonise the legal systems of Member States in relation to the various issues.

3.1 Evidentiary Effects of Decisions Taken by National Competition Authorities and National Courts. The "Follow-on Actions"

It is well established that victims of competition infringements have a right to obtain compensation for overcharging harm and lost profits. A private action can be brought either as a follow-on action to a finding of infringement by Competition Law Authorities or as a stand-alone action.

Concerning the former, the Directive seeks to strengthen the evidential value of the decisions and judgments adopted respectively by the NCAs and National Courts. Consequently, and as provided for by Article 9(1), an infringement of Competition Law established by a final decision of a NCA or by a Review Court is deemed to be *irrefutably* established for the purposes of an action for damages brought before their National Courts under Article 101 or 102 TFEU or under National Competition Law.[29]

---

[28] Herrero Suarez (2016), pp. 150–183.

[29] Calvo Caravaca and Suderow (2015), pp. 114–157.

However, where a final decision is taken in another Member State, that final decision may be presented before National Courts as at least *prima facie evidence* that an infringement of Competition Law has occurred (Article 9(2)). Although this provision could be intended to facilitate compensation actions for damages throughout the EU,[30] instead it limits the evidentiary value of foreign NCAs decisions, because they will be assessed along with any other evidence produced by the parties.[31]

3.2 Access to Evidence

As is usual in compensatory actions, the access to the proof is crucial. For this reason, the Directive establishes a detailed regulation of taking evidence. It recognises that the action for compensation "requires a complex factual and economic analysis" and, in order to provide the plaintiffs with proof of the damage whose repair is sought, it establishes detailed rules for both individuals and public bodies. With the adoption of these measures, the Directive aims to facilitate a potential claim, aimed at redressing the damages caused by the infringement of the competition rules, for which the legal text itself requires Member States that have procedural rules able to ensure the effective exercise of the Law.[32]

Regarding the disclosure of evidence (the well-known common law concept of discovery) the Directive sets out that, when there are *prima facie* evidences of prejudice, the judge may order the discover of evidence to the defendant or third parties, upon request of a claimant (Article 5(1)). The rule grants the judicial body the power to order the presentation of the evidence proposed by the plaintiff, except for the documents related to the leniency programs.

Nevertheless, this exhibition is subject to some limits. First, the plaintiff must justify his request with a reasoned motivation that contains the facts and evidence reasonably available to support the credibility of the claim for damages. On the other hand, the Directive protects confidential information. In this case, the judge must decide if the evidence that can be accessed has confidential information or not, as well as the suitable measures of protection (Article 5(3)).

As a consequence of the application of these limits, the Directive establishes a classification scheme of documents in evidentiary matters, so there are documents that have absolute protection and others of relative protection. Thus, the Directive makes a distinction between documents that can never be displayed, those included in the *black list*, documents that may be displayed in certain circumstances (*grey list*) and, finally, the other documents, which can be discovered at any time (*white list*).[33]

[30]Cisotta (2014), pp. 81–105.

[31]Casado Navarro (2016), pp. 436 ff.

[32]Martorell Zulueta (2016), pp. 304 ff.

[33]Callol García and Yuste (2015), pp. 297–315.

3.2.1 Documents Included in the Blacklist

The transaction requests (the so-called settlements) and the statements obtained in the framework of a leniency procedure cannot be discovered according to Article 6(6) of the Directive. These documents enjoy special protection in accordance with national law (Article 7(7)). The Commission has clarified that otherwise the disclosure of these documents would have a detrimental effect on the companies that cooperate under the leniency and settlement programs.

The Directive includes leniency statements (along with settlement submissions) in the *black list* of documents which national courts can *never* order a party or a third party to disclose, in order to guarantee the continued willingness of undertakings to approach competition authorities voluntarily with leniency statements or settlement submissions.

3.2.2 Documents Included in the Grey List

In relation to documents with relative protection national, Courts may order the discover of the following categories of evidence only after a Authority has closed its procedures by adopting a resolution.[34]

Thus, the documents of the *grey list*, such as the information prepared specifically for the administrative file (including responses to the information requirements) or sent to the NCA (for example, the response to a statement of objections), may only be disclosed after the Competition Authority has terminated its procedure, by adopting a resolution or otherwise (Articles 6(5) and 7(2) of the Directive).

3.2.3 Documents Included in the White List

All documents not included in the categories mentioned are part of the so-called *white list*. The Court may order their disclosure at any time, complying with the requirements of proportionality and relevance.[35]

Eventually, the practice cannot forget the important role of the European Commission and NCAs, which may intervene during the proceedings or may be required by national judges to provide their opinions or answer their questions, through the figure of the *amicus curiae*.[36]

[34]In any case, the evidence obtained through access to the file of a Competition Authority may only be used in an action for damages (Article 7(3)).

[35]Olmedo Peralta (2014), pp. 107–130; Díez Estella and Estrada Meray (2014), pp. 189–202; Martínez Moriel (2013), pp. 61–74; Fernández et al. (2005), pp. 171–188.

[36]Ordóñez Solís (2015).

4 Limitation Period of the Action to Claim Damages

As was already suggested by the Commission in 2005, the existence of different national limitation periods between the EU Member States could be one of the main obstacles in the choice of the jurisdiction where to file a claim for infringements of Competition Law.[37] One of the most controversial aspects to establish the statute of limitations to claim damages was the classification of the fault as contractual or non-contractual.[38]

Concerning infringements of the Competition Law, there are some doubts about the type of liability applicable in *antitrust* cases[39] but in accordance with the most consolidated case law we are facing non-contractual liability. Likewise, Spanish jurisprudence has decided in the same way repeatedly.[40]

To prevent those conflicts, Article 10 of the Directive sets out that Member States shall lay down rules applicable to limitation periods for bringing actions for damages. Furthermore, it expressly states that the competent authorities of Member States shall ensure that the limitation periods for bringing actions for damages were at least 5 years.[41] However, when there has been an investigation by a competition authority, either by the Commission or by the NCA, the period is interrupted and the suspension will end, at least, 1 year after the decision of infringement becomes final, or the procedure is terminated in another way (Article 10(4)).[42]

---

[37]European Commission, Damages actions for the breach of antitrust rules (2005) Staff Working Paper, at para. 7. See Canedo Arrillaga (2017), pp. 173–185.

[38]As it is known, civil liability can be contractual, when it arises from a contractual default, or non-contractual, when the responsibility derives from the breach caused by a wrongful behaviour.

[39]It is the central doctrine in Spain's academic that the liability is essentially non-contractual. In this regard, Ortíz Baquero (2011), pp. 165 ff. Peña López (2002), pp. 213–219; Alonso Soto (2013), pp. 123–133; Díez Estella and Estrada Meray (2014), p. 193; Brokelmann (2013), pp. 104 ff.

[40]See, *inter alia*, Tribunal Supremo (Sala Civil) (Supreme Court, Civil Section), of 8 June 2012, *Acor*, Rec. núm. 2163/2009, RJ\2012\9317. This meaningful judgment characterises the responsibility of the defendant as non-contractual.

[41]In Spain, the limitations for bringing actions to demand contractual liability, provided for Article 1.964 Civil Code, which was 15 years, was reduced to 5 years since the fulfillment of the obligation can be demanded, in accordance with modification carried out by Law 42/2015, of reform of the Law of Civil Procedure. On the other hand, the limitations of bringing actions to claim for damages arising from non-contractual liability is, according Article 1.968, 2nd Civil Code, one year since the injured party was aware of the damage suffered. To transpose the Directive into Spanish law, the Royal Decree-Law 9/2017, of May 26, which transposes directives of the European Union in the financial, commercial and health, and on the movement of workers provides, a legal period of five years to the exercise of actions for damages, the infringement of Competition law has ceased and the claimant becomes aware of it (Article 74).

[42]See Ordóñez Solís (2015).

5 Right to Compensation and Joint Liability of the Infringers Regarding the Damages Caused by Illegal Practices

The Directive clearly states in Article 3(1) that Member States shall ensure that any natural or legal person who has suffered harm caused by an infringement of Competition Law can claim and obtain full compensation for that harm. Article 3(2) continues to affirm that

> Full compensation shall place a person who has suffered harm in the position in which that person would have been had the infringement of competition law not have been committed. It shall therefore cover the right to compensation for actual loss and for loss of profit, plus the payment of interest.[43]

Thus, the Directive codifies CJEU's jurisprudence on the right to compensation for damages caused as a consequence of the infringement of EU Competition Law, especially in relation to the legitimacy and definition of damages.[44]

Article 11 of the Directive envisages the joint and several liability of infringers who have breached Competition Law. Thus, when several companies cooperated in the infringement of competition rules, it is expressly decided to establish, regardless of the qualification that such action is said in each Member State, that the infringers are jointly and severally liable for all the damage caused.

This general rule admits two exceptions:

1. When the infringer is a small or medium-sized enterprise (SMEs) as defined in Commission Recommendation 2003/361/EC,[45] and
2. When the infringer is a beneficiary of a *leniency program*.

In the first case, the exception only applies when the infringer caused damage to direct and indirect purchasers. In other situations, when the conduct was unlawful, but there was no damage to purchasers, the rule against the harmed will be solidarity, including SME. Furthermore, the derogation laid down in para. 2 shall not apply when the SME has led the infringement of Competition Law or has coerced other undertakings to participate therein; or the SME has previously been found to have infringed Competition Law (Article 11(3)).

In the second case, Recital 38 of the Directive states that

> it is appropriate to make provision for undertakings which have received immunity from fines from a competition authority under a leniency programme to be protected from undue

[43] However, concerning interests, the Directive does not clarify whether it refers to compensatory or delay interests, which leads us to think that this lack of unification will lead to forum shopping, in those cases in which the damages are splitted within several Member States.

[44] See Martí Miravalls (2016), pp. 321–338

[45] It is considered that a company could be a small or medium-sized enterprise when its market share in the relevant market was below 5% at any time during the infringement of Competition Law; and the application of the normal rules of joint and several liability would irretrievably jeopardise its economic viability and cause its assets to lose all their value.

> exposure to damages claims. . .It is therefore appropriate that the immunity recipient be relieved in principle from joint and several liability for the entire harm and that any contribution it must make vis-à-vis co-infringers not exceed the amount of harm caused to its own direct or indirect purchasers or, in the case of a buying cartel, its direct or indirect providers.

Thus, the beneficiary of a leniency program is not, as a general rule, jointly and severally liable. It will only assume responsibility for the damages caused to direct or indirect purchasers or providers. However, the beneficiary of a leniency program should remain fully liable to the injured parties other than their purchasers or providers should remain fully liable to the injured parties just in case when they have not been fully compensated by the other infringers.

Finally, Article 11(5) provides that

> Member States shall ensure that an infringer may recover a contribution from any other infringer, the amount of which shall be determined in the light of their relative responsibility for the harm caused by the infringement of competition law.

As a result, each infringer, even though of solidarity in its external aspect against all harmed, will respond in its internal relationship with the rest of the offenders in terms of their relative responsibility.

Regarding the question of how to determine the amount of the compensation, it seems that the Directive refers this matter to national legislation, provided that the principles of effectiveness and equivalence should be respected (Article 12(2)).

6 *Passing-on* Defense

In order to avoid compensations that exceed the damages caused, the defendant may oppose as defense that the claimant has passed on to third parties, totally or partially, the additional cost resulting from the illegal behaviour. In other words, the so-called *passing-on defense*, regulated by Article 13 of the Directive, is an instrument through which the defendant claims damages arising from an infringement of the competition rules against the plaintiff. It consists of invoking, as a defensive argument, that the claimant has passed all or part of the resulting extra cost to subsequent customers.[46]

The legal basis for this scheme is to ensure the effectiveness of the right to full compensation, laid down by Article 3. In order to achieve this goal, the Directive establishes that the infringer will be responsible for the damage caused to both direct and indirect buyers. More specifically, the Directive encourages complaints from final customers by expressly stipulating the claim by indirect purchasers (Article 12(2)).

Naturally, this legal instrument only applies to those proceedings in which the claimant is a direct purchaser, and the defendant is the alleged infringer of the competition rules, and in which the claim derives from the damages suffered by

[46]Estevan de Quesada (2016), pp. 339–354.

the direct purchaser. The harm suffered must be the premium price that the direct purchaser had to pay as a consequence of the infringement, with respect to the price that would have been paid if the infringement had not occurred.[47] In these cases, the defendant/infringer may claim as a defense against the direct purchaser the fact that he has passed on all or part of the extra cost resulting from the infringement to subsequent purchasers. In any case, the burden of proof falls on the defendant.[48]

The purpose of the passing-on defense consists in preventing the unjust enrichment of the direct purchaser, which would occur if he could claim the extra cost as compensation for damages and, at the same time, pass it on to the successive purchasers.[49] Nevertheless, the compensation is limited to a part of the damage produced, the *damnum emergens*.[50] The Directive does not consider the loss of profits suffered by the direct purchasers.[51] It is forgotten that any over-charge from direct purchases to subsequent acquirers will normally involve a lower sale, in response to lower demand, as a consequence of the price increase. Therefore, the other essential element of compensation for damage, *lucrum cessans*, is omitted. This has been criticised by the scholars, because a joint assessment of the situation created by the violation of the competition rules should be made, since antitrust damages are usually continuous damage.[52]

7 The Quantification of the Damage

The Directive is mainly aimed at ensuring that anyone who has suffered damages caused by an infringement of Competition Law by an undertaking or by an association of undertakings can effectively exercise the right to claim *full compensation* for that harm from that undertaking or association.[53] Full compensation includes actual loss and loss of profits, along with the payment of interest (Article 3(2) of the Directive), but shall not lead to *overcompensation*, whether by means of punitive, multiple or other types of damages (Article 3(3) of the Directive). Therefore, the

[47] According to Article 14(2) of the Directive, indirect buyers will have to prove that: the defendant has committed an infringement of the Competition Law; the direct buyer suffered a surcharge as a consequence of the infringement, and the indirect buyer has acquired the goods or services affected by the infringement.

[48] Article 3 of the Directive allows the infringer to require, to a reasonable extent, the evidence of the complainant or of third parties.

[49] Estevan de Quesada (2016), p. 348.

[50] As is established by the CJEU *Manfredi* case, the object of actions for compensation of damages is compensation of the damages actually caused, to be understood both the emerging damage—that is, the loss of assets suffered—and *lucrum cessans*—that is, the profit lost to be perceived, experienced by the injured party.

[51] Hernández Bataller (2016), pp. 77–98.

[52] Velasco San Pedro and Herrero Suarez (2011), pp. 593–604.

[53] Migani (2014), pp. 9 ff.

concept of *overcompensation* is closely connected with that of *overcharge*, i.e. the difference between the price actually paid and the price that would otherwise have prevailed in the absence of an infringement of Competition Law.[54] As a result, full compensation will be deducted from the combined effects of both ideas.

However, it is accepted that an injured party who has proven to have suffered harm as a result of a Competition Law infringement still needs to prove the extent of the harm in order to obtain damages. As the Directive states

> quantifying harm in competition law cases is a very fact-intensive process and may require the application of complex economic models. This is often very costly, and claimants have difficulties in obtaining the data necessary to substantiate their claims. The quantification of harm in competition law cases can thus constitute a substantial barrier preventing effective claims for compensation.

Competition Law does not establish rules on the quantification of harm caused by a Competition Law infringement. Therefore, national legal systems must determine each own rules on the quantification of the harm. However, the requirements of National Law in EU Competition Law cases should not be less favourable than those governing similar domestic actions (*principle of equivalence*), nor should they render the exercise of the Union right to damages practically impossible or excessively difficult (*principle of effectiveness*).

8 Promotion of the Extrajudicial Solutions

One of the main objectives of the Directive is the application of extrajudicial dispute resolution mechanisms, regulated by Article 18. In this regard, Recital 48 strongly supports these mechanisms, stating that

> infringers and injured parties should be encouraged to agree on compensating for the harm caused by a competition law infringement through consensual dispute resolution mechanisms, such as out-of-court settlements (including those where a judge can declare a settlement binding), arbitration, mediation or conciliation. Such consensual dispute resolution should cover as many injured parties and infringers as legally possible. The provisions in this Directive on consensual dispute resolution are therefore meant to facilitate the use of such mechanisms and increase their effectiveness.

Article 18 of the Directive is divided into three paras. The first aims to suspend the 5-year term established for filing an action for damages, until the extrajudicial dispute resolution procedure is concluded. So, the suspension of terms during the negotiations is allowed.

Article 18(2) addresses the topic of suspension, too, but from a different time perspective. That is, not before the procedure starts, but during the processing of it, in order to facilitate an out-of-court settlement of the dispute. In this case, National Courts seized with an action for damages may suspend their proceedings for up to 2 years.

---

[54] Ordóñez Solís (2015).

The Directive also allows a Competition Authority to consider that compensation paid as a result of a consensual settlement and prior to its decision imposing a fine to be a mitigating factor (Article 18(3)). This provision can only be applied in the event that the claimant files a *stand alone action*.[55] In this case, private enforcement comes before public enforcement. Therefore, the infringer could benefit from the mitigation of the fine that could be imposed later in a sanctioning public procedure.[56]

Finally, Article 19 of the Directive deals with the consequences for the parties of an out-of-court settlement regarding damages on any subsequent claims. It is intended to prevent that an infringer who pays damages through an agreed resolution of disputes be placed in a worse position compared to the co-infringers. That might happen if a settling infringer continued to be fully jointly and severally liable for the harm caused by the infringement. To avoid it, Directive lays down that

> any remaining claim of the settling injured party shall be exercised only against non-settling co-infringers

Therefore, in principle

> nonsettling co-infringers shall not be permitted to recover contribution for the remaining claim from the settling co-infringer.[57]

9 Conclusion

I would like to conclude by briefly mentioning the transposition of the Directive into Spanish Law. It has become effective in recent dates, on 26 May 2017, through Royal Decree-Law 9/2017, which modifies two basic legal texts of the Spanish legal system: Law 15/2007, on Defense of Competition, and our basic procedural Law, Law 1/2000, of Civil Procedure. The transposition has arrived late, but it must be said that it complies with the guidelines established by the Directive, so its adoption must be qualified as satisfactory.

---

[55] In other words, in those independent actions that do not derive from previous declarations of infringement by the Competition authorities.

[56] Gómez Asensio (2016), pp. 362–363.

[57] In any case, it should be necessary to consider what is established in article 19(3), in which it is expressly stated where the non-settling co-infringers cannot pay the damages that correspond to the remaining claim of the settling injured party, the settling injured party may exercise the remaining claim against the settling co-infringer.

References

Alonso Soto R (2013) La Aplicación Privada del Derecho de la Competencia. In: Font i Ribas A, Gómez Trinidad S (eds) Competencia y Acciones de Indemnización. Actas del Congreso Internacional sobre Daños derivados de Ilícitos Concurrenciales. Marcial Pons, Madrid, pp 123–133

Brokelmann H (2013) La Responsabilidad Civil por Infracción de las Normas de Defensa de la Competencia. In: Font i Ribas A, Gómez Trinidad S (eds) Competencia y Acciones de Indemnización. Actas del Congreso Internacional sobre Daños derivados de Ilícitos Concurrenciales. Marcial Pons, Madrid, pp 101–122

Callol García P, Yuste M (2015) La Directiva Comunitaria sobre Reclamación de Daños y Perjuicios derivados de Infracciones del Derecho de la Competencia. Principales novedades y potencial incidencia en el ordenamiento jurídico español. In: Recuerda Girela MA (ed) Problemas prácticos y actualidad del Derecho de la Competencia. Anuario 2015, pp 297–315

Calvo Caravaca AL, Suderow J (2015) El efecto vinculante de las resoluciones de las Autoridades Nacionales de Competencia en la Aplicación Privada del Derecho Antitrust. Cuadernos de Derecho Transnacional 7(II):114–157

Canedo Arrillaga MP (2017) La Directiva Europea relativa a acciones por daños de infracciones del Derecho de la Competencia de los Estados Miembros y de la Unión Europea. In: Prats Albentosa L, Tomás Martínez G (eds) Culpa y Responsabilidad. Thomson Reuters - Aranzadi, Navarra, pp 173–185

Casado Navarro A (2016) La Directiva 2014/104/UE sobre acciones por daños en materia de Competencia: Una apuesta por las "follow-on actions". In: Ruiz Peris J-I (ed) La Compensación de los Daños por Infracción de las normas de Competencia tras la Directiva 2014/104/UE. Directiva y Propuesta de Transposición. Thomson Reuters-Aranzadi, Navarra, pp 427–450

Cisotta R (2014) Some considerations on the last developments on antitrust damages actions and collective redress in the European Union. Competition Law Rev 10:81–105

Díez Estella F, Estrada Meray C (2014) Las acciones de daños derivadas de ilícitos anticompetitivos en España: análisis de jurisprudencia reciente. Revista de Derecho de la Competencia y la Distribución 15:189–202

Estevan de Quesada C (2016) Algunas reflexiones sobre la admisión de la "passing-on defence" en la Directiva 201/104/UE. In: Ruiz Peris J-I (ed) La Compensación de los Daños por Infracción de las normas de Competencia tras la Directiva 2014/104/UE. Directiva y Propuesta de Transposición. Thomson Reuters-Aranzadi, Navarra, pp 339–354

Fernández C, Moreno-Tapia Rivas I, López Ayuso E (2005) La eficiencia real del Derecho de la Competencia: La indemnización de los daños causados. In: Martínez Lage S, Petitbó Juan A (eds) La modernización del Derecho de la Competencia en España y la Unión Europea. Marcial Pons, Madrid, pp 171–188

Gómez Asensio C (2016) Los Acuerdos Extrajudiciales en la Directiva 2014/104/UE. In: Ruiz Peris J-I (ed) La Compensación de los Daños por Infracción de las normas de Competencia tras la Directiva 2014/104/UE. Directiva y Propuesta de Transposición. Thomson Reuters-Aranzadi, Navarra, pp 355–365

Hernández Bataller B (2016) El derecho al pleno resarcimiento como una de las claves de la Directiva 2014/104/UE. In: Ruiz Peris J-I (ed) La Compensación de los Daños por Infracción de las normas de Competencia tras la Directiva 2014/104/UE. Thomson Reuters-Aranzadi, Navarra, pp 77–98

Herrero Suarez C (2016) La Transposición de la Directiva de Daños Antitrust. Reflexiones a raíz de la publicación de la Propuesta de Ley de Transposición de la Directiva. Cuadernos de Derecho Transnacional 8(I):150–183

Hovenkamp H (2011) Federal antitrust policy. The law of competition and its practice. West, St. Paul

Martí Miravalls J (2016) Responsabilidad y plazos en el marco de las acciones de daños por infracción del Derecho de la Competencia. In: Ruiz Peris J-I (ed) La Compensación de los Daños por Infracción de las normas de Competencia tras la Directiva 2014/104/UE. Thomson Reuters-Aranzadi, Navarra, pp 321–338

Martín Aresti P (2014) Las relaciones entre el Derecho de la Competencia de la Unión Europea (arts. 101 y 102 del TFUE) y el Derecho interno español en materia de Libre Competencia. In: Tratado de Derecho de la Competencia y de la Publicidad, vol 1. Tirant lo Blanch, Valencia, pp 21–60

Martínez Moriel I (2013) La protección de la información aportada en el contexto de una solicitud de clemencia ante las acciones civiles de daños y perjuicios. Gaceta Jurídica de la Unión Europea y de la Competencia 32:61–74

Martorell Zulueta P (2016) La prueba del daño y la aplicación privada de la Competencia. In: Ruiz Peris J-I (ed) La Compensación de los Daños por Infracción de las normas de Competencia tras la Directiva 2014/104/UE. Directiva y Propuesta de Transposición. Thomson Reuters-Aranzadi, Navarra, pp 303–320

Migani C (2014) Directive 2014/104/EU: In search of a balance between the protection of leniency corporate statements and an effective private competition law enforcement. Glob Antitrust Rev 7:81–111

Müller F (2004) The New Council Regulation (EC) No. 1/2003 on the implementation of the rules on competition. Germ Law J 5(VI):721–740

Olmedo Peralta E (2014) Daños derivados de la subida de precios bajo el paraguas de un cártel (*umbrella pricing*): Una lectura jurídica del nuevo paso en la aplicación privada del Derecho de la Competencia. Revista de Derecho de la Competencia y la Distribución 15:107–130

Olmedo Peralta E (2016) La incidencia de las acciones por daños sobre la efectividad de los programas de clemencia y la estabilidad de los cárteles en el Derecho Europeo de la Competencia. In: Ruiz Peris J-I (ed) La Compensación de los Daños por Infracción de las normas de Competencia tras la Directiva 2014/104/UE. Directiva y Propuesta de Transposición. Thomson Reuters-Aranzadi, Navarra, pp 391–426

Ordóñez Solís D (2015) La Directiva 2014/104/UE, la aplicación privada del derecho de la competencia y el contexto jurisprudencial de su transposición en España. Available via EL DERECHO. http://www.elderecho.com/tribuna/mercantil/Directiva-derecho-competencia-transposicion-Espana_11_851680006.html. Accessed 28 Apr 2018

Ortíz Baquero IS (2011) La aplicación privada del Derecho de la Competencia. Los efectos civiles derivados de la infracción de las normas de Libre Competencia. La Ley, Madrid

Peña López F (2002) La responsabilidad civil y la nulidad derivadas de la realización de un ilícito antitrust. Colección de Estudios de Responsabilidad Civil, Comares, Granada

Quijano González J (2011) Derecho de la Competencia y responsabilidad por daños: Lo común y lo especial. In: Velasco San Pedro LA, Alonso Ledesma C, Echebarría Saénz M, Herrero Suarez C, Gutierrez Gilsanz J (eds) La aplicación privada del Derecho de la Competencia. Lex Nova, Valladolid, pp 479–492

Ruiz Peris JI (2016) Tiempos de cambio: Del monopolio de la aplicación pública del Derecho de la Competencia a la responsabilidad compartida. In: Ruiz Peris J-I (ed) La Compensación de los Daños por Infracción de las normas de Competencia tras la Directiva 2014/104/UE. Directiva y Propuesta de Transposición. Thomson Reuters Aranzadi, Navarra, pp 15–52

Slot PJ, Farley M (2017) An introduction to competition law, 2nd edn. Bloomsbury, Hart, Oxford

Tobío Rivas AM (2016/2017) La responsabilidad en la indemnización por daños derivados de un ilícito antitrust. Transposición de la Directiva 2014/104/UE. Actas de Derecho Industrial y Derecho de Autor 37:83–116

Torre Sustaeta MV (2014) La aplicación del Derecho de la Competencia en Europa: Intereses en juego y vías de tutela. Colección Estudios, Thomson Reuters-Aranzadi, Navarra

Velasco San Pedro LA, Herrero Suarez C (2011) La *"Passing-on defence"* ¿un falso dilema? In Velasco San Pedro LA, Alonso Ledesma C, Echebarría Saénz M, Herrero Suarez C, Gutierrez Gilsanz J (eds) La aplicación privada del Derecho de la Competencia. Lex Nova, Valladolid, pp 593–604

Marina San Martín-Calvo is Lawyer and Professor of Commercial Law at University of Burgos, Spain. She obtained a Ph.D. in International Law.

Jurisdiction and Applicable Law in Follow-on Actions

Paolo Bertoli

Abstract By the recent enactment and transposition in the EU Member States of Directive 2014/104/EU on antitrust damages actions, the EU has accomplished to couple the existing choice-of-jurisdiction and choice-of-law discipline on follow-on actions with substantive rules. The article discusses the efficiency of the private international law discipline of such actions in light of the overall goal to enhance free and undistorted competition through private enforcement of EU Competition Law rules.

1 Introduction

Infringements of EU antitrust rules, such as price-fixing cartels or abuse of a dominant position in the market (Articles 101 and 102 of the Treaty on the Function of the European Union—TFEU), adversely affect market conditions, fair competition and consumers and, at the same time, cause damages in terms of higher prices or lost profits to business and consumers (namely, the infringers' direct and indirect customers) as well as to their respective competitors and customers.

It is well established in EU Law and EU Court of Justice (CJEU) precedents that any individual or business having suffered damage as a result of a breach of EU Competition rules has the right to be fully indemnified against such harm by claiming compensation before domestic courts.

The right to compensation thus arises from EU Law and has to be exercised before domestic courts. As in the case with compensation claims for damages arising from other breaches of EU Law, historically, the modalities for the exercise of such right were left to domestic legislation and only limited at the EU level by the principles of effectiveness and equivalence. This entails that the relevant domestic rules cannot be formulated or applied in a way that makes it excessively difficult or practically impossible to exercise the right to compensation guaranteed by the TFEU or less favourably than those applicable to similar domestic actions.

P. Bertoli (✉)
University of Insubria, Como, Italy
e-mail: paolo.bertoli@uninsubria.it

S. Marino et al. (eds.), *Language and Law*,
https://doi.org/10.1007/978-3-319-90905-9_6

To he contrary, choice-of-jurisdiction and choice-of-law aspects have been regulated at the EU level for a significant period of time now, respectively by Regulations EU No 1215/2012 (so-called Brussels I Recast, formerly Regulation EC No 44/2001) on jurisdiction and the recognition and enforcement of judgments in civil and commercial matters and No 864/2007 on the law applicable to non-contractual obligations (so-called Rome II).

The recent enactment and transposition in the EU Member States of Directive 2014/104/EU on antitrust damages actions[1] has supplemented EU private international law rules with substantive rules concerning follow-on actions. Specifically, the Directive sets out rules

> fostering undistorted competition in the internal market and removing obstacles to its proper functioning

and

> necessary to ensure that anyone who has suffered harm caused by an infringement of competition law by an undertaking or by an association of undertakings can effectively exercise the right to claim full compensation for that harm from that undertaking or association.[2]

---

[1]So far, 25 Member States have communicated to the Commission that they have fully transposed the Directive: Austria, Belgium, Croatia, Czech Republic, Cyprus, Denmark, Estonia, Finland, France, Germany, Hungary, Ireland, Italy, Lithuania, Luxembourg, the Netherlands, Poland, Romania, Slovakia, Slovenia, Spain, Sweden and the United Kingdom (last updated on 13 September 2017, see http://ec.europa.eu/competition/antitrust/actionsdamages/directive_en.html). Unless otherwise noted, all the documents cited herein are available at http://eur-lex.europa.eu. See generally Maier-Rigaud (2014), Thiede (2017), Bruzzone and Saija (2017), Comoglio (2017), Wils (2017), Petrucci (2017), De Giorgi (2016), Caiazzo (2016), Giliberti (2016), Geradin (2015), Lianos et al. (2015), Villa (2015), Sansom et al. (2015), Diehl (2015), Vandenborre et al. (2014), Scharaw (2015) and Haasbeek (2015).

[2]Directive 2014/104 is aimed at removing practical obstacles to compensation for all victims of infringements of EU Competition Law. The Directive, *inter alia*, regulates the following aspects: (i) Access to evidence in follow-on actions. A party needing documents that are not in its custody, possession or control may apply for a court order for the disclosure of those documents. (ii) Proof. Final infringement decision of National Competition Authorities (NCA; just like infringement decisions by the EU Commission) will constitute full proof before civil courts in the same Member State where the infringement occurred (but not of the damages it has caused). Before courts of other Member States, it will constitute at least *prima facie* evidence of the infringement. However, the Directive sets forth a rebuttable presumption that cartels cause harm in order to facilitate compensation in light of the difficulties usually experienced in proving the harm. (iii) Limitation periods. Victims are generally allowed at least 5 years to bring damages claims, starting from the moment when they knew or could have known that they suffered harm from an infringement. This period is suspended or interrupted if a competition authority starts infringement proceedings, and victims have at least 1 year from the final decision to bring damages actions. (iv) "Passing on" defense. In follow-on cases, cartelists often argue that their customers raised the prices they charge to their own customers (indirect customers) and that, accordingly, compensation to direct customers should be decreased by the amount they passed on to indirect customers. Since it is often hard for indirect customers to prove that they suffered this pass-on, the Directive facilitates their claims by establishing a rebuttable presumption that they suffered some level of overcharge harm, to be quantified judicially. (v) Joint and several liability. Any participant to a cartel, in principle, is held

Such rules are aimed at ensuring equivalent protection throughout the Union for anyone who has suffered harm from breach of EU antitrust rules and set forth that victims are entitled to full compensation for the harm suffered, covering compensation for both actual loss and for loss of profit, plus interest.

2 Choice of Court for Follow-on Claims: The Special Ground of Jurisdiction for Non-Contractual Obligations

As far as choice of court for follow-on claims is concerned, the Brussels I Recast Regulation offers a variety of fora for claims asserted by harmed parties against infringers, as well as for claims seeking negative declaratory relief sought by the infringers themselves (so-called torpedo actions).

The general rule on jurisdiction in the Regulation is that persons domiciled in a Member State shall, whatever their nationality, be sued in the courts of that Member State (Article 4). As is well known, for purposes of such rule a company (or other legal person or association of natural or legal persons) is domiciled at the place where it has its: (a) statutory seat; (b) central administration; or (c) principal place of business.[3] Accordingly, assumed infringers of EU Competition Law may be sued at the courts of their place of domicile for the entirety of the harm caused by their infringement, and can in turn seek negative declaratory relief at the courts of the place of domicile of their clients or other potential harmed parties.

EU antitrust infringements, and especially cartels, however, are typically multijurisdictional and multi-party, since they normally involve conduct by multiple infringers located in different Member States, occurred in different Member States, and affecting customers and markets located in different Member States. Thus, the place of domicile of a defendant may not prove a suitable forum for this type of claims and ensuing proceedings, since it does not allow to concentrate jurisdiction before a single judicial authority.

Antitrust infringements amount to non-contractual obligations, and as now settled in CJEU case law,[4] follow-on proceedings can accordingly be eradicated before the judge competent for "matters relating to tort, delict or quasi-delict" pursuant to Article 7(2) of the Brussels Recast Regulation, i.e., "the courts for the place where

jointly and severally liable towards the victims for the whole harm caused by the infringement, maintaining a contribution vis-à-vis other cartelists for their share of liability. However, to safeguard the effectiveness of leniency programs, this does not apply to infringers who obtained immunity from fines in return for their voluntary cooperation with a competition authority during an investigation; these immunity recipients are normally obliged to compensate only their (direct and indirect) customers.

[3]See the thorough study by Benedettelli (2002), p. 882 ff.

[4]Case C-133/11 *Folien Fischer* [2012] ECLI:EU:C:2012:664; Case C-302/13 *LAL-Lithuanian Airlines* [2012] ECLI:EU:C:2014:2319, para. 27; Case C-352/13 *Cartel Damage Claims* (CDC) [2015] ECLI:EU:C:2015:335.

the harmful event occurred or may occur". As is well known, the expression "place where the harmful event occurred or may occur" is intended to cover both the place: (i) where the damage occurred; (ii) of the event giving rise to that damage and, thus, the defendant may be sued, at the option of the claimant(s), in the courts of either of those places.[5]

In relation to the application of those two connecting criteria to actions seeking reparation for widespread damage, the CJEU has previously held that the victim may bring an action for damages either before the Courts of the Member State of the place where the defendant is established, which have jurisdiction to award damages for all of the harm caused by the conduct, or before the courts of each Member State where the victim claims to have suffered damage, which have jurisdiction to rule solely in respect of the harm caused in the State of the seized court.[6]

The CJEU, moreover, held that Article 7(2) may also be used as a basis for an action for

> a negative declaration seeking to establish the absence of liability in tort, delict, or quasi-delict.[7]

In the recent landmark *Cartel Damages Claims* judgment, the CJEU has clarified how Article 7(2) applies in respect to follow-on claims. The claim in the main proceedings was brought before the German Courts by a Belgian company assignee of claims[8] of undertakings located in thirteen different Member States against six chemical undertakings which, with the exception of a defendant in respect of which the claim was withdrawn following a settlement, were domiciled in five Member States other than Germany. The claim was based upon the European Commission's finding that, in connection with hydrogen peroxide and sodium perborate, the defendants in the main proceedings and other undertakings participated in a cartel.

The Court first dealt with the identification of the place of the event giving rise to the damage (so-called causal event). As typical in cartel cases, the buyers were supplied by various participants in the cartel within the scope of their contractual

[5]E.g.: Case C-523/10 *Wintersteiger* [2012] ECLI:EU:C:2012:220, para. 19 and the case law cited therein.

[6]Case C-68/93 *Shevill and Others* [1994] ECR I-2355, ECLI:EU:C:1994:226, para. 33; Joined Cases C-509/09 and C-161/10, *eDate Advertising* [2011] ECR I-10269, ECLI:EU:C:2011:685, para. 42.

[7]Since the place of the harmful event "can either show a connection with the State in which the damage occurred or may occur or show a connection with the State in which the causal event giving rise to that damage took place, in accordance with the case law set out in paragraph 39 above, then the court in one of those two places, as the case may be, can claim jurisdiction to hear such an action, pursuant to point (3) of Article 5 of Regulation No 44/2001, irrespective of whether the action in question has been brought by a party whom a tort or delict may have adversely affected or by a party against whom a claim based on that tort or delict might be made": judgment *Folien Fischer*, para. 52.

[8]The Court held that "the transfer of claims by the initial creditor cannot, by itself, have an impact on the determination of the court having jurisdiction under Article 5(3) of Regulation No 44/2001": Case C-147/12 *ÖFAB* [2013] ECLI:EU:C:2013:490, para. 58.

relationships. However, the event giving rise to the alleged harm did not consist in a potential breach of contractual obligations, but in a non-contractual obligation consisting in the buyer being prevented from being supplied at a price determined by the rules of supply and demand.

The Court clarified that, in principle, the place of a causal event of loss consisting in additional costs that a buyer had to pay because a cartel has distorted market prices

> can be identified, in the abstract, as the place of the conclusion of the cartel (para. 44)

The Court went on noticing that, however, such place might not be relevant in circumstances such as those in the main proceedings since the Commission held that it was not possible to identify a single place where the cartel was concluded, because it consisted of several collusive agreements concluded during various meetings and discussions which took place in various places throughout the EU. In a similar situation, thus, Article 7(2) would not allow to establish jurisdiction at the place of the causal event, unless:

> among several agreements that, as a whole, amounted to the unlawful cartel at issue, there was one in particular which was the sole causal event giving rise to the loss allegedly inflicted on a buyer

and/or the

> referring court were to find that the cartel at issue in the main proceedings was nevertheless definitively concluded in its jurisdiction. (para. 47)

In *Melzer*, the CJEU maintained that Article 7(2) does not allow the Courts of the place where a harmful event occurred which is imputed to one of the presumed perpetrators of the damage, who is not a party to the dispute, to take jurisdiction in an action against another presumed perpetrator of that damage who has not acted within the jurisdiction of that court.[9] However, the Court explicitly derogated from this finding in *Cartel Damage Claims*, holding that in cartel cases

> there is no reason for preventing several perpetrators from being sued together before the same court. (para. 49)

Thus, the Court concluded that Article 7(2) allows to base jurisdiction

> on the basis of the causal event and with regard to all of the perpetrators of an unlawful cartel which allegedly resulted in loss

contingent upon

> the identification, in the jurisdiction of the court seized of the matter, of a specific event during which either that cartel was definitively concluded or one agreement in particular was made which was the sole causal event giving rise to the loss allegedly inflicted on a buyer.

By this finding, the Court basically duplicated the identification of the place of the causal event, which may either be the place where:

---

[9]Case C-228/11 *Melzer* [2013] ECLI:EU:C:2013:305, para. 41.

(i) the cartel was concluded (which is competent for all damages caused anywhere to any harmed parties) or
(ii) a single agreement within the cartel causing harm to a specific party was concluded (which is competent for all damages caused anywhere, but only in respect of buyers specifically harmed by such agreement).[10]

The finding under (ii) seems to apply to follow-on claims the so-called first impact rule, according to which Article 7(2) does not allow to establish jurisdiction at a place where

> the adverse consequences can be felt of an event which has already caused damage actually arising elsewhere[11]

The Court then dealt with the assessment of the place where the damage occurred. According to the Court, this is the place where the alleged damage actually manifests itself[12] and which, for loss consisting in additional costs incurred because of artificially high prices,

> is identifiable only for each alleged victim taken individually and is located, in general, at that victim's registered office.[13]

According to the Court, this place

> fully guarantees the efficacious conduct of potential proceedings, given that the assessment of a claim for damages for loss allegedly inflicted upon a specific undertaking as a result of an unlawful cartel... essentially depends on factors specifically relating to the situation of that undertaking.[14]

This finding seems to explicitly derogate from a previous finding, namely that the

> expression 'place where the harmful event occurred' does not refer to the place where the claimant is domiciled or where 'his assets are concentrated' by reason only of the fact that he has suffered financial damage there resulting from the loss of part of his assets which arose and was incurred in another [Member] State.[15]

According to the Court, moreover, the Courts so identified

> have jurisdiction to hear an action brought either against any one of the participants in the cartel or against several of them for the whole of the loss inflicted upon that undertaking as a result of additional costs that it had to pay to be supplied with products covered by the cartel concerned.

---

[10]Cf. Monico (2016), p. 1164.

[11]Case C-364/93 *Marinari* [1995] ECR I-2719, ECLI:EU:C:1995:289, para. 14; Case C-220/88 *Dumez France* [1990] ECR I-49, ECLI:EU:C:1990:8, para. 20; Corte di Cassazione (Italian Supreme Court), No 10524/1996; No 1179/2000; No 2060/2003; No 27403/2005; Saravalle (1997), p. 332; Gardella (2004), p. 129; Bariatti (2008), p. 349 ff.; Carbone and Tuo (2016), p. 126; Mankowski (2016), p. 305; Monico (2016), p. 1161.

[12]Case C-189/08 *Zuid-Chemie* [2009] ECR I-6917, ECLI:EU:C:2009:475, para. 27.

[13]Judgment *Cartel Damage Claims*, para. 52.

[14]Judgment *Cartel Damage Claims*, para. 53.

[15]Case C-168/02 *Kronhofer* [2004] ECR I-6009, ECLI:EU:C:2004:364, para. 19.

By its reference to the 'whole of the loss', it is submitted that the Court has derogated the so-called mosaic principle, according to which, as noted, the Courts of each Member State where the victim claims to have suffered damage have jurisdiction solely in respect of the harm caused in that State. However, as also clarified by the Court, the jurisdiction of the court seized by virtue of the place where the damage occurred is limited to the loss suffered by the undertaking whose registered office is located in such jurisdiction.

In the present author's view, the Court's findings have two main shortcomings. First, as discussed, the Court derogated from certain well-established principles pertaining to the application of Article 7(2), which will raise doubts as to their ongoing validity in cases different from follow-on claims. Second, if read in conjunction, the findings of the Court do not seem to allow—at least in the most frequent cases—the concentration of follow-on claims by all harmed parties before a single Court under Article 7(2). Indeed, the Court explicitly stated that neither of the following judges are competent for all the harm suffered by all damaged parties, but only for all of the harm suffered by a single damaged party:

1. the judges of the place where a single agreement within the cartel causing harm to a specific party was concluded (who are competent for all damages caused anywhere, but only in respect of buyers specifically harmed by such agreement);
2. the judges of the place where each alleged victim taken individually has its registered office (who are competent for the entirety of the harm suffered by such individual victim). On the contrary, the judges of the place where the cartel was concluded are competent for all damages caused anywhere to any harmed parties, but in practice this place is often extremely difficult to establish, if at all existent, and thus this connecting factor will allow the concentration of proceedings before a single judge under Article 7(2) only in limited circumstances.

3 *Sequitur*: *Forum* for Connected Disputes

Article 8(1) of the Brussels Recast Regulation provides that

> a person domiciled in a Member State may also be sued, where he is one of a number of defendants, in the courts for the place where any one of them is domiciled, provided the claims are so closely connected that it is expedient to hear and determine those applications together to avoid the risk of irreconcilable judgments resulting from separate proceedings.

The Court has clarified that this rule of jurisdiction is aimed at facilitating the sound administration of justice, to minimise the possibility of concurrent proceedings and thus to avoid irreconcilable outcomes if cases are decided separately.[16] To sum up, it is settled case law that, in order for Article 8(1) to apply,

---

[16]E.g., Case C-145/10 *Painer* [2011] ECR I-12533, ECLI:EU:C:2011:798, para. 77. See Marongiu Buonaiuti (2008) and Biagioni (2011).

> it is necessary to ascertain whether, between various claims brought by the same applicant against various defendants, there is a connection of such a kind that it is expedient to determine those actions together in order to avoid the risk of irreconcilable judgments resulting from separate proceedings[17]

and that

> in order for judgments to be regarded as irreconcilable, it is not sufficient that there be a divergence in the outcome of the dispute, but that divergence must also arise in the context of the same situation of fact and law.[18]

After some uncertainties, especially at the domestic level,[19] it is now settled that the rule of jurisdiction laid down in Article 8(1) is applicable without there being any need to establish separately that the claims were not brought with the sole object of ousting the jurisdiction of the courts of the Member State where one of the defendants is domiciled.[20] In other words, the Court does not require any particular test as to the existence of a genuine link or close connection between the seized Court and the facts of the case.[21] However, the foregoing rule comes with an exception, namely that Article 8(1)

> cannot be interpreted as allowing an applicant to make a claim against a number of defendants for the sole purpose of removing one of them from the jurisdiction of the courts of the Member State in which that defendant is domiciled.

Even though vaguely defined, this exception seems to allow a limited discretion for Courts not to accept jurisdiction in cases in which recourse to Article 8(1) is openly abusive in light of the circumstances of the case.[22]

Article 8(1) seems particularly suited, and is frequently invoked in practice, as a ground for jurisdiction in follow-on claims in light of their multi-party and multijurisdictional nature, which includes conduct by multiple parties causing harm of the same or similar nature to a variety of parties. Cartelists or other infringers of EU Competition Law are jointly and severally liable for the harm ensuing from their conduct and are typically summoned before the same court by several harmed parties. Cartelists or other infringers of EU Competition Law also typically file contribution claims either in the course of such proceeding or by instituting separate multi-party proceedings. They also frequently happen to file actions for negative declaratory relief against harmed parties or other cartelists. Jurisdiction in all of the foregoing proceedings is frequently based upon Article 8(1).

---

[17]See Case C-98/06 *Freeport* [2007] ECR I-8319, ECLI:EU:C:2007:595, para. 39; Case C-645/11 *Sapir and others* [2013] ECLI:EU:C:2013.228, para. 42.

[18]See judgment *Freeport*, para. 40; judgment *Painer*, para. 79; judgment *Sapir and others*, para. 43.

[19]See Corte di Cassazione (Italian Supreme Court) No 12209/1995; 785/1999; 86/2000; 13627/2001; 14287/2006; Court of Milan, 24 January 2004; Di Blase (1993), p. 26.

[20]Judgment *Freeport*, para. 54; Corte di Cassazione (Italian Supreme Court), No 25875/2008; Court of Milan, 8 May 2009.

[21]See e.g. Bertoli (2012), p. 29 ff.; Muir Watt (2016), p. 374.

[22]Case C-103/05 *Reisch Montage* [2006] ECR I-6827, ECLI:EU:C:2006:471, para. 32; and judgment *Painer*, para. 78.

In the *Cartel Damages Claim* judgment, the Court has finally spread light on the application of Article 8(1) to follow-on claims.

The Court has first clarified that the requirement that the same situation of fact and law must arise is satisfied in circumstances such as those of a follow-on action ensuing from a decision by the EU Commission. Indeed, despite the fact that the cartelists may participate in the implementation of the cartel by concluding and performing contracts under it, in different places and at different times, the cartel agreement "amounted to a single and continuous infringement" of Article 101 TFEU and Article 53 of the EEA Agreement.

The Court further held that, as regards the risk of irreconcilable judgments resulting from separate proceedings,

> since the requirements for holding those participating in an unlawful cartel liable in tort may differ between the various national laws, there would be a risk of irreconcilable judgments if actions were brought before the courts of various Member States by a party allegedly adversely affected by a cartel.[23]

As better explained below, the foregoing may or may not be true also when the cartelists are sued before the same domestic court, since they are domiciled in different Member States and their conduct and its effects may have materialised in different Member States. As a result, the choice-of-law rules of the seized Court may render different laws applicable to the various relationships at stake. However, the Court clarified that such a difference in legal basis does not, in itself, preclude the application of Article 8(1)

> provided that it was foreseeable by the defendants that they might be sued in the Member State where at least one of them is domiciled.[24]

According to the Court, such condition is fulfilled in the case of a binding decision of the Commission

> finding there to have been a single infringement of EU law and, on the basis of that finding, holding each participant liable for the loss resulting from the tortious actions of those participating in the infringement. In those circumstances, the participants could have expected to be sued in the courts of a Member State in which one of them is domiciled.[25]

As explained above, some of the parties in the main proceedings alleged that, before the action was brought, an out-of-court settlement was reached between the applicant in the main proceedings and the only defendant domiciled in Germany, and that the parties purposefully delayed the formal conclusion of that settlement until proceedings had been instituted, for the sole purpose of securing the jurisdiction of the Court seized of the case as against the other defendants in the main proceedings. The Court recalled its test as to the abusive recourse to Article 8(1) and seems to have applied it rather restrictively, holding that in order to exclude the applicability of Article 8(1), firm evidence is required that

---

[23]Judgment *Cartel Damage Claims*, para. 22.

[24]Judgment *Painer*, para. 84.

[25]Judgment *Cartel Damage Claims*, para. 24.

> at the time that proceedings were instituted, the parties concerned had colluded to artificially fulfil, or prolong the fulfilment of, that provision's applicability.

The Court went on noticing that although it is for the Court seized of the case to assess such evidence,

> it must nevertheless be made clear that simply holding negotiations with a view to concluding an out-of-court settlement does not in itself prove such collusion. However, it would be otherwise if it transpired that such a settlement had, in fact, been concluded, but that it had been concealed.

Overall, the test seems to apply in a very restrictive fashion and to capture clearly fraudulent behaviour where the applicant and that defendant had colluded to artificially fulfil, or prolong the fulfilment of, Article 8(1) applicability, not requiring a particular assessment of genuine or close links between the case at hand and the State of the seized court.

In light of the fact that, as discussed, Article 7(2) will rarely allow to concentrate follow-on claims before a single judge, recourse to Article 8(1) by suing all cartel members (or customers, for torpedo actions) before a single court is a frequent practice which the *Cartel Damages Claims* judgment seems to have substantially allowed.

4 Choice of Forum by the Parties

Contracts for the supply of goods (or provision of services) between infringers of antitrust rules and their customers may contain jurisdictional clauses and thus the issue arises whether such clauses preclude the operation of the rules on jurisdiction in Articles 7(2) and/or Article 8(1) of the Brussels I Recast Regulation.

As a preliminary matter, it is well settled that a choice of court agreement under Article 25 of the Regulation may derogate not only from the general jurisdiction under Article 4 thereof, but also from the special jurisdiction laid down in Articles 7 and 8.[26] In *Cartel Damages Claim*, the Court clarified that, in principle, the same holds true as far as cartels are concerned:

> [t]hat conclusion cannot be called into question by the requirement of effective enforcement of the prohibition of cartel agreements

because

> the Court has already held that the substantive rules applicable to the substance of a case must not affect the validity of a jurisdiction clause

and

> the court seized of the matter cannot, without undermining the aim of Regulation No 44/2001, refuse to take into account a jurisdiction clause which has satisfied the requirements

[26] E.g., Case 24/76 *Estasis Saloti di Colzani* [1976] ECR 1831, ECLI:EU:C:1976:177, para. 7.

> of Article 23 of that regulation solely on the ground that it considers that the court with jurisdiction under that clause would not give full effect to the requirement of effective enforcement of the prohibition of cartel agreements by not allowing a victim of the cartel to obtain full compensation for the loss it suffered. On the contrary, it must be considered that the system of legal remedies in each Member State, together with the preliminary ruling procedure provided for in Article 267 TFEU, affords a sufficient guarantee to individuals in that respect.[27]

In light of the foregoing, the most relevant issue seems to establish whether a choice of law clause may capture follow-on claims, which are tortious claims and not claims arising out of the contractual relationship between the cartel member and its costumer, such relationship only being the necessary factual prerequisite for the tortious claim for breach of EU Competition Law. The Court provided guidance as to how best to address this issue, clarifying that, in principle, choice of court clauses should be interpreted narrowly, since they

> can concern only disputes which have arisen or which may arise in connection with a particular legal relationship, which limits the scope of an agreement conferring jurisdiction solely to disputes which arise from the legal relationship in connection with which the agreement was entered into.[28]

Accordingly, a clause which abstractly refers to all disputes arising 'from contractual relationships' does not cover

> a dispute relating to the tortious liability that one party allegedly incurred as a result of the other's participation in an unlawful cartel.

The Court also stated the obvious principle that, by contrast, where a clause refers to disputes

> in connection with liability incurred as a result of an infringement of competition law and designates the courts of a Member State other than the Member State of the referring court, the latter ought to decline its own jurisdiction.

It is rather clear, to sum up, that follow-on claims:

1. do not arise out of the contractual relationship between a cartel member and its customer, and thus are not covered by choice-of-court agreements only capturing claims arising out of such contractual relationship;
2. are covered by choice-of-court clauses explicitly mentioning such claims. However, the Court failed to address what the solution would be when a choice of court clause encompasses all disputes 'in connection with' (as opposed to arising out of) a given contractual relationship, as tortious claims in connection with a contractual relationship (such as follow-on claims) may characterise. It is submitted that such claims are covered by choice-of court (or arbitration) agreements, unless explicitly mentioned. This reading seems better aligned both with the

---

[27]Judgment *Cartel Damage Claims*, para. 63, citing Case C-38/98 *Renault* [2000] ECR I-2973, ECLI:EU:C:2000:225, para. 23, on which see Bertoli (2005), p. 476 ff.

[28]Judgment *Cartel Damage Claims*, para. 68, citing Case C-214/89 *Powell Duffryn* [1992] ECR I-1745, ECLI:EU:C:1992:115, para. 31.

Court's suggested strict interpretation of Article 25 and with the necessity to allow the grouping of follow-on claims before a single judge (which would be jeopardised if choice-of-court—or arbitration—agreements contained in the underlying contracts between cartel members and their customers imposed to decline jurisdiction).

5 Choice-of-Law Issues

As far as choice-of-law is concerned, the Rome II Regulation (Article 6(4)) does not allow the parties to choose the law applicable to non-contractual obligations arising out of unfair competition and acts restricting free competition, including follow-on actions. This provision and the Court's findings in *Cartel Damages Claims* are thus misaligned in that the Court did find that the parties are allowed to conclude choice-of-court agreements in respect of the same matter. The prohibition to choice of law under the Rome II Regulation seems related to the fact that antitrust matters involve rights which the parties cannot dispose of and the relating fear of abusive choice of law (even though EU Competition Law is internationally mandatory and thus their application cannot be derogated by a choice-of-law clause). The Court did not share the same concerns with respect to choice-of-court clauses, which basically entail that the parties do not have a chance to secure the parallelism between competent judge and applicable law *a priori*.

Article 6(3) of the Rome II Regulation provides that the law applicable to a non-contractual obligation arising out of a restriction of Competition shall be the law of the country where the market is, or is likely to be, affected. However, when the market is, or is likely to be, affected in more than one country, the person seeking compensation for damage who sues in the court of the domicile of the defendant, may instead choose to base his or her claim on the law of the seized court, provided that the market in that Member State is amongst those directly and substantially affected by the restriction of competition out of which the non-contractual obligation on which the claim is based arises; where the claimant sues, in accordance with the applicable rules on jurisdiction, more than one defendant in that court, he or she can only choose to base his or her claim on the law of that court if the restriction of competition on which the claim against each of these defendants relies directly and substantially affects also the market in the Member State of that court.

This provision, in combination with Article 8(1) of the Brussels Recast Regulation as interpreted by the CJEU, allows claimants—under certain conditions to be ascertained on a case-by-case basis (especially the affected market test required to allow choice of the *lex fori*)—to concentrate follow-on actions in a single forum and to have such claims be governed by the substantive law of the seized court.

In perspective, in light of the enactment of Directive 2014/104 on antitrust damages actions, choice-of-law issues may become less important from a practical standpoint, since the laws of the different Member States will be harmonised, thus reducing the impact of the application of one law over another.

6 Conclusions

Articles 101 and 102 TFEU are aimed at ensuring that competition in the internal market is not distorted, and private enforcement by domestic judges in the context of follow-on proceedings is conceived as a mean to foster the efficiency of such provisions and thus free and undistorted competition. Differently from what happened in different sectors of EU Law, private international law rules aimed at providing a uniform set of rules for follow-on claims, and thus at contributing to the foregoing goals of the EU legal order, have been enacted at the EU level well before a uniform substantive discipline was achieved.

The first milestone in this process has been the Rome II Regulation, which sets forth a uniform choice of law rule aimed at identifying a single law as applicable to follow-on claims and thus at reducing uncertainty and unpredictability. The rule also allows the parties, under certain conditions, to identify and choose a single law as applicable to the several relationships to which a breach of EU competition Law typically gives rise.

The Court recently coupled the choice-of-law discipline by interpreting the long existing (and long liberally applied) choice-of-court criteria in the Brussels Recast Regulation in a very EU-antitrust-enforcement friendly manner. Specifically, the Court allowed choice of court by the parties, as well as concentration of follow-on claims before a single judge in most instances, by imposing very limited exceptions to the operation of Article 8(1) on connected proceedings, thus allowing the grouping of connected claims before the judge where a single 'anchor defendant' is domiciled.

The harmonization of the substantive provisions finally realised by Directive 2014/104 on antitrust damages and its domestic implementation might downgrade the relevance that choice of court and choice of law issues have had so far, given that harmonised substantive provisions will be present through the Member States. These will shortly no longer include the UK, a forum which has frequently been considered attractive by plaintiffs of follow-on claims for, *inter alia*, access to evidence and claimant-oriented rules on liquidation of damages.[29] Follow-on actions and private enforcement will likely continue to play a significant role in ensuring effectiveness of EU Competition Law.

References

Bariatti S (2008) Violazione di norme antitrust e diritto internazionale privato: il giudice italiano e i cartelli. Rivista di diritto internazionale privato e processuale 44:349–362

Benedettelli M (2002) Criteri di giurisdizione in materia societaria e diritto comunitario. Rivista di diritto internazionale privato e processuale 38:882–922

[29]See Bertoli (2017), p. 599 ff.

Bertoli P (2005) Corte di giustizia, integrazione comunitaria e diritto internazionale privato e processuale. Giuffré, Milano

Bertoli P (2012) Profili evolutivi della connessione attributiva internazionale. In: D'Elia G, Tiberi G, Viviani Schlein M (eds) Scritti in memoria di A. Concaro. Giuffré, Milano, pp 29–41

Bertoli P (2017) La "Brexit" e il diritto internazionale privato e processuale. Rivista di diritto internazionale privato e processuale 53:599–621

Biagioni G (2011) La connessione attributiva di giurisdizione nel regolamento CE n. 44/2001. CEDAM, Padova

Bruzzone G, Saija A (2017) Private e public enforcement dopo il recepimento della direttiva. Più di un aggiustamento al margine?. Mercato, Concorrenza, Regole 19:9–36

Caiazzo R (2016) The legislative decree of implementation of Directive 2014/104/EU on antitrust damages actions. Rivista Italiana di Antitrust 2:104–124

Carbone S, Tuo C (2016) Il nuovo spazio giudiziario europeo in materia civile e commerciale. Il regolamento UE n. 1215/2012. Giappichelli, Torino

Comoglio LP (2017) Note a una prima lettura del d.lgs. N.3 del 2017. Novità processuali e parziali inadeguatezze in tema di danno antitrust. Rivista Trimestrale di Diritto e Procedura Civile 71:991–1012

De Giorgi E (2016) Risarcimento del danno antitrust: primo commento allo schema di decreto legislativo di attuazione della Direttiva 2014/104/UE. Available via Dirittobancario. http://www.dirittobancario.it/approfondimenti/antitrust-e-concorrenza/risarcimento-del-danno-antitrust-primo-commento-allo-schema-di-decreto-legislativo. Accessed 27 Apr 2018

Di Blase A (1993) Connessione e litispendenza nella convenzione di Bruxelles. CEDAM, Padova

Diehl K (2015) Europe's new directive on antitrust damages. Glob Competition Litig Rev 8:34 ff

Gardella A (2004) Giurisdizione in materia di illecito: un passo avanti nella localizzazione del danno patrimoniale. Int Lis, 128–132

Geradin D (2015) Collective redress for antitrust damages in the European Union: Is this a reality now?. George Mason Univ Law Rev 22:1079–1101

Giliberti B (2016) Public e private enforcement nell'art. 9, co. I della direttiva antitrust 104/2014. Il coordinamento delle tutele: accertamento amministrativo e risarcimento danni nei rapporti privatistici. Rivista italiana di diritto pubblico comunitario 26:77–113

Haasbeek L (2015) The directive on antitrust damages actions. In: Raffaelli E (ed) Antitrust between EC law and National law. Bruylant-Giuffrè, Bruxelles-Milan, p 63 ff

Lianos I, Davis P, Nebbia P (2015) Damages claims for the infringement of EU competition law. Oxford University Press, Oxford

Maier-Rigaud F (2014) Toward a European directive on damages actions. J Competition Law Econ 10:341–360

Mankowski P (2016) Article 7. In: Magnus U, Mankowski P (eds) Brussels Ibis regulation. De Gruter, Köln, p 305 ff

Marongiu Buonaiuti F (2008) Litispendenza e connessione internazionale. Editoriale Scientifica, Napoli

Monico R (2016) Il private antitrust enforcement nello spazio giudiziario europeo. Rivista di diritto internazionale 99:1147–1186

Muir Watt H (2016) Article 8. In: Magnus U, Mankowski P (eds) Brussels Ibis regulation. De Gruter, Köln, p 374 ff

Petrucci C (2017) Subsidiarity in Directive 2014/104 EU on damages actions for breach of EU competition law. Eur Public Law J 23:395–421

Sansom M, Morfey A, Teague P (2015) Recent developments in private antitrust damages litigation in Europe. Antitrust Magazine, p 33 ff

Saravalle A (1997) Conseguenze dell'illecito e danni patrimoniali indiretti: il foro competente. Danno e responsabilità 2(III):332 ff

Scharaw B (2015) Commission proposal for a Directive on antitrust damages and recommendation on principles for collective redress: the road towards 'private antitrust enforcement' in the European Union. Eur Competition Law Rev 7:352–360

Thiede T (2017) Fine to follow? Private anti-trust actions in European law. China-EU Law J 5:233–263

Vandenborre I, Hoffman Lent K, Goetz T, Frese M (2014) Actions for Antitrust damages in the European union: evaluating the Commission's directive proposal. Glob Competition Litig Rev 7:1 ff

Villa G (2015) La direttiva europea sul risarcimento del danno antitrust: riflessioni in vista dell'attuazione. Corriere giuridico 32:301–309

Wils WPJ (2017) Private enforcement of EU antitrust law and its relationship with public enforcement: past, present, future. World Comp 40:3–45

Paolo Bertoli is licensed Full Professor of International Law and Director of the Research Centre on Swiss law of the University of Insubria.

Contemporary Trends in International Law in Relation to the Protection of Individuals from Multinationals' Malpractice: Greek Competition Law After the Implementation of EU Directive 2014/104

Sotirios S. Livas

Abstract Our discussion of the topic of the protection of individuals from big companies' and multinationals' malpractice, according both to the European and the Greek Competition Law, moves along two separate axes: one having to do with a presentation of the current situation prevailing in the field of the Greek Competition Law, i.e. the situation prior to the implementation of the EU Directive 2014/104 and the other related to a forecast of the possible consequences of this implementation. For this second part, we make the choice to refer ourselves to the US Alien Tort Claims Act (ATCA) and the possibility of the formation of a framework of international law rules protecting human rights from the breaches and trespasses of big companies. We conclude that when Competition Law rules fulfil their inherent goal, that is welfare of the society as a whole, they have the potential to operate as a tool of enhancing civil society vis-à-vis big companies and multinationals, thus moving in parallel with international law's endeavour to create an area of protection of human rights from their malpractice.

S. S. Livas (✉)
Department of Foreign Languages, Translation and Interpreting, Ionian University, Corfu, Greece

S. Marino et al. (eds.), *Language and Law*,
https://doi.org/10.1007/978-3-319-90905-9_7

1 Introduction—Protection of Individuals from Multinationals' Malpractice: Parallel Trajectories in International and EU Law

At the time of writing the present chapter[1] Directive 2014/104/EU[2] has just begun to be implemented in Greece. Although the Member States had to comply and bring into force the necessary legislative measures by 27th December 2016, Greece has taken a rather longer period of time to do so. Of course, a time lapse of three or even four years from the adoption of an EU directive to its transposition into Greek legislation through a national legislation measure (a law, a ministerial decision, a presidential decree) is not an unusual phenomenon at all.

The measure chosen for the transposition of the Directive is a law that was voted by the Greek Parliament on 31st January 2018. The consultation period lasted from September 14th to September 29th 2017. Following the consultation procedure, certain Directive's provisions were left out, i.e. Article 2: terminology, Article 9: effect of national decisions, Article 12: actions for damages by claimants from different levels in the supply chain, Article 14: quantification of harm, Article 15: consensual dispute resolution; in total 9 out of 16 Articles. This means that these specific Articles could not be disputed or amended through the process of open consultation.

The Law is going to provide individuals and companies the legal possibility to act against companies that have breached the competition legislation, asking for compensation in relation not only to actual damage, i.e. to positive harm, but also to consequential damage. This possibility is given not only to immediate but also to indirect purchasers, i.e. purchasers that are not directly linked to the supplier. We should note at this point that this specific provision of the Directive has proved to be the most difficult to implement. In general, though, the Greek legislator has managed to bypass the technical difficulties existing, making profit of the similarities of the Directive's provisions to the previous Greek tort regulations (Civil Code Articles 912 *et seq*).

According to the Law implementing Directive 2014/104/EU in Greece, individuals and/or companies can act in court without taking into account prior decisions of competition authorities in relation to a specific matter. The burden of proof for the amount of damage is to be brought by the plaintiff, but the court can also, in the case of scarce evidence, estimate the amount of compensation. There are also provisions in relation to the leniency programme due to small or medium-sized enterprises and in relation to consensual dispute resolution.

The competent authorities for the implementation of the Directive, i.e. the Ministry of Development and Finance and the Ministry of Justice, are going to create a totally separate judicial formation, within the Athens Courts of First Instance, with

---

[1]April 2018.

[2]Directive 2014/104/EU of the European Parliament and of the Council of 26 November 2014 on certain rules governing actions for damages under national law for infringements of the competition law provisions of the Member States and of the European Union (OJ L 349, 5.12.2014, p. 1).

jurisdiction for the whole of the country. This judicial chamber, which will try cases of both individuals and companies related to actions for compensation concerning breaches of competition legislation, will be composed of three magistrates with expertise on EU and Competition Law.

2 EU Competition Law After the Implementation of Directive 2014/104/EU: Individual Indemnification Actions Against Multinationals and Big Companies in the EU

The main feature of Directive 2014/104/EU, and, as a consequence, of the Law transposing it into Greek legislation, is the power it vests in citizens to act for compensation against firms and companies breaching the EU Competition Law. At the same time, this feature constitutes proof that the public law enforcement of Competition Law—while being necessary—is not adequate and it should be enhanced by private law enforcement rules.

The implementation of the EU legislation in Greece may give us a chance to observe the reactions of individuals in relation to the breaches of EU Competition Law by big companies and multinationals. These reactions should be interpreted in relation and in proportion to the gravity of these breaches, but in any case we will have, for the first time in Greek legal history, an imprint of the active participation of the Greek civil society, in its effort to understand, appreciate and limit the power and even, in some cases, the aggressiveness of large companies and multinationals. To assess the real and not just the imaginative measure of this imprint and the framework of the Directive's possible consequences on the regulation of the Greek market, as well as the feasibility of such an empowerment of the Greek civil society vis-à-vis the breaches of market regulations, we should examine the Directive, as well as the totality of the EU Competition Legislation, teleologically, i.e. examine its purpose and proceed to comparing it to previous relative initiatives in international law, i.e. initiatives empowering civil society vis-à-vis the market.

3 The Purpose of EU and International Competition Law: An Approach to the Roots of the Problem

As Kaplow has shown,[3] the goals and objectives of Competition Law have, for a long time, been the focus of controversy, and not just legal. Economists often prefer to stress the economic goals of competition legislation,[4] while legal theorists and

[3] Kaplow (2012), Aubert (2003) and Lorenz (2013).

[4] Bishop and Walker (1999), p. 5.

jurists also appreciate its potential social dimensions, but fail to concur in a single approach. In legal theory the debate, which is not absolutely theoretical, has to do with the choice between total welfare, i.e. the welfare of a society as a whole and the welfare of consumers only.[5]

As it is natural, if Competition Law had as an objective only the interests of consumers, the rich would benefit more. In contrast, by choosing the former (total welfare and economic equity through redistribution)[6] as the main criterion behind competition legislation, we make, in reality, the following two choices: first of all, we stress the redistributive power of Competition Law (admitting, at the same time, that this is mainly achieved via taxation) and, second, we create a link between the market and the civil society, while emphasizing the cooperative role of Competition.[7] Individuals, in this context, are seen not just as passive consumers but as active, participating citizens, who can use laws as their means and tools for self-protection, not any more against the State, but in relation to market trespasses and big corporations' breaches of law.

In this context and notwithstanding major differences in legal formulation and the nature of the relevant breaches, one could use the already existing paradigm of the US Alien Tort Claims Act (ATCA). The ATCA indicator can help us learn very interesting lessons in relation to how the society's welfare discourse can be used as an instigator of civil society empowerment against domestic and international law breaches of the regulations regarding capital flow, the power of the market and large conglomerates' behaviour. In relation to international law, suffice it to say, at this point, that the international dimension of Competition Law has already been demonstrated in relation to the global market regulation and its consequences to the global civil (not just consumers') society.[8]

4 Greek Competition Law Before the Implementation of Directive 2014/104/EU: A Historical Retrospective

The protection of free competition was regulated for a long period of time in Greece by Law 146/1914.[9] Section 1 of Law 146/1914 introduces a general clause of unfair commercial practices. According to this clause, a business practice is characterised as unfair when it meets the following criteria: it is undertaken by a competitor in the course of commercial and/or industrial and/or agricultural transactions, it enhances the position of the business entity in the relevant market vis-à-vis its competitors,

[5]Kaplow (2012), pp. 8–14; Nihoul (2012), pp. 223–224.

[6]Cseres (2005), p. 278; Whish (2003), p. 18; Motta (2004), p. 15.

[7]Kaplow (2012), pp. 30–31.

[8]Papadopoulos (2010), pp. 36–50.

[9]Unfair Competition Law 146/1914, inspired by the German legislation.

either present or potential ones, and it is contrary to fair practices, the content of which is formulated and interpreted in light of the current business morals and ethics.

As unfair practices, Greek case law and Greek legal theory have characterised the following practices:

(a) Improper solicitation of customers.
(b) Exploitation of third parties' goodwill, organisation and labor.
(c) Preventing competitors from entering the market and/or offering his products/ services.
(d) Breach of legal/contractual provisions.

Law 703/1977[10] was introduced to modernise the Competition realm and harmonise it to European practices. As Truli[11] observes, the main provisions of Law 703/1977 included: Article 1 regarding the prohibition of agreements between undertakings, decisions of associations of undertakings and concerted business practices having as their object or effect the obstruction or restriction or distortion of competition and Article 2, prohibiting the abuse of a dominant position. Both rules were drafted according to Articles 81, 82, 85 and 86 of the EC Treaty and according to EC Regulation No 17/1962. Law 703/1977 also included provisions monitoring concentrations between undertakings (Article 4(4)). Also, according to Article 9(7) of Law 703/1977, the Hellenic Competition Commission (HCC) had exclusive competence for ordering interim measures *ex officio* or upon request of the Minister of Development, when an infringement of Articles 1, 2 and 5 of the same Law or of Articles 81 and 82 of the EC Treaty seemed possible, and there existed an urgent need to prevent imminent and irreparable harm to the public interest. Furthermore, according to Article 21 of Law 703/1977, the HCC had exclusive competence to grant the exemption of Article 1(3) of the same Law (tantamount to Article 101(3) of the EU Treaty) to agreements or concerted practices falling within the scope of Article 1(1) (tantamount to Article 81(1) of the EU Treaty), following the notification procedure prescribed therein.

Responding to the increasing need for better institutions,[12] Law 703/1977 was replaced by Law 3959/2011,[13] which kept intact the main provisions of the former legislation, especially those having to do with restrictive agreements and the abuse of dominant position, and tried to harmonise the Greek legislation to European standards and to modernise the HCC' operations.[14]

The law's contribution to the delineation of the relevant market and to the definition of anti-competitive agreements cannot be underestimated. According to

[10] Tzouganatos (2005).

[11] Truli (2009), p. 188.

[12] Loukas and Nteka (2010), p. 1.

[13] Law 703/1977 had been previously amended to a greater or lesser extent by a series of acts, such as Laws 1934/1991, 2000/1991, 2296/1995, 2323/1995, 2741/1999, 2837/2000, 2941/2001, 3105/2003, 3373/2005 and 3784/2009.

[14] Truli (2012), pp. 280–285.

Article 1, all agreements between undertakings which have as their object or effect the prevention, restriction or distortion of competition in the Greek territory are prohibited. In particular, there is a strict prohibition for agreements that (a) directly or indirectly determine prices or trading conditions, (b) limit or control production, markets, technical development or investment, (c) divide markets or sources of supply, (d) apply dissimilar conditions to equivalent transactions with other trading parties, or (e) make the conclusion of contracts subject to the acceptance of additional obligations by other parties. Article 2 prohibits the abuse of dominant position in the market and states four different subcases of exploitation: imposing unfair prices or unfair trading conditions, limiting production to the prejudice of consumers, applying dissimilar conditions to equivalent transactions with other trading parties and, finally, making the conclusion of contracts subject to the acceptance of supplementary obligations by the other parties.

According to Truli,[15] the particular Law introduced some major innovations in that it abolished the involved parties' obligation to notify the competent authorities about their exemption from restrictive agreements, introduced a limitation period of 5 years for the imposition of fines, regulated the burden of proof in front of the HCC and, most importantly, strengthened the HCC's independence and effectiveness of action.

At the time of its drafting, it was noted that Law 3959/2011 lacked provisions facilitating or even permitting damages claims for antitrust infringement.[16] Nevertheless, one can safely observe that the general legislative mood prevailing in EU institutions at the time and finally leading to EU Directive 2014/104 had also permeated the formulation of Law 3959/2011. The relevant EU initiatives had started with the 2005 Green Paper on damages actions for breach of the EC antitrust rules[17] that was followed by the subsequent 2008 White Paper. We can find echoes of these initiatives and of the prevailing European *esprit des lois* in, for example, Article 35(2)—that abolished the exclusive competence of the HCC clause of Law 703/1977—, Article 25(2)(c) that considerably increased individual liability as well as in the institutional empowerment of the HCC.

The institutional lacunae of private law enforcement in the form of individuals' damages actions for Competition Law infringements is now remedied by the implementation of the Greek Law transposing Directive 2014/104/EU. As has been already pointed out, the Directive (Article 3) gives the right to

> any natural or legal person who has suffered harm caused by an infringement of competition law

to claim and obtain full compensation for that harm. Thus, Articles 101 and 102 TFEU are used as a legal basis for litigation and compensation, in cases of breach of Competition Law.

---

[15]Truli (2012), pp. 280–285.

[16]Truli (2012), p. 285.

[17]Dabbah (2003).

5 Protection of Individuals and of Social Rights in International Law Against Multinationals' Malpractice: The Grave Institutional Lacunae and the Role of the ATCA

Among others, Robertson observed that

> the most glaring illogicality of Westphalian (i.e. of state-centred) international law is that it does not apply to transnational corporations whose global activities generate more product and greater influence than most UN members will ever possess.[18]

In reality, corporate liability is a notion that has not yet entered many aspects of international law and it is characteristic that the 1998 International Criminal Court Rome statutes do not in any way refer to the human rights aspect of multinationals' international activities and especially of the breaches of law on their part. Although steps forward have been made (i.e. the US Foreign Corrupt Practices Act which has been practically reiterated in the OECD 1999 convention against company briberies, United Nations Security Council Resolution 1373 (2001) against money laundering), legal entities and their liabilities largely remain out of the realm of the control of international law. There truly exists a vacuum in international law, as indecisiveness prevails in relation to corporate liability for violations of customary international law.[19]

In the meantime, individuals can, under the ATCA, sue any company that has offices in the United States for damages suffered anywhere in the world. Although the ATCA is not, by itself, a regulation pertaining to international law, the possibility given to individuals to sue legal entities with offices in the USA is of great interest for two reasons: (a) because it can be used as a legal precedent in relation to other cases of multinationals' liability, (b) because the USA has been, until recently, the undisputed motor head of global capitalist thrust and still retains a symbolic character as the heart of capitalist development.

The ATCA dates back to 1789. It has since, and more than once, been legally interpreted in a *latu sensu* manner that permits individual claims against multinationals breaking international law. In 2004, it received the backing of the US Supreme Court decision that upheld the right of aliens to sue companies for violations of international rules which

> rest on a norm of an international character accepted by the civilised world and defined with specificity.[20]

[18]Robertson (2012), pp. 232–234.

[19]US 2nd Circuit Court of Appeals, Kiobel vs. Royal Dutch Petroleum, September 17, 2001, in Robertson (2012), pp. 235–236.

[20]Robertson (2012), p. 234.

The test case, as Robertson rightly points out, was the famous *Sosa vs. Alvarez Machain* case, in which the US Department of Justice tried, in vain, to eliminate the use of the ATCA by human rights victims.

Examples of ATCA[21] application include, among other cases, the action of Burmese villagers against UNOCAL, of South African citizens against Citibank, of Nigerians against Shell and of Indonesians against Exxon Mobil. The rulings are inconsistent, but what interests us here is the possibility given to individuals to use domestic and international law rules to act against multinationals, suing for compensation for harm. What is also important is the recognition that multinationals are slowly but surely transformed from obscure and indirect agents of international politics into subjects of international law, with their activities fully regulated in the same vein as the activities of States. In fact, the term "abstract entities" (used in the Nuremberg trials to provide a legal formula of protection for countries) has for long been used by corporations to achieve exemption from customary international law. Recent cases[22] have shown that when individuals are given the possibility to sue companies for compensation in relation to damages suffered because of corporate activities, legal manoeuvring, on the part of multinationals, starts to get restricted.

It is for this reason, as Robertson observes,[23] that many multinationals prefer to take part, by their free will, in the United Nations Global Compact initiative. Notwithstanding its voluntary character, that has made some analysts characterise it as an exercise in goodwill or as means of promotion, Global Compact could still serve as a framework of principles. These principles, together with the International Labour Organisation (ILO) set of rules[24] and the continuously expanding OECD guidelines, could form the necessary legal ground for a more effective control of the international community over corporations. The ten Global Compact principles are:

(a) in the area of Human Rights

- Principle 1: Businesses should support and respect the protection of internationally proclaimed human rights;
- Principle 2: Businesses should make sure that they are not complicit in human rights abuses.

(b) In the field of Labour relations[25]

- Principle 3: Businesses should uphold the freedom of association and the effective recognition of the right to collective bargaining;
- Principle 4: Businesses should uphold the elimination of all forms of forced and compulsory labour;

[21]Hutchens (2008).

[22]Robertson (2012), pp. 236–237.

[23]Robertson (2012), p. 237.

[24]Alston (2005).

[25]Compa and Diamond (1996).

- Principle 5: Businesses should uphold the effective abolition of child labour; and
- Principle 6: Businesses should uphold the elimination of discrimination in respect of employment and occupation.

(c) In relation to Environment

- Principle 7: Businesses should support a precautionary approach to environmental challenges;
- Principle 8: Businesses should undertake initiatives to promote greater environmental responsibility; and
- Principle 9: Businesses should encourage the development and diffusion of environmentally friendly technologies.

(d) In relation to anti-Corruption

- Principle 10: Businesses should work against corruption in all its forms, including extortion and bribery.

In parallel to these developments of an absolutely voluntary character, the UN Sub-commission for the Promotion and Protection of Human Rights has tried, since 2003, to somehow enforce its *Norms on the Responsibilities of Transnational Corporations and other Business Enterprises with Regard to Human Rights.*[26] It goes without saying that its efforts have until now been received rather coldly. One should, nonetheless, note that the notion of corporate liability has now been fully incorporated in international law, and the society's need for protection from the multinationals' and big enterprises' malpractice is now largely recognised.

6 Conclusion: Competition Law as a Possible Instrument of Civic Protection

Returning to Competition Law, Directive 2014/104/EU and the Greek implementing Law both determine the evidentiary requirements (Article 5) and available forms of compensation (Article 14) for damages. What is especially important in the compensation process, is that ultimately all damages caused by the infringement of Competition Law may be imposed on the breaching party (for example, cartel members) in order to re-establish equality of opportunity and give effect to the rules on competition (Article 4 of the Directive).[27] But if the objective is the return to normality for a deregularised—provoked by a company's breach of Competition Law—market, ultimately the purpose is a little different: upholding social values and especially welfare and enthroning liability as a core axis of compensation. Making

[26]Robertson (2012), pp. 238–239.

[27]See also Frenz (2016), pp. 626, 628–629.

use of their legal possibilities to sue infringing companies for damages, individuals actively participate in the competition process and help create a healthier, more balanced market. In the long run, Competition Law, in the form of compensation rules for individuals, could also serve as a tool of enhancing civil society vis-à-vis big companies and multinationals, thus moving in parallel to international law's endeavour to create an area of protection of human rights from their malpractice. Although this may seem right now a somehow chimerical dream, it is especially at these times of market deregulation and generalised social upheaval that we have to aspire to a new set of rules, aiming at social welfare and control of systematic malpractices. And what is especially important is that this new set of rules may be the outcome of a process of realisation that multinationals and big companies cannot stay out of the reach of law.

References

Alston P (2005) Labour rights as human rights. Oxford University Press, Oxford

Aubert C (2003) Competition Policy for countries with different development levels. Paper presented at the CEPR Competition Policy in International Markets Workshop, October 17–18 2003. www.cepr.org/meets/wkcn/6/6613/papers/Aubert.pdf Accessed 10 Apr 2018

Bishop S, Walker M (1999) Economics of EC competition law: concepts, application and measurement. Sweet & Maxwell, London

Compa L, Diamond S (eds) (1996) Human rights, labour rights and international trade. University of Pennsylvania Press, Philadelphia

Cseres K (2005) Competition law and consumer protection. Kluwer Law International, The Hague

Dabbah M (2003) The internationalisation of antitrust policy. Cambridge University Press, Cambridge

Frenz W (2016) Handbook of EU competition law. Springer, London

Hutchens LK (2008) International law in the American Courts – Khulumani vs Barklay National Bank: the decision heard "round the corporate world". German Law J 9:639–681

Kaplow L (2012) On the choice of welfare standards in competition law. In: Zimmer D (ed) The goals of competition law. ASCOLA competition law series. Edward Elgar, Cheltenham, pp 3–27

Lorenz M (2013) An introduction to EU competition law. Cambridge University Press, Cambridge

Loukas D, Nteka L (2010) The Memorandum of Understanding on Specific Economic and Competition Policy Conditionality for Granting Financial Assistance: Greek point of view. e-Competitions 37517. http://www.concurrences.com/fr/bulletin/news-issues/may-2010/The-Memorandum-of-Understanding-on. Accessed 17 Apr 2018

Motta M (2004) Competition policy, theory and practice. Cambridge University Press, Cambridge

Nihoul P (2012) Do words matter? A discussion on words used to designate values associated with competition law. In: Zimmer D (ed) The goals of competition law. ASCOLA competition law series. Edward Elgar, Cheltenham, pp 219–249

Papadopoulos A (2010) The international dimension of EU competition law and politics. Cambridge University Press, Cambridge

Robertson G (2012) Crimes against humanity – the struggle for global justice. Penguin, London

Truli E (2009) Competition in the telecommunications sector: delineation of competences between the NCA and the NRA – the example of Greece. J E-Commer Technol Commun 8:188–196

Truli E (2012) New Greek law on the protection of free competition: key changes and first impressions. Eur Competition Law Rev 6:280–285

Tzouganatos D (2005) The Objective of Upgrading the Competition Commission and the Failure of Law 3373/2005 Amending Law 703/77. Deltio Epichiriseon kai Etairion 1034–1048
Whish R (2003) Competition law, 5th edn. Lexis Nexis, London

Sotirios Livas is Associate Professor of International Law and International Relations at the Department of Foreign Languages, Translation and Interpreting of the Ionian University in Greece.

EU Competition Law in the Aftermath of Directive 2014/14 and Its Implementation in the Republic of Croatia

Ana Pošćić

Abstract The Directive on certain rules governing actions for damages under national law for infringements of Competition Law provisions of the Member States is the first Directive enacted in the field of Competition Law private enforcement. The Directive was passed on 26 November 2014, while the Member States were required to enforce laws, regulations and administrative provisions necessary to comply with the Directive by 27 December 2016. Although private enforcement is distinguished from public enforcement, they interact in many ways. The perception is however that private enforcement of Competition Law is underdeveloped, uncertain and ineffective. The purpose of this chapter is to provide insight into the Croatian rules on the damages claims, especially in light of the new Croatian Act on Actions for Damages for Infringements of Competition Law. The Act contains both substantive and procedural rules governing actions for damages for infringements of the Competition Law provisions. The chapter analyses the new rules on the damages actions and outlines the main provisions of the Act in juxtaposition to the Directive. Special emphasis is put on the substantive and procedural novelties that diverge from the present regulation.

1 Introduction

The Directive on certain rules governing actions for damages under national Law for infringements of Competition Law[1] (hereinafter: Directive) is the first Directive enacted in the field of Competition Law. It was enacted on 26 November 2014

[1]Directive 2014/104/EU of the European Parliament and of the Council of 26 November 2014 on certain rules governing actions for damages under national law for infringements of the competition law provisions of the Member States and of the European Union (OJ L 349, 5.12.2014, p. 1). See Maier – Rigaud (2014).

A. Pošćić (✉)
University of Rijeka, Faculty of Law, Jean Monnet Chair of European Public Law, Rijeka, Croatia
e-mail: aposcic@pravri.hr

S. Marino et al. (eds.), *Language and Law*,
https://doi.org/10.1007/978-3-319-90905-9_8

with the view of harmonising different procedural rules on damages claims. The best way to reach full harmonization would have been to adopt a Regulation.

Considering that rules on damage actions vary between the Member States, the European legislator decided to issue a Directive, which was seen as a compromise. Adopting a Regulation was perceived as unrealistic and a too deep intrusion into the national procedural rules. Member States were obliged to bring into force the laws, regulations and administrative provisions necessary to comply with the Directive by 27 December 2016. The last decade reveals a tendency of convergence between the national Competition Law and the EU Competition Law.

Although private enforcement is distinguished from public enforcement, there are fields of interaction between them. There is a longstanding perception that private enforcement of competition rules is underdeveloped, uncertain and ineffective.

In the seminal decision *Brasserie and Factortame*[2] the Court recognised the basic principles for the actions for damages and provided some general directions for national Courts. The Directive contains more detailed procedural and substantive issues. This area is still at the embryonic stage in most European countries as well as in Croatia.

This chapter aims to provide some insight into the Croatian rules on damages claims, especially after the new Act on Actions for Damages for Infringements of Competition Law (hereinafter: the Act)[3] came into force. The Act contains both substantive and procedural rules governing actions for damages for infringements of the Competition Law provisions.

Substantive rules concern the subject matter and scope of the application, the right to full compensation, the presumption that cartel infringements cause harm, joint and several liability of undertakings that have caused the infringement through joint behaviour, passing on overcharges, the effects of consensual settlements on subsequent actions for damages.

Procedural rules consist of definitions and rules governing the disclosure of evidence, especially the disclosure of evidence included in the file of a competition authority, the effect of the competition authorities' and the Courts' final decisions, the limitation periods, postponement of the action for damages for up to 2 years due to consensual dispute resolution in respect of the claim.

The new rules on damages actions will be analysed by outlining the main provisions of the Act in juxtaposition to the Directive. Emphasis is put on the substantive and procedural novelties.

[2]Joined Cases C-46/93 and C-48/93 *Brasserie du Pêcheur* [1996] I-1029, ECLI:EU:C:1996:79.
[3]OG 69/17.

2 Legal Sources of Competition Law in Croatia

The Constitution of the Republic of Croatia states in its Article 49(1) that the free enterprise and free markets shall form the foundation of the economic system of the Republic of Croatia. This has to be read in conjunction with para. 2 that reads

> The state shall ensure all entrepreneurs equal legal status on the market. The abuse of monopolies, as defined by law, shall be prohibited[4]

It is a principle of market economy that guarantees the freedom to compete, but also sets limits to obstructive market conduct.

The regulation of Competition issues in Croatia has begun in 1995 with the first Competition Act.[5] The subsequent act was enacted in 2003[6] with the aim to resolve some problems and discrepancies that have emerged during the implementation of the first act. The following years were devoted to struggles of becoming part of the EU. The Croatian legislator had to harmonise the Croatian competition provisions with the acquis. The Act from 2003 was seen as most harmonised. The main objection concerned problems of execution, particularly in relation to sanctions of violations by the administrative Court.[7]

The new Act of 2009[8] was meant to deal with the latter shortcomings. In this context, one of the novelties introduced was that the competent competition authority had the powers to bring direct sanctions against those that infringe market competition. The legislation came into force in 2010 with one amendment in 2013.[9] At that time Croatian Competition Law was already fully harmonised with the *acquis*. Croatian Competition Agency applied "the criteria arising from the application of the competition rules in the EU".[10] Although EU Competition Law was not applied as a primary source of law, it had a supportive role, especially in situations where legal interpretation was needed.

There are also provisions that regulate in detail certain aspects of Competition Law and that implement secondary European legislation and soft law sources.[11]

Public enforcement of competition rules is undertaken by the Croatian Competition Agency. We can generally agree that public enforcement is no longer problematic. However, possible difficulties could arise from private enforcement, which

[4]The Constitution of the Republic of Croatia, OG 56/90, 135/97, 8/98 [consolidated text], 113/00, 124/00 [consolidated text], 28/01, 41/01 [consolidated text], 55/01 [correction], 76/10 and 85/10 [consolidated text], 05/14.

[5]OG 48/95, 52/97, 89/98.

[6]OG 122/03.

[7]Petrović and Jakšić (2014), p. 357.

[8]OG 79/09.

[9]OG 80/13.

[10]It stems from the Article 70(2) of the Stabilisation and Association Agreement between the Republic of Croatia, on the one part, and the European Communities and their Member States, on the other, OG IA 14/01, 15/01, 14/02, 1/05, 7/05, 9/05, 11/06.

[11]Petrović and Jakšić (2014), p. 358.

is still undeveloped in Croatia. The new Act on Actions for Damages for Infringements of Competition Law is seen as a means to reduce the shortcomings and to promote damage claims. It has to be underlined that even before this Act, Croatia had functioning damage actions provisions.

3 The System of Private Enforcement of Competition Rules in Croatia Before the Act on Actions for Damages for Infringements of Competition Law

Before analysing the main provisions of the new Act, options of private enforcement of competition rules preceding the Act will be summarised.

The protection from breaches of competition issues is based on the general tort law provisions enforced by commercial Courts. There was only one provision dealing with private enforcement delegating the jurisdiction for antitrust damages claims to commercial Courts in accordance with the Civil Procedure Act.[12] The provision in question provided that the commercial Courts adjudicate disputes arising from the Act on Unfair Market Competition, monopolistic agreements and the disruption of equality on the single market of the Republic of Croatia (Article 34b(9)) in civil proceedings in the first instance. The wording of this provision is quite peculiar. In spite of the imprecise wording, it was assumed that the actions for breaches of competition rules fall under the jurisdiction of commercial Courts.

This is the only provision in the Civil Procedure Act referring explicitly to competition issues. General rules on non-contractual obligations from the Civil Obligations Act[13] are applicable to antitrust damage claims (Articles 1045 ff).

Croatian legislator had a choice to adopt a separate act or to implement the Directive into the existing acts. It opted for the former. It is also important to stress that unlike other EU countries, Croatia was not involved in the legislative process which led to the adoption of the Directive, for when Croatia joined the EU, the Directive has already been in force.

Generally speaking, national rules are already aligned with the rules of the Directive. There is a shortage of commercial Courts' jurisprudence in Croatia on damage actions for infringement of the Competition Law provisions.

A person who suffered damage of infringement of Competition Law has two options. It can either continue with follow-on actions or initiate stand-alone actions. Stand-alone action concerns a situation where an infringement is claimed independently of a competition authority's decision. Here the plaintiff does not rely on the Agency decision, but leaves the court to decide both on the breach of Competition Act and the claim for damages. On the other hand, the follow-on basis is a more

[12]OG 53/91, 91/92, 58/93, 112/99, 88/01, 117/03, 88/05, 2/07, 84/08, 96/08, 123/08, 57/11, 148/11, 25/13, 89/14.

[13]OG 35/05, 41/08, 125/11, 78/15.

convenient situation, where the claim relies on a prior decision by the competition authority finding liability, whereas the court does not have to struggle with finding a Competition Law infringement.

Surely the follow-on option is more convenient to the claimant because there is already a decision of the specialised body establishing the competition infringement. But if only follow-on actions were allowed, damage claims would be limited to situations where the Competition Agency has established the existence of infringement.[14]

As shall be discussed later on, before the new Act introduced special rules on facilitating access to documents, potential plaintiffs were faced with problems in collecting documents necessary to initiate damage claims.

According to the Competition Act parties to the proceedings before the Agency have the right of access to case files. Explicit access to file is reserved only to the parties to the proceedings. The Competition Act defines a party as a person upon whose request a specific proceeding has been initiated; against whom proceeding has been conducted, or a person or a group of persons on whose interests the decision taken by the Agency may exert considerable influence and whom the Agency has determined that they have the status of the party to the proceedings (Article 36). The parties have the right to access the file in its widest scope after receiving the statement of objections. It must be stressed that the Competition Act does not contain a rule permitting anyone access to the file for the purpose of antitrust damages action.

Competition Act does not contain specific provisions about the right to claim damages. A plaintiff must refer to the general provisions of Civil Obligations Act that proclaims that every person is obliged to refrain from taking any actions that may cause damage to others. There is no special rule regulating the legal standing in antitrust damages. Any natural or legal person can be a party to civil proceedings.

Everyone must prove their legal interest. For direct claimants this is usually not difficult, but for indirect claimants there can be certain complications in establishing the causal link. Proving a causal link in antitrust damage cases requires complex economic analysis based on a large number of facts and economic data. The regulation of these questions is left to national law.

According to the Civil Obligations Act, a person who has caused damage to another shall compensate it unless he has proven that the damage has not occurred as a result of his fault. Lack of duty of care shall be presumed (Article 1045) and is based on the presumed fault. We must not forget that we are referring to undertakings of whom the highest possible level of care is expected. The victim must prove the causal link; there is no presumption of causality.[15]

Regarding the types of harm, the Croatian tort law recovers actual loss, loss of profit and non-material harm (violation of privacy rights). It is evident that the Croatian legislation is broader than the Directive and recognising the principle of full compensation.

---

[14]Pecotić Kaufman (2012), p. 5.

[15]For more on this issue see Lianos (2015).

According to Civil Obligations Act there are limitation periods for the compensation of damages. The subjective limitation period is 3 years from the time the injured party became aware of the damage or the person causing the damage. The objective limitation period is set to 5 years from the moment the damage occurred.[16] A claim for compensation of damages shall run out in 3 years from the time the injured party became aware of the damage or the person causing the damage. In any case, after 5 years from the moment the damage has been caused the claimant can no longer initiate proceedings. This period is usually too short for competition claims.

4 The Croatian Act on Actions for Damages for Infringements of Competition Law

4.1 Subject Matter and Scope of the Act

Article 1 of the Croatian Act is drafted in the same terms as Article 1 of the Directive. It provides that the Act sets out certain rules necessary to ensure that anyone who has suffered harm caused by an infringement of Competition Law by an undertaking or by an association of undertakings can effectively exercise the right to claim full compensation for that harm from that undertaking or association. This is not a novelty in Croatian Law, as we already have a rule of full compensation (Article 1090 of Civil Obligations Act). The idea is to reverse the injured party's financial position to the State in which it would have been had the wrongful act not occurred.

This Act sets out rules coordinating the enforcement of the competition rules by competition authorities and the enforcement of those rules in damages actions before competent commercial Courts. This is nothing new, as the only provision on competition matters in Civil Procedure Act was on the adjudication in competition issues by the competent commercial Courts.

The subject matter is private enforcement of Articles 101 and 102 TFEU. The Articles cover antitrust issues in all aspects. State aid and merger control are left outside. According to Article 106 TFEU the right of compensation in EU Law applies also to infringement of Articles 101 and 102 by public undertakings or undertakings entrusted with special or exclusive rights. This follows from the Recital 3 of the Directive. Those articles produce direct effects in the relationship between individuals and create rights and obligations which can be enforced before the national Courts.

Article 3 enshrines familiar competition concepts and terms. It contains some definitions already known from the jurisprudence of the CJEU. The question is should we follow the same concepts as in the public enforcement case law? One example is the concept of undertaking. The concept of undertaking and the association of the undertakings should be given the same meaning according to the

[16]Article 230.

established case law. Since no definition of the notion is provided in the TFEU, its meaning has been interpreted in CJEU's case law.[17] The notion of undertaking refers to every subject engaged in economic activity regardless of its legal status and model of financing. A functional meaning of the notion has been implemented. It is possible to derive specific standards from the definition: an undertaking has to offer goods or services on the market, has to bear economic of financial risks emerging from doing business and has to have a possibility to make profits. Some difficulties in the interpretation may arise. Does the Article cover also claims addressed to group of companies that are not involved in the infringement? According to the interpretation of the Court of Justice the concept of undertaking may also encompass a group of undertakings. The Court should further clarify this, especially in light of complicated cases in which companies have subsidiaries outside the EU. Closely connected to the concept of undertaking is the concept of 'economic succession'. The latter covers a situation where the undertaking that committed the infringement has ceased to exist and its successor is responsible for its conduct. Therefore, the Croatian Courts and the CJEU should specify the boundaries of this Article. As is, this is left to interpretation and the Directive intentionally does not define the concept of 'economic succession'.

This Act, as stated, covers not only the infringement of provisions that regulate prohibited agreements and the abuse of dominant position but also the infringement of Article 101 or 102 TFEU. This means that the infringement can be the infringement of Article 101 or 102, as well as of national Competition Law. In other words, it can be an infringement of national Competition Law, but not an infringement of EU Competition Law. According to the Act, "national competition law" means provisions of national law that predominantly pursue the same objective as Articles 101 and 102 TFEU and that are applied to the same case and in parallel to EU Competition Law pursuant to Article 3(1) of Regulation No 1/2003, hence, it means infringement sanctioned by national Competition Law read in conjunction with Articles 101 and 102. It is also important to show the effect on trade.

The term court means the territorially competent commercial Court and the High Commercial Court according to the rules of organization and jurisdiction of courts.

The right to compensation is recognised for any natural or legal person. Possible claimants are consumers, undertakings and public authorities. This right may be granted to anyone who suffered harm caused by an infringement of Competition Law.

Definition of action for damages plays a central role. An action can be brought by an alleged injured party. It means that it is sufficient for a party to demonstrate that he/she has allegedly suffered harm. It also covers someone acting on behalf of one or more alleged injured parties, where national Law provides for this possibility, and also natural or legal person that succeeded in the right of the alleged injured party. The last possibility are collective actions by collective entity. The "action for damages" refers to action under national law and brought before a national court.

[17]See Bajčić and Martinović in this volume for a conceptual discussion of undertaking.

The notion of cartel has been previously defined in EU case law. The Law repeats the familiar definition of cartel as an agreement or concerted practice between two or more competitors aimed at coordinating their competitive behaviour on the market or influencing the relevant parameters of competition through practices such as, but not limited to, the fixing or coordination of purchase or selling prices or other trading conditions, including in relation to intellectual property rights, the allocation of production or sales quotas, the sharing of markets and customers, including bid-rigging, restrictions of imports or exports or anti-competitive actions against other competitors. This is a non-exhaustive list. Those are only some examples from the broad case law of EU Courts.

4.2 Right to Full Compensation

Any natural or legal person (the injured party) who has suffered harm caused by an infringement of Competition Law is able to claim and to obtain full compensation for that harm. Since the Directive is not a full harmonization Directive the Member States are free to introduce stricter rules, as long as those rules do not conflict with the principles of the Directive.

The Directive refers to the recovery of actual loss and loss of profit plus the payment of interest. The rule follows previously established case law.[18] Croatian legislator introduced a more extensive rule. According to Article 5 of the Act, damage shall imply a loss of a person's assets (pure economic loss), halting of assets increase (loss of profit) and violation of privacy rights (non-material damage) plus the payment of interest. The Croatian Act covers material and non-material damage. Interest is due from the time when the harm occurred until the time when the compensation is paid. This is in line with the Croatian general tort law principles. Non-material damage is not limited. Regarding the non-material damage, it will be interesting to see how the infringement of Competition Law can affect personal rights. This necessitates further clarification.

In practice, the recognition of non-material damages to legal persons is not so frequent. Usually, we are dealing with indirect infringements that are part of material damages.

A legal person has a right to a fair pecuniary compensation for non-material damages. In the event of the violation of personality rights, an injured party may request a disclosure of the judgment or its modification at the expenses of the defendant, or the court can order a just pecuniary compensation. It can be concluded that national rules allow for more ways of compensation than the Directive.

The divergences from the Croatian legal tradition manifest in the provision on strict liability. Infringer that caused harm by infringement of Competition Law shall

[18]Joined Cases C-295/04 to C-298/04, *Manfredi and others* [2006] ECR I-6619, ECLI:EU:C:2006:461, para. 95.

be liable for damage caused regardless of fault (Article 5). The Civil Obligations Act states that the person who caused damage to another person shall compensate for this damage, unless he has proven that the damage has not occurred as a result of his own fault (Article 1045). This could lead to unfair cases. The undertaking is always obliged to compensate for the full harm. Taking into account the nature of harmful acts committed as Competition Law infringements and the characteristics of the tortfeasor as an undertaking, the highest possible level of care is required. Had the standard of fault been kept, there would have been a possibility for the infringer to be exculpated by proving that the undertaking applied a high standard of care. This would imply a liability on the basis of a presumed fault.

It shall be presumed that cartel infringements cause harm unless the infringer rebuts that presumption.

Competition Law infringements cover not only damage to assets or infringement of personal rights but also the state of market. To bypass possible problems in interpreting and defining the concept of causal link, we should interpret it in a flexible manner. The cause must be a typical cause; one which regularly causes certain harmful consequences. An unbroken causal link must be established. The causal link must connect all three elements: the harmful act at issue, the distortion of competition and the harm to the given victim.

In order to facilitate the position of the claimant the Act says that damage caused in relation to an infringement of Competition Law in the form of a cartel shall be considered as resulting from that cartel, unless it has been proven that the cartel has not caused the damage (a presumption of causality).

4.3 *Disclosure of Evidence*

A private claimant has to produce evidence and collect data necessary for the proceedings. In this context one usually speaks of information asymmetry. The evidence is frequently held by the infringer or by a third party. According to the rules of the Civil Procedure Act, in proceedings before the Court, each party is obliged to provide facts and present evidence on which its claim is based (Article 219). Later the court will decide which of the proposed evidence shall be presented to establish the decisive facts (Article 220). Evidence comprises all facts important to render the decision and the party is obliged to furnish the document to which it refers as proof. If such documents are in the possession of a State authority or the other party, the court shall order that party to furnish the document or in the case of public documents obtain them by itself.[19]

Before the Act, the claimants had two possibilities to obtain the necessary documents: either to use the provisions of the Competition Act or the Act on the

[19]Butorac Malnar (2015), p. 150.

Right of Access to Public Information[20] with very limited reaches.[21] Now the situation has slightly changed, allowing for more options to collect the necessary data. The new Act has precise rules on the disclosure of evidence necessary for issuing damage claims and special provision of disclosure of evidence included in the file of a competition authority. It is important to note that there is an absolute ban on the disclosure of leniency statements and settlement submissions.

The Act will ease the position of possible claimants in collecting the needed information. There is a general rule with some requirements that must be met, accounting for a middle way. The claimant has to present a reasoned justification in order for the national court to be able to order disclosure of specified items of evidence. Croatian Act bans the so-called "fishing expeditions".

Articles 5 to 8 deal with different aspects of the disclosure of evidence. The disclosure of evidence has to be supported by a plausible claim. The claimant has to present reasonably available facts and evidence sufficient to support the plausibility of its claim for damages. It is a safeguard clause. Bearing in mind that competition typically implies business secrets, special questions concern the disclosure of confidential information. Now we have an explicit rule granting to national judges the power to order documents containing confidential documents. This is seen as an improvement, since until now there were no precise rules on the preservation of confidential information. According to Butorac Malnar, there are certain doubts whether a national judge has such authority or the Agency has to decide on the substance of the document.[22] It is important to note that pre-existing documents that are contained in the file of competition authority may be disclosed at any time.

The general rule on evidence disclosure is a minimum harmonisation rule. On the other hand, a ban of disclosure of leniency statements and settlement submissions is a maximum harmonization rule. All materials gained before the leniency and all materials existing independently can be disclosed. Hence, the principle of effectiveness is a guiding standard for States, courts and a benchmark for discussion.

As has been stressed, the claimant is faced with an information asymmetry. Therefore, there is a necessity to have articles giving competence to national Courts to order disclosure of evidence from parties to the proceedings and from third parties. The national Courts have the powers to order the defendant or a third party to disclose relevant evidence which lies in their control, provided that the claimant has presented a reasoned justification.

The Directive discerns different categories of evidence, whereas the Act addresses "the relevant evidence". However, the Croatian legal tradition does not distinguish categories of evidence.

Where relevant evidence is not within the control of the defendant, but is included in the file of a competition authority, it may be required by a national court to disclose the relevant evidence provided that it cannot reasonably be obtained from

[20]OG 25/13, 85/15.

[21]Butorac Malnar (2015), p. 151.

[22]Butorac Malnar (2015), p. 155.

another party or from a third party. The court has to safeguard the effectiveness of the public enforcement of Competition Law. Here the court has a lot of discretion and must decide following the principle of proportionality, especially in view of the possible costs.

There is the so-called grey list of categories of evidence, whose disclosure can be ordered by a national court only after a competition authority has closed its proceedings by adopting a decision.

Leniency statements and settlement submissions enjoy an absolute protection from disclosure (Article 9). In this context the question may arise whether the third exceptional protection applies to the immunity statement of the undertaking obtaining full immunity only or to all leniency statements. It applies to all leniency statements (immunity from fines or a reduction of fines). The last statement is of little importance for Croatia, as according to the available data, there has been only one leniency submission, notwithstanding the Act.[23] It is important to note that, we refer to leniency here in relation to cartels. The Commission calls them "the cancer of the economy". The most efficient tool to detect cartels are leniency statements. Without granting protection to the applicants detecting cartels, there would be no incentive to turn to the Commission or the national agency. Hence, leniency is the most effective tool to discourage and sanction cartels. A twofold conflict of tension arises in this context: the promotion of public or private enforcement. On the other hand, leniency statements are very useful instruments for cartel victims in initiating damage claims. There is a need to find the right balance between the two opposite goals. After the Directive, the balance has been tipped in favour of public enforcement.

Evidence obtained solely through access to the file of a competition authority can be used in an action for damages only by the natural or legal person who obtained the evidence or the person succeeding to that person's right, including the person that acquired that person's claim. There are also "sufficiently deterrent penalties" for the parties to the proceedings, but also against third parties that do not comply with a disclosure order of a national Court.

But according to Butorac Malnar

> the rights of claimants in Croatia might also be narrowed after the Act because of its rule whereby a national court may order the disclosure of evidence included in the file of a competition authority only where no party, or a third party, is reasonably able to provide that evidence.[24]

4.4 *Effect of Decisions of National Competition Agency*

The infringement of Competition Law found by a final decision of the Agency or in the administrative dispute before the High Administrative Court against the

[23]Regulation on the method of setting fines, OG 129/10.

[24]Butorac Malnar (2015), p. 155.

decisions of the Agency is deemed to be irrefutably established for the purposes of an action for damages brought before the courts (Article 11). This is full proof that the infringement has occurred.

Where the infringement of Article 101 and/or Article 102 is found by a final decision taken in another Member State, it is also deemed to be established for the purpose of actions for damages, unless proven to the contrary. It means that the infringement decision has to be assessed along with any other evidence adduced by the parties. The national courts have discretion and it is a presumption that the national court will look into the facts and reach his own conclusions on the issue of infringement. Here we have binding proof of the infringement established by Croatian Agency or Commercial Court. It remains to be seen how much weight will be given to decisions adopted by other Member States.

These are the effects of final infringement decisions adopted by the Agency or the national review courts in the framework of subsequent actions for damages before national courts. The idea is to prevent a situation where the finding of an infringement would be re-litigated in subsequent actions for damages.[25] The claimants do not have to prove the scope of the infringement again and can concentrate on the causation and the quantum of damages. According to the same Recital of the Directive this is

> to enhance legal certainty, to avoid inconsistency in the application of Articles 101 and 102 TFEU, to increase the effectiveness and procedural efficiency of actions for damages and to foster the functioning of the internal market for undertakings and consumers

4.5 Limitation Periods

According to the Directive the limitation periods for bringing actions amount to a minimum of 5 years. Croatia has followed the minimum period regarding the limitation periods for bringing actions for damages. The limitation period has changed compared to the previously applicable rules, namely instead of 3 years, the general limitation period is now 5 years.

As regards the relevant starting moment of limitation periods, it is provided that they shall not begin to run before the infringement of Competition Law has ceased and the claimant knows, or can reasonably be expected to know of the infringement of Competition Law, damage and the identity of the infringer.

The claimant must fulfil certain conditions in this regard. First, the claimant must be aware of the behaviour and of the fact that such behaviour amounts to an infringement of Articles 101 and 102. While the periods are not problematic, possible difficulties could surface in connection to the way of calculation of limitation periods; i.e. 5 years from the period when infringement of Competition Law has ceased and under three cumulative conditions. Sometimes it is difficult to establish

[25] Recital 34 of the Directive.

precisely when the infringement has ceased. The calculation of the start of the limitation period has also changed.

The limitation period is interrupted, if a competition authority takes action for the purpose of investigation or its proceedings in respect of an infringement of Competition Law to which the action for damages relates and for the duration of consensual dispute resolution process, but only with regard to those parties that are involved in the process.

The period for bringing actions shall expire within 15 years from the date the infringement of Competition Law has ceased. It is an absolute period.

4.6 Joint and Several Liability

The undertakings which have infringed Competition Law through joint behaviour are jointly and severally liable for the harm caused by the infringement of Competition Law. The consequence is that each of those undertakings is bound to compensate for the harm in full, and the injured party has the right to require full compensation from any of them until it has been fully compensated.

It is interesting to note that no limitation period is foreseen here. So, there could be a minor infringement that happened 15 years ago. It means that this seriously limits the application of the exemption and the protection given to small and medium-sized enterprises (SMEs).

Only in one situation will an immunity recipient be jointly and severally liable. It will be responsible to its direct and indirect purchasers and to other injured parties only where full compensation cannot be obtained from other undertakings that were involved in the same infringement of Competition Law.

A co-infringer should have the right to obtain a contribution from other co-infringers if it has paid more compensation than its share. The determination of that share is a relative responsibility of a given infringer, and the relevant criteria could be turnover, market share, or a role in the cartel.

An infringer may recover a contribution from any other infringer, the amount of which shall be determined in the light of their relative responsibility for the harm caused by the infringement of Competition Law. The amount of contribution of an infringer which has been granted immunity from fines under a leniency programme shall not exceed the amount of the harm it caused to its own direct or indirect purchasers or providers.

This can be an argument for defence in private litigation. But if the parties cannot obtain full compensation from other infringers, it is a sort of last resort. The Croatian Civil Obligations Act also states that if the shares cannot be determined, each infringer shall account for an equal share, unless it is just to decide otherwise in a specific case.[26] It means that all the parties who suffered harm caused by an

[26]Article 1109.

infringement of Competition Law can ask for full compensation from any undertaking involved in the infringement. This is regardless of whether the party against whom the damages claim is addressed did cause harm to the injured party. It can address its claim to the most solvent undertaking. Therefore, the undertaking can be sued in any of 28 Member States and even in the one where it has not been engaged in any activity.

4.7 Passing-on of Overcharges and Right to Full Compensation

Price increases caused by cartels or other infringements of Competition Law are often 'passed on' down the supply chain. The overcharge is defined as the difference between the price actually paid and the price that would otherwise have prevailed in the absence of an infringement of Competition Law.[27] It can be invoked by the defendant, but the defendant may try to claim that the direct purchaser did not experience any harm because it passed the overcharge on.[28]

The principle is that the indirect purchasers, consumers included, are entitled to compensation by the infringer for the harm suffered. The defendant in an action for damages can invoke as a defence against a claim for damages the fact that the claimant passed on the whole or part of the overcharge resulting from the infringement of Competition Law. This does not affect the right of an injured party to claim and obtain compensation for loss of profits due to a full or partial passing-on of the overcharge. It means that an injured party who has passed on the overcharge may still be confronted with the harm. There can be difficulties for follow-on claimants to prove the extent of harm caused.

The burden of proving that the overcharge was passed on shall be on the defendant, who may reasonably require disclosure of evidence from the claimant or from third parties (Article 15). The burden of proof is placed on the one that does not have the necessary evidence. This has to be read in conjunction with the provision of disclosure of evidence.

There is a rebuttable presumption that the indirect purchaser has shown the existence of passing-on of an overcharge to him if certain conditions are met.[29] This paragraph shall not apply where the defendant can demonstrate credibly to the satisfaction of the court that the overcharge was not, or was not entirely, passed on to the indirect purchaser.[30]

In assessing whether the burden of proof is satisfied, the court may take due account of actions for damages that are related to the same infringement, but are

[27] Article 2(20) of the Directive.

[28] Wijckmans et al. (2016), p. 59.

[29] Article 15(3) of the Act.

[30] Article 15(4) of the Act.

brought by claimants from other levels in the supply chain, judgments resulting from the previous situation and any relevant information in the public domain.[31]

The damages by claimants from different levels in the supply chain cannot lead to a multiple liability or to an absence of liability of the infringer.[32]

4.8 Quantification of Harm

The court is empowered to estimate the amount of harm, if it has been established that a claimant suffered harm, but it is practically impossible or excessively difficult to quantify it precisely on the basis of the evidence available. The claimant has to prove that the harm cannot be quantified in an exact manner. This has to be read in conjunction with the presumption specifying that cartel infringements cause harm, so the claimant can concentrate his efforts only on the quantification of the harm.

It is interesting to observe that neither the Directive, nor the Croatian Act contain such a presumption concerning damages caused by the abuse of a dominant position. It will be interesting to see how it will be applied by the national courts.

A national competition authority may, upon request of a national court, assist the national court with respect to the determination of the quantum of damages where that national competition authority considers such assistance to be appropriate. This will cover only exceptional cases because most data will come from the parties themselves. The claim will not fail simply because the harm cannot be quantified in an exact manner. The claimant must only prove that the harm cannot be precisely quantified.

Difficulties could arise in relation to the quantification of the loss of profit. It should be noted that the Commission has offered some guidance in the form of a Communication on the quantification of harm.[33] Nevertheless, it remains to be seen, whether there will be fruitful cooperation between the commercial courts and the Competition Agency.

4.9 Consensual Settlements

The last part of the Act relates to consensual dispute resolution. The limitation period for bringing an action for damages will be suspended for the duration of any

[31] Article 15(5) of the Act.

[32] Article 16 of the Act.

[33] Communication from the Commission on quantifying harm in actions for damages based on breaches of Article 101 or 102 of the Treaty on the Functioning of the European Union (OJ C 167, 3.6.2013, p. 19).

consensual dispute resolution process. The latter is considered in a broader sense encompassing arbitration, mediation and conciliation.

The suspension of the limitation period shall apply only with regard to those parties that are or that were involved or represented in the consensual dispute resolution. Limitation period may last up to 2 years.

Following the consensual settlement, the claim of the settling injured party is reduced by the settling co-infringer's share of the harm that the infringement of Competition Law inflicted upon the injured party.

Any remaining claim of the settling injured party shall be exercised only against non-settling co-infringers. Non-settling co-infringers shall not be permitted to recover contribution for the remaining claim from the settling co-infringer.

Where the non-settling co-infringers cannot pay the damages that correspond to the remaining claim of the settling injured party, the settling injured party may exercise the remaining claim against the settling co-infringer. The last possibility may be expressly excluded under the terms of the consensual settlement.

When determining the amount of contribution that a co-infringer may recover from any other co-infringer in accordance with their relative responsibility for the harm caused by the infringement of Competition Law, the court shall take due account of any damages paid pursuant to a prior consensual settlement involving the relevant co-infringer.

The idea is to avoid the situation in which settling co-infringers, by paying contribution to non-settling co-infringers, pay a total amount of compensation exceeding their relative responsibility for the harm caused by the infringement.

5 Conclusion

The new Act should be understood as a useful means in furthering private enforcement. Despite more precise and enhanced possibilities for private enforcement there are still certain doubts about the success of the Act. Likewise, there are many procedural and other difficulties in bringing Competition Law damage actions to court. Not only is there is a lack of legal tradition in many countries,[34] including Croatia, but national Courts possess very limited experience in dealing with antitrust damage claims. On the other hand, by putting emphasis on the creative role of judges, the Act calls for their continuous education and training.

Summarising, the Directive confirms the piecemeal national procedural autonomy approach,[35] while a lot of open questions still need to be resolved. Possible problems pertain to the concept of strict liability that differs from the Croatian legal tradition. The Directive, as well as the Act, do not contain rules dealing with the admissibility of economic evidence, causation and quantification of harm and a

[34] Bernitz (2016), p. 12.

[35] Cleynenbreugel (2016), p. 99.

number of factors that seem to be problematic are left outside of its scope. The issue of litigation costs is left to national procedural Law, as well as the collective redress mechanisms. The Act emphasises the role of experts in the quantification of harm.

In light of the above considerations, it can be concluded that there will still be differences among the Member States and private enforcement will probably remain subordinate to public enforcement.

References

Bernitz U (2016) Introduction to the directive on competition damages actions. In: Bergström M, Iacovides M, Strand M (eds) Harmonising EU competition litigation, the new directive and beyond, Swedish studies. Hart, Oxford, pp 3–13

Butorac Malnar V (2015) Access to documents in antitrust litigation – EU and croatian perspective. Yearb Antitrust Regul Stud 8(12):127–160

Cleynenbreugel PV (2016) Embedding procedural autonomy: the directive and national procedural rules. In: Bergström M, Iacovides M, Strand M (eds) Harmonising EU competition litigation, the new directive and beyond, Swedish studies. Hart, Oxford, pp 99–119

Lianos I (2015) Causal uncertainty and damage claims for the infringement of competition law in Europe. Yearb Eur Law 34(1):170–231

Maier – Rigaud F (2014) Toward a European directive on damage actions. J Competition Law Econ 10(2):341–360

Pecotić Kaufman J (2012) How to facilitate damage claims? Private enforcement of competition rules in Croatia – domestic and EU law perspective. Yearb Antitrust Regul Stud 5(7):13–54

Petrović S, Jakšić T (2014) Competition law. In: Josipović T (ed) Introduction to the law of Croatia. Wouters Kluwer, AH Alphen aan den Rijn

Wijckmans F, Visser M, Jaques S, Noël E (2016) The EU private damages directive – practical insights, minutes of the closed workshop 2015. Intersentia, Cambridge

Ana Pošćić is Associate Professor at the Jean Monnet Chair of European Public Law, Faculty of Law, University of Rijeka, Croatia.

EU Competition Law After Directive 2014/104/EU and Its Implementation in Italy

Silvia Marino

Abstract The admissibility of damages actions has not come as a surprise in Italy, when the Court of Justice of the European Union first upheld it in the *Courage* case. Nevertheless, Directive 2014/104/EU is to be welcome in order to grant more legal certainty in national proceedings. The Italian legislator has enacted the Directive by *decreto legislativo* 3/2017 (legislative decree). This chapter aims at analysing the new rules on private enforcement under the light of the Italian transposition and relevant praxis. It finally highlights the general line of continuity between the previous case law and the current system, and, at the same time, points out some meaningful breaks with the traditional solutions of the Italian legal system.

1 Private Remedies Against Infringements of EU Competition Law

EU Competition Law enforcement has traditionally had two facets: the public and the private enforcement. The former is envisaged in the current Article 103 TFEU, and regulated by the well-known Regulation No 1/2003,[1] which sketches in detail the role of the Commission and of the National Competition Authorities (NCAs). Furthermore, this Regulation has opened up to the development of private enforcement: Article 101(3) TFEU, on exceptions to the general cartels' prohibition, assumes direct effect, and the role of national courts is strengthened.

The Treaties already provided for one private remedy against the infringement of EU Competition Law. According to Article 101(2) TFEU, any agreement or decision fulfilling the conditions set out in Article 101(1) TFEU should be considered automatically void. The Court of Justice of the European Union (CJEU) declared its

[1]Council Regulation (EC) No 1/2003 of 16 December 2002 on the implementation of the rules on competition laid down in Articles 81 and 82 of the Treaty (OJ L 1, 4.1.2001, p. 1).

S. Marino (✉)
Department of Law, Economics and Culture, University of Insubria, Como, Italy
e-mail: silvia.marino@uninsubria.it

S. Marino et al. (eds.), *Language and Law*,
https://doi.org/10.1007/978-3-319-90905-9_9

direct effect already in the *BRT* case.[2] Further, the CJEU clearly stated in the *Courage* case[3] that an effective protection of competition within the internal market required the compensation of any damage incurred because of the infringement.[4] Subsequent case law clarified this principle: *anyone* is entitled to a damages action, even if the claimant is a consumer (*Manfredi* case[5]), or the Commission itself (*Otis* case[6]), or a person suffering damages because of the "umbrella-pricing" effect (*Kone* case[7]). Finally, the CJEU set out some principles on the limitation periods, and on the quantification of the damages (*Manfredi* case).[8]

This case law represented the basic general principles of national procedures for damages claims. Failing any EU harmonisation, damages actions were subject to (procedural and substantive) national law(s), tempered by the principles of effectiveness and equivalence, and by the rules stated by the CJEU case law. This set of applicable laws could lead to legal uncertainty. The Commission intended to overcome this situation through the adoption of a harmonising EU measure aimed at granting the same level playing field among Member States. The result of a long period of debates is Directive 2014/104/EU[9] on certain rules governing actions for damages. The deadline for the transposition was established on 27th December 2016, and at the time of writing all the Member States have communicated the national enactment measures.[10] It is therefore important to understand the impact of this Directive and of its national implementations in the Member States. This chapter focuses on the Italian experience.

---

[2]Case 127/73 *BRT* [1974] ECR 313, ECLI:EU:C:1974:6.

[3]Case C-453/99, *Courage and Crehan* [2001] ECR I-6297, ECLI:EU:C:2001:465.

[4]According to Komninos (2008), p. 165, and Jones and Sufrin (2016), p. 1060, the *Francovich* case (Joined Cases C-6/90 and C-9/90 *Francovich* [1991] I-5357, ECLI:EU:C:1991:428) was a consistent precedent, since it stated the general rule of the admissibility of damages actions for the infringement of EU Law. In the case at stake, the infringer was the State, but it can easily be an individual too, provided that the relevant EU Law provisions are directly applicable.

[5]Joined Cases C-295/04 to C-298/04, *Manfredi and others* [2006] ECR I-6619, ECLI:EU:C:2006:461.

[6]Case C-199/11, *Otis* [2012] ECLI:EU:C:2012:684.

[7]Case C-557/12, *Kone AG and Others v ÖBB-Infrastruktur AG* [2014] ECLI:EU:C:2014:1327.

[8]For further details: Domenicucci (2014), p. 179; Iannuccelli (2015), p. 131.

[9]Directive 2014/104/EU of the European Parliament and of the Council of 26 November 2014 on certain rules governing actions for damages under national law for infringements of the competition law provisions of the Member States and of the European Union (OJ L 349, 5.12.2014, p. 1). The adoption of this Directive has not been uncontested. The Commission started working on it back in 2005, the same period when the *Manfredi* case was discussed. This notwithstanding, the Directive codifies the CJEU's case law to a large extent (Pallotta 2017, p. 626). For an analysis of the backgrounds of the Directive see: Meyring (2012), p. 126; Vreck (2012), p. 278; Benacchio (2013), p. 16; Jones and Sufrin (2016), p. 1070; Rossi dal Pozzo (2017), Wils (2017), p. 21; Lianos et al. (2015), p. 33.

[10]The updated information is available at EUR-LEX. http://eur-lex.europa.eu/legal-content/IT/NIM/?uri=CELEX:32014L0104&qid=1503475032452. Accessed 19 Apr. 2018.

2 The Role of National Judges

The most important rule envisaged by Regulation No 1/2003 on the topic of private enforcement is Article 16. The provision codifies the ruling in the *Masterfood* case,[11] stating the binding effect of the Commission's decisions. The scope of the rule is extremely broad. National courts and NCAs cannot assume any measure conflicting with a Commission's decision, it being a decision finding and ordering the termination of the anticompetitive behaviour, or a commitment decision, or a finding of inapplicability.[12] Furthermore, national courts are prevented from adopting any decision that might run counter to a decision contemplated by the Commission, and to this end might stay proceedings. Actually, this seems the only reasonable solution, since national courts cannot estimate the content of the Commission's decision until it is issued.

The legal binding effect of the Commission's decision does not prevent national courts from rising doubts on its validity, according to the grounds of annulment stated in Article 263(2) TFEU. In this case, the courts have a duty to request a preliminary ruling to the CJEU, since they have no jurisdiction to declare an EU measure null and void.[13] Furthermore, national courts can always seek the cooperation of the CJEU through a preliminary ruling for the interpretation of any EU rule, such as any of the Treaties provisions, or a Commission's decision.

This rule decreases the margin of appreciation left to national judges, while strengthening the leading role of the Commission in the enforcement of EU Competition Law. At the same time, it can be extremely useful with regard to private enforcement for the injured party to prove the infringement.

Regulation No 1/2003 left the issue of the legal effects of NCAs' decisions open.[14] As we will see, Directive 2014/104 fills the gap.

---

[11]Case C-344/98, *Masterfoods Ltd v. HB Ice Cream, Ltd.* [2000] ECR I-11369, ECLI:EU:C:2000:689.

[12]The rule is so absolute that it applies to Appeal Courts, too. If a NCA's decision, or a first instance judgment is appealed, and the Commission adopts any measure in the meantime, the appeal court must overrule the decision conflicting with the Commission's subsequent decision (Case T-289/01 *Der Grüne Punkt – Duales System Deutschland GmbH* [2007] ECR II-1691, ECLI:EU:T:2007:155). The same principle cannot be extended to comfort letters, or to any non-definitive measure which does not conclude the proceedings.

[13]Case 314/85 *Foto-Frost* [1987] ECR 4199, ECLI:EU:C:1987:452.

[14]Komninos (2008), p. 77 stresses that there was no full faith and credit among NCAs and national Courts at the time of enacting the Regulation, on which a "mutual recognition" of the decisions might be grounded.

3 Damages Actions: The Italian Perspective Before the CJEU's Case Law

The admissibility of damages actions for infringements of Competition Law did not come to a surprise in Italy. The original version of Article 33(2) of Law No 287/1990 on the safeguard of the competition and the market[15] already established the functional jurisdiction of the Courts of Appeal for actions for nullity and damages for infringements of Competition Law. Interestingly, the Italian rules defining antitrust violations are modelled on Articles 101 and 102 TFEU. Therefore, Article 33 provided for damages actions for infringements of the Italian antitrust law, which was heavily based on EU Law.

Article 33(2) gave rise to considerable disputes regarding its scope of application. Briefly, it was not clear if it included only actions grounded on torts, or it extended to claims related to contractual liability, too. The answer to this question was not easy. We only need to recall the debate between two scholars,[16] the one longing to demonstrate that Article 33(2) is applicable only to claims filed by damaged undertakings (while consumer protection is part of contractual liability),[17] the other assuming a broader scope of application thereof, according to which every damaged legal or natural person—including the consumer—could take advantage of Article 33(2).[18] Although the first interpretation seemed to be prevailing initially,[19] the Supreme Court stated in 2005[20] that Competition Law protects every individual within the market, and not only undertakings. Indeed, antitrust law infringements harm free commercial competition and contractual freedom, which are public interests. Their violation amounts to torts, notwithstanding the claimant's nature and personal interests. Therefore, consumers could sue the infringer according to Article 33 of Law No 287/1990.

[15]Law of 10 October 1990, No 287, Rules on the safeguard of the competition and the market (*Gazzetta Ufficiale della Repubblica Italiana* (Italian Official Journal) [1990] 240).

[16]On these debates, more recently: Castelli (2012), p. 35; Catalozzi (2013), p. 275.

[17]Castronovo (2004a), p. 469; Castronovo (2004b) p. 1168. As a consequence, consumers should sue only their contractual counterparty before a first instance court.

[18]Libertini (2004), p. 933; Libertini (2005), p. 237.

[19]For example, Cassazione Civile sez. I (Supreme Court, Civil Section, First Chamber) 4 March 1999, No 1811; Cassazione Civile sez. I (Supreme Court, Civil Section, First Chamber) 9 December 2002, No 17475 concluded that consumers have no legal standing according to Article 33(2) of Law No 287/1990. Therefore, the first instance Court—and not the Court of Appeal—must be seized.

[20]Cassazione Civile Sezioni Unite (Supreme Court, Civil Section, Grans Chamber) 4 February 2005, No 2207. The judgment gave rise to a strong debate; for criticism: Casoria and Pardolesi (2015), I, 2752; instead, Inzitari (2005), p. 498, welcomed it. For more information on the current legal standing of consumers in Italian legal system: Fattori (2013), p. 285.

Moreover, Italian case law had already opened up to the admissibility of stand-alone damages actions. This was made clear by the Milan Court of Appeal in 1995,[21] in a claim related to an abuse of dominant position notwithstanding the absence of any previous decision by the Italian Competition Authority (ICA).

In this legal framework, the *Courage* case created a contradiction. Since Article 33(2) is an exception to the general rule, it could only be enforced within its scope of application, i.e. infringement of Italian Law. On the contrary, claims based on EU Law had to follow the general rules on jurisdiction, due to the principle of procedural autonomy of Member States, and be filed with a first instance court. A claimant complaining an infringement of EU Law was in a privileged situation, since he/she could benefit from two proceedings on the merit (first instance and appeal), because the case finds its legal ground in *Courage* (and not in Italian Law).

This consequence did not jeopardise the principle of equivalence, because plaintiffs grounding their claim on EU Law received a privileged treatment, if compared to "national law claimants". Nevertheless, it was intrinsically contradictory to provide for two different proceedings for the protection of very similar interests, codified in literally analogous provisions.

In recent years the jurisdiction to decide on private damages claim has undergone various reforms. The current situation is the following: Article 33(2) of Law No 287/1990 refers to the territorial jurisdiction of the Chambers specialised in intellectual property and commercial law, called *Tribunali delle Imprese* (Tribunals of Undertakings), established by Decree No 168/2003[22] as modified by Article 18 of Legislative Decree No 3/2017,[23] implementing Directive 2014/104. The outcome is the jurisdiction of only three *Tribunali delle Imprese*, established in Milan, Rome and Naples, for all the damages actions grounded on national or EU Competition Law. There are no differences between the enforcement of EU and Italian Competition Law.

4 The Harmonisation of Private Enforcement

4.1 The Principles of Effectiveness and Equivalence

The CJEU's contribution to the development of the private enforcement of EU Competition Law rests on the object of preliminary questions referred to it. In the absence of any EU normative measure, the CJEU cannot make up for the legislator's

[21]Court of Appeal of Milan, 18 July 1995; more recently: Court of Appeal of Milan, 11 July 2003; Cassazione Civile, sez. I (Supreme Court, Civil Section, First Chamber) 13 February 2009, No 3640.

[22]Legislative Decree 27 June 2003, No 168, Undertakings Tribunal (*Gazzetta Ufficiale della Repubblica Italiana* (Italian Official Journal) [2003] 159).

[23]Legislative Decree 19 January 2017, No 3, Implementation of Directive 2014/104 (*Gazzetta Ufficiale della Repubblica Italiana* (Italian Official Journal) [2017] 15. The first Italian complete comment of the decree is available in Meli et al. (2018), pp. 119–268.

inactivity, enacting new procedural rules. Therefore, the Court has developed the fundamental principle of procedural autonomy, as limited by the principles of equivalence and effectiveness. Briefly, Member States are free to organise their judicial system and their internal procedures, as long as they ensure an effective protection to individuals' rights, and do not discriminate between "purely national situations" and situations involving the application of EU Law.[24]

The impact of these principles is not always clear and still gives rise to many references for preliminary rulings in all the areas covered by EU Law. The harmonisation of national legislation should result in accurate rules for the sake of legal certainty, but this has not been fully the case with Directive 2014/104. Its title makes it clear that the Directive approximates only certain aspects of damages actions. For issues not contemplated by the Directive, the Member States' procedural autonomy applies.

Therefore, Article 4 of the Directive has a sort of pedagogical function, recalling the principles of equivalence and effectiveness failing any harmonised EU rule. Their impact can still be broad in the field of private enforcement. Indeed, the Directive deals only with damages actions, and not with all the possible private remedies.[25] Moreover, some issues are excluded from its scope of application, as for example causation, costs, negligence,[26] or collective redress,[27] which are fundamental issues for the proper functioning of judicial remedies. Another interesting example is local jurisdiction. For both national and cross-border disputes (i.e.,

[24]Therefore, the Directive applies to claims based both on EU Competition and/or national Competition Law (Article 2(1)(1)). Article 2(1)(b) of Legislative Decree No 3/2017 offers the same definition (Zoboli (2016)). The parallelism implements the principle of equivalence: internal and EU situations are subject to the same set of rules.

[25]Wils (2017), p. 24.

[26]Nevertheless, this should not be considered as a gap in the Directive. The CJEU's case law does not recognise any relevance to the psychological element of the violation of EU Law, whether the infringer is the State or an individual. Consequently, it should not have any weight even in the scope of application of EU Competition Law. *Contra*: Libertini (2014), p. 489, who refers to the general provisions of the Italian Civil Code and the consequent application of the principles of effectiveness and equivalence; see also: Reich (2007), p. 705.

[27]Consumer class actions can be an important tool within private enforcement, due to the frequently low value of the claims (Dunne 2015, p. 583; Scuffi 2015, p. 67; Villa 2015, p. 304). Nascimbene (2013), p. 269; Libertini (2014), p. 468, submit that the absence of EU harmonisation is a deficiency within the Directive. Article 140*bis* of the Italian Consumer Code (Decreto legislativo 6 September 2005, No 206 on the reform of the regulation for the protection of the consumer (*Gazzetta Ufficiale della Repubblica Italiana* (Italian Official Journal) Supplemento Ordinario (Ordinary integration) [2005] 162) introduces a form of opt-in class action. According to Article 1(1) of Legislative Decree No 3/2017, the harmonised rules on damages actions are applicable to class actions, too. The sole common EU measure is the Commission's Communication to the European Parliament, the Council, the European Economic and Social Committee and the Committee of the Regions "Towards a European Horizontal Framework for Collective Redress" (COM/2013/401 final). The Communication has a horizontal scope, since it is applicable to all forms of collective redress, notwithstanding the subject matter and the object of action. The Commission suggests an opt-in system.

according to the principle of equivalence), the Tribunale delle Imprese has exclusive jurisdiction and includes various districts. The general criteria for the determination of territorial jurisdiction apply, but then the jurisdiction is concentrated in these tribunals. The rule might give rise to doubts of effectiveness in cross-border cases. In the field of civil and judicial cooperation,[28] all the relevant provisions (Article 7 on contractual matters, and on torts, Article 17 on consumer contracts) enact the principle of proximity, aiming at granting the jurisdiction of a judge sitting close to the factual situation—or to the consumer for protective reasons. This is the reason why these provisions determine both international and territorial jurisdiction.[29] The Italian rule on the exclusive jurisdiction of specialised courts risks frustrating this aim, because of the broad extension of the jurisdiction.[30] The CJEU has already accepted the specialisation of the courts in specific and sensitive disputes,[31] insofar as it helps achieving the objective of a proper administration of justice and does not run counter to the principle of proximity. Although the case dealt with maintenance obligations, the same reasoning seems to be applicable to other subject matters, such as Competition Law, where the specialisation can justify the concentration, to the extent that the proximity is not completely lost. The same is true when the enforcement of a foreign judgment is at stake.[32]

Quite reasonably, the Italian legislator did not implement or mention the principles established in Article 4 in that they are a consolidated and undisputed part of general EU Law.

4.2 The Right to Full Compensation

Article 3 of the Directive establishes the right to full compensation. This should include any harm suffered by the claimant, with particular regard to actual loss, loss of profit and payment of interest. It excludes any overcompensation not aimed at fully compensating the harm, such as punitive or multiple damages. Through this rule, the European Union has definitively shown its aversion towards non-compensative damages.[33] The wording of the provision is so clear that it can easily be considered as having direct effect. This means that even Member States

[28] Regulation (EU) No 1215/2012 of the European Parliament and of the Council of 12 December 2012 on jurisdiction and the recognition and enforcement of judgments in civil and commercial matters (recast) (OJ L 351, 20.11.2012, p. 1).

[29] Case C-386/05 *Color Drack* [2007] ECR I-3699, ECLI:EU:C:2007:262.

[30] Supposing that the place where the harmful event has occurred (Article 7(1)(2)) is Palermo, we wonder how Tribunale delle Imprese of Naples can be considered close to the factual situation.

[31] Joined Cases C-400/13 and C-408/13 *Sanders and Huber* [2015] ECLI:EU:C:2014:2461.

[32] Case C-283/16 *M.S.* [2017] ECLI:EU:C:2017:104.

[33] The position of the Court in *Manfredi* was less clear-cut, but stressed the compensative aim of the damages action.

admitting non-compensative damages are prevented from awarding punitive or multiple damages in these claims.

Nevertheless, the quantification and the proof of harm may be a problem. Article 17 of the Directive tries to simplify their ascertainment. Firstly, it provides a duty not to make it extremely difficult or rather impossible to exercise the right to damages due to the procedural rules on the burden and the standard of proof. Secondly, it admits a margin of appreciation for national courts, if the quantification is impossible, or not reasonably possible. Thirdly, in cartel cases the Directive states a rebuttable presumption that cartel infringements cause harm. Finally, a national court may request the cooperation of a NCA to determine the harm.

This rule must be read in conjunction with the Communication from the Commission on quantifying harm in actions for damages,[34] which offers some guidelines to national courts for its concrete determination. The Guidelines aim at suggesting some methods to assess it with the highest precision, such as comparative analysis, or simulations.[35]

Italian Legislative Decree No 3/2017 defines damages in Article 1(2) as including actual loss, loss of profit and payment of interest. Damages may not have an over-compensative function. This definition strictly depends on the notion of damages accepted within the Italian legal system, which have a restorative and compensative function.[36] Therefore, this is coherent with the approach endorsed in the Directive.[37] Moreover, Article 14(1) of Legislative Decree No 3/2017 refers back to Articles 1223, 1226 and 1227 of the Italian Civil Code, providing for a total parallelism among damages actions for competition law infringements, torts[38] and contractual liability. The solution seems perfectly consistent with the Directive, except for one issue.

[34]Communication from the Commission on quantifying harm in actions for damages based on breaches of Article 101 or 102 of the Treaty on the Functioning of the European Union (OJ C 167, 3.6.2013, p. 19).

[35]The preference among various methods depends necessarily on the information available for each single case at stake: Caprile (2016), p. 697. In the Italian *Brennercom* saga, the experts in economics, required to assist the judge, presented structured opinions on the economic methods for the quantification of harm; Carli (2017), p. 105. The methods are contested from both a practical and an economic perspective, but according to Buccirossi (2014), p. 323, the outcome of the analysis should be subject to an evaluation of its intrinsic consistency, rationality and solidity. Indeed, a "but for" analysis requires a comparison with a hypothetical situation, which leads to practical difficulties and uncertainties: Dunne (2015), p. 592; Rose and Bailey (2013), p. 1249; Al Mureden and de Pamphilis (2017), p. 140; Lianos et al. (2015), p. 161.

[36]The Italian legal system does not provide for the award of punitive or multiple damages. Therefore, the application of foreign law and the recognition of a foreign judgment may give rise to practical difficulties, insofar as the overcompensation has deterring functions. For further details see Busnelli (2009), p. 909.

[37]Villa (2015), p. 302; Bruzzone and Saija (2017), p. 14.

[38]Article 2056 of the Italian Civil Code on torts refers to the very same provisions on the quantification of harm, which are included in the chapter devoted to obligations in general.

According to Article 1227 of the Italian Civil Code, the quantification of damages might be reduced, if the victim behaved in a negligent fashion, causing a harm or an aggravation of harm. There is no corresponding provision in the text of the Directive. This raises a question whether Article 1227 of the Italian Civil Code is compatible with the notion of damage endorsed in the Directive. The question is not theoretical: the rule has already been applied in a national case on an abuse of dominant position, since the victim willingly contributed to the antitrust behaviour.[39] The question is open, since the CJEU's case law does not provide a final answer. Indeed, the CJEU has stated that the subjective/psychological element in torts under EU Law is generally irrelevant in analysing the infringer's conduct; there is no case law on the issue regarding the victim.[40] In *Manfredi*, the CJEU took the lack of contractual freedom of the victim and his/her psychological status into due consideration. Notwithstanding the unclear legal framework, a tentative answer is still possible. If we stress the compensative function of restoration, the exclusion from compensation of certain harms should be acceptable.[41] If the victims' behaviour creates new or unforeseeable damages, or increases the damages already produced, or does not prevent at least part of harmful consequences, the infringer is not under a duty to restore this kind of avoidable damages: these are not a direct consequence of the infringement, but of the victim's negligence.

As regards the quantification of harm, some ICA's praxis shows a particular attention for the consequences of the infringement, in the light of the cooperation with national courts. One example thereof is the very well-known case of the car insurance cartel.[42] The ICA's decision is not limited to ascertaining the infringement, but aims at determining its impact on the market and on the consumers (these being direct victims of the cartel). This decision gave rise to a high number of follow-on damages actions, which grounded the quantification of harm on the analysis contained in the ICA's decision. In one of these cases, the Court of Appeal of Naples awarded damages for 19.68 euro, i.e. about the 20% of the price applied.[43] The determination of the impact of the cartel on the market by a highly specialised body as the ICA or NCAs in general might prove extremely helpful for national judges. The Italian Supreme Court has already confirmed the correctness of a reference to the ICA's decisions even for the quantification of the harm caused,[44] but the claimant

[39]Court of Appeal of Milan, 11 July 2003.

[40]Case C-224/01 *Köbler* [2003] ECR I-10239, ECLI:EU:C:2003:513; Case C-173/03 *Traghetti del Mediterraneo* [2006] ECR I-5177, ECLI:EU:C:2006:391.

[41]Al Mureden and de Pamphilis (2017), p. 135.

[42]ICA Decision No 8546, 28 July 2000.

[43]Court of Appeal of Naples, First Civil Chamber, 27 April 2005, No 1310/05: Osti and Prostaro (2012), p. 242.

[44]Cassazione Civile, sez. III (Supreme Court, Civil Section, Third Chamber) 2 February 2007, No 2305; Cassazione Civile 23 April 2014, No 9116; Cassazione Civile, sez. I (Supreme Court, Civil Section, First Chamber) 22 May 2013, No 12551; Cassazione Civile, sez. I (Supreme Court, Civil Section, First Chamber) 28 May 2014, No 11904.

must give evidence of the existence of harm, which is not an automatic consequence of the infringement.[45]

If this becomes the common praxis of the ICA, Article 14(3) of Legislative Decree No 3/2017 might prove quite useless in follow-on actions. This article empowers national courts to ask specific questions on the quantification of harm, although the ICA's decisions might already give sufficient guidelines for courts. Nevertheless, if a national court still has doubts as to the quantification, it can resort to the ICA provided that its questions are specific.

5 The Notion of Victim and the Legal Standing

The definition of harm is strictly linked to the notion of the victim of the infringement. Provided that the restoration has compensative functions, only persons suffering harm can claim for damages. The CJEU has been very clear on this point, especially in two very peculiar cases. In *Otis* the Commission claimed for damages.[46] In *Kone*, the claimant was a purchaser from a non-cartelist in a cartelised market, who increased prices taking advantage of the cartel itself. The admissibility of such an action is of great relevance. Every damaged person has the right to sue, although he/she has no factual or legal relationship whatsoever with the infringer(s).

Nevertheless, the victims must demonstrate that they suffered damages. If "anyone" has legal standing for the damages action, the claimant must prove to be a victim of the infringement. Therefore, the notion of claimant depends on the admissibility of the passing-on defence.[47]

In this framework, Article 14 of the Directive is dedicated to indirect purchasers, and admits the "offensive passing-on". According to quite common procedural rules (amounting to general principles in Italy), the claimant/indirect purchaser must give evidence that the overcharge has been passed on. This can be a *probatio diabolica*, an extremely hard burden of the evidence for the claimant. Indeed, the overcharge might depend on many factors, as a modification of the market, or an increase of the price of instrumental goods.[48] The indirect purchaser, probably a consumer, might not be able to prove that the overcharge has been passed on. At the same time, the

[45]Casszione Civile, sez. I (Supreme Court, Civil Section, First Chamber) 19 September 2013, No 21480; Court of First Instance of Milan, 26 May 2016, No 6666. This schizophrenic approach of the Supreme Court brings uncertainties in the first instance and appeals Courts regarding the legal value of the ICA's decision (Giudice di Pace di Lecce, 30 January 2003; Giudice di Pace di Roma, 21 March 2003, No 13638), or in the request of the proof thereof in follow-on cases, too (Court of Appeal of Naples, 14 April 2008, No 1430).

[46]For an Italian case note: Botta (2013), p. 11.

[47]Meyring (2012), p. 135; Rose and Bailey (2013), p. 1242; Whish and Bailey (2015), p. 317. The topic of the passing-on is not new in a comparative perspective: the first cases were decided in the USA in the mid-1960s Harris and Sullivan (1979), p. 269.

[48]Harris and Sullivan (1979), p. 272.

direct purchaser might not have a concrete interest in suing the provider notwithstanding the damage, for example in order not to hamper commercial relationships. Direct purchasers might even benefit from the infringement, even though they were not responsible for it.[49] In these cases, it would be rather impossible to enforce EU Competition Law through private actions.

Therefore, a rebuttable provision eases the burden of proof. The indirect purchaser must give evidence that: the defendant has infringed Competition Law; its outcome is an overcharge for the direct purchaser; the indirect purchaser has purchased goods or services which are the object of infringement, or which are derived from or contained in it. The defendant might prove that the overcharge has not been passed on, or not entirely. This presumption is extremely useful for the indirect purchaser, with special regard to the consumer.[50] In follow-on actions—which are the most frequent—the claimant needs to prove a causal link leading from the infringer to the direct purchase, and to give evidence of the purchase (which can be simply a bill or an invoice, for example). In any case, only the overcharge for direct purchasers is relevant: indirect purchasers do not need to give evidence of the total or partial pass-on through the commercial chain that lead to them.[51] The presumption is rebuttable: the infringer can prove the opposite, because it is the party having more technical competences on both the product or service, and the market at stake.

Article 14 of the Directive is so clear and precise that Article 12 of Legislative Decree No 3/2017 only reproduces it and even simplifies the wording.

This rule considers only one kind of damaged party, the indirect purchaser, and not all the possible classes of damaged persons ("anyone"). Therefore, standard rules concerning the burden of proof must be applied to all the other victims. This seems reasonable if we think of one cartelist (as in *Courage*), or one competitor losing part of the market. Nevertheless, the burden of the proof might be extremely difficult in respect of other categories of injured persons, such as the providers or suppliers of the infringer, or the competitor excluded from the market as a direct consequence of the infringement; not to mention its workers, who lost their job because of the bankruptcy,[52] or the consumer, who has not purchased the product of the cartel

[49] Afferni (2009), p. 500; Wils (2017), p. 19; Ashton (2018), p. 43.

[50] The scope of protection of EU Competition Law and the role of the consumer are still debated; see, recently: Andriychuk (2009), p. 77; Parret (2010), p. 339; Iannuccelli (2015), p. 13; Ioannidou (2015), p. 79.

[51] The standard rules on the burden of proof require the evidence of the quantification of the overcharge. The Directive and its Italian implementation do not provide for any simplification thereof. The Commission has published the *Study on the Passing-on of Overcharges*, offering some possible economic approach to its quantification. In this case, too, the national Court has a duty to scrutinise economic models, and would need a technical expert to assist in its evaluations.

[52] Afferni (2009), p. 510; Frignani (2012), p. 53, challenge the admissibility of a damages claim presented by the former workers of the excluded undertaking(s) presuming that it is not too direct an effect of the cartel. The authors submit that a purchase under the umbrella-pricing effect is not an immediate consequence of the cartel, too, but still the purchaser is a victim of the cartel according to the *Kone* case.

because of the price increase. All these damages are different from an overcharge and hit persons that might not have had any relationship with the infringer. Still, there is no simplification for them of the burden of evidence, and they need to show that they are victims of the infringement. In some cases this seems rather impossible.[53]

6 The Notion of Defendant

According to Article 2(1)(2) of the Directive, the infringer is

> the undertaking or the association of undertakings which has committed an infringement of competition law.

Legislative Decree No 3/2017 contains the very same definition. Noteworthy, there is no mention of any previous Commission's or NCAs' decision ascertaining the infringement and the infringer: the Directive covers both follow-on and stand-alone actions.

Especially (but not only) in cartel cases, the infringer can be more than one undertaking and its correct identification may not always be easy for an injured private party. Article 11 of the Directive tries to help the claimant in identifying the defendant. Indeed, it provides that the undertakings taking jointly part in an infringement are jointly and severally liable for the harm caused. In this respect, Article 9 of Legislative Decree No 3/2017 refers to Article 2055 of the Italian Civil Code, which introduces the general principle of joint liability in torts. The rule offers greater protection to victims, who may sue only one cartelist in order to recover the whole damage.

Two exceptions balance this aim with two other different interests. First, joint liability is not applicable to direct and indirect purchasers if the infringer is a small or medium-sized enterprise, provided that the market share was below 5% and the application of joint and several liability would jeopardise its economic stability and cause the loss of its economic value.[54] These conditions are very strict.[55] The exception is barely applicable in abusive cases, since undertakings having a dominant position on the market commonly have more than a 5% market share. The natural scope of application of the provision is therefore the cartel, where the participation of at least two undertakings is required. What if some of the infringers are small or medium-sized enterprises, and some not? The exception does not seem applicable, because the rule refers in a very general way to the infringer. If this is

[53]Castelli (2012), p. 70.

[54]The Commission's proposal did not envisage such exceptions and the subsequent preparatory measures do not justify them (Wils 2017, p. 28).

[55]Schepisi (2017), p. 91.

true, the scope of application of the exception is extremely limited (only in cartels between small or medium-sized enterprises).

Article 9 of Legislative Decree No 3/2017 reproduces the principles established by the Directive, but adds one more exception.[56] Probably it is justified by the fact that most of the undertakings having their seat in Italy are small or medium-sized enterprises according to the definition of the Directive. Therefore, joint and several liability is limited even when the claimant is not a direct or indirect purchaser. More precisely, the victim has a duty to ask for compensation first from the other cartelists; if this effort is unsuccessful, then the small or medium-sized enterprise can be sued for the entire damage caused. In absence of any similar provision in the Directive, and any margin of appreciation to Member States in the implementation of the rules on the liability of the small or medium-sized enterprises, this national rule may give rise to doubts as to its incompatibility with EU Law.

In any case, the exception to joint and several liability does not apply if the infringer/defendant had a leading role in the cartel, or coerced the other cartelists, or had already violated Competition Law. In these cases, there is no need to protect a party that seriously breached EU Competition Law.

The second exception to joint and several liability applies when the infringer is an immunity recipient. The *rationale* behind it is to favour whistle-blowers, who are subject to a more favourable treatment in private enforcement, too, if compared to that of the other infringers. These undertakings are subject to joint and severable liability towards their direct and indirect purchasers; in the other cases, they are liable to the extent that the victim has not been able to recover full compensation from the other cartelists.[57]

According to the Directive, joint and several liability means that the infringer/defendant may recover the amount of the compensation paid for the other infringers. This amount must be determined having due regard to each one's liability within the infringement. This is a general rule under Italian law: Article 9(3) of Legislative Decree No 3/2017 refers to Article 2055(2) of the Italian Civil Code.

Once more, a few exceptions are established in favour of the immunity recipient. The amount of its contribution cannot exceed the harm it caused to its direct or indirect purchasers, or providers. Its liability within the cartel has no relevance. The Italian implementation of these rules is only apparently incomplete: although it clarifies the limitations of the contribution towards purchasers and providers, it refers once more back to Article 2055 of the Italian Civil Code, which, as mentioned above, clearly provides for the proportional liability of the parties. Very importantly, the third para. is not referred to: it provides for equal liability, if it is not possible to demonstrate its exact percentage. The Directive does not envisage such simplification of the burden of proof, and there is no reference to the Italian standard rule within the Legislative Decree No 3/2017.

---

[56] De Cristofaro (2018), p. 541.

[57] Ameye (2016), p. 405.

7 The Disclosure of Evidence

7.1 The General Rules

Accessing documents is the first pre-condition for the claimant to be able to file a successful complaint. Indeed, it might prove impossible to give satisfactory evidence of undertakings' liability, especially in stand-alone actions.[58] The Italian Supreme Court has stated that the burden of proof cannot be interpreted too narrowly in these cases: the opposite would amount to a *de facto* impossibility to demonstrate the violation. Therefore, the Court must make use of all its *ex officio* powers already recognised by Italian civil procedure in order to ascertain the infringement, without prejudice to the principles of the adversary system and of the burden of proof.[59] In follow-on cases, the disclosure of evidence might still help the claimant to demonstrate the other essential elements of liability, i.e. causation and harm.

The disclosure of evidence cannot be without limits or conditions. Indeed, other conflicting interests might be at stake, as those related to secret or industrial information, or connected with a leniency programme. A right balance of all the interests is necessary.

Therefore, Articles 5 and 6 of the Directive are devoted to the disclosure of evidence. Article 5 establishes general principles when the evidence is under the control of the defendant or a third party. The judge may order the disclosure, provided that the claimant has requested it and has offered reasonable justification and evidence of a consistent factual framework to support his/her claims. Therefore, the victims have a specific duty to justify their requests, and to submit any reasonable evidence of the infringement in support. These conditions aim at preventing "fishing expeditions", where the applicant has no idea of the kind and of the contents of the documents to be found.

In particular, national courts may order the disclosure of a specified item of evidence, or of categories of evidence. This last part of the rule has a great impact in the Italian legal system. Indeed, under Italian civil procedure, it is not possible to order the disclosure of "categories of evidence", but only of single items of evidence. In implementing this provision, Article 3 of Legislative Decree No 3/2017 provides for an exception to the general rules on evidence established in Article 210 of the Italian Code of Civil Procedure. The court must be precise in its order. It must indicate the specific item of evidence, or the relevant categories of evidence of the request or of the disclosure order. A "category" is determined according to some common characteristics, such as the nature, the relevant period, the object or the content of the items of evidence. For example, the national Court may order the disclosure of all the mail exchanged between X and Y in the years 2015/2016

[58] Biavati (2007), p. 105.

[59] Cassazione Civile, sez. I (Supreme Court, Civil Section, First Chamber) 4 June 2015, No 11564: Geraci (2015), p. 537; Di Via and Leone (2015), p. 233.

concerning the fixing of product A prices,[60] or the invoices issued in year 2016. The disclosure of categories can be extremely helpful to claimants, while demonstrating an infringement of Competition Law. Such openness is welcome, and the wide Italian definition gives a reasonable margin of appreciation to judges.

The disclosure might nevertheless be limited to safeguard the other interests involved. Article 5(3) of the Directive grants a margin of appreciation to national courts. The Court must verify the solidity of the request, and the facts and evidence already available to support it. On the other hand, it must balance the scope and the costs of the disclosure, for third parties too, in order to avoid a generic search for information which is not useful in the context of the proceedings. Correctly, the Directive makes it clear that the interest for an undertaking not to be sued in a damages action is not an interest to be judicially protected. Finally, it must verify if the evidence contains confidential or reserved data. In this case, the court is responsible for determining the means to protect the secrecy. The party or the third parties involved have a right to be heard before a national court.

These guidelines to the discretion of judges are extremely precise. Italy has implemented them, pointing out the means to protect confidential information. The court can indeed order the disclosure, adding some specific measures, as the duty of secrecy, the possibility to hide the confidential parts of documents, private hearings with a closed audience, the limitation of the number of persons authorised to access the evidence, and a summary of the evidence by experts. Legislative Decree No 3/2017 offers a definition of confidential information, including personal, commercial, industrial or financial information, as commercial secrets. Such a definition is so broad that it risks hampering the margin of appreciation left to Courts by the Directive. This is even more so because Article 5(8) of the Directive leaves to Member States the possibility to allow for a broader disclosure of the evidence, while the Italian definition seems to restrict it. Therefore, it should be interpreted accordingly to the softer approach endorsed by the Directive, looking at it as a list of the information that might (and not must) be confidential. The only category of documents immediately covered by confidentiality under the Directive is that containing the communications between the party and his/her lawyer.

[60]The general rule in Italian civil procedure would require the determination of every single item of evidence. The request—and the order—would most probably look like "the email sent on . . .between X and Y, concerning the methods of calculation of the price of product A in the first half of 2015". It can be very easily submitted that claimants cannot be so precise in their request to the judge. If they were, they would barely need the disclosure of documents.

7.2 Disclosure of the Evidence Contained in the File of a Competition Authority

The documents contained in the file of a NCA are a special kind of evidence under the control of a third party. Nevertheless, the NCA is not a third party whatsoever but the main national body responsible for public enforcement. Therefore, Article 6 of the Directive balances the needs of public enforcement, which may require confidentiality, with the purposes of private enforcement, which instead requires the availability of all the existing documents in favour of the victim(s).

The special rule applies only to NCAs: Article 6(2) leaves Regulation No. 1049/2001 unaffected.[61] Since it covers the public access to the Commission's files, the institution is not subject to the Directive.

Article 6 aims at limiting the margin of appreciation granted to judges by Article 5. Therefore, there is a "black list" of non-accessible documents, i.e. leniency statements and settlement submission. The *rationale* behind it is not to put the whistle-blower in a worse position compared to the other cartelists/infringers for disclosing confidential information to the NCA. A damages action would better succeed against this undertaking, since it permitted access to (confidential) documents under its control. In the balance between public and private enforcement, the former prevails, because leniency programmes have an extremely practical impact on the discovery of antitrust behaviours. Indeed, the ICA follows the same approach.[62]

The prohibition to disclose these documents overrules the decision in *Pfleider* and *Donau Chemie*.[63] This should not come as a surprise. As already made clear, judge-made law aims at filling the gaps of written law, according to the principles of effectiveness and equivalence.[64] Legislative measures must not be bound by case law. Very often the EU legislator has codified the CJUE's case law, even within Directive 2014/104, but this is a free choice in the determination of the normative content.

In addition to the "black list", Article 6(5) of the Directive provides for a "grey list", i.e. documents that can be disclosed after the termination of the NCA's proceedings. This rule aims at granting the effectiveness of the on-going public enforcement. These are documents prepared specifically for the proceedings, or drafted by the NCA, or finally settlement submissions that have been withdrawn. These documents are all drafted or prepared in light of the public enforcement proceedings: it

[61]Regulation (EC) No 1049/2001 of the European Parliament and of the Council of 30 May 2001 regarding public access to European Parliament, Council and Commission documents (OJ L 145, 31.5.2001, p. 43). For its application to Competition cases: Komninos (2008), p. 108; Rose and Bailey (2013), p. 1227; Pace (2014), p. 247; Iannuccelli (2015), p. 131.

[62]Schettino (2013), p. 154.

[63]Case C-360/09, *Pfleiderer AG v Bundeskartellamt* [2011] ECR I-5161, ECLI:EU:C:2011:389; Case C-536/11, *Donau Chemie* [2013] ECLI:EU:C:2013:366. Further: Bastianon (2013), p. 111.

[64]Chieppa (2014), p. 285.

means that pre-existing documents that have been submitted during the NCA's proceedings are not covered by this exception.[65]

Article 6(4) lists a set of grounds to be taken in consideration to evaluate the proportionality of the order, which are strictly linked to public enforcement efficiency. Still, the national court can order the disclosure of the evidence to verify if it corresponds to the documents in the black or in the grey list. The same rules apply if only part of the documents may be subject to disclosing restrictions.[66]

In order to avoid abusive behaviours, the same restrictions apply when a person has the documents or knows their contents because of his/her participation in the NCA's administrative proceedings.

Article 6 is extremely precise, too, and the Italian legislator has implemented it with quite the same wording (Article 4). Article 4(8) of the legislative decree is nevertheless a key provision, which is not provided for (but neither prohibited) by the Directive. It gives the national court the power to stay the proceedings until the NCA (any, not only the ICA) has come to a final decision,[67] or until the appropriate moment, insofar as a party has requested the disclosure of a grey list document and the stay might be useful for the effectiveness of public enforcement. The stay of proceedings might be useful for public enforcement, which can continue without external interferences, and for private enforcement, too: indeed, a stand-alone action might become a follow-on claim, where the infringement can be considered as ascertained and documents are more accessible.

8 The Effects of National Competition Authorities' Decisions

The Directive fills the gap left by Article 16 of Regulation No 1/2003, and approximates national laws in a field where different solutions were adopted.[68] Italian case law recognised the standing of preferential evidentiary tool/privileged evidence to ICA's final decisions.[69] The Italian legal system does not recognise the category of

[65]Ameye (2016), p. 403.

[66]Article 8 of the Directive gives Member States the duty to provide for effective sanctions for the infringement of disclosure orders. These are established in Article 6 of Legislative Decree No 3/2017, which provides for administrative sanctions.

[67]The possible stay of proceedings was provided only in the case of stand-alone class actions (Article 140*bis* of the Italian Consumer Code). Legislative Decree No 3/2017 avoids any difference or discrimination between individual claims and collective redress (Zoboli 2016).

[68]Cortese (2014a), p. 145.

[69]Cassazione Civile, sez. I (Supreme Court, Civil Section, First Chamber) 13 February 2009, No 3638; Cassazione Civile, No 3640/2009; Cassazione Civile, sez. III (Supreme Court, Civil Section, Third Chamber), 20 June 2011, No 13486; Cassazione Civile, sez. III (Supreme Court, Civil Section, Third Chamber), 22 September 2011, No 19262.

privileged evidence, but rather that of legal evidence and simple evidence.[70] Privileged evidence is therefore a creation of case law aimed at recognising a meaningful (but not very clear) value to ICA's decisions before a court. Therefore, the claimant had to introduce the ICA's decision into the proceedings, but the defendant could overcome it by producing different evidence. According to the division between administrative and civil justice in Italy, it was very difficult to recognise the legal binding effects of the ICA's decision: nevertheless, case law has shown a trend to rest on it.

The Directive takes a step forward. According to Article 9, the decision of the NCA (of the State of the judge seized) and/or the judgment deciding on an appeal against it shall have a legal binding effect as regards the ascertainment of the infringement. No evidence to the contrary is admitted. In the opinion of the present author, any kind of final decision containing the ascertainment of the infringement may produce this effect. There are doubts whether a commitment decision should contain such a statement. The answer should be in the affirmative, although the statement is implicit: the NCA would not ask the undertaking(s) (and the undertaking(s) would not accept) to change its/their behaviour, unless it amounted to an infringement of Competition Law.[71]

Article 7 of Legislative Decree No 3/2017 is more complex. Indeed, there are two main issues in Italy. First, the judge is subject only to the law (and not to the administration or to administrative measures); second, justice has a limited jurisdiction in the review of administrative measures.[72] Administrative courts cannot review facts but only the reasoning, the solidity and the *rationale* behind the administrative decision, finally stating if the decision is valid or invalid, but (simplifying) not if it is right or wrong. In competition cases, facts are of the utmost importance, and a fault in their ascertainment can lead to completely different results. Failing a full review by the administrative judge, it would seem inconsistent to bind the civil judge, seized of a damages action, to the fact-finding contained in an administrative decision.

The Italian legislator has overcome this contradiction by extending the jurisdiction of the administrative judge against the ICA's decisions. This amounts to a clear exception to the general role of administrative justice in Italy. The administrative judge can directly verify the facts established in the ICA's decisions, and evaluate the technical issues when there is no real margin of appreciation and these elements may invalidate the decision. This does not mean that the administrative judge is granted full-review powers, but that the blatantly wrong ascertainment of the facts, or the

---

[70] Frignani (2013), p. 441.

[71] Pera (2012), p. 69; Pera (2013) p. 387; Chieppa (2014), p. 281. Instaed, Radicati and Russo (2011), p. 1047, and Castelli (2012), p. 120, argue that these decisions do not contain any evaluation of the supposed infringers' conduct.

[72] Benacchio (2011), p. 560; Rordorf (2014), p. 784; Siragusa (2014), p. 298; Morbidelli (2015), p. 7; Villa (2015), p. 306; Giliberti (2016), p. 77; Trotta (2013), p. 361, analyse these issues in the light of the coordination between public and private enforcement in Italy.

clearly wrong application of technical rules might render the decision invalid.[73] Still, some scholars suggest that there might be some doubt on the independence of the NCAs, due to their statutory functions to pursue Competition Laws policies.[74]

Moreover, Article 7(1) of Legislative Decree No 3/2017 clarifies that the legal binding effect concerns the type of infringement and its impact, but not the causal link and the existence of damage. Article 9 of the Directive does not specify these limits, but refers only to the infringement. We might suppose that the Directive does not cover other requirements for the civil liability of undertakings, too.[75] Nevertheless, as specified above, Italian Courts give utmost consideration to the ICA's decisions as regards the quantification of the harm, too. This case law is not overruled by Legislative Decree No 3/2017, but it means that the determination and the quantification of the harm, established by the ICA's decision, does not produce a legal binding effect. Still, the ICA's decision can be privileged evidence of the causal link and the existence of harm.

The Report accompanying the Draft Legislative Decree No 3/2017 adds that civil courts might not be bound by the Italian antitrust authority's decisions, if they consider the decisions invalid (and not subject to appeal). The question arises on the legal value of the Report, which does not have the same value as a statute in Italy. Although the administration and administrative justice serve public purposes, legal certainty would be seriously undermined if a civil judge declared an ICA's decision null and void.

The same legal effects cannot be granted to foreign NCAs' decisions. Indeed, the EU has not experimented with true administrative cooperation among Member States yet. National substantive and procedural laws are not harmonised, and there seems to be no possibility to approximate them in the near future. Moreover, automatic recognition would restrict the Member States' procedural autonomy and jeopardise the defendant's right to judicial protection.[76] Consequently, it is not possible to grant legal binding effects to public acts issued abroad. Nevertheless, EU Competition Law benefits from the cooperation system between the Commission and the NCAs, and among NCAs (Articles 11 ff. of Regulation No 1/2003). It cannot be argued that the foreign public enforcement systems are completely unknown and obscure.

Therefore, foreign NCAs' decisions must be considered at least as *prima facie* evidence of the infringement, to be assessed along with other evidence (Article 9

[73]The full-review jurisdiction of a first instance court seems more consistent with the case law of the European Court of Human Rights, Case No 43509/08, *A. Menarini Diagnostics S.R.L. v. Italy*, according to which Article 6(1) of the European Convention of Human Rights requires at least one instance, decided by a court, where the case is again reviewed in fact and in law. On the impact of this judgment on the Italian legal system: Siragusa and Rizza (2013), p. 408; Zagrebelsky (2014), p. 1196.

[74]Pallotta (2017), p. 633.

[75]Nascimbene (2017).

[76]Bariatti and Perfetti (2009), p. 26. These concerns seem typical of the Southern EU countries (Cortese 2014b, p. 105).

(2) of the Directive). This rule leaves a margin of appreciation in the implementation. The UK and Germany already granted legal binding effects to foreign NCAs' decisions.[77] This solution presumes a high level of mutual trust between Member States.[78]

There is no precedent in the Italian experience. Italy has therefore opted for a *minimum* implementation. Article 7(2) states that the decision may be presented as evidence, among other things, of the infringement against the infringer. It may cover the kind of infringement and its impact.

The Directive has allowed the Italian legal system, which did not even consider the last instance administrative judge's final decision as irrebuttable, to take a big step forward. This new coordination might help victims in providing evidence of the first element of tort, i.e. misconduct.

9 The Passing-on Defence and the Causal Link Between the Harmful Event and the Damage

While qualifying the notion of claimant, we have discussed the offensive passing-on in favour of indirect purchasers. In parallel, the Directive admits the passing-on defence, too, i.e. the possibility for the infringer to give evidence that the direct purchaser has passed on the overcharge partly or fully. The burden of proof lies on the defendant, who may also require the disclosure of evidence (Article 13).

The *rationale* behind the rule is that only the victims can be granted damages. In this sense, the evidence of the passing-on of overcharge has already been admitted by Italian case law.[79] Article 11 of Legislative Decree No 3/2017 has implemented this rule.

The general admissibility of the passing-on defence might create under or over compensation, if more damaged parties file more claims against the same defendants in different Courts. Indeed, the offensive passing-on rule benefits from a rebuttable presumption: the indirect purchaser will quite often be able to prove that the overcharge has been passed on. On the contrary, the other damaged parties must give evidence of the passing. Finally, the infringer must prove the passing-on.

---

[77]Germany used two different approaches in follow-on and stand-alone cases. In the first, the aim of consistency was pushed to the greatest extent granting the primacy to public enforcement. In the second, the national Court was under no obligation to stay the proceedings and to wait for the *Bundeskartellamt* decision (OLG Düsseldorf VI-W (Kart) 6/06). As for UK case law see Whish and Bailey (2015), p. 335.

[78]Nascimbene (2017) analyses the principle of mutual trust in civil and judicial cooperation, assuming that it is so strong in this field that no differences between national and foreign NCAs decisions should be admitted. The similarities of NCAs' duties and commitments lead Pallotta (2017), p. 636 to the same conclusion.

[79]Court of Appeal of Cagliari, 23 January 1999; Court of Appeal of Turin, 6 July 2000; Court of Appeal of Milan, 11 July 2003.

Therefore, the final determination of the fact—whether the overcharge has actually been passed on—might depend on the available evidence and on the judges' margin of appreciation. Indirect purchasers may be considered victims due to the presumption in some jurisdictions, but at the same time the infringer may not be able to demonstrate that the overcharge has been passed on within a different dispute. These results would be contradictory.[80] Therefore Article 15 of the Directive tries to coordinate different damages actions. National courts seized of damages actions must take into consideration other actions pending in different jurisdictions, filed by claimants from other levels of the supply chain, the judgments stemming from these actions and other information resulting from the public enforcement. This rule does not jeopardise the application of Article 30 of Regulation No 1215/2012 on international pending related actions.[81]

Since the Directive's provision is very specific and clear, too, Article 13 of Legislative Decree No 3/2017 only rephrases it, adding a reference to Articles 39 and 40 of the Italian Civil Procedural Code on the *lis pendens* and related actions, whenever two or more claims are simultaneously filed with more Italian Courts.

These are the sole rules on the causal link between the event and the harm. The general regulation is left to the Member States, risking at jeopardising the approximating effect of the Directive.[82] It is therefore interesting to recall that Italian case law has recognised the role of privileged evidence to the ICA's decisions analysing the causal link.[83] Therefore, the defendant has the burden to prove the 'interruption' of the causal link, i.e. an unforeseeable fact or set of facts that finally caused the harm. These circumstances cannot be the same as those already analysed and overcome in the ICA's decision, as, for example, the change of the market prices, or the risk increase in insurance contracts.[84]

As mentioned above, the ICA's decisions now bind the judge with respect to the violation ascertainment, and not to the other requirements of damages actions.

---

[80]Meyring (2012), p. 145; Lianos et al. (2015), p. 231.

[81]Under specific circumstances, the first judge seized may have jurisdiction to hear the related cases, too, if its national procedural law admits the consolidation thereof. Article 7 of Law 31 No 218 of May 1995, Reform of the system of private international law (*Gazzetta Ufficiale della Repubblica Italiana* (Italian Official Journal) [1995] 128), is devoted to the coordination of international pending actions, if the claim is filed in a non-Member State of the EU. EU Law does not require any coordination with Third States, and it does not seem of the utmost importance in this field even from a national perspective. Indeed, if the foreign judgment risks jeopardising the EU rules on Competition Law, it must not be recognised for contrast with EU public policy (Case C-126/97 *Eco Swiss* [1999] ECR I-3055, ECLI:EU:C:1999:269). EU Competition Law requires a stricter approach to international coordination in general.

[82]EU Law in general does not seem to provide a theory of the causal link in torts: Ashton (2018), p. 174; Caprile (2016), p. 691; Lianos et al. (2015), p. 69.

[83]Cassazione Civile, No 2305/2007; Cassazione Civile, sez. III (Supreme Court, Civil Section, Third Chamber) 21 March 2011, No 6347.

[84]Cassazione Civile, No 13486/2011; Cassazione Civile, sez. III (Supreme Court, Civil Section, Third Chamber) 10 May 2011, No 10211; Cassazione Civile, No 11904. In the insurance cases, the claimant only needed to present the ICA's decision and to prove the insurance contract.

Nevertheless, it is not excluded that these decisions can still have the role of privileged evidence as to the other elements of the tort, although some Italian scholars have seriously contested this outcome.[85] If this remains the Italian practice, consumers can easily demonstrate a tort in follow-on actions related to cartels. Indeed, the ICA's or the Commission's decision is binding and might be privileged evidence of the causal link, the harm is presumed and the judge can quantify it *ex aequo*, using a margin of appreciation if other more economical methods prove impossible.[86]

10 Consensual Settlements

The Directive does not promote consensual settlements, which are therefore left to the general regulation of mediation, i.e. Directive 2008/52[87] and Directive 2013/11 in consumer cases.[88] These Directives provide quite a complete framework for mediation as a method for non-judicial dispute resolution. Damages claims may be settled through mediation, as all other civil claims.

Nevertheless, the process of alternative dispute resolution (ADR) might be time-consuming and affect the limitation period. Therefore, Article 18 provides for a suspension of limitation periods in any ADR or arbitration cases. In the former, the limitation period is suspended for all the duration of the non-judicial process in favour of the parties involved. For the latter, a maximum 2-year suspension may be granted. In the case of consensual settlement, the NCA might reduce penalties.

Article 15 of Legislative Decree No 3/2017 refers to the already enacted general rules on suspension in the case of ADRs, and makes it clear that this period is not to be included in the reasonable duration of proceedings. The Legislative Decree also grants the 2-year suspension in the case of arbitration.[89]

Article 19 of the Directive establishes the effects of a settlement on other possible damages actions. The rule is again quite precise and clear, and Article 16 of the Legislative Decree No 3/2017 just rephrases it. The infringer must benefit from the settlement: the part of harm included therein is deducted from the total harm caused. If the injured party has suffered other harms, actions can be filed only against other co-infringers. Still, the liability is joint and several: if the non-settling co-infringers

[85] Palmieri (2011), p. 2674, and Frignani (2012), p. 429, observe that this approach jeopardises the right of the infringer's judicial defence.

[86] Villa (2015), p. 308, suggests stopping this automatism in the legislation implementing the Directive, but nothing in Legislative Decree No 3/2017 seems to prevent such interpretation.

[87] Directive 2008/52/EC of the European Parliament and of the Council of 21 May 2008 on certain aspects of mediation in civil and commercial matters (OJ L 136, 24.5.2008, p. 3).

[88] Directive 2013/11/EU of the European Parliament and of the Council of 21 May 2013 on alternative dispute resolution for consumer disputes and amending Regulation (EC) No 2006/2004 and Directive 2009/22/EC (OJ L 165, 18.6.2013, p. 63).

[89] Bastianon (2017), p. 158; Zuffi (2018), p. 555.

cannot pay the damages, the settling co-infringer is still liable, unless this liability is excluded in the consensual settlement. According to Article 16(4) of Legislative Decree No 3/2017, the general rule of the proportionality between the participation in the tort and the infringer's liability is safe. The national court must take due account of previous settlements of actions among co-infringers subsequent to the exercise of joint and several liability by a damaged party.

11 Limitation Periods

Article 10 of the Directive aims at approximating limitation periods, codifying the principles established in *Manfredi*.[90] The case law of the Italian Supreme Court is already consistent with Article 10. Accordingly, limitation periods begin to run when the damaged party knows, or is expected to know, of the existence of infringement.[91] The publication of an ICA's decision might be a relevant moment, though this is not always the case because, otherwise, the damaged party may have to wait for the ICA's decision and too many years may pass between the infringement and the claim.

Article 10 of the Directive establishes that limitation periods last at least 5 years, starting from the moment when the damaged party knows, or is expected to know of the misconduct, of the harm and of the infringer's identity. If a case is being examined by a NCA or by the Commission, the limitation periods are suspended, and the suspension ends at the earliest 1 year (in Italy, 1 year) after the final infringement decision. This rule shows a clear favour for damages actions. We recall that the judge, seized with a damages action, might even stay the proceedings. Therefore, the Directive aims at simplifying follow-on actions, which are clearly more practical for both the claimant and the judge, strengthening the role of the NCAs even within private enforcement.[92] Nevertheless, the application of this rule may cause enormous delays in the recovery of the damage. Indeed, the final infringement decision is defined as "an infringement decision that cannot be, or that can no longer be, appealed by ordinary means" (Article 1(1)(12) of the Directive). Years may elapse between the beginning of the examination by the NCA or the Commission, and the final judgment from a last-instance court on the legitimacy and validity of that decision.

Article 8 of Legislative Decree No 3/2017 rephrases the Directive's provision.

---

[90] Nascimbene and Rossi dal Pozzo (2008), p. 513.

[91] Court of First Instance of Turin, 22 December 1998; Cassazione Civile, sez. III (Supreme Court, Civil Section, Third Chamber) 6 December 2011, No 26188; Cassazione Civile, No 2305/200.; Cassazione Civile, sez. III (Supreme Court, Civil Section, Third Chamber) 3 April 2013, No 8110; Cassazione Civile, No 12551/2013; Cassazione Civile, sez. III (Supreme Court, Civil Section, Third Chamber) 10 December 2013, No 27527.

[92] Rordorf (2014), p. 784.

Moreover, in case of joint and several liability, the limitation periods should be reasonably long to allow the injured parties to bring actions against the infringer or the co-infringer(s). Accordingly, Article 9(4) of the Legislative Decree No 3/2017 establishes that the limitation period begins after the ascertainment of the impossibility to obtain recover from the infringer or the co-infringers.

12 Final Remarks

The Italian transposition of the Directive is quite on time and seems generally correct. Two factors have contributed to the Italian legislator's precision. First, civil jurisdictions have already experienced both stand-alone and follow-on actions. In a functional interpretation of substantive civil law and civil procedural law, the case law had already achieved some of the results which are nowadays codified in the Directive. Therefore, the Directive did not have an earthquake effect in the Italian legal system.

Second, the Directive harmonises only *certain* aspects of damages actions, i.e. not all the remedies within private enforcement, and not the whole procedure for damages actions. This choice can be justified by the principle of proportionality: the EU can enact only the measures which are necessary to reach the EU objectives. Therefore, a complete new civil procedure would have appeared unproportioned.[93]

The Italian legislator did not add much to the topics approximated, except for the rationalisation of territorial jurisdiction and the retroactive effect of part of legislative decree-rules on disclosure and on limitation periods connected to arbitration, which are applicable to proceedings filed as from 26 December 2014, when the Directive entered into force. According to Article 19 of the Legislative Decree No 3/2017, these provisions should be characterised as procedural rules (while Article 22 of the Directive prohibits the retroactive effect of substantive rules).

The Directive seems to aim at consumers' protection and help individuals bring successful actions. Still, it does not consider one of the most important obstacles, i.e. the costs of the proceeding. If the damages amount to less than 20 euro, as awarded by the Court in Naples, the consumer is not pushed to act, neither in a follow-on case, nor in a stand-alone single action. Collective redress might be a possible solution, but at the same time, the Directive and the Italian legislation do not promote this system.

It is doubtful whether the Directive really leads to an increase in the number of damages actions that might result in private remedies being considered as a type of *enforcement* of EU Competition Law. Although rules on disclosure and on the effect of NCAs' decisions are of the utmost importance, there are still too many gaps that do not make these actions interesting enough.[94] The particular position of the parties

---

[93]Reich (2007), p. 738.

[94]Giannaccari (2017), p. 143.

other than direct and indirect purchasers, the exclusive effects of the abuse of dominant positions, the costs, the usefulness of class actions, are some of the key elements that the Directive failed to consider, but that can be extremely important for a successful action. Their regulation is left to Member States, and different national legislations risk creating again legal fragmentation and uncertainty.

In recent years, private enforcement seems to have become less fashionable, after the first enthusiastic statements at the beginning of 2000. The Directive might come a bit late in this framework, and it has too limited a scope. Hopefully, it constitutes a new incitement to injured parties' claims. The on-time and correct Italian implementation might be a good opportunity to obtain satisfaction and full compensation of the damages suffered.

References

Afferni G (2009) La traslazione del danno nel diritto antitrust nazionale e comunitario. Concorrenza e mercato 16:494–521

Al Mureden E, de Pamphilis M (2017) Valutazione dei danni. In: Manzini P (ed) Il risarcimento del danno nel diritto della concorrenza. Giappichelli, Torino, pp 126–157

Ameye E (2016) Damages: thorny issues for National Courts despite the EU anti-trust damages directive. In: Beneyto JM, Maillo J (eds) The fight against Hard Core Cartels in Europe. Bruylant, Bruxelles, pp 400–418

Andriychuk O (2009) Can we protect competition without protecting consumers. Competition Law Rev 6:77–87

Ashton D (2018) Competition damages actions in the EU. Elgar, Cheltenham

Bariatti S, Perfetti L (2009) Prime osservazioni sulle previsioni del 'Libro Bianco in materia di azioni per il risarcimento del danno per violazione delle norme antitrust' della Commissione e del codice del consumo. In: Nascimbene B, Rossi dal Pozzo F (eds) Il private enforcement delle norme sulla concorrenza. Giuffrè, Milano, pp 3–30

Bastianon S (2013) La tutela dei privati e l'accesso alle informazioni riservate. In: Tesauro G (ed) Concorrenza ed effettività della tutela giurisdizionale tra ordinamento dell'Unione europea e ordinamento italiano. ESI, Napoli, pp 111–120

Bastianon S (2017) Composizione consensuale delle controversie. In: Manzini P (ed) Il risarcimento del danno nel diritto della concorrenza. Giappichelli, Torino, pp 158–170

Benacchio GA (2011) Alcune questioni in tema di risarcimento del danno antitrust nella giurisprudenza nazionale e comunitaria. In: Ajani G, Gambaro A, Graziadei M, Sacco R, Vigoriti V, Waelbroeck M (eds) Studi in onore di Aldo Frignani: nuovi orizzonti del diritto comparato europeo e transnazional. Jovene, Napoli, pp 555–572

Benacchio GA (2013) Il private enforcement del diritto europeo antitrust: evoluzione e risultati. In: Pace LF (ed) Dizionario sistematico della concorrenza. Jovene, Napoli, pp 16–26

Biavati P (2007) Il diritto processuale e la tutela dei diritti in materia di concorrenza. Riv. trim. dir. proc. civ. 61:97–117

Botta M (2013) Commission acting as plaintiff in cases of private enforcement of EU competition law: Otis. Common Mark Law Rev 50:1105–1118

Bruzzone G, Saija A (2017) Private e public enforcement dopo il recepimento della direttiva. Più di un aggiustamento al margine?. Mercato Concorrenza Regole 19:9–36

Buccirossi P (2014) Riflessioni intorno alla guida pratica per la quantificazione del danno. Concorrenza e mercato 21:323–330

Busnelli FD (2009) Deterrenza, responsabilità civile, fatto illecito, danni punitivi. Europa e diritto privato 12:909–946

Caprile (2016) L'applicazione diretta degli artt. 101 e 102 da parte dei giudici nazionali. In: Frignani A, Bariatti S (eds) Disciplina della concorrenza nella UE. Wolters Kluwer, CEDAM, Padova, pp 679–710

Carli C (2017) Brennercom vs. Telecom: atto secondo. Mercato Concorrenza Regole 45:105–116

Casoria M, Pardolesi R (2015) Disciplina della concorrenza, private enforcement e attivismo giudiziale: dopo la dottrina, il diritto delle corti?. Foro Italiano 140:I, 2752–2757

Castelli L (2012) Disciplina antitrust e illecito civile. Giuffré, Milano

Castronovo C (2004a) Antitrust e abuso di responsabilità civile. Danno e responsabilità 9:469–474

Castronovo C (2004b) Responsabilità civile antitrust: balocchi e profumi. Danno e responsabilità 9:1168–1174

Catalozzi P (2013) Il giudice competente nel processo antitrust. In: Pace LF (ed) Dizionario sistematico della concorrenza. Jovene, Napoli, pp 275–282

Chieppa R (2014) L'impatto delle nuove regole sull'accesso al fascicolo dell'autorità. Concorrenza e mercato 24:279–285

Cortese B (2014a) Defining the role of courts and administrative bodies in private enforcement in Europe: United in diversity?. In: Cortese B (ed) EU competition law. Between public and private enforcement. Wolters Kluwer, Alphen aan den Rijn, pp 145–178

Cortese B (2014b) The difficult relationship between administrative authorities and the judiciary in antitrust private enforcement. In: Cortese B (ed) EU competition law. Between public and private enforcement. Wolters Kluwer, Alphen aan den Rijn, pp 102–107

De Cristofaro M (2018) Innovazioni e prospettive nella dimensione processuale che sta al cuore del *private antitrust enforcement*. Nuove leggi civili commentate 41:523–554

Di Via A, Leone P (2015) Italy. In: Knoble Gotis I (ed) The private competition enforcement review. Law Business Research, London, p 233

Domenicucci DP (2014) Preliminary rulings and competition law: some reflections for National Judges. In: Cortese B (ed) EU competition law. Between public and private enforcement. Wolters Kluwer, Alphen aan den Rijn, pp 179–221

Dunne N (2015) Courage and compromise: the directive on antitrust damages action. Eur Law Rev 40:581–597

Fattori P (2013) La legittimazione attiva e passiva all'azione antitrust. In: Pace LF (ed) Dizionario sistematico della concorrenza. Jovene, Napoli, pp 283–289

Frignani A (2012) L'onere della prova nelle cause risarcitorie da illecito antitrust. In: Benacchio GA, Carpagnano M (eds) I rimedi civilistici agli illeciti anticoncorrenziali. Private enforcement of competition law. CEDAM, Padova, pp 53–58

Frignani A (2013) La difesa disarmata nelle cause follow on per danno antitrust. La Cassazione in guerra con se stessa. Mercato Concorrenza Regole 41:429–447

Geraci A (2015) Condotta anticoncorrenziale e perimetrazione del mercato rilevante. Il diritto industriale 23:537–545

Giannaccari A (2017) In tema di private enforcement: sulla rotta giusta. Mercato Concorrenza Regole 45:143–148

Giliberti B (2016) Public e private enforcement nell'art. 9, co. I della direttiva antitrust 104/2014. Il coordinamento delle tutele: accertamento amministrativo e risarcimento danni nei rapporti privatistici. Rivista italiana di diritto pubblico comunitario 26:77–113

Harris RG, Sullivan LA (1979) Passing on the monopoly overcharge: a comprehensive policy analysis. Univ Pa Law Rev 128:269–360

Iannuccelli P (2015) La responsabilità delle imprese nel Diritto della concorrenza dell'Unione europea e la direttiva 2014/104. Giuffrè, Milano

Inzitari B (2005) Abuso da intesa anticoncorrenziale e legittimazione aquiliana del consumatore per lesione alla libertà negoziale. Danno e responsabilità 10:498–505

Ioannidou M (2015) Consumer involvement in private EU competition law enforcement. Oxford University Press, Oxford

Jones A, Sufrin B (2016) EU competition law. Text, cases and materials. Oxford University Press, Oxford

Komninos AP (2008) EC private antitrust enforcement. Hart, Oxford

Lianos I, David P, Nebbia P (2015) Damages claims for the infringment of EU competition law. Oxford University Press, Oxford

Libertini M (2004) Ancora sui rimedi civili conseguenti ad illeciti antitrust. Danno e responsabilità 9:933–941

Libertini M (2005) Ancora sui rimedi civili conseguenti ad illeciti antitrust (II). Danno e responsabilità 10:237–251

Libertini M (2014) Diritto della Concorrenza dell'Unione Europea. Giuffrè, Milano

Meli V et al (2018) La nuova disciplina del risarcimento dei danni per violazione della normativa antitrust: profili sostanziali (Parte I). Nuove leggi civili commentate 41:119–268

Meyring B (2012) European Union. In: Knoble Gotis I (ed) The private competition enforcement review. Law Business Research, London, p 126

Morbidelli G (2015) Della necessaria distinzione tra accertamento dei fatti e giudizio di attendibilità. Riflessioni nascenti dal caso Novartis-Roche. Giust Amm It 12:7–38

Nascimbene B (2013) Interaction between leniency programmes and damages actions in antitrust law: perspective for collective redress. World Competition 36:269–283

Nascimbene B (2017) La vincolatività del provvedimento di condanna dell'Autorità garante successivamente alla direttiva sul private enforcement (Direttiva 2014/104/UE). Available via EUROJUS http://rivista.eurojus.it/la-vincolativita-del-provvedimento-di-condanna-dellautorita-garante-successivamente-alla-direttiva-sul-private-enforcement-direttiva-2014104ue/. Accessed 17 Mar 2018

Nascimbene B, Rossi dal Pozzo F (2008) L'azione di risarcimento antitrust e la «prescrizione» nel diritto comunitario e nel diritto nazionale. Diritto del commercio internazionale 22:513–523

Osti C, Prostaro A (2012) Italy. In: Knoble Gotis I (ed) The private competition enforcement review. Law Business Research, London, p 242 ff

Pace LF (2014) The Court of Justice 'Antitrust Enforcement Negative Harmonisation Framework' and the CDC and Pfleiderer Judgments: 'Another Brick in the wall'. In: Cortese B (ed) EU competition law. Between public and private enforcement. Wolters Kluwer, Alphen aan den Rijn, pp 241–255

Pallotta O (2017) Public e private antitrust enforcement alla luce della direttiva 2014/104/UE: l'equilibrio alterato. Studi sull'integrazione europea 12:621–640

Palmieri A (2011) Intese restrittive della concorrenza, sanzionate dall'Agcm, fra imprese assicuratrici, e danni alla massa degli assicurati per indebito aumento del premio. Foro Italiano 136.I, 2674–2679

Parret L (2010) Shouldn't we know what we are protecting? Yes we should! A plea for a solid and comprehensive debate about the objectives of EU competition law and policy. Eur Competition J 6:339–376

Pera A (2012) Decisioni con impegni e private enforcement nel diritto antitrust. Mercato Concorrenza Regole 40:69–116

Pera A (2013), Le decisioni con impegni e il rilievo per l'antitrust private enforcement. In: Pace LF (ed) Dizionario sistematico della concorrenza. Jovene, Napoli, pp 379–387

Radicati L, Russo F (2011) Decisioni di accettazione degli impegni e private enforcement del diritto antitrust. Diritto del commercio internazionale 25:1047–1058

Reich N (2007) Horizontal liability in EC law: hybridization of remedies for compensation in case of breaches of EC rights. Common Mark Law Rev 44:705–742

Rordorf R (2014) Il ruolo del giudice e quello dell'Autorità nazionale della Concorrenza e del Mercato nel risarcimento del danno antitrust. Le Società 28:784–789

Rose V, Bailey D (2013) BELLAMY & CHILD European Union Law of Competition. Oxford University Press, Oxford

Rossi dal Pozzo F (2017) La direttiva sul risarcimento del danno da illecito antitrust. Armonizzazione delle regole nazionali in tema di private enforcement o occasione mancata?.

Available via EUROJUS http://rivista.eurojus.it/la-direttiva-sul-risarcimento-del-danno-da-illecito-antitrust-armonizzazione-delle-regole-nazionali-in-tema-di-private-enforcement-o-occasione-mancata/ Accessed 17 Mar 2018
Schepisi C (2017) Responsabilità in solido. In: Manzini P (ed) Il risarcimento del danno nel diritto della concorrenza. Giappichelli, Torino, pp 91–107
Schettino A (2013) Il difficile rapporto tra private e public enforcement: il caso dell'accesso agli atti nei programmi di clemenza. Studi sull'integrazione europea 8:153–174
Scuffi M (2015) Brevi note in tema di class action alla luce della direttiva 104/2014. In: Benacchio GA, Carpagnano M (eds) L'applicazione delle regole di concorrenza in Italia e nell'Unione europea. Editoriale Scientifica, Napoli, pp 67–73
Siragusa M (2014) L'effetto delle decisioni delle autorità nazionali della concorrenza nei giudizi per il risarcimento del danno: la proposta della Commissione e il suo impatto nell'ordinamento italiano. Concorrenza e mercato 21:297
Siragusa M, Rizza C (2013) Violazione delle norme antitrust, sindacato giurisdizionale sull'esercizio del potere sanzionatorio da parte dell'autorità di concorrenza e diritto fondamentale a un equo processo: lo "stato dell'arte" dopo le sentenze Menarini. KME e Posten Norge Giur Comm 40:408–456
Trotta A (2013) Il rapporto tra il giudizio civile e gli atti dell'AGCM e della Commissione. In: Pace LF (ed) Dizionario sistematico della concorrenza. Jovene, Napoli, pp 361–367
Villa G (2015) La direttiva europea sul risarcimento del danno antitrust: riflessioni in vista dell'attuazione. Corriere giuridico 32:301–309
Vreck B (2012) Overvierw of Europe. In: Foer AA, Cuneo JW (eds) The international handbook on private enforcement of competition law. Elgar, Cheltenham, p 278
Whish R, Bailey D (2015) Competition law. Oxford University Press, Oxford
Wils WPJ (2017) Private enforcement of EU antitrust law and its relationship with public enforcement: past, present, future. World Comp 40:3–45
Zagrebelsky G (2014) Le sanzioni Consob, l'equo processo e il ne bis in idem della CEDU. Giur. it 114:1196–1200
Zoboli L (2016) Private enforcement: verso il recepimento della direttiva sul risarcimento del danno da illecito antitrust. Available via EUROJUS http://rivista.eurojus.it/la-vincolativita-del-provvedimento-di-condanna-dellautorita-garante-successivamente-alla-direttiva-sul-private-enforcement-direttiva-2014104ue/. Accessed 17 Mar 2018
Zuffi B (2018) L'incentivazione del ricorso ai metodi di composizione alternativa (*consensual settlements*) nelle liti risarcitorie antitrust. Nuove leggi civili commentate 41:555–585

Silvia Marino is Professor of European Union Law at the University of Insubria, Varese and Como, Italy, and Coordinator of the Project "Training Action for Legal Practitioners: Linguistic Skills and Translation in EU Competition Law".

Part II
Linguistic Aspects of Drafting, Translating, Interpreting and Implementing EU Competition Law

Legal Languages in Contact: EU Legislative Drafting and Its Consequences for Judicial Interpretation

Agnieszka Doczekalska

Abstract "United in diversity"—the motto of the European Union (EU)—points out the paradoxes both drafters and interpreters of EU law cope with. On the one hand, diversity (including diversity of cultures and languages) is respected and protected by EU law. On the other hand, EU law is required to be applied uniformly in all Member States, thus creating the union of languages and cultures. The chapter investigates how this paradoxical combination of diversity and unity is obtained by means of language use during legislative drafting and judicial interpretation processes. In particular, the analysis focuses on whether linguistic equality can be attained when EU law is drafted and interpreted. If all EU official languages are in use throughout the legislative process, and none of them has a dominant position, especially, none of them influences radically the wording of other language versions, then all language versions of an EU legal act should equally shape the meaning of this act. Consequently, the unity reflected in the uniform interpretation of EU law (the same meaning of all language versions of an EU legal act in all Member States) can be achieved through linguistic diversity manifested in the multilingual nature of EU legislation.

1 Introduction

The use of languages throughout legislative drafting and interpretation of European Union (EU) laws reflects the motto of the EU "Unity in diversity".[1] Linguistic diversity results from the requirement that EU legal acts are drawn up, enacted and published in 24 official languages. Unity is expressed by the expectation that multilingual legal acts, which are created throughout the legislative process in which all languages are used by means of translation and interpretation, render the

[1] https://europa.eu/european-union/about-eu/symbols/motto_en.

A. Doczekalska (✉)
Law School, Kozminski University, Warsaw, Poland
e-mail: adoczekalska@alk.edu.pl

S. Marino et al. (eds.), *Language and Law*,
https://doi.org/10.1007/978-3-319-90905-9_10

same meaning in all language versions. Judges retrieve this meaning from all language versions (diversity) of a legal act which is to be uniformly applied (unity) in all the Member States. The chapter investigates how this paradoxical combination of diversity and unity is obtained by means of language use during the legislative drafting and judicial interpretation processes.

The practice of legislative drafting and legal interpretation of EU laws creates the ground where legal languages stay in contact and might influence each other. The chapter distinguishes two types of contact:

- Type I: the contact of EU official languages, and
- Type II: the contact of EU legal languages and Member States' official (legal) languages.

Both types can be observed during the legislative drafting and interpretation of EU laws. EU law is drafted in 24 EU official languages (Type I contact) which have the status of official languages in one or more Member States and are also used to draw up national law (Type II contact). Hence, EU legislative drafters must create new legal terms for EU concepts or use national legal terminology with great care.[2] Moreover, the contact of Type II can be also detected when EU legal acts use not only autonomous EU concepts and terms but also terms which denote national legal concepts of Member States. The established case law of the Court of Justice of the European Union (hereinafter CJEU; previously the European Court of Justice (ECJ)) requires language versions of EU legal acts to be taken into consideration during the judicial interpretation process, and in particular, requires that none of the versions are read in isolation. Hence EU official languages stay in the contact and influence each other (Type I contact). On the other hand, what allows for Type II language contact is the application of EU law (especially, direct application in the case of regulations) and its interpretation within legal systems of Member States by national courts, which reconstruct legal norms sometimes from both national and EU secondary legal acts and take into consideration national law while interpreting EU law.

Having the above observations in mind, the first part investigates the use and reciprocal influence of languages during the legislative process. In order to find out whether all languages participate in the drafting process in the same way and to the same degree, the meaning of official and working language status is analysed and then the practice of how EU languages are actually used in the EU institutions is examined. The focus is on the language use in three main EU institutions participating in the legislative drafting, namely the European Commission, the European Parliament and the Council of the European Union. The CJEU whose legal interpretation of EU law is binding, uses only French as its working language,[3] whereas

---

[2]Guideline 5 of *Joint Practical Guide,* European Union (2015).

[3]McAuliffe (2012), p. 203; Schilling (2010), p. 1475.

all EU official languages can become procedural languages.[4] The chapter does not address the language regime in the CJEU but discusses, in the second part, the issue of language versions of EU legal acts and their importance when determining the meaning of EU legal provisions.

2 Legislative Drafting by EU Institutions

2.1 All Equal? The de jure *and* de facto *Status of EU Languages*

The Treaty on the Functioning of the European Union (TFEU) in Article 342 (former Article 290 of the Treaty establishing the European Community) confers the competence of determining the rules governing the languages of the institutions of the Union to the Council. This competence does not cover the language system of the CJEU which is allowed to stipulate its own rules in the Statute of the Court. In its very first Regulation[5] adopted in 1958, the Council granted the status of official and working languages of EU institutions (EEC institutions then) to four languages: Dutch, French, German and Italian (Article 1), which were the official languages of the founding six Member States of the EU.[6] Since 1958, Regulation No 1/1958/EEC was amended several times due to successive enlargements which increased the number of EU (EC) official languages and due to the transformation of the European Economic Community into the European Community and then the European Union, which also resulted in the renaming of the Official Journal.

The second recital of the Regulation explains why Dutch, French, German and Italian were granted the status of official languages. Firstly, these are the languages in which the Treaty[7] was drafted. Secondly, these are official languages in one or more of the Member States. Consequently, when a new Member State whose official language has not been yet recognised as an official language of the EU, joins the European Union, the official language of a Member State gains the status of EU official language as well. If a Member State has more than one official languages and one of them already has the status of EU official language, other official language (s) of the Member State might not be granted official status in the EU. Turkish, which, together with Greek, is an official language of Cyprus, is an example of an

[4]See Chapter 8 (Articles 36–42) of the Rules of Procedure of the Court of Justice (OJ L 265, 29.9.2012, p. 1).

[5]Council Regulation (EEC) No 1 of 15 April 1958 determining the languages to be used by the European Economic Community (OJ 17, 6.10.1958, p. 385); referred to further as Regulation No 1/1958/EEC.

[6]Belgium, France, Germany, Italy, Luxembourg and the Netherlands.

[7]Then Treaty establishing the European Economic Community (Rome Treaty), since 2009 the Treaty on the Functioning of the European Union.

official language of a Member State that did not become an official language of the EU.

Until 2007, Irish, the first official language of Ireland, could also serve as an example of the above-mentioned situation. The accession of the Republic of Ireland and the United Kingdom in 1973 resulted in granting the status of the EU's official language to English, which was recognised as a national official language in both countries. At that time, Ireland accepted that Irish would be only the language of the Treaties but not an official and working language of the EU institutions. However, in 2004 Ireland requested the recognition of Irish as an official and working language of the EU. The Council granted such a status to Irish in 2005 pursuant to Regulation No 920/2005/EC amending Regulation No 1/1958/EEC.[8] The Regulation entered into force in 2007. Thus, Irish gained the status of an EU official and working language 34 years after Ireland joined the EC.

Malta, which joined the EU in 2004, has two official languages, namely Maltese and English; its linguistic situation is, thus, comparable to the Irish one. However, at the time of the accession negotiations, Malta requested that Maltese be an official and working language of the EU.

Regulations, directives or decisions adopted under the ordinary legislative procedure, Council and Commission regulations, Council and Commission directives addressed to all the Member States and Council and Commission decisions which do not specify to whom they are addressed can enter into force and be published in the Official Journal only if the text has been drafted in all the official EU languages (see Articles 4 and 5 of Regulation No 1958/1/EEC).[9] There is an exception from these general rules which refers to the Irish language, the only language that became an official language of the EU a long time after the accession of Ireland. Council Regulation No 920/2005/EC, which granted Irish the status of official language and working language of the institutions of the Union, provided as well that, for practical reasons and on a transitional basis, the EU institutions are not obliged to draft or translate all acts. Only regulations adopted jointly by the European Parliament and the Council must be drafted and published in the Official Journal in all the official EU languages, including Irish. This derogation is temporary and renewable. It was established for 5 years starting 1 January 2007 (Article 2(1) of Regulation No 920/2005/EC), and then extended twice; firstly, in 2010, for a period of 5 years until 31 December 2016 (Council Regulation No 1257/2010/EU)[10] and secondly, in

[8]Council Regulation (EC) No 920/2005 of 13 June 2005 amending Regulation No 1 of 15 April 1958 determining the languages to be used by the European Economic Community and Regulation No 1 of 15 April 1958 determining the language to be used by the European Atomic Energy and introducing temporary derogation measures from those Regulations (OJ L 156, 18.6.2005, p. 3).

[9]Council of the European Union (2016), p. 50.

[10]Council Regulation (EU) No 1257/2010 of 20 December 2010 extending the temporary derogation measures from Regulation No 1 of 15 April 1958 determining the languages to be used by the European Economic Community and Regulation No 1 of 15 April 1958 determining the languages to be used by the European Atomic Energy Community introduced by Regulation (EC) No 920/2005 (OJ L 343, 29.12.2010, p. 5).

2015, for various periods of time (from 1 to 5 years),[11] depending on the act concerned (Council Regulation No 2015/2264/EU).[12] Council Regulation No 2015/2264/EU aims at the gradual reduction of derogation to apply Regulation No 1958/1/EEC, which should result in the application of Regulation No 1958/1/EEC without a derogation as of 1 January 2022. However, the Council may extend derogation measures once again.

To sum up, at least one official language of a Member State is recognised as an official language of the European Union. However, in the case of bilingual or multilingual countries where some official languages are also official languages of other Member States and therefore already have or will have the status of an official language of the EU, the recognition of other official languages of a Member State as EU official languages requires such a Member State's request (Article 8 of Regulation No 1/1958/EEC) and then a decision by the Council (Article 342 TFEU). Since not all Member States in the situation described above request such a recognition, not all official languages of the Member States have the same status in the European Union.

Nowadays 28 languages have been granted the status of official and working languages. Regulation No 1/1958/EEC distinguishes official languages from working languages, but does not specify the meaning of these terms in the legal definition. However, its provisions explain their meaning. Besides Article 1 granting the status of official language, the term "official language" is used in Articles 2, 4, and 5. Regulation No 1/1958/EEC mentions explicitly the term 'working languages' only in Article 1. However, Articles 6 and 7 refer to working, not official, languages. Taking into consideration Regulation No 1/1958/EEC, EU official languages can be described as languages in which regulations and other documents of general application must be drafted (Article 4), in which the Official Journal must be published (Article 5). The concept of EU official languages also covers languages of documents which a Member State or a person subject to the jurisdiction of a Member State send to EU institutions (Article 2). According to Article 6, EU institutions may stipulate in their rules of procedure which of the languages are to be used in specific cases. Article 7 requires the CJEU to decide in its rules of procedure which languages are to be used in the Court's proceedings.

[11]The derogation is provided until 31 December 2016 for Directives adopted by the European Parliament and the Council, until 31 December 2017 for Decisions adopted by the European Parliament and the Council, until 31 December 2019 for Directives adopted by the Council which are addressed to all Member States, Regulations adopted by the Council, Decisions adopted by the Council which do not specify to whom they are addressed, until 31 December 2020 for Regulations adopted by the Commission, Directives adopted by the Commission which are addressed to all Member States, Decisions adopted by the Commission which do not specify to whom they are addressed (see Annex to Council Regulation No 2015/2264/EU).

[12]Council Regulation (EU, Euratom) No 2015/2264 of 3 December 2015 extending and phasing out the temporary derogation measures from Regulation No 1 of 15 April 1958 determining the languages to be used by the European Economic Community and Regulation No 1 of 15 April 1958 determining the languages to be used by the European Atomic Energy Community introduced by Regulation (EC) No 920/2005 (OJ L 322, 8.12.2015, p. 1).

The wording of Article 1 puts forward equality between languages, whereas the expression "which of the languages" applied in Article 6 suggests that not all working languages must necessarily be used equally by EU institutions.[13] According to Adrey, Article 1 expresses language equality, whereas Article 6 institutional glottopolitical autonomy.[14] The latter might result in potential linguistic inequality. In other words, all EU official languages have the status of working languages, but it may happen that not all of them are used in practice. Therefore, *de jure* working languages which have a formal status of working languages are distinguished from *de facto* working languages which are actually used in the EU institutions. The latter are named "procedural languages" in the Commission.

2.2 Drafting or Translation? The Use of EU Legal Languages Throughout the Legislative Process

The Commission, the Council and the Parliament, namely the EU institutions involved in the legislative drafting, have applied Article 6 of Council Regulation No 1/1958/EEC and, in their Rules of Procedure, have adjusted language use arrangements to their needs. The solutions described in the Rules of Procedures and applied in practice seek to achieve a balance between linguistic diversity and equality, which is ensured by the use of all official languages (the policy of full multilingualism), and practical capabilities and actual needs. None of the institutions specify which languages are their working languages. However, the Parliament, the Commission and the Council approve situations in which not all 24 languages are used.

While discussing language use during the legislative drafting, three questions should be taken into consideration:

1. Firstly, which languages are used in oral communication during discussions over a legislative proposal;
2. Secondly, which language is used for the drafting of a legislative proposal and then translated from
3. Finally, which languages are used in written communication and at what stage of the legislative process; especially which documents are available in all languages and when are language versions of a legal act prepared: throughout the legislative process or only towards its end.

Before any drafting starts, a legislative proposal is discussed. Furthermore, discussions over a proposal continue during negotiations in the Council and in the Parliament. The institutions' Rules of Procedure arrange for language use rather in written than oral communication (with the exception of the Parliament's Rules of

[13]See the analysis of wording by Adrey (2009), p. 52.

[14]Adrey (2009), pp. 52, 54.

Procedure). However, some information is provided in other documents (decisions, reports, memos or answers to Parliament Members' questions).

The Commission deliberately decided not to introduce any detailed provisions on language use in its Rules of Procedure in order to allow committees to choose solutions that suit their real needs best.[15] The Commission indicates English, French and German as procedural languages,[16] which are used during internal meetings. However, German speakers confirm that German is used very rarely, since only English and French actually play the role of vehicular[17] and drafting languages.[18] Hence, although the Commission declares respect towards the equality of official and working languages,[19] they are not equally used during oral communication in the Commission.

As far as the Council and the Parliament are concerned, the language regime of oral communication depends on the nature and level at which meetings are organised.[20] The European Parliament's Rules of Procedure provide that all Members have the right to speak in the official language of their choice in the Parliament (Rule 158.2).[21] Their speeches are simultaneously interpreted into the other official languages and into any other language that the Bureau may consider to be necessary (Rule 158.2).[22] However, interpretation is provided according to the "resource-efficient full multilingualism" policy adopted by the Parliament in 2014.[23] Interpretation is provided in the order of priority and full multilingualism assured for meetings of parliamentary bodies, especially for plenary sittings and priority political meetings.[24] Interpretation for administrative meetings is granted only when resources are available and it is justified by actual needs.[25]

---

[15] Special Report No 9/2006 concerning translation expenditure incurred by the Commission, the Parliament and the Council together with the institutions' replies (OJ C 284, 21.11.2006, p. 21).

[16] European Commission (2013).

[17] A vehicular language is a language used for communication between speakers of different languages; some authors underline that vehicular language is used in "certain established contexts and situations" Cherubim (2006) after Laakso et al. (2016), p. 13.

[18] Ban (2013).

[19] The Commission answer to Oral Question No 53 by Alfredo Antoniozzi (H-0159/05) on the subject of the use of Italian in the EU institutions; and to Written Questions E-3124/03 by Mrs Muscardini (UEN) and E-2111/04 by Mrs Reynaud.

[20] Gazzola (2006), p. 398.

[21] Procedure of the European Parliament, 8th parliamentary term, January 2017.

[22] Some derogations from Rule 158 are provided in Rules 106.4a, 113.4 and 159 of the Rules of Procedure. The provisions of Rule 158.1 and 158.2 are repeated in Article 7 of the Decision of the European Parliament (EC, Euroatom) of 28 September 2005 adopting the Statute for Members of the European Parliament (OJ L 262, 7.10.2005, p. 1) which ensures linguistic diversity and opposes discrimination against any of the official languages.

[23] The Code of Conduct on Multilingualism. Bureau Decision of 16 June 2014, available at www.europarl.europa.eu/pdf/multilinguisme/coc2014_en.pdf (Accessed 20 Mar 2018).

[24] Article 2 of the Code of Conduct on Multilingualism.

[25] Article 2 of the Code of Conduct on Multilingualism.

As far as the Council is concerned, all 24 working languages might be used during meetings of national ministers. The same applies to European Council meetings since Member States' representatives can speak any official EU language of their choice and interpretation into other languages is provided.[26] The Committee of Permanent Representatives (COREPER) on the other hand, works usually only in French, English and German.[27] The language regime of the Council's working groups and preparatory bodies is based on the request-and-pay system which aims at reducing the cost of interpretation. According to this system, Member States, which partially pay for interpretation, decide whether they need interpretation and for which languages.[28]

To sum up, the equality of working languages is fulfilled by the fact that each working language can be used in oral communication in the EU institutions. However, not necessarily all of them are used in practice during meetings. The more formal the debate is, the more languages are usually involved.[29]

Regardless of the number of languages involved in the debates, documents are first drafted in one language and then translated into others. From a practical standpoint, it is not possible to prepare a legislative act simultaneously in 24 languages.[30] Therefore, language versions of EU law are prepared by means of translation, although after they are published in the Official Journal of the EU and enter into force, none of the versions may be regarded as a translation. They are all equally authentic versions of a legal act. To evaluate whether linguistic equality during the legislative process is assured, it is important to establish in which language documents, and especially proposals, are first drafted. Legislative proposals were previously prepared in French and nowadays they are drawn up in English. Baaij[31] estimates that approximately 95% of legislation adopted in the co-decision procedure is drafted in English. The use of English may put non-native speakers at a disadvantage.[32] It is true, in the sense that those who do not know English cannot actually participate in the drafting of the very first version of a legal act. However, they can debate and influence the content of the document when they receive it in the language they know. Nevertheless, since legislation is often drafted by non-native English speakers, this language is misused and shaped by non-native influences. Such influences are much less observed in the case of other languages into which only native speakers translate English texts.

English as a lingua franca of the EU institutions does not belong only to native speakers of English but also to those who have a mother tongue other than English.

[26] Gazzola (2006), p. 398.

[27] Fenet (2001), p. 247.

[28] Doczekalska (2009), p. 351.

[29] Truchot (2003), p. 102.

[30] Such practice is applied in Canada where English and French versions of a bill are co-drafted at the same time. See for instance Labelle (2000) and Šarčević (2005), pp. 277–292.

[31] Baaij (2013) after Dragone (2006), p. 100; Frame (2005), p. 22.

[32] Phillipson (2003), pp. 21, 131.

The latter influence the development of English as well. The predominant position of English could mean that this language will influence the development of other languages. Since English is the main language in which legislative proposals are discussed, new concepts are first denoted in English. However, translators into other languages not always choose calques or borrowings from English. Sometimes a descriptive equivalent is preferred.[33]

The use of English by non-native speakers and native speakers who have started to lose "touch with their language after years of working in a multilingual environment"[34] resulted in the major changes that English has undergone and in the development of EU English.[35]

Since drafting at the same time in 24 languages is not feasible, the only way to guarantee linguistic equality is to provide the translation of documents throughout the legislative process. A legislative proposal is not a final legal act. It undergoes changes and amendments as a result of difficult negotiations. Therefore, not only a final act should be available in all languages just before its enactment but also other texts[36] produced during the legislative process ought to be translated. Not all documents produced by the EU institutions are translated or require translation.[37] Sometimes translation is provided only in a few languages (e.g. the Commission prepares some documents only in three procedural languages). In respect of three EU institutions (i.e. the Commission, the Parliament and the Council), the most important legal documents drawn up during the legislative process are available in all the official languages. As far as the Commission is concerned, legislative proposals, explanatory memoranda, reports required by legal texts, Communications by the Commission (including white and green papers), follow-up reports of Council decisions are translated into all languages.[38]

The European Parliament requires all the official language versions of documents which are published in the Official Journal of the European Union or which are voted on in plenary.[39] The European Parliament's Rules of Procedure provide that all

[33]Compare, for instance, equivalents of the term *flexicurity* in French (*flexicurité*) or Spanish (*flexiseguridad*) and in Lithuanian (*darbo rinkos lankstumo ir užimtumo garantijų pusiausvyra*) or Polish (*model elastycznego rynku pracy i bezpieczeństwa socjalnego*).

[34]European Commission (2018).

[35]See examples from Gardner (2016).

[36]These texts encompass, for instance, amendments and modifications to the legislative proposal, modified and amended versions of the proposals, reports (e.g. reports of the Committee on Legal Affairs or other responsible committees), opinions and joint texts of the Council and the Parliament.

[37]For instance, Commission replies to written questions by Members of the European Parliament are translated into their language and into one procedural language (Special Report No 9/2006 concerning translation expenditure incurred by the Commission, the Parliament and the Council together with the institutions' replies (OJ C 284, 21.11.2006, p. 21).

[38]Special Report (2006), p. 21. Other documents translated into all languages include: announcements of State aid and antitrust procedures published in the Official Journal, as well as the subsequent final decisions published in the Official Journal, anti-dumping decisions, calls for tenders or for manifestation of interest and press releases (Special Report (2006), p. 21).

[39]Special Report (2006), p. 22.

documents of the Parliament are drawn up in the official languages (Rule 158.1). Amendments must be available in all the official languages before they can be put to the vote (Rule 169.6). The Parliament can decide otherwise, but not if such a decision would place any Member which uses "a particular language at an unacceptable disadvantage" (Rule 169.6).

As far as the Council is concerned, documents discussed at ministerial meetings are required in all official languages (Article 14 of the Council's Rules of Procedure).[40] However, the Council can decide otherwise on grounds of urgency. Then, if translations are not available, any member of the Council may oppose discussion.

The number of official and working languages does not allow for the simultaneous drafting of all language versions of legislative documents. However, languages are present and in contact during the legislative process due to translation. From a legal standpoint, language versions of legal acts are equally authentic and even if drawn up by means of translation, they cannot be referred to as translations. On the other hand, translation ensures full multilingualism (even if controlled) and language equality.[41]

3 All Authentic? Judicial Interpretation of EU Law

Despite how they have been drafted, all language versions of EU legislative acts are equally authentic. Hence, they have the same legal force and effect. Therefore, it is assumed that the same meaning is rendered in all language versions.[42] Equal authenticity requires that EU legal acts are "interpreted in the light of the versions in all the official languages".[43] If all language versions are compared and taken into consideration at the interpretation process, all of them shape the meaning of the legal provision in question and influence each other at the semantic level. Similarly to the analysis of contact between languages during the legislative process, the investigation of interpretation should involve the question which languages are considered in order to establish the meaning of EU legal provisions. In particular, the following issues should be addressed:

- firstly, whether all 24 language versions are actually compared by the CJEU and/or national courts of Member States, and
- secondly, whether any language version has a dominant position during the interpretation process, i.e., if not all language versions are compared, it is more

[40]Especially draft legislation at certain milestone stages, agendas for the Council, documents for adoption or discussion by the Council agenda, opinions of the legal service; Council minutes should have all language versions. See *The Annex to the Guide for producing documents for the Council and its preparatory bodies*.

[41]For more details see Doczekalska (2008).

[42]Derlén (2016), p. 55.

[43]Case 29/69 *Erich Stauder* [1969] ECR 419, ECLI:EU:C:1969:57, para. 3.

often considered or in the case of discrepancies between language versions, its meaning is chosen.

When the CJEU formulated for the first time the requirement of interpretation "in the light of the versions in all the official languages" in case *Stauder*, EEC law was authentic only in four languages. Thus, the comparison of all language versions was achievable in practice. The requirement has been repeated in the *CILFIT* case, in 1982, when law was authentic in eleven languages. The Court stated then that

> Community legislation is drafted in several languages and that the different language versions are all equally authentic[, a]n interpretation of a provision of Community law thus involves a comparison of the different language versions.[44]

Since then, the number of authentic language versions of EU law raised to 24 and it is doubtful that courts profoundly analyse all of them, even if they take all versions into consideration.

The analysis of CJEU judgments from 1960 to 2010 conducted by C.J.W. Baaij[45] reveals that the Court actually mentions the comparison of language versions only in 3% of judgments. As regards national courts, Advocate General Jacobs and Advocate General Stix-Hackl noted that the comparison of all language versions

> would put a disproportionate effort on the part of the national courts[46]

and would be

> a practically intolerable burden on the national courts.[47]

The analysis of national courts' interpretation practice in some Member States reveals that actually up to three or four language versions are compared.[48] Versions in English, French, German and in a language of the national court are usually chosen.[49] The information which language versions have been analysed for interpretation purposes can be retrieved from the text of judgments where judges explain their interpretation decisions. If the meaning is clear and the same in all language versions, the reference to the comparison of language versions is unnecessary. Therefore, the lack of such a reference does not mean that the analysis of all or some language versions has not been undertaken. Even if some language versions seem to be more often considered than others, it does not confirm their dominant position. Linguistic inequality in the interpretation process would arise, if the courts

[44]Case 283/81 *Srl CILFIT* [1982] ECR 3415, ECLI:EU:C:1982:335, para. 18.

[45]Baaij (2011), (2012), pp. 217–233.

[46]Opinion of Advocate General Jacobs delivered on 10 July 1997 in Case C-338/95 *Wiener S.I. GmbH v Hauptzollamt Emmerich* [1997] ECR I-06495, ECLI:EU:C:1997:352, para. 65.

[47]Opinion of Advocate General Stix-Hackl delivered on 12 April 2005 in Case C-495/03 *Intermodal Transports BV v Staatssecretaris van Financiën* [2005] ECRI-08151, ECLI:EU:C:2005:215, para. 99.

[48]Derlén (2009), Doczekalska and Jaśkiewicz (2014), pp. 66–76.

[49]The analysis included British, German, Danish courts Derlén (2009) and Polish administrative courts Doczekalska and Jaśkiewicz (2014), pp. 66–76.

constantly preferred the meaning of one or some language versions over others. It is not the case of interpretation practice in the CJEU. If there is divergence between the versions of EU legal act, the CJEU searches for the meaning uniform to all versions

> by reference to the purpose and general scheme of the rules of which the provision in question forms part.[50]

The requirement to consider all language versions is difficult to fulfil in practice, while it also causes some theoretical problems. Firstly, it can be regarded as contrary to the rationale for multilingualism, according to which the existence of 24 equally authentic language versions of a legal act guarantees that its addressees may obtain their knowledge about their legal rights and obligations just from one language version. EU citizens may not be required to be fluent in 24 languages to understand EU law. If all language versions of a legal act must be read together to find out the meaning of this act, the principle of legal certainty may be jeopardised.

Secondly, the requirement is contrary to the presumptions[51] of equal (the same) meaning and intent, on which the principle of equal authenticity is based.[52] If all language versions have the same meaning, then the comparison of all of them is needless. The interpretation of one language version should be sufficient. It would also support the right of EU citizens to follow only one language version of EU legal act.

To address the above paradoxes, the meaning of the requirement to interpret EU law "in the light of the versions in all the official languages" and to compare different language versions should be clarified. The explanation has been provided already in the judgment in the *Stauder* case, where the CJEU for the first time required all language versions to be taken into consideration and noted that

> owing to uniform application and according to uniform interpretation, it is impossible to consider one version of the text in isolation.[53]

Consequently, the requirement of the interpretation "in the light of the versions in all the official languages" does not mean that all 24 versions must de facto be compared but that, especially in the case of divergences between them, none of the versions may be discarded and the uniform meaning must be found for all language versions. The uniform interpretation and application of EU law in all Member States guarantee linguistic equality and legal certainty.

The uniform interpretation of EU law is possible because the EU has developed its own autonomous legal system.[54] The EU legal autonomy makes it possible to create new autonomous concepts, the meaning of which is specific to EU law. Each

---

[50] For instance: para. 14 of the judgment in Case 30/77 *Regina v Bouchereau* [1977] ECR 1999, ECLI:EU:C:1977:172.

[51] The presumptions are indicated by Strandvik (2016), p. 146.

[52] Doczekalska (2009), pp. 365–370.

[53] Case 29/69 *Erich Stauder* [1969] ECR 419, ECLI:EU:C:1969:57, para. 3.

[54] Para. 3 of the judgment of the Court of 15 July 1964, Case 6/64 *Flaminio Costa v E.N.E.L.* [1964] ECR 1141, ECLI:EU:C:1964:66.

legal system has its own conceptual and terminological system. Autonomous concepts are denoted by system-bound terms with no equivalent in other legal systems and their legal languages.[55] Therefore, legal translation is the most challenging type of translation. However, translation within EU legal systems should be an easier task since the same concept should be denoted in 24 languages. Translators need to look for terms in their languages, not for equivalent legal concepts in their national legal systems.

The EU legal system is an integral part of the Member States' legal systems.[56] Therefore, although independent and autonomous, EU law and national law influence each other. Consequently, in spite of the terminological and conceptual autonomy of EU law explicitly confirmed in the *CILFIT* case,[57] very few concepts developed within EU legal systems are actually new and original. Although they are EU autonomous concepts, their creation was inspired by and rooted in the Member States' legal systems. Therefore, sometimes it is not easy to evaluate whether the concept is autonomous and EU specific meaning should be ascribed to it or rather the concept belongs to the Member State's national law and its meaning should be established in national doctrines and case law. In the case of doubt, national courts can ask the CJEU for a preliminary ruling. However, as the case law in the area of competition law illustrates, sometimes it is not easy even for the CJEU to find out whether the concept in question is an autonomous concept of EU law.[58]

4 Conclusions

Each official language of an EU Member State may be recognised by the Council of the European Union as an official and working language of EU institutions. Currently, Council Regulation No 1/1958/EEC (Article 1) grants this status to 24 languages. The wording of Article 1 and its literal (linguistic) interpretation assures equality between languages. The formal linguistic equality allows all languages to be used in the same way and to the same extent in the legislative drafting process. As a

[55]Šarčević (1997), pp. 149, 158.

[56]Šarčević (1997), pp. 149, 158.

[57]Para. 19 of the *CILFIT* Judgment, states that "Community law uses terminology which is peculiar to it" and that "legal concepts do not necessarily have the same meaning in Community law and in the law of the various Member States".

[58]See para. 155 of Joined Cases T-122/07 to T-124/07 *Siemens Österreich* [2011] ECR II-793, ECLI:EU:T:2011:70, where the General Court indicates that "the concept of 'joint and several liability for the payment of fines' is an autonomous concept which must be interpreted by reference to the objectives and system of competition law of which it forms part [...]" and para. 67 of Case C-231/11P *Siemens Österreich* [2014] ECLI:EU:C:2014:256, where the CJEU stated that "the General Court erred in law by finding, at paragraph 155 of the judgment under appeal, first, that the concept of joint and several liability for the payment of fines is an autonomous concept".

result and pursuant to Article 4 of Council Regulation No 1/1958/EEC, regulations and documents of general application are drafted in all official languages. The linguistic equality should be reflected not only in legislative drafting but also in legal interpretation. In particular, the CJEU does not derive its interpretation of EU law from only one language version but takes other versions into consideration. This approach should ensure the uniform interpretation of EU law.

The chapter indicates, however, a few exceptions to linguistic equality. Firstly, not all official languages of EU Member States enjoy the status of official and working languages of EU institutions. Turkish, an official language of Cyprus, and Luxemburgish, an official language of Luxembourg, are not official and working languages of the EU. Irish, which is the first official language of Ireland, was not recognised as an EU official and working language until 2007. Secondly, the Council allowed for the exception to the requirement provided by Articles 4 and 5 Council Regulation No 1/1958/EEC, and as regards Irish, the EU's official language, not all documents of general application are drafted and published in this language in the Official Journal. Moreover, although all EU official languages also have a status of working languages of EU institutions, not all working languages are used with the same intensity. Article 1 Council Regulation No 1/1958/EEC makes it possible to use any working language(s) in the EU institutions, whereas Article 6 allows the institutions to decide which of the languages will be used in specific cases. As a result, the distinction between *de jure* and *de facto* working languages is made. The former are languages which enjoy the status of working language in accordance with Regulation No 1/1958/EEC, the latter are languages which are actually used by the institutions.

Although some elements of hierarchy between languages can be observed in the legislative drafting process, interpretation aims at finding a uniform meaning for all language versions despite how a particular version has been prepared. As regards the interpretation of EU law, although the equal authenticity principle requires all language versions to be compared, the analysis of the CJEU's and national courts' judgments reveals that not always this requirement is fulfilled. However, it is not the number of language versions which have been compared that ensures linguistic equality but whether all of them have the same meaning.

References

Adrey JB (2009) Discourse and struggle in minority language policy formation: Corsican language policy in the EU context of governance. Palgrave Macmillan, Basingstoke

Baaij CJW (2011) Presentation on the consequences of discrepancies between language versions in cases of the European Court of Justice. DGT, European Commission, 8 June 2010

Baaij CJW (2012) Fifty years of multilingual interpretation in the European Union. In: Tiersma PM, Solan LM (eds) The Oxford handbook of language and law. Oxford University Press, Oxford, pp 217–233

Baaij CJW (2013) The EU policy on institutional multilingualism: between principles and practicality. Int J Lang Law, 1. https://www.languageandlaw.de/jll/article/view/4/4. Accessed 23 Feb 2018

Ban C (2013) Management and culture in an enlarged European Commission: from diversity to unity. Palgrave Macmillan, New York

Cherubim D (2006) *Das Konzept der "Verkehrssprache" und die frühen geographischen* Berichte über Nordeuropa. In: Arold A (ed) Deutsch am Rande Europas. Tartu University Press, Tartu, pp 13–31

Council of the European Union (2016) Comments on the Council's Rules of Procedure European Council's and Council's Rules of Procedure. http://www.consilium.europa.eu/en/documents-publications/publications/council-rules-procedure-comments/. Accessed 20 Jan 2018

Derlén M (2009) Multilingual interpretation of European Union law. Kluwer Law International, Alphen aan den Rijn

Derlén M (2016) Single text or a single meaning. In: Šarčević S (ed) Language and culture in EU law: multidisciplinary perspectives. Routledge, New York, pp 53–72

Doczekalska A (2008) All originals: fiction and reality of multilingual legal drafting in the European Union and Canada. Unpublished PhD thesis, Florence

Doczekalska A (2009) Drafting and interpretation of EU law – paradoxes of legal multilingualism. In: Grewendorf G, Rathert M (eds) Formal linguistics and law. Mouton de Gruyter, Berlin, pp 339–370

Doczekalska A, Jaśkiewicz J (2014) Wykładnia aktów wielojęzycznego prawa pochodnego Unii Europejskiej przez polskie sądy administracyjne. Zeszyty Naukowe Sądownictwa Administracyjnego 5:66–76

Dragone S (2006) The quality of Community legislation and the role of the European Commission legal revisers. In: Pozzo B, Jacometti V (eds) Multilingualism and the harmonization of European law. Kluwer Law International, Alphen aan den Rijn, pp 99–106

European Commission (2013) Memo of 26.09.2013. Frequently asked questions on languages in Europe. IP/13/875. http://europa.eu/rapid/press-release_MEMO-13-825_en.htm. Accessed 23 Feb 2018

European Commission, Directorate-General for Translation (2018) English style guide. A handbook for authors and translators in the European Commission. https://ec.europa.eu/info/sites/info/files/styleguide_english_dgt_en.pdf. Accessed 23 Feb 2018

European Union (2015) Joint Practical Guide of the European Parliament, the Council and the Commission for persons involved in the drafting of legislation within the Community institutions. Publications Office of the European Union, Luxembourg

Fenet A (2001) Diversité linguistique et construction européenne. Revue trimestrielle de droit européen 37(2):235–269

Frame I (2005) Linguistic oddities in European Union legislation: don't shoot the translator. Clarity 53:22–24. http://www.clarity-international.net/journals/53.pdf. Accessed 20 Jan 2018

Gardner J (2016) Misused English words and expressions in EU publications. https://www.eca.europa.eu/Otherpublications/EN_TERMINOLOGY_PUBLICATION/EN_TERMINOLOGY_PUBLICATION.pdf. Accessed 21 Mar 2018

Gazzola M (2006) Managing multilingualism in the European Union: language policy evaluation for the European Parliament. Lang Policy 5:393–417

Labelle A (2000) La corédaction des lois fédérales au Canada. Vingt ans après: quelques réflexions. In: Proceedings, conference on legal translation, history, theory/ies and practice. ESTI-ASTTI, Geneva and Bern. http://www.tradulex.com/Actes2000/LABELLE.pdf. Accessed 9 Apr 2018

Laakso J, Sarhimaa A, Spiliopoulou Åkermark S, Toivanen R (2016) Towards openly multilingual policies and practices: assessing minority language maintenance across Europe. Multilingual Matters, Bristol

McAuliffe K (2012) Language and law in the European Union: the multilingual jurisprudence of the ECJ. In: Tiersma PM, Solan LM (eds) The Oxford handbook of language and law. Oxford University Press, Oxford, pp 200–216

Phillipson R (2003) English-Only Europe? Challenging language policy. Routledge, New York
Schilling T (2010) Multilingualism and multijuralism: assets of EU legislation and adjudication? Germ Law J 12(7):1460–1491
Special Report No 9/2006 concerning translation expenditure incurred by the Commission, the Parliament and the Council together with the institutions' replies (2006) OJ C 284, 21.11.2006, pp 1–39
Strandvik I (2016) On quality in EU multilingual lawmaking. In: Šarčević S (ed) Language and culture in EU law: multidisciplinary perspectives. Routledge, New York, pp 141–167
Šarčević S (1997) New approach to legal translation. Kluwer Law International, The Hague
Šarčević S (2005) The quest for legislative bilingualism and multilingualism: Co-drafting in Canada and Switzerland. In: Gémar JC, Kasirer N (eds) Jurilinguistique: entre langues et droits Jurilinguistics: between law and language. Les Édition Thémis, Montréal, Bruylant, Brussels, pp 277–292
Truchot C (2003) Languages and supranationality in Europe: the linguistic influence of the European Union. In: Maurais J, Morris MA (eds) Languages in a globalising world. Cambridge University Press, Cambridge, pp 99–110

Agnieszka Doczekalska is an Assistant Professor at the Law School of Kozminski University in Warsaw (Poland). She obtained Ph.D. in Law at the Law Department of the European University in Florence (Italy).

Language and Translation in EU Competition Law: Insights from English, Greek, Italian and Spanish Versions of Legislative Texts

Vilelmini Sosoni

Abstract The present chapter seeks to explore EU Competition Law concepts and terms, such as *exploitative abuses, concerted practice, vertical agreements, leniency,* and *undertaking*, in English, Greek, Italian and Spanish. It draws on the analysis of a multilingual parallel corpus of EU Competition legislation and aims to investigate the strategies used for the formation of terms and their translation under the light of EU Law autonomy and uniform interpretation and the EU's policy of multilingualism. In so doing, it also aspires to establish whether the sought-after unified deterritorialised and hybrid legal culture in the EU can actually exist.

1 Introduction

The autonomy of European Union (EU) Law together with its supremacy and direct effect are key to European integration. Autonomy, in particular, is of paramount importance as it contributes to the creation of the sought-after unified deterritorialised and hybrid legal culture[1] which helps construct a common European identity, which, in turn, concerns the "constitution of a new community with the characteristics and beliefs of *Europeanness*".[2] The autonomy of EU Law is synonymous with a *sui generis* supranational legal system, distinct from both national and international law, with its own growing body of legal concepts and terms.[3] A new conceptual system is thus born which can only be expressed by language.

Yet, language use in the EU is particularly complex and governed to a great extent by the policy of multilingualism which is built on the principles of democracy and

[1]cf. McAuliffe (2011) and Biel (2014a).

[2]Fiorito (2013), p. 9.

[3]Gombos (2014).

V. Sosoni (✉)
Department of Foreign Languages, Translation and Interpreting, Ionian University, Corfu, Greece
e-mail: sosoni@ionio.gr

S. Marino et al. (eds.), *Language and Law*,
https://doi.org/10.1007/978-3-319-90905-9_11

transparent governance and aims at providing EU citizens with access to legislation in their native tongues.[4] The policy was enshrined in the very first Council Regulation of the European Economic Community, adopted in 1958.[5] In essence, it requires that the EU publishes its legislation and all major policy documents in all the official EU languages so that EU citizens, government entities and private organisations are able to understand the rights and obligations that EU membership confers upon them.[6] The main feature of EU multilingualism is the mandatory equal treatment of all the official languages. In fact, although English is the language for most of the draft legislation of the EU, and thereby acts as the basis of much of the post-enactment translation into the official languages, in theory there is no Source Text (ST) and no Target Text (TT), i.e. no translation. This is known as the principle of equal authenticity[7] or plurilinguistic equality.[8] In view of the fact that EU Law has supremacy over national law, this egalitarian approach to all the official languages is politically necessary as it guarantees that all EU citizens are equal before the law. In legal terms, although in most other cases a translated legal text is an informative text which loses its prescriptive nature and has no legal force, in the case of EU Law all 24 language versions have authoritative status[9] and are deemed equally valid and authentic, i.e. they form a single legal instrument. The importance of Regulation No 1/1958/EEC for legislation to be drafted in all the official languages and the equal authenticity of all language versions has also been acknowledged by the Court of Justice of the European Union (CJEU) in the *CILFIT* case.[10]

Within that particularly complex context, the present chapter seeks to explore EU Law concepts and terms—in particular EU Competition Law concepts and terms—in English, Greek, Italian and Spanish on the basis of the analysis of a multilingual corpus of EU Competition legislation. In particular, it aims to investigate the strategies used for the formation of terms and their translation under the light of

[4]Baaij (2012), p. 16.

[5]Council Regulation (EEC) No 1 of 15 April 1958 determining the languages to be used by the European Economic Community (OJ 17, 6.10.1958, p. 385); referred to further as Regulation No 1/1958/EEC.

[6]Somssich et al. (2010), p. 1.

[7]Šarčević (1997), p. 64.

[8]van Els (2001).

[9]cf. Cao (2010), p. 73.

[10]See also paras. 18, 19 and 20 in Case 283/81 *Srl CILFIT* [1982] ECR 3415, ECLI:EU:C:1982:335, which states that: "To begin with, it must be borne in mind that Community legislation is drafted in several languages and that the different language versions are all equally authentic. An interpretation of a provision of Community law thus involves a comparison of the different language versions. It must also be borne in mind, even where the different language versions are entirely in accord with one another, that Community law uses terminology which is peculiar to it. Furthermore, it must be emphasized that legal concepts do not necessarily have the same meaning in Community law and in the law of the various Member States. Finally, every provision of Community law must be placed in its context and interpreted in the light of the provisions of Community law as a whole, regard being had to the objectives thereof and to its state of evolution at the date on which the provision in question is to be applied".

EU Law autonomy and uniform interpretation and the EU's policy of multilingualism. In so doing, it also wishes to establish whether the sought-after unified deterritorialised and hybrid legal culture in the EU can actually exist.

2 The Interface of Language and Law in the EU

2.1 EU Law and the Concept of Autonomy

Unlike the civil law and common law legal systems, the legal system of the EU draws on the traditions of Roman Law and—since the accession of the United Kingdom in 1973—on common law, particularly in the area of attention to precedent. There are three types of EU Law: primary law—which includes treaties—, secondary law—which includes interinstitutional agreements, such as Regulations, Directives, Decisions, Recommendations, and Opinions—and tertiary law—which includes the decisions of the CJEU. These three types of EU Law, known as the *acquis* or body of EU Law, represent the full set of distributive, constituent and regulatory European policies[11] and constitute a melting pot for national legal systems, languages and cultures, interpreted and applied through different institutions and procedures. It is, thus, often termed a hybrid legal system.[12]

Its hybridity is interlinked with the concepts of autonomy, supremacy and direct effect of EU Law, all of which are key to achieving, among others, European integration. Autonomy, in particular, is a fundamental and structural principle of the EU legal order.[13] In simple terms, it refers to self-rule and its importance lies in the fact that it oversteps the traditional divide between international law and domestic law. As Molnár points out

> the autonomy of Union law can be basically conceived in two ways: vis-à-vis either international law (*external aspect of autonomy*) or the domestic legal systems of the Member States (*internal aspect of autonomy*).[14]

The EU legal autonomy makes it possible to create new autonomous concepts,[15] the meaning of which is specific to EU Law and which are denoted by system-bound terms with no equivalent in other legal systems and their legal languages.[16] In other words, these concepts enjoy a status of semantic independence, i.e. their meaning is

---

[11]Kaeding (2007), p. 3.

[12]cf. Koskinen (2000), p. 63; Mattila (2006), p. 108; Biel (2014a).

[13]cf. Barents (2004), Szurek (2007), pp. 57–92; de Witte (2010), pp. 141–155; van Rossem (2013).

[14]Molnár (2016), p. 433.

[15]See also para. 19 in Case *CILFIT*, which states that "Community law uses terminology which is peculiar to it" and that "legal concepts do not necessarily have the same meaning in Community law and in the law of the various Member States".

[16]Šarčević (1997), pp. 149, 158.

not to be equated with the meaning that they possess in domestic or international law.[17]

Yet, in practical terms, it has been found that very few concepts developed within EU legal systems are actually new and original or as Kjaer argues "stating autonomy does not automatically result in autonomy".[18] As Mattila aptly observes, there are in essence three types of concepts within the conceptual system of EU Law: (1) general legal concepts, (2) concepts known in one or more Member States' legal systems and (3) original concepts (created within the framework of the EU).[19] However, the creation of these "original concepts", i.e. EU autonomous concepts, is rooted in the Member States' legal systems. Like in the case of international law, these concepts "reflect back"[20] on the national systems, potentially modifying or redefining them.[21] As a result, legal terms that originally represented national legal concepts are increasingly used with reference to supranational law. Therefore, sometimes it is not easy to evaluate whether a given concept is autonomous within EU Law or whether the concept belongs to the Member State's national law and its meaning should be established in national doctrines and case law. In cases of doubt, national courts can ask the CJEU for a preliminary ruling; in many cases, though, it is not easy even for the CJEU to establish whether the concept in question is an autonomous concept of EU Law.[22]

2.2 The Complexity of EU Legal Language

These autonomous legal concepts cannot be embodied and represented in any way other than by using linguistic signs. In other words, they need "linguistic clothing". A legal norm and its linguistic expression are, thus, inseparable from each other. Yet, this embodiment is no easy task, especially under the EU's policy of multilingualism and principle of plurilinguistic equality. If a legal concept is to be interpreted and applied uniformly by everyone, it has to be communicated (a) with exactly the same meaning in 24 languages, without any distortions,[23] free from any semantic or cultural connotations or traditions a given linguistic sign might have in that language and (b) in such a way that the same legal effect be reached in all circumstances. From

[17]Letsas (2004), p. 282.

[18]Kjær (2015), p. 105.

[19]Mattila (2006), p. 119.

[20]Giannoni (2003), p. 223.

[21]Catenaccio (2008), p. 260.

[22]See, for instance, para. 155 of Joined Cases T-122/07 to T-124/07 *Siemens Österreich* [2011] ECR II-793, ECLI:EU:T:2011:70, where the General Court indicates that "the concept of 'joint and several liability for the payment of fines' is an autonomous concept which must be interpreted by reference to the objectives and system of competition law of which it forms part".

[23]Gombos (2014).

the point of lawmaking, challenges emerge mostly due to the fact that each Member State has its own legal system and that the overall approach and the specific concepts of these are sometimes as different from each other as, for instance, the common law system used in England and the continental law system used in Germany. On the other hand, in the case of languages spoken in more than one Member States, a single language may represent more than one legal systems. For instance, English is the language of the common law system of England but also of the continental law system in Malta and Scotland. The case of Scotland is in fact particularly puzzling as England and Scotland are parts of one and the same Member State, i.e. the United Kingdom of Great Britain and Northern Ireland. Nevertheless, even legal systems similarly based on continental law may display differences in their legal concepts and terminology, which is partly explained by the different "lifeworld"—to use Habermas' term[24]—, i.e. the different paths the culture and traditions of each country have taken so far and, partly, by differences inherent in the way the community of speakers of a certain language construct and view the world and create concepts through which to label its phenomena.

Moreover, and from a purely linguistic perspective, the language of EU Law in its attempt to express new and pan-European concepts inevitably becomes a new legal variant of the official languages,[25] a Eurolect,[26] which is characterised by a specific language or style.[27] Eurolect is perceived as a multilingual legal language realised in distinct legal varieties of national languages with an interdependent conceptual system. Like EU Law, it is also considered to be hybrid at the intersection of underlying cultures and languages,[28] neutralised and deculturalised[29] so that it can facilitate multilingual translation[30] and uniform interpretation and application of EU Law in all Member States; this, in turn, is deemed to guarantee linguistic equality and legal certainty.

Eurolect is also shaped by a number of factors which come at play when drafting and translating legislation, i.e. non-native speaker (NNS) drafting, collective multilingual drafting and drafting by native speakers who work in multilingual environments,[31] use of controlled language prescribed in the institutional drafting guidelines with a view to achieving homogeneity and consistency but also with a view to minimising translation problems and inaccuracies.[32] As Biel observes, there is an

---

[24]Habermas (1981).

[25]According to de Corte (2003), p. 70, the emergence of Eurolect "is inevitable in that the legal system set up by the Treaties requires a specific Community language".

[26]cf. Koskinen (2000), Sosoni (2011) and Biel (2014a).

[27]cf. Trosborg (1997), Koskinen (2000) and Tosi (2005).

[28]Trosborg (1997), p. 147; Tirkkonen-Condit (2001).

[29]Caliendo (2004), p. 163.

[30]Pozzo (2012), p. 1198.

[31]Wagner et al. (2010), p. 76; Sosoni (2011), p. 87.

[32]Biel (2014b), pp. 6–7.

> institutionalisation of translation and high standardisation and formulaicity of EU texts with norms devised to rationalise, standardise and control the translation process.[33]

By extension, EU legal language is affected by a clear preference for literal translation strategies and avoidance of cultural adaptation.[34]

3 The Curious Case of EU Competition Law

It emerges from the discussion above that EU Law is unique, that the drafting and translation of EU legal texts is particularly complex and that the language used therein is a new legal variant with inherent idiosyncrasies.

The focus of this study is on EU Competition Law which promotes the maintenance of competition within the European Single Market by regulating anti-competitive conduct by companies to ensure that they do not form cartels and monopolies that would damage the interests of society.[35] The main authority for applying competition law within the EU is the Directorate General for Competition of the European Commission, although State aids in some sectors, such as agriculture, are handled by other Directorates General.

Nowadays, European Competition Law derives mainly from Articles 101 to 109 of the Treaty on the Functioning of the European Union (TFEU),[36] as well as a number of Regulations and Directives. Four main policy areas include:

a. Cartels or control of collusion and other anti-competitive practices.
b. Market dominance or prevention of the abuse of dominant market positions.
c. Mergers, control of proposed mergers, acquisitions and joint ventures involving companies that have a specified amount of turnover in the EU.
d. State aid, control of direct and indirect aid given by EU Member States or through State resources to companies.

Within EU Law, the case of EU Competition Law is particularly complex due to its hybrid nature given that it is positioned at the intersection of finance, economics

[33] Biel (2014b), p. 7.

[34] cf. Garzone (2000), p. 6; Koskinen (2000), pp. 54–56; Wagner et al. (2010), p. 64; Sosoni (2012), p. 87.

[35] In the words of the Directorate General for Competition of the European Commission, the EU Competition Law's aim is "to provide everyone in Europe with better quality goods and services at lower prices. Competition policy is about applying rules to make sure companies compete fairly with each other. This encourages enterprise and efficiency, creates a wider choice for consumers and helps reduce prices and improve quality. These are the reasons why the EU fights anticompetitive behaviour, reviews mergers and state aid and encourages liberalisation". Overview: making markets work better, available at http://ec.europa.eu/competition/general/overview_en.html (Accessed 20 Feb 2018).

[36] Articles 101 to 109 of the Treaty on the Functioning of the European Union (OJ C 167, 3.6.2013, p. 88).

and law and includes numerous financial and economic terms, but also due to historical and socio-political reasons. First of all, the foundations of EU Competition Law were laid right from the beginning, with the predecessor of the EU, the Treaty establishing the European Coal and Steel Community (ECSC)[37] which was created in 1951. Given that the ECSC was born in the aftermath of World War II, it was of great importance to the founding fathers that Germany would not resume the strong position in the coal and steel market that it had enjoyed before the war. In order to deal with this, the ECSC was established, creating a legal community where control over the industry was exercised within a single regime, and the services of those industries affected were placed in the hands of the community. Since the ECSC existed to control industries, it became clear to the founding fathers that it would be necessary to create some form of competition regulation. This was ensured with Articles 65 and 66 of the ECSC Treaty. Article 65[38] prohibited anti-competitive behaviour and banned cartels, while Article 66 included a provision on concentrations (i.e. mergers), and another on the abuse of a dominant position by firms.[39]

These articles were, however, inspired by the United States (US),[40] where modern competition policy was born with the adoption of the Sherman Antitrust Act by the US Congress in 1890 and also with the adoption of the Clayton Act and the Federal Trade Commission Act in 1914. These Acts, first, restrict the formation of cartels and prohibit other collusive practices regarded as being in restraint of trade. Second, they restrict the mergers and acquisitions of organisations that could substantially lessen competition. Third, they prohibit the creation of a monopoly and the abuse of monopoly power. The US did not officially take part in the negotiations because the negotiators wanted to avoid the danger of the project being seen as US-controlled, but they did play a role, as they provided the drafters of the Treaty with basic ideas,[41] while many claim that they in fact set as a condition for their withdrawal from Germany the introduction of a Competition Law.[42]

---

[37]Treaty establishing the European Coal and Steel Community. No longer in force, Date of end of validity: 23.7.2002. ELI: http://data.europa.eu/eli/treaty/ceca/sign, (Accessed 20 Feb 2018); referred to further as ECSC Treaty.

[38]In particular, Article 65(1) of the Treaty establishing the European Coal and Steel Community states: "All agreements between undertakings, decisions by associations of undertakings and concerted practices tending directly or indirectly to prevent, restrict or distort normal competition within the common market shall be prohibited, and in particular those tending:

(a) to fix or determine prices;
(b) to restrict or control production, technical development or investment;
(c) to share markets, products, customers or sources of supply."

[39]Papadopoulos (2010), p. 13.

[40]cf. Harding and Joshua (2003), p. 94; Warlouzet and Witschke (2012), Patel and Schweitzer (2013) and Buch-Hansen and Levallois (2015).

[41]Gerber (2010), p. 342.

[42]cf. Maher (2000), p. 155.

German law was, thus, also key in the drafting and interpretation of the competition provisions.

Under the light of the US competition policy inspiration, the influence of the English language[43] on EU Competition Law is unquestionable. Yet, the paradox is that Articles 65 and 66 were enacted before the accession of the UK to the EU, so they were drafted in French, which was the main drafting language at the time, and to a lesser degree in German. It becomes apparent that the birth of EU Competition Law terminology is very complex and cannot be studied without taking into account this broader socio-political and historical framework within which it was developed and has been applied.

4 Naming Concepts and Creating Terms

In the sections that follow, an attempt is made to explore EU Competition Law concepts by investigating the strategies used for their naming and for their translation.[44] In the present section, the main term formation strategies are analysed and discussed.

According to Valeontis and Mantzari,[45] terms are the linguistic representation of concepts.[46] However, contrary to the situation prevailing in general language or Language for General Purposes (LGP), where the arbitrariness of the linguistic sign is fully acceptable, special languages or Languages for Special Purposes (LSPs)[47] endeavor to make the process of designation systematic, based on certain specified

---

[43] American English rather than British English due to the US influence.

[44] In light of the importance of meaning for legal translation in the EU context, it has been claimed that comparative law and translation theories may not be the most relevant theories to apply, cf. Kjær (2015), p. 92; terminological approaches have been shown to be more appropriate since they place meaning at the forefront and address the issue of conceptualisation, cf. Bajčić (2017), p. 129.

[45] Valeontis and Mantzari (2006), p. 5.

[46] According to Picht and Draskau (1985), p. 96 a concept is commonly defined as an element of thought, a mental construct that represents a class of objects. Concepts consist of a series of characteristics that are shared by a class of individual objects; these characteristics, which are also concepts, allow human beings to structure thought and to communicate. In order to communicate concepts and their supporting propositions, speakers use written or oral linguistic signs made up of a term or group of terms, or some other type of symbols. A distinction between words and terms is made by Sager et al. who claim that "The items which are characterised by special reference within a discipline are the 'terms' of that discipline and collectively they form its 'terminology'" (p. 75).

[47] According to Picht and Draskau (1985), p. 3 an LSP is a "formalised and codified variety of language, used for special purposes in a legitimate context – that is to say, with the function of communicating information of a specialist nature at any level – at the highest level of complexity, between initiate experts, and, at lower levels of complexity, with the aim of informing or initiating other interested parties, in the most economic, precise and unambiguous terms possible". LGP, on the other hand, is a general reservoir on which the LSPs of the various special areas draw.

linguistic rules, so that terms reflect the concept characteristics they refer to as precisely as possible. The aim of the systematisation of these principles is to achieve transparency and consistency in the linguistic representation of knowledge. According to ISO 704:2009,[48] the general recommendations which should be observed when connecting concepts to terms are linguistic appropriateness, linguistic economy and derivability.

As far as the methods for term formation or term formation mechanisms are concerned, ISO 704:2009 identifies the following three:

a. Creating new forms/Neologisms/Neoterms
b. Using existing forms, and
c. Translingual borrowing.

The first two are used mainly for primary term formation and the third for secondary term formation. The analysis of primary and secondary term formation mechanisms mentioned in the sections that follow is based on ISO 704:2009.[49]

4.1 Creation of New Forms to Name New Concepts/Neologisms/Neoterms

a. Derivation: The process of derivation is the formation of a new term by adding one or more affixes to a root or to a word, e.g. *proportionality, appreciability, επικουρικότητα* [subsidiarity],[50] *competitor, risarcimento* [compensation].
b. Compounding:

> Compounding involves combining existing words or word elements to create a new form that contains two or more roots but designates a single concept. Compounds may be complex terms, phrases or blends. The elements of the complex term or phrase often include qualifiers to a superordinate term in the form of adjectives, proper names, noun or verbal qualifiers, and may be joined by a hyphen or by fusing, or may not be joined at all. Blends result from fusing two or more words, after one or more of them have been clipped[51]

[48]ISO 704:2009, Terminology Work: Principles and Methods (2009). ISO 704 is a standard that was produced by Subcommittee SC1 of the ISO Technical Committee (TC) 37. It "establishes the basic principles and methods for preparing and compiling terminologies both inside and outside the framework of standardization, and describes the links between objects, concepts, and their terminological representations. It also establishes general principles governing the formation of designations and the formulation of definitions. Full and complete understanding of these principles requires some background knowledge of terminology work. The principles are general in nature and this document is applicable to terminology work in scientific, technological, industrial, administrative and other fields of knowledge" (2009), p. v.

[49]ISO 704:2009, Terminology Work: Principles and Methods (2009), pp. 51–55; cf. Valeontis and Mantzari (2006), pp. 5–8; Krimpas (2017).

[50]Back-translations are provided by the author in square brackets in all cases of non-English terms.

[51]ISO 704:2009, Terminology Work: Principles and Methods (2009), pp. 51–52.

e.g. *Member State, cyclical change, άδεια εκμετάλλευσης* [operating licence], *attivi materiali* [tangible assets], *cross-holdings, non-reciprocal agreement, flexicurity*.

c. Abbreviated Forms: Shortening serves the purpose of creating more concise forms—especially for frequently used terms—and also of creating names that are easy to remember for lengthy terms which are not clearly recognisable as terminological units. The following types of abbreviated forms can be distinguished:

   i. Short form: The short form is an abbreviated form of a complex term or name of considerable length in words. It uses fewer words in order to designate the same concept, e.g. full form: *Court of Justice of the European Communities* = short form: *Court.*
   ii. Abbreviation: Created by omitting words or parts of the words of which a term consists, e.g. full form: *number* = abbreviation: *No.*
   iii. Clipped form: A clipped term is formed by truncating the front, middle or back portion of a single-word term, e.g. full form: *parachute* = clipped form: *chute,* full form: *prefabricated house* = clipped form: *prefab.*
   iv. Initialism: Initialisms are formed from the first letters of each of the elements of a complex term or name. They are always pronounced letter by letter, e.g. *TFEU, ECSC, EEA*.
   v. Acronym: Acronyms are formed by combining the initial letters or syllables of all or several of the elements of a complex term or name. Acronyms are always pronounced syllabically just like regular words, e.g. *EFTA, ECOFIN, Coreper*.

4.2 Using Existing Forms

a. Conversion: This term-formation mechanism involves changing the syntactic category (e.g. grammatical function) of existing forms, e.g. using an adjective as a noun (very common in Greek) or a noun as a verb (which never occurs in Greek, but is quite frequent in English),[52] e.g. *bail* (NOUN)/bail (VERB), *reserve* (VERB)/*reserve* (NOUN), *market* (NOUN)/*market* (VERB).
b. Terminologisation: This is a general procedure through which a word or phrase from the general language or Language for General Purposes (LGP) is transformed into a term designating a concept in a special language or Language for Special Purposes (LSP), e.g. *appeal* in LGP refers to "a request to the public for money, information, or help", while in LSP it means "a request made to a court of law or to someone in authority to change a previous decision".[53]

[52] Valeontis and Mantzari (2006), p. 7.

[53] Definition of *appeal*, Cambridge Dictionary, available at https://dictionary.cambridge.org/dictionary/english/appeal (Accessed 20 Feb 2018).

c. Semantic transfer within a special language: It is the process whereby an existing term in an LSP is used in order to designate a different concept, by an analogous extension. In the case of the EU, we could say that this also involves the recontextualisation of concepts from national discourses and use of existing terms with an extension of their semantic meaning.[54] This is quite risky given that many terms in EU legal texts appear identical to terms commonly used in national legislation, although they refer to different concepts. An example of this is the term *EU citizenship*[55] which does not have the usual meaning that we associate it with. Although it invariably refers to a national of a particular country, in the EU context its meaning had changed to denote certain privileges conferred on nationals of any EU Member State, such as a right to vote in local elections in other Member States. The different meaning of this concept even provoked strong debates among Member States after it was introduced by the Maastricht Treaty in 1992 and even led to its temporary non-ratification.[56] The term *foreclosure* is an interesting example from the realm of EU Competition Law. It is used in UK law and it refers to the

> remedy available to a mortgagee when the mortgagor has failed to payoff a mortgage by the contractual date for redemption. The mortgagee is entitled to bring an action in the High Court, seeking an order fixing a date to pay off the debt; if the mortgagor does not pay by that date he will be foreclosed, i.e. he will lose the mortgaged property. If, after this order (a foreclosure order nisi) is made, the mortgagor does not pay on the date and at the place (usually a room in the Royal Courts of Justice) named, the foreclosure is made absolute and the property thereafter belongs to the mortgagee. However, the court has discretion to allow the mortgagor to reopen the foreclosure and thereby regain his property.[57]

In EU Competition Law, though, the term *foreclosure* is used to describe any instance where actual or potential rivals' access to supplies or markets is hampered or eliminated as a result of the merger, thereby reducing these companies' ability and/or incentive to compete. As a result of such foreclosure, the merging companies—and, possibly, some of its competitors as well—may be able to profitably increase the price (14) charged to consumers. These instances give rise to a significant impediment to effective competition and are therefore referred to hereafter as 'anticompetitive foreclosure'.[58]

d. Transdisciplinary borrowing: In transdisciplinary or internal borrowing, a term from one subject field is borrowed and used to designate a new concept in another subject field within the same language. Take for example the term *entity* in business which means

[54] cf. Gombos (2014).

[55] For an extensive discussion of EU citizenship see, for instance, Wiener (1997), Shaw (1997, 2007) and O'Leary (1998).

[56] Čavoški (2017), p. 68.

[57] Definition of *foreclosure*, Oxford Dictionary of Law (2003), p. 207.

[58] Guidelines on the assessment of non-horizontal mergers under the Council Regulation on the control of concentrations between undertakings (OJ C 265, 18.10.2008, p. 6).

> an organization established as a separate existence for the purposes of taxes. Corporations, limited liability companies, and sole proprietorships are types of common business entities[59]

and the term *entity* in law which means

> an association, corporation, partnership, proprietorship, trust, or individual that has legal standing in the eyes of law. A legal entity has legal capacity to enter into agreements or contracts, assume obligations, incur and pay debts, sue and be sued in its own right, and to be held responsible for its actions.[60]

4.3 *Translingual Borrowing*

Legal translation needs to meet two types of equivalence: communicative equivalence and legal equivalence. According to the principle of legal equivalence, legal translation will seek to achieve identity of meaning between original and translation, i.e., identity of propositional content as well as identity of legal effects,[61] while at the same time pursuing the objective of reflecting the intent of the original author. In that sense, faithfulness to the original text is considered of paramount importance in legal translation. In the case of EU multilingual law, however

> the principle of fidelity to the source text is losing ground to the principle of fidelity to the single instrument[62]

and the success of translation is determined by its uniform interpretation and application. Under that light, at the terminological level, literal equivalents are preferred.[63] Literal equivalents fall under the category of translingual borrowing, which involves the introduction of terms which exist in one language into another language by means of direct borrowing and loan translation or calques.

a. Direct borrowing: This mechanism refers to the full adoption of terms from a given language during the process of secondary term formation. The borrowed term can be identical to the one of the source language, e.g. the borrowing of the term *acquis* from French into English, or it can differ in terms of pronunciation, spelling and declination, e.g. the borrowing of the indeclinable loan word *στούντιο* [studio] from English into Greek. The term *dumping* is a very interesting case in the context of EU trade policy, since it is borrowed directly from English in almost all of the EU official languages. In Danish, Dutch, Czech, German,

[59]Definition of *business entity*, Business Dictionary, available at http://www.businessdictionary.com/definition/business-entity.html (Accessed 20 Feb 2018).

[60]Definition of *legal entity*, Business Dictionary, available at http://www.businessdictionary.com/definition/legal-entity.html (Accessed 20 Feb 2018).

[61]Sager (1993), p. 180.

[62]Šarčević (1997), p. 112.

[63]cf. Garzone (2000), p. 6; Biel (2007), p. 154.

Italian, Maltese, Spanish, Croatian, French, Polish, Portuguese, Romanian, Slovakian and Slovenian it is transferred in Latin characters without any change, while in Greek, Bulgarian, Gaelic, Estonian, Hungarian, Latvian, Lithuanian and Swedish it is either transferred with slight morphological changes or is transliterated. Interestingly, in Finnish, the term used to refer to *dumping* is *polkumyynti*, which is neither a transliteration nor a translation of the English term *dumping*. It is a blend of the terms *polkuhinta* [very low price] and *myynti* [selling, trading].[64] Another interesting point that is worth mentioning with respect to the term formation mechanism of direct borrowing is that in law borrowing from Latin is common and is used predominantly for primary term formation. For instance, a company formed under community legislation is named *societas Europaea*, which also known as *European company*.

b. Loan translation/Calque: Interlingual borrowing most often occurs via loan translation or calque. The morphological elements of a term or whole words from the source language are translated literally, i.e. "word for word", in order to form a new term in the target language (TL), e.g. *online* in English becomes *en ligne* in French, *acquis communautaire* in French becomes *κοινοτικό κεκτημένο* in Greek and *acervo comunitario* in Spanish.

In the cases of direct borrowings and loan translations/calques, a clarification is often provided in the form of an additional word, notes or glosses. Sometimes even couplets are used, that is, citations of the source text in parenthesis, preceded by the literal equivalent.[65]

Apart from translingual borrowing, another strategy employed by legal translators is the use of functional equivalents, i.e. terms in the TL which denote a concept or institution, the function of which is the same or similar as that in the source legal system.[66] Yet, in the EU context, although the use of functional equivalents may sometimes be necessary in order to ensure a proper understanding of EU legislation, most often than not they denote concepts of particular legal traditions that have different scopes of application in national laws than in EU Law.[67] In other words, they can be misleading; for that reason, supranational, neutral terms without any "immediate" national connotations are preferred.[68]

---

[64]Special thanks to Professor Mikhail Mikhailov from the University of Tampere who helped me identify the strategy for the formation of the Finnish term *polkumyynti*.

[65]Jopek-Bosiacka (2013), p. 120.

[66]Alcaraz Varó and Hughes (2002), pp. 184–185; Šarčević (1988), pp. 456–459.

[67]Kjær (2014), p. 434; Bajčić (2017), p. 132.

[68]cf. Wagner et al. (2010), p. 65; Prieto Ramos (2014), p. 319.

5 Material and Methodology

In order to study how terms are actually formed in EU Competition Law, a corpus-based approach is adopted.[69] In particular, a multilingual parallel corpus[70] of EU Competition legislation is used. This was partly compiled in the framework of the project *Training action for legal practitioners: Linguistic skills and translation in EU Competition Law*. More specifically, jurists and linguists[71] from the five participating academic institutions[72] compiled, *inter alia*, a list of key EU Competition legislation texts; then, the linguists downloaded the English, Italian, Spanish, Polish, Greek and Croatian versions of those key legislative texts from the EUR-Lex[73] and Curia[74] websites and converted them into text files with UTF-8 encoding. For the purposes of the present study, the English corpus (Corpus A), the Greek corpus (Corpus B), the Italian corpus (Corpus C) and the Spanish corpus (Corpus D) were extended, and each includes 35 legal acts, i.e. 19 Regulations, 15 Directives and Articles 101–109 TFEU. With the exception of Articles 101–109, the rest of the legal acts were all drafted during the period after the UK's accession to the EU. i.e. after 1 January 1973; in particular, the oldest legal act in the corpus is Directive 98/6/EC of the European Parliament and of the Council of 16 February 1998 on consumer protection in the indication of the prices of products offered to

[69]A distinction between corpus-based and corpus-driven language study was introduced by Tognini-Bonelli (2001), pp. 84–85 who notes that corpus-based studies typically use corpus data in order to explore a theory or hypothesis, with the aim to validate it, refute it or refine it, while corpus-driven studies use the corpus as the sole source of a given hypothesis about language. A corpus-based approach is used in this study, since an assumption is made about the formation and translation strategies of terms on the basis of the existing bibliography which claims that the use of literal equivalents is preferred when translating EU legal texts.

[70]Several types of multilingual corpora can be distinguished. Unfortunately, the terminology used to describe the different types is inconsistent and confusing, cf. Baker (1995, 1999), Hartmann (1996), Johansson (1998). For the purposes of this study, we use the typology and terminology put forward by McEnery and Hardie (2012) who distinguish between multilingual comparable corpora and multilingual parallel corpora. They define a comparable corpus as one which contains components in two or more languages that have been collected using the same sampling method—but are not translations of each other—, while they define a parallel corpus as one which contains source texts and their translations. Although, as pointed out in 10.1, in theory there is no ST and no TT, in practical terms approximately 95% of the legislation adopted in the co-decision procedure is drafted in English, cf. Dragone (2006), p. 100. The English version is, therefore, used as the ST in almost 95% of the cases.

[71]I would like to extend my thanks to Stavros Kozobolis, PhD candidate at the Department of Foreign Languages, Translation and Interpreting of the Ionian University for compiling the Greek corpus and for helping extend the Spanish and Italian corpora.

[72]Università degli Studi dell'Insubria, Uniwersytet Warszawski, Ionian University, University of Rijeka-Jean Monnet Inter-University Centre of Excellence Opatija and Universidad de Burgos.

[73]http://eur-lex.europa.eu/homepage.html (Accessed 20 Feb 2018).

[74]https://curia.europa.eu (Accessed 20 Feb 2018).

Table 1 The multilingual parallel corpus of EU Competition legislation

	Number of files	Number of tokens	Number of types	TTR
Corpus A (English)	35	531,260	7328	0.013
Corpus B (Greek)	35	544,678	15,935	0.029
Corpus C (Italian)	35	558,449	11,062	0.019
Corpus D (Spanish)	35	601,961	11,467	0.019

consumers,[75] while the most recent one is Directive (EU) 2016/943 of the European Parliament and of the Council of 8 June 2016 on the protection of undisclosed know-how and business information (trade secrets) against their unlawful acquisition, use and disclosure.[76] This means that, on the basis of the fact that approximately 95% of the legislation adopted in the co-decision procedure is drafted in English,[77] all the legal acts of Corpus A were most probably drafted in English. Under the light of the above, the focus in the present study is on term formation in English, while translation is discussed with respect to English, Greek, Italian and Spanish.

Following the classification of legal texts according to their function, the corpora consist of prescriptive texts with a normative purpose[78] and equal legal force, i.e. they are all equally authentic legal texts, irrespective of their original status. By virtue of this process, such texts "are not mere translations of the law, but the law itself".[79] The audience is very wide and may include: politicians, civil servants, judges, lawyers, and other law professionals, and also natural and legal persons who need to abide by it and are affected by it.

The tools used for the building and analysis of the corpora were *Sketchengine*[80] and *YouAlign*.[81]

As can be seen in Table 1, the Type to Token Ratio (TTR)[82] is 0.013 in the English corpus (Corpus A), 0.019 in the Italian and Spanish corpora (Corpus C and Corpus D) and 0.029 in the Greek corpus (Corpus B). Given that the corpora were not lemmatized, this variation can be attributed to the fact that Greek, Italian and Spanish are more inflectional languages than English, i.e. they have more inflectional variants of a base form than English.

[75]Directive 98/6/EC of the European Parliament and of the Council of 16 February 1998 on consumer protection in the indication of the prices of products offered to consumers (OJ L 80, 18.3.1998, p. 27).

[76]Directive (EU) 2016/943 of the European Parliament and of the Council of 8 June 2016 on the protection of undisclosed know-how and business information (trade secrets) against their unlawful acquisition, use and disclosure (OJ L 157, 15.6.2016, p. 1).

[77]Dragone (2006), p. 100.

[78]Šarčević (1997), p. 11; Cao (2007), pp. 9–10.

[79]Šarčević (1997), p. 20.

[80]https://www.sketchengine.eu/ (Accessed 20 Apr 2018).

[81]https://youalign.com/ (Accesses 20 Apr 2018).

[82]The TTR rather than the Standardised Type to Token Ratio (STTR) is used in the present analysis because the corpora are of similar size.

As the aim of the study was to explore EU Competition Law terms, the first step after the compilation of the corpora was to identify key legal terms related to competition in the EU in the English corpus (Corpus A). This identification involved automatic as well as manual methods. We first used Sketchengine in order to extract keywords/terms—including multi-words—against two reference corpora, i.e. EUR-Lex 2/2016 Corpus and DGT Eng Corpus, and then we sorted the lists manually. We left out LGP lexical items, e.g. *fulfil, accumulate, conformity, organisation, indent, jeopardise, function, paragraph, systemically, four-month period*; prepositional phrases, e.g. *in accordance with, pursuant to*; technical and scientific terms, e.g. *aquaculture, emissions, algorithmic, information society, urban development, digital content*; general business and financial terms, e.g. *insolvency, credit institution, liquidity, SME*; general EU terms, e.g. *directive, proportionality, subsidiarity, European Commission, European Parliamen*t, and general legal terms, e.g. *provision, amend, unlawful, authorise, national law, third party*. The manual sorting and analysis led to the identification of the 10 most frequently used terms.

The renderings of those terms in the Greek, Italian and Spanish corpora were then identified with the help of *YouAlign* and *Sketchengine*. First, *YouAlign* was used to create bilingual aligned tmx files. Then, those files were uploaded on *Sketchengine* for the creation of parallel corpora and the extraction of terms.

6 Analysis of English Terms and Their Greek, Spanish and Italian Translations

The key EU Competition Law terms in English, Greek, Italian and Spanish appear in Table 2.

Table 2 Key EU Competition legislation terms

English	Greek	Italian	Spanish
aid	ενίσχυση	aiuto	ayuda
concentration	συγκέντρωση	concentrazione	concentración
concerted practice	εναρμονισμένη πρακτική	práctica concertada	pratica concordata
de minimis aid	ενίσχυση de minimis	aiuto de minimis	ayuda de minimis
dominant position	δεσπόζουσα θέση	posizione dominante	posición dominante
enforcement system	σύστημα επιβολής κυρώσεων	sistema di esecuzione	sistema de aplicación
exploitative abuse	καταχρηστική εκμετάλλευση ισχύος στην αγορά	abuso di sfruttamento	abuso de explotación
leniency	επιεικής μεταχείριση	clemenza	clemencia
undertaking	επιχείρηση	impresa	empresa
vertical agreement	κάθετη συμφωνία	accordo verticale	acuerdo vertical

6.1 Term Formation in EU Competition Law: Insights from English

First, it arises from the analysis that the origin of the terms is often blurred; it cannot always be safely established whether they are neologisms or whether they constitute products of a semantic transfer within the legal language with the corresponding concepts having been recontextualised from the national systems of the EU Member States or from another system outside the EU borders. This is mainly due to the historical and sociopolitical reasons mentioned in 10.3. Secondly, the analysis of the ten terms under attention reveals three main types of term formation: (a) formation through semantic transfer and recontextualisation, (b) creation of new terms to name new concepts, i.e. neologisms, and (c) translingual borrowing.

6.1.1 Semantic Transfer and Recontextualisation

The term *concentration* is used for the first time in EU Law in the ECSC Treaty, in French. However, the term was widely used in US Law which, as pointed out already, inspired the enactment of Articles 65 and 66 of the ECSC Treaty regarding competition. In US Antitrust Law, *concentration* generally refers to the concentration of economic power in the hands of fewer than before; it essentially refers to mergers and acquisitions. In EU Competition Law, a *concentration* is more concretely defined, i.e. it arises

> where two or more previously independent undertakings merge (merger), where an undertaking acquires control of another undertaking (acquisition of control), or where a joint venture is created, performing on a lasting basis all the functions of an autonomous economic entity (full-function joint venture).[83]

This all-encompassing definition means that the term *concentration* applies to various types of transactions, such as mergers, acquisitions, takeovers and joint ventures that cede significant control of operational and financial management to the parent body.[84]

The second case of term formation through semantic transfer is the term *vertical agreement*. In US Antitrust Law and in particular under the 1890 Sherman Act, the 1914 Federal Trade Commission Act and the 1914 Clayton Act—which continue to regulate the conduct and organisation of business corporations—there are two types of agreements, i.e. horizontal agreements between competing businesses that include price fixing, and vertical agreements between sellers and buyers that include engaging in resale price maintenance.[85] In EU Competition Law, a *vertical agreement* refers to an

---

[83]Articles 3(1) and (2) of Council Regulation (EC) No 139/2004 of 20 January 2004 on the control of concentrations between undertakings (OJ L 24, 29.1.2004, p. 1).

[84]cf. Alese (2008).

[85]cf. van den Bergh (2016).

> agreement or concerted practice entered into between two or more undertakings each of which operates, for the purposes of the agreement, at a different level of the production or distribution chain, and relating to the conditions under which the parties may purchase, sell or resell certain goods or services.[86]

The term was thus inspired by US Antitrust Law, but the concept was recontextualised and adapted to the specific needs and circumstances of EU Competition Law.

The third term formed through semantic transfer is *concerted practice*. It refers to the coordination between undertakings which, without having reached the stage of concluding a formal agreement, have knowingly substituted practical cooperation for the risks of competition. Article 101(1) TFEU[87] prohibits agreements and concerted practices which have as their object or effect the prevention, restriction or distortion of competition—except where pro-competitive benefits produced by that agreement outweigh the restrictive effects on competition. These general prohibitions and exceptions are elaborated upon in guidelines published by the European Commission,[88] while the meaning of *concerted practice* has been the subject of much judicial consideration.[89] The origin of the concept is particularly blurred; several scholars have hypothesised that the concept of *concerted practice* in EU Competition Law was directly imported from US Antirust legislation. For instance, Goyder[90] has asserted that none of the European Member States had a concept equivalent to "concerted actions" or "concerted practices" in their domestic laws prior to the enactment of the relevant Articles in the Treaty of Rome. However, in 1953 France issued an executive order prohibiting anti-competitive practices, including "actions concertées" [concerted actions]. Theories that try to interpret the meaning of the concept of "concerted practices" in Article 101 of the Treaty of Rome are therefore incomplete when they only look at the US Sherman Act or US common law. The legislative history surrounding the implementation of concerted actions in France should not be forgotten, as France had a key role during the drafting of the Treaty of Rome in 1957. The complexity and specificity of the concept and its linguistic embodiment thus become apparent as does the recontextualisation of the concept and its transfer into the EU Competition Law conceptual system.

The term *enforcement system* is also formed through semantic transfer. It is originally related to a sociopolitical concept which refers to the process of ensuring compliance with laws, regulations, rules, standards, or social norms. In US Antitrust Law, enforcement is based on criminal law, with financial and custodial penalties

---

[86]Commission Regulation (EU) No 330/2010 of 20 April 2010 on the application of Article 101 (3) of the Treaty on the Functioning of the European Union to categories of vertical agreements and concerted practices (OJ L 102, 23.4.2010, p. 1).

[87]Article 101(1) TFEU.

[88]Communication from the Commission—Guidelines on the application of Article 101 of the Treaty on the Functioning of the European Union to technology transfer agreements (OJ C 89, 28.3.2014, p. 3).

[89]Joined opinion of Mr Advocate General Mayras delivered on 2 May 1972, ECLI:EU:C:1972:32.

[90]Goyder (1993), p. 88.

against individuals. Private enforcement also plays a significant role and victims of anticompetitive behaviour are awarded damages treble the amount of the actual damage suffered. In EU Competition Law, however, the term refers to the system of competition law enforcement, both public and private, which pursues three interconnected objectives: injunctive, punitive (deterrent) and compensatory[91] and in which companies are penalised with fines.

A study of the English terms also reveals that there is a case of terminologisation combined with semantic transfer. In particular, the term *leniency* in LGP refers to "the fact or quality of being more merciful or tolerant than expected"[92]; in law, it refers to a legal transaction in which a defendant pleads guilty in exchange for some form of leniency. It often involves a guilty plea to lesser charges or a guilty plea to some of the charges if other charges are dropped. Such bargains are not binding on the court.[93] *Leniency*, however, is used within EU Competition Law with a very specific meaning. It refers to the Commission's leniency policy whereby a participant in a secret cartel, independently of the other undertakings involved in the cartel, cooperates with an investigation of the competition authority, by voluntarily providing presentations regarding that participant's knowledge of, and role in, the cartel in return for which that participant receives, by decision or by a discontinuation of proceedings, immunity from, or a reduction in, fines for its involvement in the cartel.[94]

6.1.2 Creation of New Terms to Name New Concepts

From the ten terms under attention in this study, only two terms were originally created to name new concepts in English in the realm of EU Competition Law. A case of creation of a new term to name a new concept through compounding and direct borrowing from Latin is the term *de minimis aid*. It refers to aid not exceeding a certain fixed amount below which it is deemed not to fall within the scope of Article 107(1) TFEU, and therefore being exempt from the requirement laid down in Article 108(3) TFEU to notify the European Commission in advance.[95]

Exploitative abuse is another term which was originally created in EU Competition Law through compounding in order to name a new concept, i.e. the direct or indirect imposition of unfair purchase or selling prices or other unfair trading

[91]Komninos (2008), p. 7.

[92]Definition of *leniency*, English Oxford Living Dictionary, available at https://en.oxforddictionaries.com/definition/leniency (Accessed 20 Apr 2018).

[93]cf. Cobb (2006), p. 140.

[94]cf. http://ec.europa.eu/competition/cartels/leniency/leniency.html (Accessed 20 Feb 2018).

[95]Commission Regulation (EU) No 1407/2013 of 18 December 2013 on the application of Articles 107 and 108 of the Treaty on the Functioning of the European Union to de minimis aid (OJ L 352, 24.12.2013, p. 1).

conditions. The EU has for many years prohibited exploitative abuse, in contrast with the U.S. where Antitrust Law consciously lacks an equivalent prohibition.[96]

6.1.3 Translingual Borrowing

In EU Competition Law, borrowing in English takes place from French and German, given that these two were the original drafting languages of the EU. In the corpus under attention, a case of translingual borrowing is the term *undertaking*, derived from the German *Unternehmen*. The term is not defined in the Treaties, but its meaning is reasonably settled as a result of case law. It generally refers to any entity engaged in an economic activity, i.e. an activity consisting in offering goods or services on a given market, regardless of its legal status and the way in which it is financed. To qualify, no intention to earn profits is required, nor are public bodies by definition excluded. Historically, the CJEU has sought to maximise the application of EU Competition Law by taking a broad definition of the term in order to include many different types of businesses. The traditional definition in *Höfner* provides that the

> concept of an undertaking encompasses every entity engaged in an economic activity, regardless of the legal status of the entity and the way in which it is financed.[97]

Another case of borrowing is the term *aid*. It was introduced in Article 92 of the 1957 Treaty establishing the European Economic Community (now Article 107 TFEU). Its meaning is understood under the light of the broad historical framework within which the Treaty was signed.[98] In 1957, the governments of France, Germany, Italy and the Benelux initiated an ambitious experiment in economic and political cooperation, which aimed at the creation of an ever closer union among the peoples of Europe. The principle behind this effort was the agreement to establish a common market, since governments believed that the dismantling of barriers to cross-border economic activity would lead to a better standard of living for all and, by extension, to peace in the continent. Although the main aim of the Treaty was the elimination of "barriers", it also included other measures which were deemed important for the establishment of a common economic space. One of these was the provision of government assistance, i.e. State aid. All Community governments provided economic assistance to one degree or another, to address national economic and social challenges, but Treaty negotiators recognised that in order to make the most of the potential of a continental market, governments could not be provide public assistance without constraint. To address the risks posed by such provision, government negotiators incorporated into the Treaty a body of rules designed to limit aid provision while at the same time preserving it as a tool of national policy. These are found in Articles

[96]Shiraishi (2017).

[97]Case C-41/90 *Klaus Höfner and Fritz Elser v Macrotron GmbH* [1991] ECR I-1979, ECLI:EU:C:1991:161.

[98]cf. Doleys (2009).

90–92. Article 90(1) stipulates what measures constitute State aid within the meaning of the Treaty. It also stipulates that such measures are subject to a general prohibition, which is neither absolute nor unqualified. In brief, in EU Competition Law, *aid* refers to a very specific concept, i.e. State aid which is defined as an advantage in any form whatsoever conferred on a selective basis to undertakings by national public authorities that could potentially distort competition and trade in the EU. The definition of State aid is very broad because "an advantage" can take many forms. It is anything which an undertaking could not get on the open market. Although State aid is prohibited, there are cases when it is beneficial to the economy and supports growth and other policy objectives. Therefore, subsidies granted to individuals or general measures open to all enterprises are not covered by this prohibition and do not constitute State aid (examples include general taxation measures or employment legislation).

Another case of translingual borrowing in EU Competition Law is the term *dominant position*. Like in the case of *aid*, the term was borrowed from French. The term *position dominante* appeared for the first time in Article 86 of the ECSC Treaty[99] and states that

> any abuse by one more undertakings of a dominant position within the common market or in a substantial part of it shall be prohibited as incompatible with the common market in so far as it may affect trade between Member States.

In addition, the meaning of the term was clearly defined by the CJEU in *Hoffmann-La Roche*, one of the first Article 82 cases: the dominant position

> relates to a position of economic strength enjoyed by an undertaking, which enables it to prevent effective competition being maintained on the relevant market by affording it the power to behave to an appreciable extent independently of its competitors, its customers and ultimately of the consumers. Such a position does not preclude some competition, which it does where there is a monopoly or quasi-monopoly, but enables the undertaking, which profits by it, if not to determine, at least to have an appreciable influence on the conditions under which that competition will develop, and in any case to act largely in disregard of it so long as such conduct does not operate to its detriment.[100]

In general, under EU Competition Law, it is not illegal to hold a dominant position, since a dominant position can be obtained by legitimate means of competition, for example by inventing and selling a better product. Yet, Article 102 TFEU does not allow companies to abuse their dominant position, e.g charge unreasonably high price, deprive smaller competitors of customers by selling at artificially low prices they cannot compete with, obstruct competitors in the market (or in another related market) by forcing consumers to buy a product which is artificially related to a more popular, in-demand product, refuse to deal with certain customers or offering special discounts to customers who buy all or most of their supplies from the dominant company and make the sale of one product conditional on the sale of another product.

---

[99]The ECSC Treaty was the only Treaty drafted exclusively in French on the initiative of the French foreign minister Robert Schuman (Felici (2010), p. 96).

[100]Case 85/76 *Hoffman-La Roche* [1979] ECR 461, ECI:EU:C:1979:36.

6.2 Saying (Almost) the Same Thing?

It also arises from the analysis that during the translation or production of "language versions" a systematic attempt is made to produce terms which are similar in form; literal equivalents, loan translations/calques and direct borrowings rather than functional equivalents are thus preferred in 77% of the cases. Thus, *aid, concentration, de minimis aid, dominant position* and *vertical agreement* are all translated literally in Greek, Italian and Spanish. Naturalness in the TL or conformity to TL conventions, norms and readers' expectations do not appear to be particularly important, since marked simple and complex terms are often preferred as long as they are similar in all languages and help differentiate EU Competition Law concepts from general legal concepts. For instance, in Greek, the term *dominant position* is translated as *δεσπόζουσα θέση* rather than *κυρίαρχη θέση*. Both *δεσπόζουσα* and *κυρίαρχη* back-translate as "dominant", but the adjective *δεσπόζουσα* creates a marked complex term which clearly designates a new concept within the realm of EU Competition Law.

This observation is in line with the EU norms to rationalise, standardise and control the translation process and also avoid the use of national and culture-specific terms mentioned in Sect. 2.2. It can also explain the alienation that exists between the public and the Community-level conceptual structure and terminology.[101]

In a few cases and as can be seen in Table 3, a discrepancy was observed between the term in English and the term in another language, notably Greek. For instance, the term *enforcement system* is rendered literally in Italian and Spanish, i.e. *sistema di esecuzione, sistema de aplicación*. In Greek, however, it is translated as *σύστημα επιβολής κυρώσεων* which back-translates as "system of imposing sanctions". The Greek term is more specific, more concrete as it refers to a system of imposing sanctions and clearly does not convey the same meaning as the English, Italian and Spanish terms—which are more general and convey all three dimensions of the related concept i.e. the injunctive, the punitive and the compensatory ones. Similarly, *exploitative abuse*

Table 3 Literal equivalents of EU Competition Law terms

English	Greek	Italian	Spanish
aid	ενίσχυση	aiuto	ayuda
concentration	συγκέντρωση	concentrazione	concentración
concerted practice		práctica concertada	pratica concordata
de minimis aid	ενίσχυση de minimis	aiuto de minimis	ayuda de minimis
dominant position	δεσπόζουσα θέση	posizione dominante	posición dominante
enforcement system		sistema di esecuzione	sistema de aplicación
exploitative abuse		abuso di sfruttamento	abuso de explotación
leniency		clemenza	clemencia
undertaking			
vertical agreement	κάθετη συμφωνία	accordo verticale	acuerdo vertical

[101] Koskinen (2000), p. 61.

and *leniency* are translated literally in Italian and Spanish, but in Greek the terms are more informative, more descriptive. In particular, *exploitative abuse* is rendered as *καταχρηστική εκμετάλλευση ισχύος στην αγορά* which back-translates as "abusive exploitation of power in the market". The informative dynamism of the Greek term is stronger than its English, Italian and Spanish counterparts. The term *leniency* is rendered in Greek as *επιεικής μεταχείριση* which back-translates as "lenient treatment". The term "επιείκεια" would be a literal rendering and like the English, Italian and Spanish terms would be natural and transparent; yet, it is very general and can refer to the fact or quality of being more merciful or tolerant than expected. The more informative rendering may be due to an attempt to create a marked complex term which clearly designates the concept of leniency within the realm of EU Competition Law, i.e. the total or partial reduction of fines applied to firms that cooperate with antitrust authorities in cartel investigations. Another example of a divergent translation is *concerted practice.* The term is translated literally in Spanish and Italian, i.e. *pratica concordata* in Spanish, *práctica concertada* in Italian. In Greek, however, it is translated as *εναρμονισμένη πρακτική*. The Greek term which back-translates as "harmonised practice" is more vague and can be misinterpreted as it bears positive connotations. Finally, the most interesting case is the term *undertaking*. As already discussed in 6.1.3, the English term is preferred over *enterprise, business, company*, etc. to refer to any entity engaged in an economic activity regardless of its legal status and the way in which it is financed. Yet, the Greek, Italian and Spanish terms, namely *επιχείρηση, impresa and empresa* all back-translate as enterprise and are more restricted than *undertaking*.

6.3 Discussion

The analysis of the term formation strategies reveals that in 50% of the terms under attention, English EU Competition Law terms are formed through recontextualisation of a concept from a national discourse with the use of the corresponding term with an extension of its semantic meaning. This inevitably creates ambiguity and vagueness, which are both types of indeterminacy.[102] It also emerges from the analysis that a systematic attempt is made by EU translators to produce terms which are similar in form; thus, literal equivalents, loan translations/calques and direct borrowings rather than functional equivalents are preferred in 77% of the cases under attention. Still, some discrepancies in meaning are observed, which, in turn, may give rise to disputes. In cases of indeterminacy or disputes, the sole authority to interpret EU Law is the CJEU which promotes the uniform interpretation and application of EU Law by ascertaining the meaning of disputed provisions referred to it by national courts in references for a preliminary ruling. Disputed provisions include those which are unclear or ambiguous in the language version of the referring national court or are alleged to diverge from the other language versions. In considering questions of interpretation, the CJEU may

[102] cf. Bajčić (2017), p. 43; Schilling (2011), p. 1464.

choose from literal, contextual, comparative and teleological methods. In fact, teleological methods, which are understood as broad "purposive" methods and require the CJEU to view legislation taking into account the entire setting and spirit of the *acquis communautaire,* are widely used by the CJEU and are increasingly employed by national courts in interpreting EU Law.[103]

7 Conclusion

The analysis of the corpus offers an overview of the complexity of term formation and translation within the legislative system of the EU and highlights the demanding role of lawmakers, translators and all those involved in interpreting and implementing EU legislation. It becomes clear from the terms discussed that EU Competition Law discourse is particularly complex and idiosyncratic as the related concepts are unique, born at the intersection of legal cultures and systems. In addition, within that context and as the analysis highlighted, EU translators resort to literal renderings and neologisms which enable lawmakers and judges to differentiate EU from national concepts and ensure the preservation of the unity of the single instrument in all authentic texts and, by extension, the uniform interpretation and application of EU legislation by the national courts in all Member States.[104] It appears, after all, that in the EU the Members States' lifeworlds can converge through the cross-fertilisation of law concepts—and ultimately law systems—and that a unified deterritorialised and hybrid legal EU culture can actually exist.

References

Alcaraz Varó E, Hughes B (2002) Legal translation explained. St. Jerome, Manchester

Alese F (2008) Federal antitrust and EC competition law analysis. Ashgate, Aldershot

Baker M (1995) Corpora in translation studies. An overview and some suggestions for future research. Target 7:223–243

Baker M (1999) The role of corpora in investigating the linguistic behaviour of professional translators. Int J Corpus Linguist 4:281–298

Baaij CJW (2012) Fifty years of multilingual interpretation in the European Union. In: Tiersma PM, Solan LM (eds) The Oxford handbook of language and law. Oxford University Press, Oxford, pp 217–233

Bajčić M (2017) New insights into the semantics of legal concepts and the legal dictionary. John Benjamins, Amsterdam. https://doi.org/10.1075/tlrp.17

Barents R (2004) The autonomy of community law. Kluwer Law International, The Hague

Biel Ł (2007) Translation of multilingual EU law as a sub-genre of legal translation. In: Kierzkowska D (ed) Court interpreting and legal translation in the enlarged Europe. Translegis, Warsaw

---

[103] Holland and Webb (2016), p. 344.

[104] Šarčević and Gotti (2006), p. 14.

Biel Ł (2014a) Lost in the Eurofog. The textual fit of translated law. Peter Lang, Frankfurt am Mein. https://doi.org/10.3726/b11383

Biel Ł (2014b) The textual fit of translated EU law: a corpus-based study of deontic modality. Translator 20(2):1–24

Buch-Hansen H, Levallois C (2015) The scale and geography of collusion in the European market: a longitudinal view. J Common Mark Stud 53(4):737–752

Cao D (2007) Translating law. Multilingual Matters, Clevedon

Cao D (2010) Legal translation. In: Gambier Y, van Doorslaer L (eds) Handbook of translation studies. John Benjamins, Amsterdam

Caliendo G (2004) EU language in cross-boundary communication. Textus 17:159–178

Catenaccio P (2008) Implementing Council Directive 1993/13/EEU on unfair terms in consumer contracts in Great Britain: a case for intra-linguistic translation? In: Bhatia VK, Candlin CN, Allori PE (eds) Language, culture and the law. The formulation of legal concepts across systems and cultures. Peter Lang, Bern, pp 259–280

Čavoški A (2017) Interaction of law and language in the EU: challenges of translating in multilingual environment. JoSTrans – J Spec Transl 27:58–74. http://www.jostrans.org/issue27/art_cavoski.php. Accessed 20 Apr 2018

Cobb RJD (2006) Justice and public safety reference manual: a practical guide to justice and public safety agencies and their information systems. Lulu.com

de Corte F (2003) The contribution of freelance translators. In: Tosi A (ed) Crossing barriers and bridging cultures. Multilingual Matters, Clevedon, pp 67–72

de Witte B (2010) European Union Law: how autonomous is its legal order? Zeitschrift für öffentliches Recht 31:141–155

Doleys T (2009) Fifty years of moulding Article 87: The European Commission and the development of EU State Aid Law & Policy (1958–2008). Paper presented at the ESRC Workshop the European Union and State Aid: The Present Crisis and Beyond, Norwich, 9–10 July 2009

Dragone S (2006) The quality of Community legislation and the role of the European Commission legal revisers. In: Pozzo B, Jacometti V (eds) Multilingualism and the harmonization of European law. Kluwer Law International, Alphen aan den Rijn, pp 99–106

Felici A (2010) Translating EU law: legal issues and multiple dynamics. Perspectives 18(2): 95–108. https://doi.org/10.1080/09076761003668289

Fiorito L (2013) How to build Europe with words: the discursive construction of European identity in the EU's founding treaties. Giapeto editore, Italy

Garzone G (2000) Legal translation and functionalist approaches: a contradiction in terms? In: Legal translation: history, theory/ies and practice. Proceedings of the International Colloquium. University of Geneva, Geneva, pp 395–414

Gerber D (2010) Global competition: law, markets and globalization. Oxford University Press, Oxford

Giannoni DS (2003) The UNCITRAL model and Italian statute law: a linguistic and topical description. In: Bhatia VK, Candlin CN, Gotti M (eds) Legal discourse in multilingual and multicultural contexts: arbitration texts in Europe. Peter Lang, Bern, pp 221–246

Gombos K (2014) EU law viewed through the eyes of a national judge. http://ec.europa.eu/dgs/legal_service/seminars/20140703_gombos_speech_en.pdf. Accessed 17 Feb 2018

Goyder DG (1993) EC competition law. Clarendon Press, Oxford

Habermas J (1981) The theory of communicative action (trans: McCarthy T). Polity, Cambridge

Harding C, Joshua J (2003) Regulating cartels in Europe: a study of legal control of corporate delinquency. Oxford University Press, Oxford

Hartmann RRK (1996) Contrastive textology and corpus linguistics: on the value of parallel texts. Lang Sci 18:947–957

Holland J, Webb J (2016) Learning legal rules. Oxford University Press, Oxford

ISO (2009) ISO 704:2009. https://www.iso.org/standard/38109.html. Accessed 17 Feb 2018

Johansson S (1998) On the role of corpora in cross-linguistic research. In: Johansson S, Oksefjell S (eds) Corpora and cross-linguistic research: theory, method and case studies. Rodopi, Amsterdam, pp 1–24

Jopek-Bosiacka A (2013) Comparative law and equivalence assessment of system-bound terms in EU legal translation. Linguistica Antverpiensia 12:110–146

Kaeding M (2007) Better regulation in the European Union: lost in translation or full steam ahead. Leiden University Press, Leiden

Kjær AL (2014) New challenges to the theory of legal translation: transnational legal communication and the autonomization of international law. Translator 20(3):430–436. https://doi.org/10.1080/13556509.2014.927700

Kjær AL (2015) Theoretical aspects of legal translation in the EU: the paradoxical relationship between language, translation and the autonomy of EU law. In: Šarčević S (ed) Language and culture in EU law: multidisciplinary perspectives. Ashgate, Surrey, pp 91–107

Komninos AP (2008) EC private antitrust enforcement: decentralised application of EC competition law by National Courts. Hart, Oxford

Koskinen K (2000) Institutional illusions: translating in the EU Commission. Translator 6(1): 49–65. https://doi.org/10.1080/13556509.2000.10799055

Krimpas PG (2017) ISO 704:2009 and equivalents of English financial terms in lesser-used languages: the case of Greek. Perspectives 25(3):397–416. https://doi.org/10.1080/0907676X.2017.1287206

Letsas G (2004) Autonomous concepts: how to interpret the ECHR. Eur J Int Law 15(2):279–305. https://doi.org/10.1093/ejil/15.2.279

Maher I (2000) Re-imaging the story of European competition law. Oxford J Legal Stud 20(1): 155–166 https://doi.org/10.1093/ojls/20.1.155

Mattila HES (2006) Comparative legal linguistics (trans: Goddard C). Ashgate, Aldershot

McAuliffe K (2011) Hybrid texts and uniform law? The multilingual case law of the Court of Justice of the European Union. Int J Semiot Law 24:97–115. https://doi.org/10.1007/s11196-010-9188-3

McEnery T, Hardie A (2012) Corpus linguistics: method, theory and practice. Cambridge University Press, Cambridge

Molnár T (2016) The concept of autonomy of EU law from the comparative perspective of international law and the legal systems of Member States. In: Hungarian yearbook of international law and European law 2015. Eleven International Publishing, The Hague, pp 433–459

O'Leary S (1998) The options for the reform of European Union citizenship. In: O'Leary S, Tilikainen T (eds) Citizenship and nationality status in the New Europe. Institute for Public Policy Research, London

Papadopoulos AS (2010) The national and international dimensions of competition law and policy. In: Papadopoulos A (ed) The international dimension of EU competition law and policy. Cambridge University Press, Cambridge, pp 7–51

Patel KK, Schweitzer H (eds) (2013) The historical foundations of EU competition law. Oxford University Press, Oxford

Picht H, Draskau J (1985) Terminology: an introduction. University of Surrey, Guildford

Pozzo B (2012) Multilingualism and the harmonization of European private law: problems and perspectives. Eur Rev Priv Law 20:1185–1198

Prieto Ramos F (2014) International and supranational law in translation: from multilingual lawmaking to adjudication. Translator 20(3):313–331. https://doi.org/10.1080/13556509.2014.904080

Sager JC (1993) Language engineering and translation: consequences of automation. John Benjamins, Amsterdam

Šarčević S (1988) Translation of legislation with special emphasis on languages of limited diffusion. In: Nekeman P (ed) Translation, our future. XIth World Congress of FIT. Euroterm, Maastricht, pp 455–462

Šarčević S (1997) New approach to legal translation. Kluwer Law International, The Hague

Šarčević S, Gotti M (2006) Introduction. In: Gotti M, Šarčević S (eds) Insights into specialized translation. Peter Lang, Frankfurt am Mein, pp 9–23

Shiraishi T (2017) The exploitative abuse prohibition. Antitrust Bull 62(4):737–751

Somssich R, Várnal J, Bérczi A (2010) Lawmaking in the EU multilingual environment. European Commission, Directorate General for Translation, Brussels
Sosoni V (2011) Training translators to work for the EU institutions: luxury or necessity? JoSTrans – J Spec Transl 16:77–108 http://www.jostrans.org/issue16/art_sosoni.php. Accessed 17 Feb 2018
Sosoni V (2012) A hybrid translation theory for EU texts. Vertimo Studijos 5:76–89. https://doi.org/10.5281/zenodo.1048190
Shaw J (1997) The many pasts and futures of citizenship in the European Union. Eur Law Rev 22(6):554–572
Shaw J (2007) EU citizenship and political rights in an evolving European Union. Fordham Law Rev 75(5):2549–2578
Schilling TJR (2011) Multilingualism and Multijuralism: assets of EU legislation and adjudication? German Law J 12:1460–1491
Szurek S (2007) Du particularisme à l' autonomie? Esquisse des rapports du droit international et du droit communautaire. Annuaire de droit européen 5:57–92
Tirkkonen-Condit S (2001) EU project proposals as hybrid texts: observations from a Finnish research project. Across Lang Cult 2(2):261–264
Tognini-Bonelli T (2001) Corpus linguistics at work. John Benjamins, Amsterdam
Tosi A (2005) EU translation problems and the danger of linguistic evaluation. Int J Appl Linguist 15(3):384–388
Trosborg A (1997) Translating hybrid political texts. In: Trosborg A (ed) Text typology and translation. John Benjamins, Amsterdam, pp 145–158. https://doi.org/10.1075/btl.26.12tro
Valeontis KE, Mantzari E (2006) The linguistic dimension of terminology: principles and methods of term formation. In: 1st Athens international conference on translation and interpretation translation: between art and social science, HAU, Athens, 13–14 October 2006. http://www.eleto.gr/download/BooksAndArticles/HAU-Conference2006-ValeontisMantzari_EN.pdf. Accessed 26 Feb 2018
van den Bergh R (2016) Vertical restraints: the European part of the policy failure. Antitrust Bull 61(1):167–185. https://doi.org/10.1177/0003603X15625122
van Els TJM (2001) The European Union, its institutions and its languages: some language political observations. Curr Issues Lang Plann 2(4):311–360. https://doi.org/10.1080/14664200108668030
van Rossem WJ (2013) The autonomy of EU law: more is less? In: Wessel RA, Blockmans S (eds) Between autonomy and dependence. The EU legal order under the influence of international organisations. TMC ASSER PRESS, The Hague, pp 13–46
Wagner E, Bech S, Martínez JM (2010) Translating for the European Union Institutions, 2nd edn. St. Jerome, Manchester
Warlouzet L, Witschke T (2012) The difficult path to an economic rule of law: European competition policy, 1950–91. Contemp Eur Hist 21(3):437–455
Wiener A (1997) Making sense of the new geography of citizenship in the European Union. Theory Soc 26:529–560

Vilelmini Sosoni is Assistant Professor of Economic, Legal and Political Translation at the Department of Foreign Languages, Translation and Interpreting of the Ionian University in Greece.

A Mutual Learning Exercise in Terminology and Multilingual Law

Martina Bajčić and Adrijana Martinović

> *Whatever criticism is leveled at the language of the law for its notoriously imprecise and equivocal terms, it does appear that lawyers choose their words more carefully than non-lawyers, including the selection of vague or ambiguous terms which serve a useful function by virtue of their lack of precision.*—Lewis (1972), p. 316.

Abstract While it is true that legal language strives for precision, legal concepts are often vague. This seeming paradox can be observed in light of the fact that legal concepts need to be applied to different real-life situations in order to account for the changing social circumstances. By focusing on the important role of terminology in general, and concepts in particular, for the mechanism of the law, this chapter poses the following question: How do courts cope with vague concepts of EU Law and inadequate terms in translations of EU Law? Emphasis is placed on EU Competition Law concepts from the dual perspective of law and language. Applying terminology as a linguistic discipline which studies terms, concepts and the conceptual structure, can further understanding of EU Competition Law concepts. On the other hand, examining how the Court of Justice of the EU grapples with the meaning of vague EU Law concepts and how it resolves divergences between language versions in its case law, provides valuable assistance for legal practitioners, and translators. With this in mind it can be claimed that to overcome vagueness and linguistic discrepancies, lawyers and linguists need to engage in a continuous exercise of mutual learning.

M. Bajčić (✉)
University of Rijeka, Faculty of Law, Department of Foreign Languages, Rijeka, Croatia
e-mail: martina@pravri.hr

A. Martinović
University of Rijeka, Faculty of Law, Department of EU Public Law, Rijeka, Croatia
e-mail: adrijana@pravri.hr

S. Marino et al. (eds.), *Language and Law*,
https://doi.org/10.1007/978-3-319-90905-9_12

1 Introduction: No Terminology, No Law

It is well known that language is the lawyer's most important tool.[1] Law cannot exist without being communicated to the people subject to it.[2] Recognized as "the most linguistic of institutions",[3] law has been studied in close connection to language by both lawyers and linguists, which has led to the birth of legal linguistics, or law and language studies, as an interdiscipline offering a

> common platform from which researchers from other fields than law cooperate with legal scholars with a view to elucidating the blind spots of conventional legal studies.[4]

For the purpose of studying law in close connection to language, it is important to endorse a broader view of linguistics as including semantics, pragmatics and terminology. After all, legal norms and legal institutions are expressed by legal concepts and legal terms. Studying the use and application of legal terms (pragmatics) also sheds light on the meaning of legal terms and concepts (semantics) in a domain, which lies at the core of Terminology[5] as a linguistic discipline. Departing from this background, the first part of this chapter explains the important role of Terminology in the mechanism of the law. Section two defines terms and concepts. Emphasis is placed on synonymy and polysemy of legal terms in different languages and their effect on legal certainty. Shifting the focus to the implications of multilingualism of EU Law, the third section sheds light on different methods of legal interpretation used by the CJEU in cases of divergences between language versions on hand of EU Competition Law cases. Finally, the fourth section zooms in on examples of vague concepts of EU Competition Law. The meaning and implications of vagueness in law and linguistics are briefly sketched. Assuming that national law practitioners, but also legal translators, would benefit from a higher level of interdisciplinarity in the study of legal language, the authors employ both legal and linguistic approaches in their analysis of EU Competition Law concepts. With its repertoire of examples of terms in different languages, the present chapter has a twofold purpose: on the one hand, it attempts to elucidate the importance of Terminology for legal practitioners in the EU and, on the other, by applying the methods and principles of Terminology, to further understanding of EU Competition Law.

---

[1] Tiersma (1999), p. 1.

[2] Engberg and Kjær (2011), p. 7. Vernengo stated that law as language is a technique of communication serving the function of bridging divergences and enabling understanding between opponents: 'Als Sprache ist das Recht eine Kommunikationstechnik, die zur Überbrückung von Divergenzen und zur Verständigung von Gegnern dient'. See Vernengo (1965), p. 295.

[3] Gibbons (2004), p. 1.

[4] Engberg and Kjær (2011), pp. 7–8.

[5] In the remainder of this chapter we use Terminology with an upper-case latter to refer to the linguistic discipline, and terminology with a lower-case letter when referring to a body of terms used in a domain.

2 Terminology

Despite the fact that Terminology has long established itself as a discipline in its own right, researchers from other fields still tend to deflate the notion to a "body of terms used in a particular field". This view does not necessarily hamper the importance of what can be dubbed applied terminology or terminology work or terminology management, including standardization as a prescriptive terminology activity or nomenclature; or the creation of terminological resources among others. However, there is more to terminology than *terms*, i.e.

> words that are assigned to concepts used in the special languages that occur in subject-field or domain-related texts.[6]

A term is hence a verbal designation of a general concept in a specific subject field, whereas a concept is a unit of knowledge created by a unique combination of characteristics.[7] Concepts, not terms, are central to Terminology as a discipline concerned with classification, structure of a conceptual field and the problem of defining and delineating concepts from other related concepts. In this regard, Terminology has to tackle semantics as long recognized by Eugen Wüster.[8]

The broad label special or specialized language is used to denote a language that covers a specific field and is prototypically used among field specialists.[9] In terms of a special language, the language of the law has been described as

> the customary language used by lawyers in those common law jurisdictions where English is the official language.[10]

As observed by Lewis,[11] legal terms often sound like ordinary English, however, their meaning in the argot of the law may vary. For this reason, law students sometimes feel they are being taught not only law, but a foreign language as well.[12] Albeit these observations refer to (legal) English, they hold true for other (legal) languages. In addition to legal terms, it is important to shed more light on the underlining legal concepts, which frame legal knowledge. Acknowledging this central role of concepts, Wüster regarded special language as a language of concepts, i.e., of purpose.[13] Observed in this light, meaning, classification and defining of concepts form integral parts of Terminology. In a similar vein, establishing the

---

[6] Wright (1997), p. 13.

[7] ISO 1087-1:2000.

[8] A pioneer in terminological work, Eugen Wüster (1898–1977) brought the study of specialized languages to a higher level. See Wüster (1974), in Picht and Schmitz (2001), p. 12.

[9] Martin and van der Vliet (2003), p. 333.

[10] Mellinkoff (1963), p. 3.

[11] Lewis (1972), p. 307.

[12] Lewis (1972), p. 307.

[13] Wüster (1974), in Picht and Schmitz (2001), p. 12.

meanings of concepts and the problem of defining vague concepts are part and parcel of legal interpretation in the multilingual context of EU Law.

2.1 *Synonymy and Polysemy of Legal Terms*

Bearing in mind the distinction between term and concept, a term is said to identify a concept. Legal terms act as signposts for legal practitioners to determine which legal concept is denoted by a given legal term. Using the correct legal term is of vital importance for legal practitioners and courts; indeed, it appears that lawyers choose their terms more carefully than non-lawyers.[14] After all, inadequate terms can lead to undesired legal effects and undermine legal certainty as will be illustrated in subsequent sections. Mindful of the importance of legal terminology, lawyers are conservative in their use of language[15] and resist language change.[16] This is not surprising, considering the normative nature of law.

The relationship between term and concept is by no means a straightforward one, as the following example illuminates. Article 10 of the Convention on the Service Abroad of Judicial and Extrajudicial Documents in Civil or Commercial Matters signed in The Hague on 15 November 1965 (the Hague Service Convention) states:

> Provided the State of destination does not object, the present Convention shall not interfere with – a) the freedom to **send** judicial documents, by postal channels, directly to persons abroad (emphasis added).[17]

In the US, the Convention's use of the term *send* created a split in the Circuit Courts over whether documents sent via Article 10(a) to a foreign defendant constituted valid service of originating process. In this context judges at US courts use the term *serve*, rather than *send*. Faced with the latter term, they were uncertain as to the meaning of the concept conveyed by the term *send*. In Terminology, the definition describes the concept, not the term. Because of that, meaning is also to be established at the concept level.[18] This example is telling of another paradox of legal language. On the one hand, legal language strives for precision, clarity of expression and consequently, unambiguous terms. On the other hand, the nature of law manifests itself in the necessity to apply legal concepts to different real-life situations in order to regulate different behaviours and changing social circumstances. Because of that, legal concepts can be vague and indeterminate, and their meanings contingent on interpretation in order to ascertain whether or not a certain concept can be

[14] Lewis (1972), p. 307.

[15] Lewis (1972), p. 315.

[16] Mellinkoff (1963), p. 295.

[17] Available at: https://www.hcch.net/en/instruments/conventions/full-text/?cid=17. Accessed: 1 Feb 2018.

[18] This is not in contradiction to the cognitive linguistics view of language as encompassing both linguistic and extralinguistic level.

considered as a member of a legal category. Observed in this light, US courts had to ascertain if 'sending documents' can be deemed to constitute valid service. The courts in the Second Circuit took the view that sending documents via Article 10 (a) is valid service.[19] However, other courts in the 5th and 8th Circuits have taken the view that sending documents in the mail to overseas defendants lacks the formality necessary for service of process.[20] Finally, according to the 9th Circuit,

> sending the documents pursuant to Article 10(a) has sufficient formality when the forum court also authorises mail service in a similar domestic action and when the procedural rules for mail service are followed.[21]

This example has demonstrated that, not only are legal concepts sometimes vague in terms of their meanings, but the interpretation of their meaning may vary as well. The question we are pursuing here, is, to what extent Terminology, and a greater awareness of Terminology can assist legal practitioners in the task of legal interpretation especially in a multilingual setting as the EU.

The above mentioned paradox of legal language is also evident in the example of synonymy. Neither synonymy, nor polysemy can be blotted out completely from special languages, despite the fact that both synonymy and polysemy undermine legal certainty, in that a judge might be insecure whether two terms (used in a legislative text) refer to the same concept or not. This runs counter to univocity as the basic principle of Terminology, positing that one term denotes one concept only. Though this one-on-one relation accounts for a precondition of effective, precise and smooth communication among experts, it is sometimes hampered by synonymy and polysemy. EU Competition Law is not devoid of polysemous terms. As a matter of fact, some of its most instrumental concepts are couched in polysemous terms such as *competition, merger, concentration, leniency, aid,* in the sense that the latter have different or slightly distinct meanings in Competition Law, as opposed to other legal fields, or in contrast to their general language meanings. The term *aid* here is a poignant example, because it is often used in the plural in EU Competition Law (e.g. State aids). However, in its general meaning of 'assistance' it is commonly used in the singular as an uncountable noun.[22] It is instructive to note that, in the realms of Terminology, polysemy is treated as homonymy (when one term denotes two different concepts), owing to the fact that a term's semantic value is determined based on the relationship of the term and the conceptual system.[23] Furthermore, Wüster insisted upon differentiating *Mehrsinnigkeit* ('more senses') and

---

[19]See Mutual Benefits Offshore Fund v. Zeltser (2016 NY Slip Op 04344, N.Y. App. Div.); Ackermann v Levine, 788 F.2d 830 (2nd Cir 1986).

[20]See Nuovo Pignone v. Storman Asia M/V, 310 F.2d 374, 384 (5th Cir. 2002); Bankston v. Toyota Motor Corp., 889 F.2d 172 (8th Cir 1989).

[21]See Brockmeyer v. May, 383 F.3d 798 (9th Cir. 2004).

[22]In plural, the noun is commonly used to refer to a disease (AIDS) or to devices that help you do something (e.g. 'hearing aids' or 'teaching aids', see Gardner (2016), p. 12).

[23]Cabré (1999), p. 108.

Mehrdeutigkeit ('more than one meaning', polysemy).[24] Observed in this light, *Mehrdeutigkeit*, not *Mehrsinnigkeit*, refers to special languages[25] and manifests itself in legal terms which are used in legal language, albeit to denote different legal concepts in different legal fields (e.g. *proportionality* or *subsidiarity*).[26]

An example will illustrate the problems of synonymous terms in legal language. The German language version of Regulation 2377/80[27] uses two different terms: *Werktag* and *Arbeitstag*, while Regulation 1182/71,[28] which establishes uniform general rules for the application of terms such as working days or public holidays in the Commission's or Council's acts, used only *Arbeitstag*. The English version of both Regulations used one term only, namely *working day*. This led to uncertainty in legal practice, and the Administrative Court in Frankfurt requested a preliminary ruling on the question, whether the "concept 'Werktag'" in the German language version of Article 8(a) of Regulation 2377/80 should be interpreted as being synonymous with the concept 'Arbeitstag' in the German language version of Article 2.2. of Regulation 1182/71 and thereby exclude Saturdays.[29] The question is hence, do *Werktag* and *Arbeitstag* have the same reference? The German term *Werktag* calls for further clarification in this regard. Although in everyday language it's regarded as synonymous with *Arbeitstag* (namely as having the same reference), in the legal context the prevailing opinion is that it includes Saturdays, which is not the case with *Arbeitstag*,[30] for Saturday is not intrinsic to the content or reference of the expression *Arbeitstag*. One can see how the use of two different terms in this context leads to legal uncertainty. In what follows, we shall see how the CJEU resolves such uncertainties.

---

[24]See Wüster (1985), pp. 79–83. We are aware of potential ambiguity of 'meaning' and different approaches to meaning in philosophy of language employing other notions such as sense, reference, content, proposition. However, it is difficult, due to short space, to probe into different semantic vs. reference theories here.

[25]Bajčić (2017), p. 57.

[26]For a discussion of interdisciplinary, polysemous legal terms see Bajčić (2011).

[27]Commission Regulation (EEC) No 2377/80 of 4 September 1980 on special detailed rules for the application of the system of import and export licences in the beef and veal sector (OJ L 241, 13.9.1980, p. 5) as amended by the Commission Regulation (EEC) No 2798/81 of 28 September 1981 amending for the third time Regulation (EEC) No 2377/80 on special detailed rules for the application of the system of import and export licences in the beef and veal sector (OJ L 275, 29.9.1981, p. 24).

[28]Regulation (EEC, Euratom) No 1182/71 of the Council of 3 June 1971 determining the rules applicable to periods, dates and time limits (OJ L 124, 8.6.1971, p. 1).

[29]Case VG Frankfurt am Main 1987-01-22, I/2 E 1326/84.

[30]The German Federal Holiday Act (BurlG) is often referred to by German courts as a means of clarification in this regard: 'Nach § 3 Abs. 2 Bundesurlaubsgesetz (BUrlG) gelten als Werktag „alle Kalendertage, die nicht Sonn- oder gesetzliche Feiertage sind'. In keeping with a judgment of the Higher Regional Court Hamm (Oberlandesgericht Hamm), in everyday language Saturday is regarded as a working day, whereas *Werktag* should not be used synonymous with *Arbeitstag* (AZ: 2 Ss OWi 127/01): 'Der Begriff sei nicht mit "Arbeitstag" gleichzusetzen, sondern vielmehr als Gegensatz zum Begriff "Sonn- und Feiertag" zu verstehen'.

3 EU Multilingual Adjudication

Drawing on the above example, it can be argued that the relation between an abstract term (expression) and the real world (content, reference) poses the main (linguistic) challenge to legal interpretation. The interpretive practice of courts in terms of the legal approach to meaning brings to the fore two contradictory poles of law's normativism on the one hand, and descriptivism in language studies, on the other. The normative interests of the law resonate in the fact that meaning in law is ascribed to a legal norm or established in the event of several plausible meanings, rather than described (as semantic theories purport to do). It is therefore often claimed that lawyers are less concerned with linguistic categories (e.g. syntax, phonology, semantics), placing greater weight on what can be dubbed the conceptualization of legal problems (e.g. is a student a worker; is Saturday a working day). However, this does not render the legal approach devoid of semantics or linguistics; in fact, resorting to linguistics, and Terminology tools, might enable a better understanding of the process of legal interpretation, in particular in the multilingual context.

3.1 Multilingualism and Cases of Doubt

As the above example demonstrates, it is impossible that 24 official language versions of EU legislation always convey the same meaning, even though they should refer to the same concept in order to enable uniform application and interpretation of EU Law. Equal authenticity[31] of each official language version actually prohibits reliance on one single version in that no version can override other language versions.[32] In this section we investigate how the Court resolves divergences between language versions which result from the sheer impossibility of conceptual congruence among 24 languages (also known as multilingual concordance) and the fact that legal translation is imperfect.

In the above mentioned *Werktag* case, the Court referred to the *Stauder* judgment stating that, in the interest of a uniform interpretation of Community law, the provision should be interpreted in the light of all the language versions. *Stauder*,[33] a signature case for linguistic discrepancies concerned the Commission's decision on the programme of subsidised butter addressed to Member States. The German version provided that beneficiaries of the Commission measure are entitled to butter at reduced price in exchange for a *coupon issued in their names* i.e., in the German version: "*. . . nur gegen einen auf ihren Namen ausgestellten Gutschein. . .*", whereas

[31]On the principle of equal authenticity see for instance Baaij (2018), p. 28; Šarčević (2013); Mišćenić (2016), p. 90, Bajčić (2017), pp. 93–94 and Doczekalska in this volume.

[32]See e.g. Case C-372/88 *Milk Marketing Board* [1990] ECR I-1345, ECLI:EU:C:1990:140, para. 18; Case 19/67 *van der Vecht* [1967] ECR 445, ECLI:EU:C:1967:49.

[33]Case 29/69 *Stauder* [1969] ECR 419, ECLI:EU:C:1969:57.

the French and Italian versions mentioned only a "*bon individualisé*" or "*buono individualizzato*" (individualised coupon), and the Dutch version "*op naam gestelde bon*". A German recipient believed that the fact that he had to present a coupon to the seller with his name on it, according to the German text, violated his human rights, most notably his human dignity. The Court of Justice took a stance which is still upheld and followed as 'good law' even five decades later:

> When a single decision is addressed to all the MS the necessity for uniform application and accordingly for uniform interpretation makes it **impossible to consider one version of the text in isolation** but requires that **it be interpreted on the basis of both the real intention of its author and the aim it seeks to achieve, in the light in particular of the versions in all four languages**. (para. 3 of the judgment, emphasis added)

Let's not forget that at the time of *Stauder* there were four official language versions (English, French, German, Dutch), whereas as of July 1, 2013 there are 24 official languages of the EU: Bulgarian, Croatian, Czech, Danish, Dutch, English, Estonian, Finnish, French, German, Greek, Hungarian, Irish, Italian, Latvian, Lithuanian, Maltese, Polish, Portuguese, Romanian, Slovak, Slovenian, Spanish and Swedish.

The right to rely on one language version was central to the case *Ferriere Nord*[34] at the heart of which was the wording of Article 101 TFEU (then Article 85 EC) regarding cooperation between companies distorting competition. According to the Italian language version, agreements between undertakings will be prohibited, if they have both as object and effect the prevention, restriction or distortion of competition.[35] However, according to other language versions, the criteria were named alternatively, not cumulatively; in other words, the agreements should have either as their object or effect, the prevention, restriction or distortion of competition. Demonstrating once again that a plaintiff who refers to his right to rely on one language version has little success,[36] the Court stated that one of the criteria here was sufficient and thereby confirmed that uniform interpretation of Article 101 TFEU makes it impossible to look at just one language version of this text in isolation. Uniform interpretation and application is essential, especially given that rules on competition in internal market fall under the Union's exclusive competences. In cases of doubt, a provision must be interpreted and applied in the light of the other language versions which have to be recognised as having the same weight,

[34]Case C-219/95P *Ferriere Nord* [1997] ECR I-441, ECLI:EU:C:1997:375.

[35]The Italian version reads as follows: 'Sono incompatibili con il mercato comune e vietati tutti gli accordi tra imprese, tutte le decisioni di associazioni di imprese e tutte le pratiche concordate che possano pregiudicare il commercio tra Stati membri e che abbiano per oggetto e per effetto di impedire, restringere o falsare il gioco della concorrenza all'interno del mercato comune' however, the English language version refers to alternative, not cumulative criteria: 'the following shall be prohibited as incompatible with the common market: all agreements between undertakings, decisions by associations of undertakings and concerted practices which may affect trade between Member States and which have as their object or effect the prevention, restriction or distortion of competition within the common market'.

[36]Derlén (2009), p. 32.

regardless of the size of the population of the Member States using the language in question.[37]

Another case concerning Article 101 TFEU illustrates the comparison of other language versions, case *Robert Bosch*.[38] The case concerned the meaning of the term *affect*, that is the term *beeinträchtigen* in the German version:

> Mit dem Gemeinsamen Markt unvereinbar und verboten sind alle Vereinbarungen zwischen Unternehmen, Beschlüsse von Unternehmensvereinigungen und aufeinander abgestimmte Verhaltensweisen, welche den Handel zwischen Mitgliedstaaten zu beeinträchtigen geeignet sind und eine Verhinderung, Einschränkung oder Verfälschung des Wettbewerbs innerhalb des Gemeinsamen Marktes bezwecken oder bewirken, insbesondere

While the German term means 'to influence negatively', like the Italian *pregiudicare*, English and French *affect* and *affecter* mean 'influence in whatever way'. The Court agreed with the opinion of AG Legrande that the wording in question should be interpreted as meaning "influence in whatever way" bearing in mind the importance of retaining broader competence over competition law cases.[39]

In conclusion, it can be said that there is no legal certainty until a case is resolved by the Court. Likewise, reinforcing the important role of concepts for law, and in spite of the comparison of languages, the Court determines the meaning of the concept, not the German, English or Italian term.[40] When an inconsistency in various language versions is detected

> [t]he only way of overcoming [it] is by setting aside the wording and, by relying upon a systematic or purposive reading of the text of the law, reformulating the rule.[41]

3.2 *National Courts and the Duty to Compare*

Another point to be considered in this context is the national courts' duty to compare different language versions. According to Bobek,[42] the (in)famous guidelines postulated by the CJEU in the *CILFIT* case[43]—also discussed elsewhere in this

[37] See Case C-296/95 *EMU Tabac* [1998] ECR I-1605, ECLI:EU:C:1998:152.

[38] Case 13/61 *Robert Bosch* [1962] ECR 45, ECLI:EU:C:1962:11.

[39] Opinion of the Advocate General Lagrande of 27 Feb 1962, Case 13/61 *Robert Bosch*, EU:C:1962:3.

[40] Legal scholars have underscored that in fact equally authentic language versions have equal status, but not the same meaning (cf. Baaij (2018), p. 28).

[41] Bobek (2011), p. 139.

[42] Bobek (2011), p. 141.

[43] (1) Community legislation is drafted in several languages and the different language versions are all equally authentic. An interpretation of a provision of Community law thus involves a comparison of the different language versions. (2) Community law uses terminology which is peculiar to it. (3) Legal concepts do not necessarily have the same meaning in Community law and in the law of the various Member States. (4) Every provision of Community law must be placed in its context and interpreted in the light of the provisions of Community law as a whole, regard being had to the

volume—apply to national courts as well. What's more, national courts should ask if the wording of the national language version represents the true meaning of a given provision.[44] Recent cases settled by the Croatian Competition Agency, and adjudicated by the Croatian High Administrative Court as the highest instance for competition cases, explicate the importance of comparing different language versions to filter out translation mistakes which can lead to unwanted legal effects. Article 5 (2) of the Council Regulation (EC) No 1/2003 of 16 December 2002 on the implementation of the rules on competition laid down in Articles 81 and 82 of the Treaty in its English version reads as follows:

> Where on the basis of the information in their possession the conditions for prohibition are not met they may likewise decide that there are **no grounds for action on their part**. (emphasis added)

The Croatian version:

> Ako na temelju informacija koje posjeduju nisu ispunjeni uvjeti za izricanje zabrane, nacionalna tijela za tržišno natjecanje mogu također odlučiti da **ne postoji temelj za *pokretanje postupka***. (emphasis added)

Relying on the Croatian version of Article 5(2) of the Regulation which states "no grounds for initiating proceeding" and not "no grounds for action on their part", the High Administrative Court maintained that, once the Croatian Competition Agency has initiated the proceeding, it cannot terminate it, but close it by taking a decision on the merits. However, in conformity with the Regulation, where national competition authorities establish that there is no evidence that the alleged infringement had been committed, they may only close the proceeding without taking a decision on the merits. This view was also confirmed by the CJEU.[45] Had the Croatian court compared other language versions[46] of Article 5(2), it would most likely interpret it in the following way:

---

objectives thereof and to its state of evolution at the date on which the provision in question is to be applied (paras. 18–20 Case 283/81 *CILFIT* [1982] 3415, ECLI:EU:C:1982:335).

[44]Derlén (2009), p. 160.

[45]Cf. Case C-375/09 *Tele 2 Polska* [2011] ECR I-3055, EU:C:2011:270. The European Commission is exclusively empowered to take a negative decision within the meaning of Articles 101 and 102 of the Treaty. If the national law would provide for an obligation by the national authority to take a negative decision in the sense of Articles 101 and 102 of the Treaty, such a provision of national law would contravene with EU law.

[46]See for instance, German, Slovene, Italian and French:

DE Sind die Voraussetzungen für ein Verbot nach den ihnen vorliegenden Informationen nicht gegeben, so können sie auch entscheiden, dass für sie kein Anlass besteht, tätig zu werden.

SL Kadar na podlagi razpoložljivih informacij pogoji za prepoved niso izpolnjeni, se lahko odločijo, da ni nobenega vzroka za njihovo ukrepanje.

IT Qualora, in base alle informazioni di cui dispongono, non sussistono le condizioni per un divieto, possono anche decidere di non avere motivo di intervenire.

FR: Lorsqu'elles considèrent, sur la base des informations dont elles disposent, que les conditions d'une interdiction ne sont pas réunies, elles peuvent également décider qu'il n'y a pas lieu pour elles d'intervenir.

> Where in the proceedings initiated pursuant to Article 101 or 102 of the Treaty the CCA establishes that there is no distortion of competition, it should not and it may not decide on the merits but terminate the proceeding in line with the interpretation provided by the EU Court cited before.[47]

It should be noted that the initiative for correcting the Croatian version of Regulation No 1/2003 came from the Croatian Competition Authority, which resulted in the Croatian corrigendum to the Regulation concerned published in the Official Journal of the EU L 173/108 of 30 June 2016. Article 5(2) now reads as follows:

> Ako na temelju informacija koje posjeduju nisu ispunjeni uvjeti za utvrđivanje zabrane, nacionalna tijela za tržišno natjecanje mogu također odlučiti da **ne postoji temelj za njihovo daljnje postupanje**. (emphasis added)

Further empirical research is certainly needed to establish how Croatian national courts deal with vague legal terms (also referred to as general or abstract terms)[48] or linguistic discrepancies resulting from translations of EU *acquis*. However, judging from this example, courts will not be too enthusiastic to compare different language versions of the same document and will instead rely solely on the wording of the text in their national language. This is partly understandable, as they are used to interpreting vague legal terms in the national, Croatian legal context using their native language. Still, this is precisely what the Court of Justice in *Stauder* warned against. Although in the discussed example a corrigendum was made, many other cases calling for a comparison of different language versions will not be about incorrect translation, but about vague and indeterminate terms.

4 Vagueness and Legal Uncertainty

As mentioned earlier, one of the paradoxes of legal language is evident in the need for precision and clarity on the one hand, and inherent vagueness of some legal concepts on the other, which poses difficulties for legal interpretation. In its everyday, general language meaning, 'vague' is used in the sense of 'not clear', 'not having a precise meaning', 'not clearly defined' or 'not sharply outlined'.[49] People tend to use vague in the sense of uninformative or incomplete.[50] In different spheres, vagueness of expression takes on different features. Whereas in political discourse it can be described as the art of giving the appropriate amount of information, vagueness poses an array of both linguistic and legal challenges to legal interpretation, as well as to legal translation. Not only is vagueness a linguistic phenomenon

[47] Available at: http://www.aztn.hr/en/7178/. Accessed: 1 Feb 2018.

[48] Baaij (2018), p. 45.

[49] Available at: https://www.merriam-webster.com/dictionary/vague. (Accessed 1 Feb 2018).

[50] Endicott (2001), p. 57. For an extensive study of vagueness in law see Endicott's seminal book *Vagueness in Law*.

that can lead to ambiguity and polysemy, but also a source of legal uncertainty and legal indeterminacy. A distinction can be made between semantic vagueness in the former case, and pragmatic, in the latter. According to Bix, law lends itself to "all types of semantic and pragmatic vagueness and every imaginable combination thereof"[51] A (legal) term is considered vague if its meaning is underdefined and subject to more than one possible interpretation.[52] Observed from a legal perspective, vagueness is described in terms of imprecision, uncertainty and indeterminacy and poses a threat to legal communication, because, unlike ambiguity, it cannot be resolved through linguistic context.[53]

4.1 Vagueness of EU Competition Law Concepts

On the example of EU Competition Law concepts of *undertaking* and *economic activity* attempt is made to elucidate the consequences of vague concepts in the practice of (multilingual) law, by drawing on the principles and methods of Terminology with a view of gaining a better understanding, and in turn furthering the uniform application of law by legal practitioners in the EU.

What exactly then constitutes an undertaking for the purpose of EU Competition Law? Considering the above account of vagueness in law, *undertaking* can be regarded as a vague, indeterminate concept due to the following reasons. First, there is no statutory definition of undertaking at the level of EU primary law. In consequence, there appears to be no single answer as to what constitutes an undertaking (e.g. in the sense of an exhaustive list or a set of essential, unequivocal features as *differentia specifica*), which may lead to legal uncertainty. Second, its meaning has been established by the CJEU on a case-to-case basis, because of which, the scope of the concept grew with each new case, rendering it extensive. This is also due to the fact that *undertaking* is an autonomous concept of EU Law whose meaning is to be interpreted autonomously at the level of EU Law, independent of national law meanings. Needless to say, interpreting the meaning of undertaking in line with national laws, or equating it with natural or legal personality under national law—would have provided some legal certainty and facilitated the identification of undertaking in EU Competition Law.[54] As is, courts still grapple with the concept's meaning. In keeping with the cognitive linguistics view and Terminology, to understand the meaning of *undertaking* it is necessary to conceptualize it as part of its wider conceptual structure, including its related concepts and even domains in which it is conceptualized. Basic principles of internal market and freedom of

[51]Bix (2016), p. 134.

[52]Frade (2005), p. 137.

[53]Bajčić (2017), p. 43.

[54]Jones (2012), p. 7.

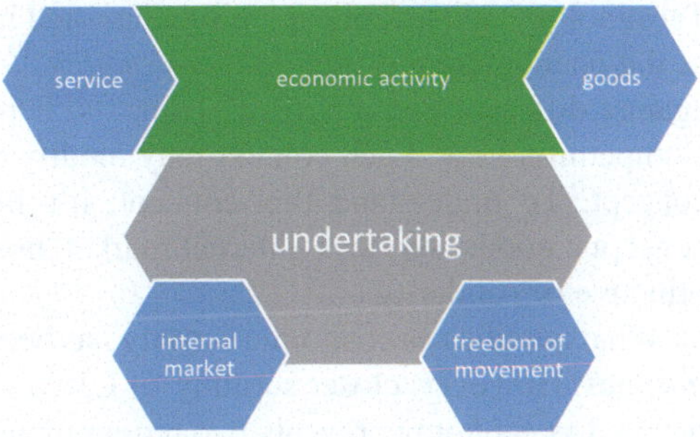

Fig. 1 The conceptualization of undertaking

movement are central to understanding competition law concepts. The latter conceptualization can be illustrated in the following way (Fig. 1):

Relying on settled case law of the CJEU, there appear to be nuanced ways of conceptualizing an *undertaking*, or to be more precise, of an entity qualified as an undertaking for the purpose of EU Competition Law. Nevertheless, one feature looms large in this regard, namely *economic activity*. Owing to the CJEU's interpretation, economic activity crystallised as the *differentia specifica* of undertaking. However, the concept of economic activity is also underdefined. In broadest terms, it comprises "offering goods and services in a given market", though the exercise of some economic activity transcends the concepts of 'goods' (having positive or negative market value) and services (offered for remuneration).[55] According to Hatzopoulos, although economic theory offers helpful classifications of this concept, they 'have barely made it into any legal instrument'.[56] *Economic activity* can also be regarded as a vague concept, in that it has been interpreted differently in the context of competition law rules, as opposed to the internal market rules.[57] This runs counter to the principle of coherence enshrined in Article 7 TFEU stating that:

> The Union shall ensure consistency between its policies and activities, taking all of its objectives into account and in accordance with the principle of conferral of powers.

Aware of the importance of a uniform interpretation of this concept, the CJEU has on many occasions drawn parallels between the internal market and competition rules. Note that Hatzopoulos states that competition law is part of the broader concept of internal market—ever since the entry into force of the Treaty of Lisbon—which commands a uniform interpretation of the same terms.[58] From the perspective of

[55]See Hatzopoulos (2011), p. 2.

[56]Hatzopoulos (2011), p. 3.

[57]Case C-355/00 *Freskot* [2003] ECR I-5263, ECLI:EU:C:2003:298; Case C-309/99 *Wouters* [2002] ECR I-1577, ECLI:EU:C:2002:98.

[58]If internal market and competition rules could be thought to stand on parity and independently from each other, the Lisbon Treaty has clearly subdued the latter to the former: undistorted competition has disappeared, as such, from the aims of the EU (Articles 3(3) TEU and 3(1)(b) TFEU) and has been relegated to Protocol 27, according to which 'the internal ... market includes a system ensuring that competition is not distorted'. See Hatzopoulos (2011), p. 13.

Terminology, a concept can be subclassified in more than one way, which is known as the phenomenon of *multidimensionality*.[59] The meaning of a concept is profiled against different extralinguistic contexts, here: the context of internal market and Competition Law. Each context may modify the conceptualization of a vague legal concept. To understand this concept, it's necessary to understand other related concepts: goods, services, internal market, non-economic activities, social function, principle of solidarity.

What qualifies as economic activity has been the bone of contention in many legal disputes. However, closer scrutiny of CJEU's case law on what renders an activity pursued as economic, reveals two requirements which must be met for an activity to qualify as economic. First, the activity should consist in offering goods and services in a given market.[60] Second, the entity offering goods and services should be bearing the financial risks of the activity.[61] These conditions make for a very extensive concept of 'undertaking'. Indeed, by analyzing relevant case law, it is evident that undertaking can include one or more legal persons[62] (parent companies and subsidiaries); an individual,[63] a State or public body (e.g. social insurance provider, healthcare management body),[64] partnerships, sporting associations[65] *inter alia*.[66] The Court's conceptualization of undertaking can be illustrated by means of ontological[67] relationships resembling a simple taxonomy (Fig. 2):

The figure illustrates that economic activity can be singled out as the 'essential feature', i.e. the most salient feature that makes an entity to qualify as undertaking for the purpose of EU Competition Law. However, economic activity is not considered in isolation of the context: the subsequent use of the purchased goods of services

---

[59]Faber and López Rodrĭguez (2012), p. 26.

[60]e.g. Case C-205/03P *FENIN* [2006] I-6295, ECLI:EU:C:2006:453.

[61]Cf. Hatzopoulos (2011), pp. 18–19. On the first requirement see, for instance *FENIN* judgment. The second requirement was highlighted in the following CJEU's cases: *Wouters*, paras. 48-9; Case C-244/94 *FFSA* [1995] ECR I-4013, ECLI:EU:C:1995:392, para. 21; Case C-364/92 *SAT Fluggesellschaft* [1994] I-43, ECLI:EU:C:1994:7, para. 9.

[62]Case C-266/93 *Bundeskartellamt v Volkswagen and VAG Leasing GmbH* [1995] I-3477, ECLI: EU:C:1995:345.

[63]See e.g. Case *Wouters*, EU:C:2002:98; European Commission, case *RAI/UNITEL* (OJ L 157, 15.6.1978, p. 39); *French Beef* (OJ L 209, 19.8.2003, p. 12).

[64]Case C-41/90 *Höfner and Elser* [1991] ECR I-1979, ECLI:EU:C:1991:161; Case *FFSA*; Case C-67/96 *Albany* [1999] ECR I-5751, ECLI:EU:C:1999:430; Case C-475/99 *Firma Ambulanz Glöckner* [2001] ECR I-8089. ECLI:EU:C:2001:577.

[65]Case T-193/02 *Laurent Piau v Commission* [2005] ECR II-209, ECLI :EU:T:2005:22.

[66]For a detailed analysis of case law on the meaning of undertaking see: Jones (2012). For the purpose of this Chapter prominent CJEU's cases include: Case *Höfner and Elser*; Case 19/61 *Mannesman AG* [1962] ECR 357, ECLI:EU:C:1962:31; Joined Cases 17/61 and 20/61 *Klöckner-Werke AG and Hoesch AG* [1962] ECR 325, ECLI:EU:C:1962:30.

[67]Greatly simplified, an ontology is a conceptualization of a specific field. Ontologies resemble taxonomies in that they display taxonomic or hierarchical structure of a domain. Providing for context-rich representations of concepts, they are often employed in terminological resources, e.g. databases.

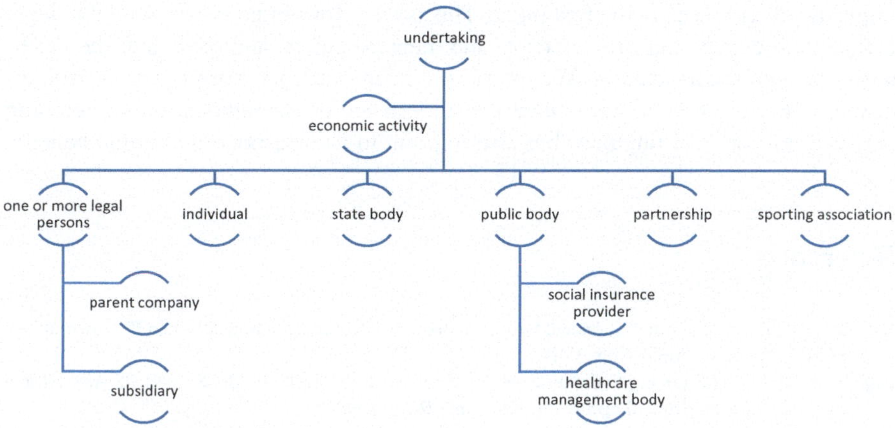

Fig. 2 A taxonomic representation of undertaking

matters,[68] as well as the social function of the entity involved[69]; or existence and implementation of the principle of solidarity.[70] All of these related concepts contribute to the legal conceptualization of economic activity and in turn, paint a more realistic picture of the concept of undertaking in EU Competition Law. Gaining a deeper understanding of the meaning of vague legal concepts and the way in which courts establish their meanings is instrumental to ensure their uniform application Union-wide. In our opinion, this is important not just from the perspective of legal practitioners in EU Member States, but for the work of legal translators as well.

5 Conclusion

The interpretation and application of law in the multilingual EU environment require a special approach and skills grounded in both law and linguistics. Legal practitioners of different legal backgrounds are responsible for overcoming vagueness intrinsic to many legal concepts and uncertainty resulting from this vagueness, but also from inadequate usage of legal terms. In a multilingual context, this is not possible by relying solely on one language version of the text. Even though each language version is equally authentic, in cases of doubt one version will not be enough to establish the true meaning of a concept, as we have seen. While it is the task of the Court of Justice of the EU to ensure uniform interpretation of EU Law, the real responsibility and challenge lies with national legal practitioners to recognize

[68]e.g. Case *FENIN*.

[69]e.g. Joined Cases C-159/91 and C-160/91 *Poucet and Pistre* [1993] ECR I-637, ECLI:EU:C:1993:63; Case C-218/00 *Cisal* [2002] ECR I-691, ECLI:EU:C:2002:36.

[70]e.g. Case *Albany*; Case C-350/07 *Kattner* [2009] ECR I-1513, ECLI:EU:C:2009:127.

linguistic divergences in the first place. This is why Terminology is essential in legal language: it concentrates on concepts and their meanings, and feeds into the mechanism of legal interpretation. We return to our introductory warning: no Terminology, no law, in order to accentuate the importance of continuous mutual learning between lawyers and linguists, but also to point to a corresponding mutual benefit.

References

Baaij CJW (2018) Legal integration and language diversity. Rethinking translation in EU lawmaking. Oxford University Press, New York

Bajčić M (2011) The conceptualization of legal terms in different fields of law: the need for a transparent terminological approach. Res Lang 9(I):81–93

Bajčić M (2017) New insights into the semantics of legal concepts and the legal dictionary. John Benjamins, Amsterdam

Bix BH (2016) Legal interpetation and the philosophy of language. In: Solan LM, Tiersma PM (eds) The Oxford handbook of language and the law. Oxford University Press, pp 145–159

Bobek M (2011) The multilingualism of the European Union Law in the National Courts: beyond the textbooks. In: Kjær –L, Adamo S (eds) Linguistic diversity and European democracy. Ashgate, Great Britain, pp 123–142

Cabré MT (1999) Terminology. Theory, methods and applications. John Benjamins, Amsterdam

Derlén M (2009) Multilingual interpretation of European Union Law. Wolters Kluwer, Alphen aan den Rijn

Endicott T (2001) Vagueness in law. Oxford University Press, Oxford

Engberg J, Kjær AL (2011) Approaches to language and the law – some introductory notes. Hermes J Lang Commun Stud 46:7–10

Faber P, López Rodrĭguez CI (2012) Terminology and specialized language. In: Faber P (ed) A cognitive linguistic view of terminology and specialized language. De Gruyter Mouton, Berlin, pp 9–33

Frade C (2005) Legal multinominals: recovering possible meanings from vague texts. In: Bhatia VK et al (eds) Vagueness in normative texts. Peter Lang, Bern, pp 133–157

Gardner J (2016) Misused English words and expressions in EU publications. European Court of Auditors. Available via ECA. https://www.eca.europa.eu/Other%20publications/EN_TERMINOLOGY_PUBLICATION/EN_TERMINOLOGY_PUBLICATION.pdf. Accessed 20 Nov 2017

Gibbons J (2004) Introduction. Taking legal language seriously. In: Gibbons J et al (eds) Language in the law. Orient Longman, India, pp 1–16

Hatzopoulos V (2011) The concept of economic activity in the EU Treaty. From ideological dead-ends to workable judicial concepts. College of Europe Research Papers in Law. Available via COLEUROPE. https://www.coleurope.eu/study/european-legal-studies/research-activities/research-papers-law. Accessed 15 Nov 2017

Jones A (2012) The boundaries of the concept of undertaking. Eur Competition J 8(2):301–331

Lewis OC (1972) Symposium: law, language, and communication – introduction. Case West Res Law Rev 23:307 ff

Martin W, van der Vliet H (2003) Design and production of terminological dictionaries. In: van Sterkenburg P (ed) A practical guide to lexicography. John Benjamins, Amsterdam, pp 333–350

Mellinkoff D (1963) The language of the law. Little, Brown and Co, Boston

Mišćenić E (2016) Legal translation vs. legal certainty in EU law. In: Mišćenić E, Raccah A (eds) Legal risks in EU law. Springer, Cham, pp 87–107

Picht H, Schmitz K-D (2001) Terminologie und Wissensordnung. Ausgewählte Schriften aus dem Gesamtwerk von Eugen Wüster. TermNet, Wien

Šarčević S (2013) Multilingual lawmaking and legal (Un)certainty in the European Union. Int J Law Lang Discourse 3(1):1–29
Tiersma P (1999) Legal language. The University of Chicago Press, Chicago
Vernengo RJ (1965) Recht und Sprache. Archiv für Rechts- und Sozialphilosophie. Beiheft Neue Folge 4:293–297
Wright SE (1997) Term selection: The initial phase of terminology management. In: Wright SE, Budin, G (eds) Handbook of terminology management, vol 2. John Benjamins, Amsterdam, pp 13–25
Wüster E (1974) Die allgemeine Terminologielehre – Ein Grenzgebiet zwischen Sprachwissenschaft, Logik, Ontologie, Informatik und den Sachwissenschaften. Linguistics 119: 61–106
Wüster E (1985) Einführung in die allgemeine Terminologielehre und terminologische Lexikographie. Infoterm, Kopenhagen

Martina Bajčić is Assistant Professor, Department of Foreign Languages, University of Rijeka Faculty of Law, Croatia.

Adrijana Martinović is Assistant Professor, Department of EU Public Law, University of Rijeka Faculty of Law, Croatia.

Binomials in EU Competition Law

Katja Dobrić Basaneže

Abstract This chapter investigates binomial expressions in EU legal language from a bilingual corpus-based perspective, where one of the languages involved in the analysis is a language of lesser diffusion. By investigating binomial expressions in two parallel corpora of EU Competition Law (English and Croatian), the chapter focuses on the semantic relationship between the constituents so as to account for the deletions in the language which does not dispose of the same binomial structures. Since EU Law in general and EU legal translation in particular is characterised by hybridity, an attempt is made to detect non-typical binomials. The chapter also investigates whether these binomials, although some of them invented for the purpose of conveying the meaning of the concepts of EU Law, can still be considered more idiomatic in one language than in the other.

1 Introduction

Binomial expressions have thus far been given significant attention in the research on legal language. This especially holds true for legal English, where they have originally been used to facilitate communication.[1] Today, however, many binomials represent "worthless doubling",[2] while the Plain English campaign has been discouraging the use of binomials "which are purely aesthetic in nature or, in essence, unmotivated semantically".[3] Surprisingly and contrary to their legal tradition, binomials are not as frequent in English present-day legislation.[4] Moreover, it seems that some English varieties tend to

[1]Danet (1980), p. 469.

[2]Mellinkoff (1963), p. 363.

[3]Kopaczyk (2017), p. 161.

[4]Kopaczyk (2017), p. 174.

K. Dobrić Basaneže (✉)
University of Rijeka, Faculty of Law, Department of Foreign Languages, Rijeka, Croatia
e-mail: kdobric@pravri.hr

S. Marino et al. (eds.), *Language and Law*,
https://doi.org/10.1007/978-3-319-90905-9_13

employ their own inventory of binomials more frequently than the binomials which stand a chance of appearing in the UK legislation too.[5]

Since translated EU Law is very often characterised by hybridity, we expect that the inventory of binomials discussed in this chapter would not necessarily be typical of legal English used by native speakers outside the EU institutions and might thus be regarded as one of the characteristics of hybrid language.[6]

We thus expect that many of these sequences do not combine by linguistic convention, but are created through "individualized reference to concepts or participants",[7] or in this case, through reference to the concepts of Competition Law. Needless to say, this stability of sequences is also preserved in the target language, thus making these word strings[8] untypical of both the source and target language. The chapter also focuses on the extent to which variations and deletions are permitted[9] with regard to the translation of binomials in the context of EU Competition Law and it does so by adopting a corpus-based perspective. In addition, it attempts to detect some instances of the Bad Simple English (BSE)[10] trend, where one (or both) constituent(s) of binomials is not used in keeping with the English grammar rules. Since it is deemed that "linguistic aspects of hybrid languages have not been investigated in a systematic manner",[11] this chapter attempts to fill a gap in this regard. Given the fact that it focuses on parallel corpora of English and Croatian Competition Law, the chapter represents a useful resource for both practicing translators and lawyers in developing strategies for the translation of binomials.

2 Typology of Binomial Expressions

The term *binomial* was first defined by Malkiel in 1959 as

> a sequence of two words pertaining to the same form-class, placed on an identical level of syntactic hierarchy, and ordinarily connected by some kind of lexical link.[12]

---

[5]Kopaczyk (2017), p.173.

[6]Schäffner and Adab (2001).

[7]Monzó Nebot (2017), p. 114.

[8]Cao (2007).

[9]Šarčević (1997), p. 183.

[10]The term *Bad Simple English* (BSE) was coined by German scientists to refer to the bad English used in science so as to encourage the abolition of "an English-only rule at meetings attended only by speakers of German" (German scientists fear BSE—Bad Simple English. https://www.expatica.com/de/news/country-news/German-scientists-fear-BSE-Bad-Simple-English_132114.html. Accessed 29 Mar 2018).

[11]Trklja (2017), p. 90.

[12]Malkiel (1959), p. 113 cited in Gustafsson (1984), p. 124.

Consequently, many authors have proposed their own definitions of binomials,[13] thus also creating an abundance of terms to denote the same concept (*binomials, binominals, doublets, binomial pairs, paired forms, couplets, conjoined phrases, nominal stereotypes, word strings*). While some argue that binomials contribute to the all-inclusiveness[14] and preciseness[15] of legal language, others consider them worthless[16] and pleonastic.[17] Nonetheless, they are a distinctive feature of legal language, which is why, despite the centuries-old urge towards their reduction to single words, they 'insinuate themselves into the lawyer's subconscious'.[18] Needless to say, they also reflect the "specific legal cultures"[19] in which they are embedded and "structure our social experience".[20]

Binomial expressions may be extended into larger units of meaning, "thus making up larger fixed sequences"[21] with "the additional constituents being (either) almost obligatory or more or less optional".[22] Bukovčan points out that

> doublets can be extended to trinomial and multinomial expressions representing a special type of phraseological unit which call for in-depth linguistic and extralinguistic study.[23]

Enumeration is another style marker of legal language and encompasses "listing more than two syntactically and semantically interrelated elements",[24] and, hence, these larger chunks of enumerated elements may sometimes represent extended binomial expressions. For instance, the binomial *fees and charges* may become part of the enumeration *to pay all costs, fees, charges, disbursements and expenses*, the latter listing all types of amounts that are to be paid.

Although there are different typologies of binomial expressions, in this chapter they will be classified according to the word classes of their constituents.[25] Additionally, the semantic relationship between constituents[26] will also be taken into consideration so as to justify the use of binomial expressions. In this regard, Gačić[27] distinguishes between doublets and triplets, that is, sequences of synonymous units (e.g. *agreed and declared*; *force and effect*; *give, devise, and bequeath*), and

---

[13] Gustafsson (1984), Bhatia (1993) and Bukovčan (2009).

[14] Bhatia (1993).

[15] Gustafsson (1984).

[16] Mellinkoff (1963).

[17] Lewis and Mrčela (2016).

[18] Mellinkoff (1963), p. 363.

[19] Bukovčan (2009), p. 62.

[20] Monzó Nebot (2017), p. 109.

[21] Gabrovšek (2011), p. 21.

[22] Ibid., p. 20.

[23] Bukovčan (2009), p. 63.

[24] Ibid., p. 74.

[25] Gustafsson (1984).

[26] Bukovčan (2009).

[27] Gačić (2009).

binomial and multinomial expressions, hence, sequences of antonymous units or sequences which contribute to the all-inclusiveness of legal language (e.g. *advice and consent*; *by or on behalf of*; *executed and signed*; *freehold conveyed or long lease granted*; *jointly and severally*). For the purpose of this chapter, sequences of synonymous units will be treated as binomials proper,[28] and hence, redundant, while sequences of antonymous units or sequences which contribute to the all-inclusiveness of legal language, although very often pleonastic, will be treated as indispensable to legal language.

3 Binomials and Legal Translation

Legal translation is often defined as "an act of communication in the mechanism of the law"[29] that is receiver-oriented. In our case, given the fact that with EU translations the translated legal text very often has the same legal force as the original (as is the case with primary law and legislative texts of secondary law), the type of translation involved is the normative[30] or institutional[31] one. Despite the fact that in the context of supranational institutions, such as the EU, the process of legal translation is facilitated by developing standardised legal terminology in the official languages of the Member States, legal translators might still encounter many pitfalls, especially when translating from English. We are well aware of the fact that, although the correct translation of terms constitutes the very essence of legal translation, very often

> the Achilles heel of the operation remains the creation of the appropriate LSP environment for the term in the target language[32]

in order to

> make the text appear as written by an expert and not by a layman.[33]

Furthermore, a collocational error in legal translation indicates

> the lack of specialized professional knowledge and either provokes unpleasant comments or leads to losing a client.[34]

It seems, however, that in this type of institutional translation, other tendencies prevail:

---

[28]Kopaczyk (2009).

[29]Šarčević (1997), p. 55.

[30]Cao (2007).

[31]Koskinen (2008).

[32]Picht (1987), p. 154.

[33]Aguado de Cea (2007), p. 190.

[34]Matulewska (2013), p. 96.

> [T]ranslated law uses untypical collocational patterns and is marked by a lack of phraseological rigor. The referencing patterns in translated language are significantly more varied and are a close reflection of SL patterns with little effort on the part of translators to overcome interference. It significantly decreases the textual fit of translated law to nontranslated legal language in the area where difference may not be attributed to the multilingualism-related constraints, conceptual lacunas or asymmetry between languages.[35]

The importance of studying legal phraseology was thus never in doubt, given the fact that

> legal translation is not only a question of terminology, but also a problem of phraseological conventions.[36]

As a matter of fact, standardised expressions such as binomials, can help us grasp "the stylistic preferences in legal drafting".[37] These expressions, however, are problematic when translating between unrelated legal systems, because the target language often does not contain the word strings with the units bearing a similar meaning. After all, language is "inextricably intertwined with the legal system",[38] hence, some scholars claim legal English and common law are inseparable.[39] Many terms and phraseological units can thus be understood only against a common law background. Translations in EU context, however, are not produced within the target culture[40] and are often perceived as strange outside the EU. Very often, and this especially applies to the English versions, they are referred to as 'hybrid texts'.[41] This hybridity in turn results in a mixture of word combinations, including both the ones combining according to the phraseological conventions of common law English and the invented ones, "relatively unknown to native English speakers outside the EU institutions".[42] It thus follows that, although many scholars have argued it is advisable to translate binomial expressions "in any way compatible with the target-language conventions"[43] in the context of EU translations, it is sometimes necessary to reproduce the same hybridity in the target text as well, especially since in law, "sometimes each and every word may carry different legal meanings and legal consequences".[44] It is thus expected that institutional translations of legal texts contain both semantically unmotivated binomials typical of the language they originated from and the invented ones, which are in our case motivated both by the EU translation policies and the genre of EU Competition Law.

---

35 Biel (2014), p. 190.

36 Goźdź–Roszkowski and Pontrandolfo (2017), p. 4.

37 Ibid., p. 3.

38 Kjær (2007), p. 508.

39 Triebel (2009), p. 149.

40 Koskinen (2011), p. 57.

41 Trosborg (1997).

42 Gardner (2016), p. 3.

43 Alcaraz Varó and Hughes (2002), p. 40.

44 Cao (2007), p. 90.

4 Corpus

As suggested by Bowker and Pearson, corpus linguistics is "an approach or a methodology for studying language use".[45] Due to the easy access to a large collection of texts, corpus linguistics has become an important tool for studying phraseology. It involves the study of naturally occurring language by means of electronic corpora. One of the first definitions of the term *corpus* thus suggests that

> a corpus is a collection of pieces of language text in electronic form, selected according to external criteria to represent, as far as possible, a language or language variety as a source of data for linguistic research.[46]

In order to answer our research questions, the corpus designed for the purpose of this study represents a collection of EU legal texts on Competition Law in English and their Croatian translations. Since from the perspective of translation studies we can differentiate between four types of corpora,[47] our corpus consists of source texts and their translations and can thus be categorised as a parallel one. The corpus consists of texts collected for the purpose of the project *Training Action for Legal Practitioners: Linguistic Skills and Translation in EU Competition Law*, but is, for the purpose of this chapter, restricted to the English and Croatian texts only. Since, however, Croatian translations are not available for all English texts, the design of the English corpus very much depended on the availability of their Croatian counterparts, so as to balance both the size and the content of the corpora. Nevertheless, given the fact that corpora designed for the purpose of studying special-purpose languages (LSP) can be smaller than those used for studying general-purpose languages (LGP),[48] it can be claimed that the English corpus of Competition Law (EnCompLaw) of 278,493 and the Croatian one (CroCompLaw) of 229,398 words are of sufficient size.

In terms of content, on the other hand, both corpora can be subdivided into two groups:

1. The most important EU legislation on Competition Law
2. EU Commission's decisions, guidelines and notices relevant for Competition Law

Considering the above proposed criteria for corpus design and the availability of Croatian language versions, the first group consists of 22 instruments, of which one can be classified as primary legislation (*Treaty rules on competition law*) and the rest as secondary legislation encompassing sixteen regulations and five directives. Since regulations "are the most centralising of all EU instruments",[49] they also prevail in

[45] Bowker and Pearson (2002), p. 3.
[46] Sinclair (2005), p. 16.
[47] Biel (2010), pp. 3–4.
[48] Bowker and Pearson (2002), p. 48.
[49] Chalmers et al. (2010), p. 98.

the corpus. The second part of the corpus, on the other hand, mainly consists of soft law instruments, and includes seven notices, two guidelines and one decision. The corpus thus consists of sixty-four texts, with each subcorpus accounting for the half of the total corpus. Finally, in terms of publication dates, all texts were published in the time period from 2001 to 2015.

5 Methodology

Both EnCompLaw and CroCompLaw were queried by means of Sketch Engine.[50] Since all binomial expressions are either joined by 'and' ('i') or 'or'('ili'), it was decided that the search for binomials would start from these conjunctions, that is, from their collocation candidates. Given the fact that binomial expressions always occur in contiguous sequences, we only included one token[51] from the right and one from the left when computing collocation candidates. In addition, minimum frequency of occurrence was set at three, although this chapter also takes some variations of the basic binomial into consideration that occur in the corpus less than expected (e.g. *pažljivo i nepristrano* as the variation of the more frequent *nepristrano i pažljivo*). Since the queries that are taken as the starting point for searching the corpus can fulfil a variety of syntactic functions (e.g. joining two clauses), it was also necessary to analyse the concordances of collocation candidates (see Fig. 1), thus making the analysis a semi-automatic one.

Additionally, the programme also listed some collocation candidates, which were eliminated based on our linguistic intuition (e.g. *which*). Since, however, the list of Croatian binomial expressions did not produce a complete match with the English list of binomials, we also needed to rely upon our intuition when searching for the missing translation equivalents. Here we presupposed that at least one of the constituents of the English binomial might be rendered by one word and by providing a *prima facie* translation[52] of the constituent, we examined its wider context in CroCompLaw, hence, its concordances. A case in point may be illustrated by the English binomial *obsolete or uncompetitive*, which is in CroComp not rendered as a binomial, but through two independent clauses (*je zastarjela ili nije više konkurentna*). Finally, three additional corpora available in Sketch Engine were consulted for the purpose of referencing, the British National Corpus (BNC) of 96,134,547 for English and hrwac 2.2[53] of 1,210,021,198 words for Croatian. The English binomials were also verified against the British Law Report Corpus of

[50]Kilgariff et al. (2014).

[51]The smallest unit of a corpus; each word from and punctuation can be considered as a separate token (Sketch Engine Keywords. https://www.sketchengine.eu/my_keywords/token/. Accessed 21 Mar 2018).

[52]Carvalho (2008), p. 10.

[53]Ljubešić and Klubička (2014).

Fig. 1 Concordances of the collocation candidate *concerned*

8,515,749 words. No similar comparison could have been carried out for Croatian units since to date there are no legal corpora for Croatian. The Croatian web corpus, however, does include texts from the legal domain and is therefore a relevant comparison point.

6 Results

Given the fact that the main objective of the chapter is to focus on all binomial types and the way they are rendered in the two parallel corpora, a list of binomials ordered in terms of their frequency is not produced. In this chapter binomial expressions are, as noted above, categorised taking into account the word classes of their constituents. Additionally, a distinction is made between binomials, trinomials and enumerations. It is thus natural that the list in the Appendix does not correspond to the list ordered in terms of frequency (see Table 1). The latter is, however, taken into account when elaboration is made on the typicality and non-typicality of binomials, which is additionally confirmed through the comparison with reference corpora.

Table 1 The most frequent English binomials and their frequency (per million words)[a] in the BNC and British Law Report Corpus

Binomials in EnCompLaw joined by 'and'	Frequency (per million) in EnCompLaw	Frequency (per million) in the BNC	Frequency (per million) in the British Law Corpus
Research and development	435.15	6.60	0.50
Fishery and aquaculture	164.65	0	0
Small and medium-sized	85.27	0.74	0
Agreements and practices	85.27	0.01	0.10
Open, transparent and non-discriminatory	70.56	0	0
Goods and services	58.80	5.73	7.57
Culture and heritage	52.92	0.05	0
Information and evidence	32.34	0.09	1.10
Establishment and operation	32.34	0.01	0
Fines and periodic penalty payments	32.34	0	0
Rights and obligations	29.40	1.05	10.80
Agreements and concerted practices	26.46	0.01	0

[a]Frequency per million is also called normative or relative frequency (hereinafter: RF)

Results suggest that both binomials joined by 'and' and the ones joined by 'or' mostly consist of nominal pairs. It thus seems that Gustafsson's claim[54] on the typicality of nominal pairs in legal language also applies to what can be dubbed EU legal language. Less frequently found in the corpus are adjectival pairs, although they also occur significantly enough. Contrary to Gustafssson's findings, where there is total absence of adverbs, in EU Competition Law there are ten instances of adverbial pairs. Verbal pairs, on the other hand, are least represented in the corpus (see Fig. 2).

A similar picture is also depicted by trinomial pairs, which again mostly consist of nouns and adjectives. Verbal trinomials, on the other hand, are least frequent (see Fig. 3).

Finally, it seems that enumerations in EU legal English are not as frequent as in common law legal English. As a matter of fact, there is only one instance of a nominal and one instance of a verbal enumeration (see Fig. 4).

It must be pointed out, however, that variations and modifications of one binomial were not given a separate count, for they carry only one meaning and are often

[54]Gustafsson (1984), p. 132.

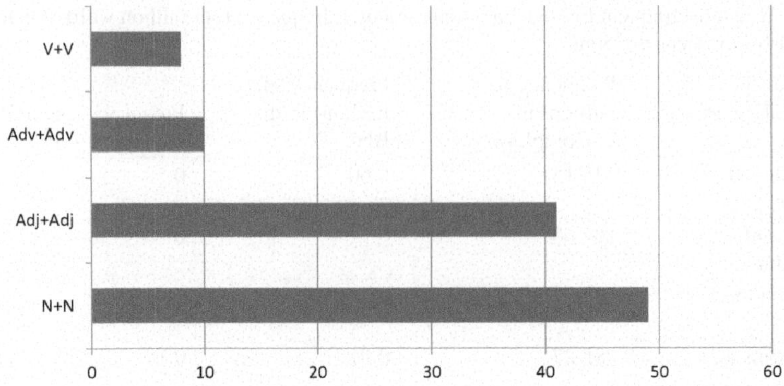

Fig. 2 Frequency and types of binomials

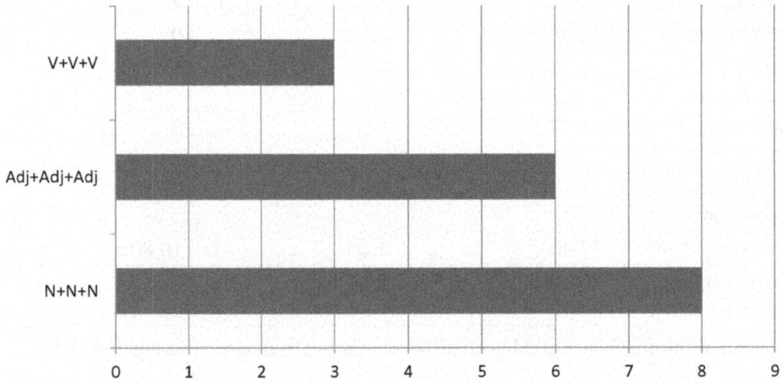

Fig. 3 Frequency and types of trinomials

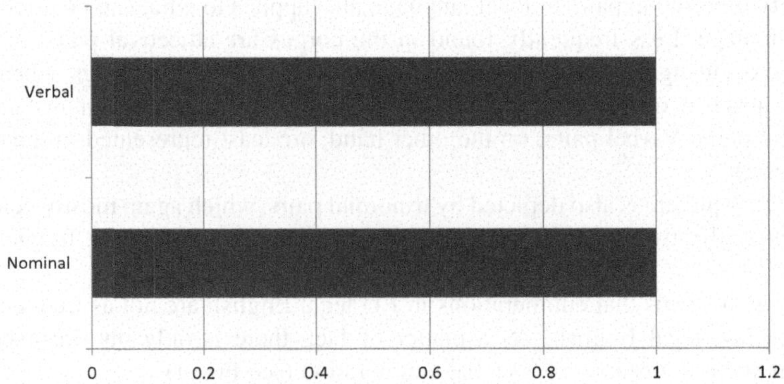

Fig. 4 Frequency and types of enumerations

rendered in the target language in a lesser number of variants. This was, for instance, the case with the binomial *in whole or in part*, which witnesses additional five variants in EnCompLaw (*fully or partly, partly or fully, entirely or partly, partly or entirely, wholly or mainly*), but is in CroCompLaw rendered through two variants only (*u cijelosti ili djelomično* or *djelomično ili potpuno*). Furthermore, due to the differences between languages involved in the analysis, there are cases when an English binomial is rendered through different means in Croatian, which is why the starting point for the analysis were the data from EnCompLaw.

7 Analysis and Discussion

While most binomials and trinomials from EnCompLaw are in CroCompLaw rendered in their full forms (see Appendix), thus preserving both the word order and the degree of their idiomaticity (e.g. *open, transparent and non-discriminatory* – *otvoren, transparentan i nediskriminirajući*; *to improve, substitute or replace* – *poboljšati, nadomijestiti ili zamijeniti*), some witness more variations, which applies to both the degree of their reversibility and modifications. Constituents of the binomials *impartial and dillligent* (*pažljivo i nepristrano*); *national or regional* (*nacionalan ili regionalan*) seem to be less restrictively combined than, for instance, constituents in the binomials *agreements or practices* (*sporazumi ili usklađena djelovanja*); *books or records* (*poslovne knjige ili dokumentacija*); *mergers or acquisitions* (*spajanja ili preuzimanja*). Numerous expressions, as suggested by the above example *in whole or in part*, also witness modifications of their constituents. By the same token, the English binomial *experience and testing* allows modifications of the second constituent in CroCompLaw (*iskustvo i testiranje/ispitivanje*). Similar examples include *incorrect or misleading* (*netočan ili obmanjujući*; *netočan ili zavaravajući*), *directly or indirectly* (*izravno ili neizravno*; *neposredno ili posredno*; *posredno ili neposredno*), *intentionally or negligently* (*namjerno ili iz nehaja*; *namjerno ili nepažnjom*); *to record and compile* (*bilježiti i prikupljati*; *evidentirati i prikupljati*) and clearly point to the fact that the Croatian language is more prone to variations and modifications of binomials than English. Furthermore, these examples reveal the

> relative stability of legal word combinations that apply not only to varying degrees of stability of *different* word combinations, but also to varying degrees of stability of *one and the same* word combination, depending on the situation and use.[55]

The situation and use are in turn portrayed through the wider context of these expressions, which very often suggests that some extensions are obligatory and some optional.[56] This is the case with the binomial *small and medium-sized* (*mala i*

[55]Kjær (2007), p. 514.

[56]Gabrovšek (2011), p. 20.

srednja), which is exclusively used as a modifier of the noun *enterprises* (*poduzeća/poduzetnici*). Along the same lines, the adjectival pair *tangible and intangible* (*materijalni i nematerijalni*) is always accompanied by the noun *assets* (*imovina*), while *single and continuous* (*jedinstvena i trajna*) always precede the noun *infringement* (*povreda*). The 'distinctive meaning'[57] of these expressions thus emerges only in their wider context and suggests that their extensions are impossible to leave out, "thus rendering the basic binomial somewhat suspect as to its very existence".[58]

The existence of most binomials in EnCompLaw and CroComplaw is conditioned by the genre of EU Law. It is thus highly unlikely that the enumeration *frameworks, guidelines, communications and notices* (*okviri, smjernice, komunikacije i obavijesti*) would occur outside the context of the EU. This can easily be proven by consulting the BNC and the British Law Report Corpus, which witness no instances of the above enumeration. Likewise, the Croatian counterpart *okviri, smjernice, komunikacije i obavijesti* is non-existent in the Croatian web corpus. It also seems that the field of Competition Law provides for its own inventory of binomials, as witnessed by the example *trade and competition* (*trgovina i tržišno natjecanje*) or *open, transparent and non-discriminatory* (*otvoren, transparentan i nediskriminirajući*). Similarly, the trinomial *prevention, restriction or distortion* represents the essence of fair trading and reflects the purpose of the *Treaty Rules on Competition*, given that they prohibit:

> all agreements between undertakings, decisions by associations of undertakings and concerted practices which may affect trade between Member States and which have as their object or effect the *prevention, restriction or distortion of competition* within the internal market (Article 101(3) of the Treaty on The Functioning of the European Union (TFEU); emphasis added)

Another example which accounts for the non-typicality of English binomials is *rescuing and restructuring* (*sanacija i restrukturiranje*), which in EnCompLaw forms part of the extended unit of meaning,[59] hence, *State aid for rescuing and restructuring firms in difficulty*. This binomial only occurs as a verbal pair in EnCompLaw (RF 14.70), but it can also take the form of a nominal binomial, as supported by the text of the Commission's *Guidelines on State aid for rescuing and restructuring non-financial undertakings in difficulty*.[60] In fact, in CroCompLaw this verbal binomial is rendered as a nominal one (*sanacija i restrukturiranje*). As noted above, uniqueness of these expressions is confirmed by the data from the BNC, the British Law Report Corpus and hrwac 2.2., which either reveal no occurrences of the above binomials or, if they do, these directly refer to the genre of (EU) Competition Law. The BNC and the British Law Report Corpus thus prove our supposition that the binomial *rescuing and restructuring* is typical neither of general nor of legal

[57] Sinclair (2004).

[58] Gabrovšek (2011), p. 24.

[59] Sinclair (2004).

[60] Guidelines on State aid for rescuing and restructuring non-financial undertakings in difficulty (2014/C 249/01).

English. The Croatian web corpus, however, does witness a significant number of occurrences (RF 0.10) of the binomial *sanacija i restrukturiranje*, most of which concern the context of State aid and some of them refer to other both legal and non-legal contexts (e.g. *sanacija i restrukturiranje hrvatske brodogradnje; sanacija i restrukturiranje u glavama državnih i drugih dužnosnika*). This in turn suggests that the Croatian binomial is more stable than the English one, given the fact that the latter reveals zero frequency both in the BNC and the British Law Report Corpus. A case in point can also be illustrated by the trinomial *open, transparent and non-discriminatory*, which is non-existent both in the BNC and the British Law Report Corpus. The combination of the constituents of this trinomial cannot altogether be attributed to the tendency of EU legal language towards providing its own inventory of word combinations, but might also be influenced by the American English variety and the US,[61] to whom the EU "is likely to look for guidance"[62] with respect to the field of Competition Law. Since Member States are obliged to transpose EU Directives in their national laws, it is natural that this trinomial was reinvented in Croatian legal texts, given the fact that all four occurrences[63] from hrwac 2.2. refer either to the websites of agencies reporting on the norms and regulations of the Republic of Croatia or to the decisions of the Croatian government on the adoption of rules with respect to Commission's communications related to Competition Law.

Another case of hybridity can be reported by some instances from EnCompLaw which witness distorted English language use. This distortion might be attributed to French, which used to be the main working language in the EU and from which many false friends were derived. Yet, nowadays, EU texts are drafted mostly in English, though by non-native speakers of English "who also come from different cultural backgrounds and all work in English".[64] They thus enrich the EU texts with the expressions from their mother tongue-languages.[65] All this creates confusion for translators, since they need to identify whether an expression should be construed pursuant to the language of the text or to the meaning the draftsmen had in mind. A case in point may be illustrated by the binomial *actual or potential*, where *actual* might either be used to refer to *current* or *happening now* or to *real* or *existing*, the latter being the English meaning of the term:

---

[61]The EU and the US advance work to promote open, transparent and non-discriminatory investment policies. http://trade.ec.europa.eu/doclib/press/index.cfm?id=837 (Accessed 26 Apr 2018).

[62]Furse (2004), p. 2.

[63]Although Table 1 suggests that the trinomial *otvoren, transparentan i nediskriminirajući* does not occur in hrwac 2.2., we must keep in mind that what is expressed in the table is relative frequency, which refers to how often we may assume "we will see the word per *x* words of running text" (Statistics in corpus linguistics. https://corpora.lancs.ac.uk/clmtp/2-stat.php (Accessed 26 Apr 2018)). In cases of large corpora, it may thus be the case that a word or word combination does occur in the corpus, but its relative frequency is negligible.

[64]Sosoni (2012), p. 82.

[65]Robertson (2014), p. 156.

Ex. 1: *In view of the above, PCT argues that the ports mentioned in the opening decision cannot be considered as actual or potential substitutes for the PCT container port as regards the provision of stevedoring services for transshipment traffic in the eastern Mediterranean.*

Ex. 2: *Even where the licensor is not an actual or potential supplier on the product market and the licensee is not an actual or potential competitor on the technology market, it is relevant to the analysis whether the licensee owns a competing technology, which is not being licensed.*

Croatian translators have, however, opted for the English meaning and have thus translated the binomial as *stvaran ili potencijalan*. If the draftsmen, alternatively, wanted to imply the meaning of *current*, the confusion could have been avoided by choosing *current* or *present*[66] as the first constituent and thus avoid

> the use of terminology that is unknown to native speakers and either does not appear in dictionaries or is shown in them with a different meaning.[67]

Likewise, although the binomial *goods or services* is usually used in plural, data from EnCompLaw reveal three instances where the noun *goods* is used in singular:

Ex. 3: *'Product' means a good or a service, including both intermediary goods and services and final goods and services.*

As a matter of fact, Collins Dictionary also suggests that the noun *goods* can sometimes take the singular form in the fields of economics, where it refers to

> commodities that are tangible, usually movable, and generally not consumed at the same time as they are produced.[68]

It is deemed, however, that this form is rarely used when *goods* combines with other words, especially since data from the BNC reveal only one occurrence of *a good or service*, the latter referring to an EU context:

Ex. 4: *To recapitulate, it is clear that differences in national legislation may not only have the effect of preventing a good or service produced in one state being sold in another, but may also distort conditions of competition between manufacturers or suppliers located in different Member States of the Community.*

It thus follows that binomials in EU Law are often not typical of EU legal English, which also results in only few instances of semantically unmotivated binomials in the corpus. Their obvious redundancy is in turn brought to the fore through their translation equivalents in CroCompLaw. The binomial *terms and conditions* is reduced to a single word (*uvjeti*). In fact, this binomial also seems to be one of the

---

[66]Gardner (2016), p. 10.

[67]Ibid., p. 4.

[68]Collins Online Dictionary. https://www.collinsdictionary.com/dictionary/english/goods. Accessed 27 Mar 2018.

few semantically opaque binomials in the UK and Scottish legislation,[69] which suggests that complaints against verbosity of legal documents have borne fruit. Similarly, the binomial *joint and several* (*liability*) is in Croatian rendered as *solidarna* (*odgovornost*), since, as supported by the UK Insurance Factsheet,[70] *joint and several* can be used interchangeably with *in solidum*. Furthermore, as rightly asserted by Adams:

> the word *joint* is subsumed by *several* – if you're able to go after each obligor separately, it follows that you can go after them all. So nothing is accomplished by using the phrase *joint and several*. Sure, *joint* is redundant rather than pernicious, but why perpetuate the confusion?[71]

Some binomial expressions, although not directly purporting their redundancy, can be considered pleonastic when analysing the semantic field of their constituents. Butt and Castle[72] thus suggest that the trinomial *easements, rights and privileges* may be reduced to a single word (*right*), since all three words imply the meaning of *right*. The same line of interpretation may be applied to our binomial *right or power* since the constituent *power* also refers to "the legal *right* or authorization to act or not act".[73] Croatian linguists suggest that the majority of these expressions can be classified as pleonastic, given the fact that

> the base word is determined by the determinants which encompass the whole semantic field of the base word.[74]

Although such redundant expressions should be avoided,[75] they ensure that the meaning is understood properly,[76] which is why the full rendering is also preserved in Croatian (*prava ili ovlasti/ovlaštenja*). As a matter of fact, such expressions contribute to the preciseness of legal message and very often the relationship between the constituents of such binomials is one of contiguity, hence, "one meaning is an extension of the other".[77] Thus, for instance, the meaning of constituents of the binomial *research and development* are also contiguous, for every research also includes contributions to or developments of a field. In other words, research should be innovative, as suggested by the trinomial *research, development and innovation*, although we cannot claim that all research is innovative, hence, the relationship of contiguity.

---

[69]Kopaczyk (2017).

[70]UK Insurance Factsheet. https://www.ace-cae.eu/fileadmin/New_Upload/3._Area_2_Practice/Insurance_webpage/UK_Insurance_Factsheet_Edit_171018.pdf. Accessed 20 Mar 2018.

[71]Adams (2012).

[72]Butt and Castle (2006), p. 9.

[73]Garner (2004), p. 3708.

[74]Hudeček et al. (2011), p. 60.

[75]Petrović (2005), p. 50.

[76]Hudeček et al. (2011), p. 43.

[77]Kopaczyk (2017), p. 166.

Since law is a social science, however, it can never be as precise as mathematics. Mellinkoff[78] claims that the tendency towards precision is deeply rooted in the language of law due to: (1) the traditional way of saying things (e.g. *last will and testament*), (2) the way of precedent and (3) the required way prescribed by law draftsmen. It seems, however, that as far as legislative texts are concerned, both the EU and the UK ones, the law draftsmen have changed their preference for the formulaic expressions analysed in this chapter. Corpus data thus suggest that there are only two instances of binomials proper, that is, the ones whose existence cannot be justified neither in terms of their contributions to precision nor all-inclusiveness (e.g. *terms and conditions*; *joint and several*). The rest of the inventory listed in the Appendix are semantically motivated either by complementation (e.g. *goods or services*), contiguity (e.g. *authorisations and approvals*), antonymy (e.g. *supply and demand*) or hyponymy (e.g. *fishery and aquaculture*). For this reason, translators usually do not use deletions when translating binomials from EU Law into Croatian and thus safely preserve both the word order of the binomials and their overall meaning.

Exceptions can be detected only in a small number of cases, where the binomial pattern is rendered through different means. Worth discussing is the binomial *obsolete or uncompetitive*, whose formulaicity is disrupted in CroCompLaw, given the fact that the translator opted for an independent clause *više nije konkurentna* instead of choosing the constituent *nekonkurentna*:

Ex. 7: *The parties will therefore be considered to be competitors if at the time of the conclusion of the agreement it is not obvious that the licensee's technology is obsolete or uncompetitive.*

Ex. 8: *Stoga će se sudionici smatrati tržišnim natjecateljima ako u vrijeme sklapanja sporazuma nije očito da je tehnologija stjecatelja licence zastarjela ili više nije konkurentna.*

Since, however, "relying on one language version [...] runs counter to legal certainty",[79] the task of the translator is to consult as many language versions as possible. The choice of the Croatian translator can thus be justified by the German version, which reveals the same pattern as the Croatian one:

Ex. 9: *Folglich werden die Parteien als Wettbewerber betrachtet, wenn bei Abschluss der Vereinbarung nicht ersichtlich ist, dass die Technologie des Lizenznehmers* ***überholt oder nicht mehr wettbewerbsfähig ist***. (emphasis added)

The examples discussed in this chapter therefore suggest that binomials are more typical of the English language even in the EU context, where the "language itself is used in subtly different ways".[80] Albeit, as shown by this study, their patterns are mostly kept in the target language, sometimes they are expressed through alternative

[78]Mellinkoff (1963), p. 296.
[79]Bajčić (2017), p. 98.
[80]Robertson (2014), p. 156.

means of which the target language disposes, thus, on one hand, increasing the degree of their variations and modifications and, on the other, where the binomial structure is not preserved, decreasing their idiomaticity.

8 Concluding Remarks

Recent research in binomial expressions has shown that legislative texts have reduced wordiness and that noun binomials are rather infrequent, regardless of their legal tradition.[81] This especially applies to the instances of synonymous pairs which "confuse an issue that should be immediately clear".[82] Needless to say, if the number of such binomials in legal English bound to a common law background has decreased, it is not surprising that in EU legal texts there are even fewer such instances, as shown by this study. Their superfluousness is visible when consulting the languages which do not typically employ such binomials, such as Croatian. On another front, this hybridity of EU English also results in the hybridity of phraseological units, part of which conform to the phraseological patterning of English and part of which are invented and thus also reinvented in other language versions. As asserted by Sosoni:

> the aim as regards text production in the EU is not the production of functional TTs which respect the TL and TC conventions and norms, but the production of 'versions', which respect the 'sameness format', i.e. the literal rendering and the closest possible syntax and lexis, as well as the very specific instructions issued by the EU institutions.[83]

This pursuit for sameness is aspired to in all language versions so as to preserve the principles of both equal authenticity and standardization. Since, however, not all binomial expressions are preserved in all language versions to the same extent, their status remains questionable. This on one hand becomes visible when one language disposes of significantly more variants of one binomial than the other (as is most often the case with Croatian), but comes especially to the foreground, when the structure of the binomial is not retained. Albeit the efforts at standardization are reflected in terminology, syntax, punctuation and orthography,[84] it seems that they are less considerable in terms of phraseology. Data presented in this chapter have shown that English binomials are mostly preserved in the Croatian language, but are less restricted in terms of their combinations and thus reveal more variants as regards their reversibility and modifications. Translators will thus not be frowned upon when failing to preserve the idiomaticity of these expressions in other languages, for it seems that this type of phraseological units is not conditioned by legal constraints.[85]

---

[81] Kopaczyk (2017), p. 174.

[82] Mellinkoff (1963), p. 398.

[83] Sosoni (2012), p. 87.

[84] Robertson (2014), p. 161.

[85] Kjær (2007).

This study has been limited to binomial expressions in EU legislative texts and soft law instruments, but has excluded the case law of the CJEU. Future research might profit from investigating binomial expressions in the language of judgments to see whether 'phraseological, idiosyncratic conventions that typically recur in judicial discourse'[86] create new binomials or rather preserve the norm-conditioned[87] ones.

Binomials in EU Competition Law

Binomials in EnCompLaw joined by 'and'	Translation equivalents in CroCompLaw
Nominal binomials	
Research and development	istraživanje i razvoj
Fishery and aquaculture	ribarstvo i akvakultura
Agreements and practices	sporazumi i postupanja
Goods and services	roba i usluge
Culture and heritage	kultura i (kulturna) baština
Information and evidence	podatci i dokazi
Establishment and operation	osnivanje i djelovanje uspostava i djelovanje
Fines and periodic penalty payments	novčane kazne i periodični penali
Rights and obligations	prava i obveze
Agreements and concerted practices	sporazumi i usklađena djelovanja
Heating and cooling	grijanje i hlađenje
Subject matter and purpose	predmet i svrha
Imports and exports Export and import	uvoz i izvoz izvoz i uvoz
Authorisations and approvals	dozvole i odobrenja
Land and buildings Premises and land	zemljišta i zgrade zgrade i zemljišta
Research and knowledge-dissemination	istraživanje i širenje (znanja)
Rules and practices	pravila i praksa
Costs and revenues	troškovi i prihodi
Conditions and obligations Obligations and conditions	uvjeti i obveze obveze i uvjeti
Supply and distribution	nabava i distribucija
Interpretation and application	tumačenje i primjena
(In the interests of) clarity and rationality	(radi/zbog/u svrhu) jasnoće i racionalnosti
Terms and conditions	uvjeti
Experience and testing	iskustvo i testiranje/ispitivanje
Effectiveness and equivalence	učinkovitost i jednakovrijednost

(continued)

[86]Pontrandolfo (2015), p. 153.

[87]Kjær (2007).

Binomials in EnCompLaw joined by 'and'	Translation equivalents in CroCompLaw
Secrecy and substantiality	tajnost i značajnost
Trade and competition	trgovina i tržišno natjecanje
Products and technologies	proizvodi i tehnologije
Undertakings and consumers	poduzetnici i potrošači
Rules and procedures	pravila i postupci
Rights and principles	prava i načela
Supply and demand	ponuda i potražnja
Nature and content	karakter i sadržaj
Adjectival binomials	
Small and medium-sized (enterprises)	mala i srednja (poduzeća/poduzetnici)
Tangible and intangible (assests)	materijalna i nematerijalna (imovina)
Active and passive	aktivni i pasivni
Public and private	javni i privatni
Single and continuous (infringement)	jedinstvena i trajna (povreda)
Impartial and diligent	nepristrano i pažljivo pažljivo i nepristrano
Economic and non-economic	ekonomski i neekonomski
Vague and generic	nejasno i općenito
New and innovative	nova i inovativna (tehnologija)
Neighbouring and separate (market)	susjedno i različito (tržište)
Unilateral and reciprocal Reciprocal and non-reciprocal	jednostran i uzajaman jednostran i recipročan
Significant and useful	bitan i koristan
Complete and correct	cjelovit i točan potpun i točan
Joint and several (liability)	solidarna (odgovornost)
Immediate and effective	neposredno i stvarno (izvršenje odluke) odmah i stvarno (vraćena)
Financial and organisational	financijska i organizacijska
General and specific	opći i posebni
Valid and enforceable	valjan i primjenjiv
Open and non-discriminatory	otvoren i nediskriminirajući
Clear and realistic (exit strategy)	jasna i ostvariva (izlazna strategija)
Fair and non-discriminatory	pošteni i nediskriminirajući
Reasonable and prudent (hypothesis)	razumna i promišljena (pretpostavka)
Technical and economic	tehnički i gospodarski
Insufficient and contradictory (statement of reasons)	nedostatno i proturječno (obrazloženje)
Artistic and cultural; Cultural and artistic	umjetnički i kulturni kulturni i umjetnički
Clear and precise	jasan i nedvosmislen

(continued)

Binomials in EnCompLaw joined by 'and'	Translation equivalents in CroCompLaw
Adverbial binomials	
Jointly and severally (liable)	solidarno (odgovoran)
Actively and passively	aktivno i pasivno
Clearly and unequivocally	jasno i nedvosmisleno
Verbal binomials	
To record and compile	bilježiti i prikupljati evidentirati i prikupljati
To record and transcribe	snimiti i zapisati snimiti i prepisati
To rescue and restructure	sanacija i restrukturiranje

Binomials in EnCompLaw joined by 'or'	Translation equivalents in CroCompLaw
Nominal binomials	
Agreement(s) or practice(s)	sporazumi ili postupanja
Goods or services A good or a service	roba ili usluge roba ili usluga
Product(s) or service(s)	proizvodi ili usluge
Person(s) or undertaking(s)	poduzetnici ili udruženja poduzetnika
Rights or powers	prava ili ovlaštenja prava ili ovlasti
Fine(s) or periodic penalty payment(s)	novčane kazne ili periodični penali
Project or activity	projekt ili djelatnost
Production or distribution	proizvodnja ili distribucija
Sectors or activities	sektori ili djelatnosti
Price or quantity	cijena ili količina
Books or records	poslovne knjige ili dokumentacija
Purchasers or providers	kupci ili dobavljači
Import(s) or export(s)	uvoz ili izvoz
Mergers or acquisitions	spajanja ili preuzimanja
Memorandum or articles of association	statut ili društveni ugovor
Creation or strengthening (of a dominat position)	stvaranje ili jačanje (vladajućeg položaja)
Adjectival binomials	
One or more	jedan ili više
Direct or indirect	izravan ili neizravan neposredan ili posredan
Natural or legal (person)	pravna ili fizička (osoba)
Actual or potential	stvaran ili potencijalan stvaran ili mogući
Incorrect or misleading	netočan ili obmanjujući netočan ili zavaravajući
Exclusive or special (right) Special or exclusive (right)	isključivo ili posebno (pravo) posebno ili isključivo (pravo)
New or improved New or significantly improved	nov ili unaprijeđen nov ili znatno poboljšan
Public or private	javni ili privatni

(continued)

Binomials in EnCompLaw joined by 'or'	Translation equivalents in CroCompLaw
Judicial or administrative	sudski ili upravni
(In) written or electronic (form)	(u) pisanom ili elektroničkom obliku (u) tiskanom ili elektroničkom obliku
Purchase or selling (prices)	nabavne ili prodajne (cijene) proizvodne ili prodajne (cijene) kupovne ili prodajne (cijene)
Full or partial	potpun ili djelomičan
Obsolete or uncompetitive	zastarjela ili nije više konkurentna
Continuous or periodic (activity)	trajna ili periodična (djelatnost)
National or regional Regional or national	nacionalna ili regionalna
Adverbial binomials	
Directly or indirectly	izravno ili neizravno neposredno ili posredno posredno ili neposredno
In whole or in part Fully or partly Partly or fully Entirely or partly Partly or entirely Wholly or mainly	u cijelosti ili djelomično djelomično ili potpuno
Upstream or downstream	uzlazno ili silazno
Inside or outside	unutar ili izvan
Intentionally or negligently	namjerno ili iz nehaja namjerno ili nepažnjom
Individually or jointly	samostalno ili zajedno samostalno ili zajednički
Jointly or individually	zajedno ili samostalno pojedinačno ili zajednički
Verbal binomials	
To indicate or impose (penalties)	navesti ili izreći (kazne)
To appoint or remove	imenovati ili smijeniti postaviti ili smijeniti
To annul or suspend	poništiti ili ukinuti
To exclude or hinder	isključiti ili stvarati prepreku
Plan or put into effect	planirati ili provesti

Trinomials in EnCompLaw joined by 'and'	Translation equivalents in CroCompLaw
Nominal trinomials	
Agreements, decisions and practices	sporazumi, odluke i usklađena djelovanja
Production, processing and marketing	proizvodnja, prerada i stavljanje na tržište
(Aid for) research and development and innovation (Aid for) research, development and innovation	(potpore za) istraživanje i razvoj i inovacije (potpore za) istraživanje, razvoj i inovacije

(continued)

Trinomials in EnCompLaw joined by 'and'	Translation equivalents in CroCompLaw
Transparency, equal treatment and effective monitoring	transparentnost, jednaki tretman/postupanje i učinkoviti nadzor/praćenje
Adjectival binomials	
Open, transparent and non-discriminatory	otvoren, transparentan i nediskriminirajući
Smart, sustainable and inclusive Sustainable, smart and inclusive	pametan, održiv i uključiv održiv, pametan i uključiv
Uniform, transparent and simple (application)	jedinstvena, transparentna i jednostavna (primjena)

Trinomials in EnCompLaw joined by 'or'	Translation equivalents in CroCompLaw
Nominal trinomials	
Products, services or technologies	proizvodi, usluge ili tehnologije
Products, processes or services	proizvodi, procesi ili usluge
Rectification, amendment or supplement	ispravak, izmjena ili dopuna
Prevention, restriction or distortion (of competition)	sprječavanje, ograničavanje ili narušavanje (tržišnog natjecanja)
Adjectival trinomials	
Incorrect, incomplete or misleading	netočan, nepotpun ili zavaravajući/obmanjujući
Legislative, regulatory or administrative	zakonodavni, regulatorni ili upravni
Administrative, managerial or supervisory (body)	upravno, upravljačko ili nadzorno (tijelo)
Verbal trinomials	
To improve, substitute or replace	poboljšati, nadomjestiti ili zamijeniti
Purchase, sell or resell	proizvoditi, prodavati ili preprodavati kupovati, prodavati ili preprodavati
To cancel, reduce or increase	ukinuti/poništiti, smanjiti ili povećati

Enumerations in EnCompLaw joined by 'and'	Translation equivalents in CroCompLaw
Nominal enumerations	
Frameworks, guidelines, communications and notices	okviri, smjernice, komunikacije i obavijesti

Enumerations in EnCompLaw joined by 'or'	Translation equivalents in CroCompLaw
Verbal enumerations	
To manufacture, purchase, sell or resell	proizvoditi, kupovati, prodavati ili preprodavati

References

Adams K (2012) Exploring "Joint and Several". Available via ADAMSDRAFTING. http://www.adamsdrafting.com/exploring-joint-and-several/. Accessed 20 Mar 2018

Aguado de Cea G (2007) A multiperspective approach to specialized phraseology: internet as a reference corpus for phraseology. Avalable via UPM. http://oa.upm.es/6176/1/A_multiperspective_approach_to_specialized_phraseology_(Art%C3%ADculo_en_libro_The_

Texture_of_Internet_Netlinguistics_in_Progress,_Cambridge_2007)_pdf. Accessed 11 Oct 2015
Alcaraz Varó E, Hughes B (2002) Legal translation explained. St. Jerome Publishing, Manchester
Bajčić M (2017) New insights into the semantics of legal concepts and the legal dictionary. John Benjamins, Amsterdam
Bhatia V K (1993) Analysing genre. Longman, Harlow
Biel Ł (2010) Corpus-based studies of legal language for translation purposes: methodological and practical potential. In: Heine C, Engberg J (eds) Reconceptualizing LSP. Online Proceedings of the XVII LSP Symposium 2009. http://bcom.au.dk/fileadmin/www.asb.dk/isek/biel.pdf. Accessed 11 Dec 2014
Biel Ł (2014) Lost in the Eurofog: the textual fit of EU translated law. Peter Lang, Frankfurt am Main
Bowker L, Pearson J (2002) Working with specialized language. A practical guide to using corpora. Routledge, London
Bukovčan D (2009) Binominal expressions in the German and English language of criminal law. In: Sočanac L, Goddard C, Kremer L (eds) Curriculum, multilingualism and the law. Nakladni zavod Globus, Zagreb, pp 61–78
Butt P, Castle R (2006) Modern legal drafting. A guide to using clearer language. Cambridge University Press, Cambridge
Cao D (2007) Translating law. Multilingual matters. Clevedon, Buffalo
Carvalho L (2008) Translating contracts and agreements from a corpus linguistics perspective. Cult Juridicas 3(1):1–15
Chalmers D, Davies G et al (2010) European Union Law, 2nd edn. Cambridge University Press, Cambridge
Danet B (1980) Language in the legal institution process. Law Soc Rev 14(3):445–564
Furse M (2004) Competition law of the EC and the EU. Oxford University Press, Oxford
Gabrovšek D (2011) "Micro" phraseology in action: a look at fixed binomials. ELOPE 8:1):19–1):29
Gačić M (2009) Riječ do riječi: lingvistička istraživanja odnosa engleskoga i hrvatskog jezika na području prava i srodnih disciplina. Profil International, Zagreb
Gardner J (2016) Misused English Words and Expressions in EU publications. Available via ECA. https://www.eca.europa.eu/Other%20publications/EN_TERMINOLOGY_PUBLICATION/EN_TERMINOLOGY_PUBLICATION.pdf. Accessed 20 Mar 2018
Garner BA (ed) (2004) Black's Law Dictionary. West Publishing Company, St. Paul
German scientists fear BSE – Bad Simple English. https://www.expatica.com/de/news/country-news/German-scientists-fear-BSE-Bad-Simple-English_132114.html. Accessed 29 Mar 2018
Goźdź–Roszkowski S, Pontrandolfo G (2017) Introduction: cross–linguistic approaches and applications to phraseology in legal and institutional discourse. In: Goźdź–Roszkowski S, Pontrandolfo G (eds) Phraseology in legal and institutional settings. A corpus–based interdisciplinary perspective. Routledge, London, pp 1–8
Gustafsson M (1984) The syntactic features of binomial expressions in legal English. Interdisciplinary J Study Discourse 4(1–3):123–142
Hudeček L, Lewis K et al (2011) Pleonazmi u hrvatskome standardnom jeziku. Rasprave Instituta za hrvatski jezik i jezikoslovlje 37(1):41–72
Kilgariff A, Baisa V et al (2014) The sketch engine: ten years on. Lexicography:1–30
Koskinen K (2008) Translating Institutions. An ethnographic study of EU translation. St. Jerome, Manchester
Koskinen K (2011) Institutional translation. Handb Transl Stud 2:54–60
Kjær A L (2007) Phrasemes in legal texts. In Burger, H, Dobrovol'skij, D et al (eds) Phraseologie/Phraseology. Ein internationales Handbuch zeitgenössischer Forschung/An international handbook of contemporary research. de Gruyter, Berlin, pp 506–515
Kopaczyk J (2009) Multi-word units of meaning in 16th-century legal Scots. In: McConchie RW, Honkapohja A, Tyrkkö J (eds) Selected proceedings of the 2008 symposium on new approaches

in English Historical Lexis (HEL-LEX2). Cascadilla Proceedings Press, Somerville, MA, pp 88–95
Kopaczyk J (2017) Terms and conditions: a comparative study of noun binomials in UK and Scottish legislation. In: Goźdź-Roszkowski S, Pontrandolfo G (eds) Phraseology in legal and institutional settings. A corpus-based perspective. Routledge, London, pp 160–177
Lewis K, Mrčela M (2016) Pravno nazivlje i hrvatski jezik. Udruga hrvatskih sudaca, Zagreb
Ljubešić N, Klubička F (2014) {bs,hr,sr}WaC – Web corpora of Bosnian, Croatian and Serbia. http://nlp.ffzg.hr/data/publications/nljubesi/ljubesic14-bs.pdf. Accessed 20 Mar 2018
Malkiel Y (1959) Studies in irreversible binomials. Lingua 8:113–160
Matulewska A (2013) Legilinguistic translatology. A parametric approach to legal translation. Peter Lang, Bern
Mellinkoff D (1963) The language of the law. Wipf and Stock Publishers, Oregon
Monzó Nebot E (2017) The out-grouping society: phrasemes othering underprivileged groups in the International Bill of Human Rights (English-French-Spanish). In: Goźdź-Roszkowski S, Pontrandolfo G (eds) Phraseology in legal and institutional settings. A corpus-based perspective. Routledge, London, pp 109–125
Petrović B (2005) Sinonimija i sinonimičnost u hrvatskome jeziku. Hrvatska sveučilišna naklada, Zagreb
Picht H (1987) Terms and their LSP Environment – LSP Phraseology. Meta 32(2). Available via ERUDIT. http://id.erudit.org/iderudit/003836ar. Accessed 11 Oct 2015
Pontrandolfo G (2015) Investigating judicial phraseology with COSPE: a contrastive corpus-based study. In: Fantinuoli C, Zanettin F (eds) New directions in corpus-based translation studies (Translation and Multilingual Natural Language Processing 1). Language Science Press, Berlin, pp 137–161
Robertson C (2014) EU legislative texts and translation. In: Cheng L, Sin King K, Wagner A (eds) The Ashgate handbook of legal translation. Routledge, London, pp 156–175
Sinclair JM (2004) Trust the text: language, corpus and discourse. Routledge, London
Sinclair JM (2005) Corpus and text - basic principles. In: Wynne M (ed) Developing linguistic corpora: a guide to good practice. Oxbow Books, Oxford, pp 1–16
Šarčević S (1997) New approach to legal translation. Kluwer Law International, The Hague
Schäffner C, Adab B (2001) The idea of the hybrid text and translation: contact as conflict. Across Lang Cult 2:167–180
Sosoni V (2012) A hybrid translation theory for EU texts. Transl Stud 5:76–89
Triebel V (2009) Pitfalls of English as a contract language. In: Olsen F, Lotz A et al (eds) Translation issues in language and law. Palgrave Macmillan, Hampshire, pp 147–182
Trklja A (2017) A corpus investigation of formulaicity and hybridity in legal language: a case of EU case law texts. In: Goźdź-Roszkowski S, Pontrandolfo G (eds) Phraseology in legal and institutional settings. A corpus-based perspective. Routledge, London, pp 89–108
Trosborg A (1997) Translating hybrid political texts. In: Trosborg A (ed) Text typology and translation. John Benjamins, Amsterdam, pp 145–158

Katja Dobrić Basaneže is Senior Lecturer, Department of Foreign Languages, University of Rijeka, Faculty of Law, Croatia

Collocations of Terms in EU Competition Law: A Corpus Analysis of EU English Collocations

Łucja Biel, Agnieszka Biernacka, and Anna Jopek-Bosiacka

Abstract The objective of this chapter is, first, to identify key terms in EU Competition Law in English and, secondly, to identify and examine their collocational environment via the corpus methodology. The first part of the chapter presents a theoretical background on EU English as a supranational variety of English due to the increased mediation of content through translators and non-native English-speaking authors. The chapter next discusses the role of collocations, focusing on collocations of legal terms and collocations in EU English. Section 4 describes the EU Competition Corpus (1.5 million words), comprised of EU legislation, case law and "praxis" documents on Competition Law. The corpus was used to extract term-node candidates (103 terms). Their collocational environment was analysed through words sketches and concordances in Sketch Engine and WordSmith. The analysis has focused on the following aspects of collocations: semantic prosodies, collocational ranges (combinatory potential), derivational productivity, international prefixes, Latinisms, premodification by *–ing* and *–ed* participles, adjectives with negative connotations, deverbal and deadjectival nouns and an atypical grammatical behaviour of certain patterns. Last but not least, the chapter draws attention to a high variation of terminology and phraseology at various levels, which contributes to the hybridity of EU English.

1 Introduction

A leading British linguist J. R. Firth observed, famously, that "You shall know a word by the company it keeps!",[1] which could be paraphrased in the context of legal language as "You shall know a *legal term* by the company it keeps". Collocations and other phraseological units are known to cause problems to non-native speakers

[1] Firth (1957), p. 11.

Ł. Biel (✉) · A. Biernacka · A. Jopek-Bosiacka
University of Warsaw, Institute of Applied Linguistics, Warsaw, Poland
e-mail: l.biel@uw.edu.pl; a.biernacka@uw.edu.pl; a.jopek-bosiacka@uw.edu.pl

S. Marino et al. (eds.), *Language and Law*,
https://doi.org/10.1007/978-3-319-90905-9_14

of languages and, thanks to the advent of new computational methods of analysis, they have recently received increased attention from researchers and practitioners in the fields of language teaching and learning, language for special purposes (LSP), translation studies, terminology and terminography. Considering that English is the dominant working language of the European Union (EU), the purpose of this chapter is first, to empirically identify key terms in EU Competition Law in English, next to identify and examine their collocational environment as part of glossary compiling activity.[2] To make the study more accurate and systematic, we will use quantitative methods of corpus linguistics and corpus analysis software.

2 EU English as a Supranational Variety of English

Starting with the Scandinavian accessions in 1995 and accelerated by the 2004 accessions of Central and Eastern European countries, English grew to become the main procedural language of the European Union's institutions—the lingua franca of the European Union.[3] With the exception of the Court of Justice of the European Union,[4] English dethroned French from the dominant position it had held since the 1950s and currently is the main source language of documents. This means that most documents are first prepared in English and next translated into other languages. In the case of the European Commission, 81% of the output was translated from English and only 4.5% from French in 2013.[5] This rate is even higher for the Council of the European Union, where over 90% of documents translated by its General Secretariat in 2016 were translated from English.[6]

The idea of a procedural language, which clearly favours one language over the others, is inconsistent with the EU's multilingualism policy which is intended to promote respect for linguistic diversity[7] (and "figures like a mantra"[8]) and to presume an equal treatment of 24 official languages. Owing to practical considerations and budgetary constraints, the declared policy is in stark contrast with actual practices.[9] The multilingualism policy imposes an obligation to ensure that regulations and "documents of general application" are available in all the official

[2]See Chap. 15 in this volume.

[3]Seidlhofer (2010) and Pozzo (2012a, b).

[4]McAuliffe (2017).

[5]European Commission (2014). See also Robinson (2017), p. 243, who observes that first drafts of EU legislation are written and examined by lawyer-linguists mainly in English.

[6]Hanzl and Beaven (2017), p. 140, fn 1.

[7]Article 3, Consolidated version of the Treaty on European Union (TEU) (OJ C 326, 26.10.2012, p. 13).

[8]Seidlhofer (2010), p. 360.

[9]Seidlhofer (2010), p. 356; Biel (2017).

languages.[10] This is in practice applied quite narrowly to legislation, case law and some document types and the multilingualism policy tends to be restricted to the legal validity and authenticity of the EU-wide legislation. Thus, as already noted, most documents are drafted in English (the English version is a *de facto* original[11]) and are selectively translated, if legally required or if need be, into other official languages. A considerable body of EU documents exists only in English (and sometimes in French as well). The institutions themselves refer to this selective translation practice euphemistically as "controlled full multilingualism" or "a pragmatic approach to multilingualism"[12] and they prefer to refer to "language versions" rather than to the (English) original and translations. The academia is generally more critical in its assessment by referring to this selective approach as "hegemonic multilingualism"[13] and even as "unilingualism", given the overuse of English as a procedural language.[14] The dominance of English as a procedural language is also manifested in more informal contexts where English is often a preferred working language inside the EU's institutions, including the European Commission's Directorates General and its Directorate General for Competition, where most internal work is done in English. English may also be chosen by expert groups, as was the case with experts drafting the European Civil Code.[15] English also dominates in the EU institutions' social media.[16] The choice of English over other languages is a natural consequence of the popularity of English in Europe (and beyond), with English being studied as a foreign language by 96% of students in general upper secondary education in EU-28.[17] Some claim, though, that English should be viewed as complementary to and not competitive with other official languages[18] because it is a medium of cross-cultural communication for speakers who do not share the first language (L1).[19]

English used in the EU is different from standard British English and tends to be regarded as a distinct hybrid variety of English,[20] known under a number of names: EU English, Euro-English, and Eurish. Its properties are manifested most clearly at

[10]Articles 5 and 6, Council Regulation (EEC) No 1 of 15 April 1958 determining the languages to be used by the European Economic Community (OJ 17, 6.10.1958, p. 385).

[11]Derlén (2015), p. 68.

[12]Biel (2017), pp. 39–41, for further discussion.

[13]Krzyżanowski and Wodak (2011).

[14]Mattila (2013), p. 33.

[15]Glanert (2008), p. 168.

[16]Koskinen (2013).

[17]http://ec.europa.eu/eurostat/statistics-explained/index.php/Foreign_language_learning_statistics.

[18]Seidlhofer (2010), p. 365.

[19]Modiano (2017), pp. 314, 323.

[20]Modiano (2017), p. 314, see also Doczekalska this volume.

the conceptual/terminological level[21] due to the supranational nature of the EU Law, but also at the stylistic and grammatical levels.[22]

The distinctiveness of EU English is caused by an interplay of factors connected with the various types of mediation of content through translators and non-native speaker authors; hence, extreme filtering through other working languages. This phenomenon is typical of all EU variants of legal languages; however, because of its status as the main procedural language, the degree of mediation is incomparably higher for English.[23] First, EU English started to take shape in the 1970s when the UK joined the European Economic Community and had to translate the acquis from the then official languages (French, Dutch, German, Italian). Thus, it was affected by the translation process and interference from other languages from the very beginning.[24] Secondly, documents are prepared, negotiated and drafted in a multistage and multilingual manner,[25] with a text going back and forth, with the help of translators and interpreters,[26] through various languages and back to English. Even though translators working for the EU institutions are well-trained professionals, this multistage multilingual processing of texts inevitably leaves traces in the fabric of the final target text, mainly in the form of an overuse or underuse of certain linguistic patterns as a result of interference.[27] Thirdly, and more importantly, the key reason for the hybridity and distinctness of EU English is that it is chosen as a preferred language of professional communication within the EU not only by native speakers of English, who constitute a small minority of the EU staff,[28] but, largely, by non-native speakers. In most cases, EU texts are written by non-native speakers of English[29] and even if they are, the fact that native speakers work in the EU institutions' multilingual environment may adversely affect their language competence.[30] This results in a shift in the ownership of the language and its appropriation by non-native speakers, which is a natural process for lingua francas.[31] Non-native

---

[21]Catenaccio (2008), p. 276; Pozzo (2012b), p. 1196, Robertson (2012), p. 1237, Modiano (2017), p. 322.

[22]Salmi-Tolonen (1994); Crystal (2003), p. 182; Gardner (2017).

[23]This phenomenon applies also to French.

[24]Biel (2014), p. 64, Gardner (2017), p. 149.

[25]Doczekalska (2009), p. 360.

[26]Koskinen (2008), p. 63, on code-switching in multilingual institutions.

[27]Biel (2014).

[28]E.g. in respect of the European Commission, 3.1% of its staff has declared British as their first nationality (plus 1.8%—Irish nationality and 0.5%—Maltese), cf. *Statistical Bulletin for the Commission* on 1.10.2017, https://ec.europa.eu/info/sites/info/files/statistical-bulletin-staff-by-nationality-dg_en.pdf (Accessed 28 Dec 2017). It should be noted that according to Gardner (2017), p. 150, the UK staff has reduced rapidly by about 50% since 2004 and further reductions may be expected after Brexit.

[29]cf. Wagner et al. (2002), p. 70; Tosi (2002), p. 178; Gardner (2017), p. 150; Hanzl and Beaven (2017), p. 141.

[30]cf. Tosi (2002), p. 184, Wagner et al. (2002), p. 76.

[31]cf. van Els (2001), p. 344; Seidlhofer (2010), p. 362.

speakers transfer elements from their own native languages but also introduce errors. Typical errors in EU English concern disjunctive word order (e.g. adverbials placed between the verb and its object), incorrect punctuation (defining and non-defining relative clauses), an excessive use of nominalisation at the expense of verbs, incorrect prepositions (overuse of *of*), problematic use of verbs (preference for simple present tenses, *shall* and the passive voice), as well as lexical errors, including calques and other borrowings, especially from French[32] and culture-specific lexical usage transferred from national languages.[33] Yet, Modiano warns against perceiving EU English as a simplified and limited contact language, considering this view as "misleading and condescending" because it "unjustifiably marginalizes" a large group of proficient continental users of English in the EU context.[34] Since non-native use may impede comprehension and reduce readability,[35] EU institutions have started to invest more resources in English-language editing by native speakers. For example, the European Commission intends to increase the editing of its major initiatives from 12% in 2015 to 65% in 2020.[36] Thus, some improvement may be expected in the coming years. It should be appreciated, though, that editing is not always possible for political reasons—as noted aptly by Gardner:

> final versions of important publications are often adopted at a senior or political level, and significant changes cannot be made after adoption, even if major language errors are involved.[37]

Finally, EU English goes through neutralisation[38] and deculturalisation, that is a reduction of cultural embedding typical of lingua francas[39] so that it can be used as a neutral meta-language,[40] "a go-between" which has been "reinvented" and accommodated to facilitate multilingual translation[41] and meet "the communicative needs of the member states".[42] Obviously, it is an open question to what degree such neutrality is successfully achieved. Neutralisation concerns in particular the terminological level, where as a rule, drafters tend to avoid system-specific terms of national law[43] and replace them with neutral terms—neologisms and generic terms in a specialised sense[44] and modified terms, to better reflect their supranational nature

---

[32] Gardner (2017), pp. 153–162.

[33] Modiano (2017), p. 322.

[34] Modiano (2017), p. 322.

[35] Gardner (2017), p. 154.

[36] European Commission (2016).

[37] Gardner (2017), p. 150.

[38] Caliendo (2004), p. 163.

[39] van Els (2001), p. 329.

[40] Šarčević (2010), pp. 34–35.

[41] Pozzo (2012b), p. 1198, Crystal (2003), p. 182, Robertson (2010), pp. 3, 6.

[42] Schäffner (2000), p. 3.

[43] In particular, the traditional terminology may be perceived as "loaded" in some national contexts, cf. Whittaker (2006), p. 60.

[44] Mattila (2013), pp. 157–158, Šarčević (2018), p. 21.

and to signal that they are autonomous concepts.[45] The supranational nature of EU legal terms stems from the independence and hybridity of EU Law, which is a meeting point of the Member States' legal cultures,[46] a "*tertium comparationis* juxtaposing and combining very different legal systems, cultures and styles".[47] It shares features of both common law (e.g. precedents) and civil law.[48] As a result, its terminology is "peculiar" to EU Law (supranational) and may have different meanings than in national law,[49] which is particularly visible in the case of English due to its common law foundation.

In this context, Brexit naturally poses questions as to the status of English in the EU after the UK leaves. English is the official language in Ireland and Malta, the countries which notified Irish and Maltese as EU official languages. For practical and financial considerations, as well as due to the strong preference for English as a core tool of EU communication, it is unlikely that the dominance of English in EU institutions will be affected substantially. Interestingly, Modiano argues that Brexit will in fact strengthen the role of English within the EU by putting non-native speakers on an equal footing, and the UK will no longer be there as guardians:

> [w]hen Britain leaves the EU, the sociolinguistic space for a European variety (or varieties) of English will become even more unambiguous, given the absence of Britain as an arbiter of correctness and standardization.[50]

This may accelerate linguistic nativisation and create space where new linguistic features function as identity markers for the EU speech community.[51]

3 Why Do Collocations Matter?

3.1 What Are Collocations?

Collocations are known under a number of names, i.e. prefabricated units, prefabs, phraseological units, lexical chunks, multi-word units.[52] Collocations may be defined broadly[53] as a regular co-occurrence of lexical units,[54] or more specifically with reference to legal language, as a co-occurrence of a term (which functions as a

[45] cf. Bajčić (2017), p. 83.

[46] Šarčević (2007), p. 44.

[47] Jopek-Bosiacka (2011), p. 26.

[48] Robertson (2012), p. 1237, see also Šarčević (2001), p. 43.

[49] Case 283/81 *CILFIT* [1982] ECR 3415, ECLI:EU:C:1982:335.

[50] Modiano (2017), p. 314.

[51] Modiano (2017), pp. 319–321.

[52] Wray (2002), p. 9.

[53] The term collocation is often used as a synonym of phraseology/phraseme and covers idioms, proverbs, etc. Partington (1998).

[54] Baker (1992), p. 47.

node) with other linguistic elements referred to as collocates. The most typical and basic collocational patterns, as confirmed by our study, are:

- a verb plus a noun (a term)
  e.g. *to distort competition, claim compensation,*
- an adjective plus a noun
  e.g. *unfair competition, dominant position,*
- a noun plus a noun
  e.g. *leniency programme, action for damages.*

Such collocational patterns often form larger recurrent sequences through noun phrases and prepositional phrases, e.g. *an infringement of competition law*.

With the advent of corpora, collocations are now predominantly identified through the frequency criterion (known as the frequency-based approach)[55] and statistical measures. This means that collocations need to meet certain recurrence thresholds to show that their co-occurrence is not random but conventionalised. In other words, a word sequence needs to be sufficiently frequent to be regarded as a collocation.

As demonstrated repeatedly by corpus linguistics over the last two decades or so, language use is characterised by a large number of recurrent patterns of co-occurring words. This means that language use is formulaic and highly patterned[56] and composed of a large number of prefabs which are stored and activated by users as single choices rather than constructed from scratch.[57] Such patterns tend to be processed semi-automatically and subconsciously. It is worth noting that the degree of formulaicity and prefabrication is much higher in legal language, which is often referred to as "frozen"[58] and "fossilized".[59]

This high degree of prefabrication of languages combines with cross-linguistic differences in prefabricated patterns, in particular collocational patterns and ranges, which, as a result, overlap partially across languages.[60] These two factors make collocations problematic in particular to language learners[61] and translators,[62] who are prone to collocational errors as a result of interference. A more proficient use of collocations is associated with more advanced stages of foreign language (L2) development thanks to reduced processing effort[63] and contributes to fluency and the perception of output as native-like.[64] For this reason legal professionals who

[55]Nesselhauf (2005), p. 12.

[56]Stubbs (2004), p. 111.

[57]Sinclair (1991), p. 110.

[58]Bhatia et al. (2004), p. 206.

[59]Alcaraz and Hughes (2002), p. 9.

[60]cf. Larson (1998[1984]), Baker (1992), p. 48, Hatim and Munday (2004), p. 251.

[61]cf. Howarth (1998).

[62]cf. Newmark (1981), p. 180, Larson (1998[1984]), p. 160, Mauranen (2000).

[63]Nesselhauf (2005), p. 2.

[64]cf. Howarth (1998) and Nesselhauf (2005).

are non-native speakers of English should pay more attention to collocations to improve their communication skills.

3.2 Collocations of Legal Terms

Compared to general language, collocations in specialised languages are more restricted—in other words, they are fixed.[65] This means they have fewer variants and synonyms, which is due to the property of terms to develop preferences for certain collocates out of a range of possible synonyms.[66] The degree of collocational fixedness is even higher in legal language. Similarly to legal terms, collocations may be system bound, that is unique to a given legal system, e.g. *to lift the corporate veil* (UK) and *to pierce the corporate veil* (US).[67] Collocations are often sanctioned in legislation and replicated in lower-ranking genres as set phrases in an idiom-like manner,[68] thus establishing intertextual links to the higher-ranking texts and functioning as "implicit quotation from other text in a genre chain in the legal domain".[69] This bars, to some extent, against the synonymy and variability of legal collocates.

One of the main functions of legal collocations is to embed legal terms in text; hence, their name as term-embedding collocations.[70] Term-embedding (i.e. terminological) collocations establish links between terms and elements of conceptual frames, in particular verbal collocations are used to build "scripts" and "scenarios" with action, e.g. *to distort competition, to restrict competition, to affect competition, to impede competition, to eliminate competition, to protect competition, to restore competition.* Furthermore, it has been established that collocations organise texts: they are "main organising features of text"[71] and they divide a text into units of meaning.[72]

3.3 EU English and Collocations

Even though the EU institutions show a growing interest in increasing the naturalness of EU language,[73] some degree of foreignness and unnaturalness of terms and

[65] Meyer and Mackintosh (1994), Heid (1994), Partington (1998), p. 17, L'Homme (2000).

[66] L'Homme (2000), p. 91.

[67] cf. Biel (2012), p. 227.

[68] cf. Biel (2014), p. 47.

[69] Kjær (2007), p. 512.

[70] Biel (2014), p. 44.

[71] Partington (1998), p. 19.

[72] Teubert (2010), p. 357.

[73] Biel (2017).

collocations is unavoidable. As a result of non-native influences on EU English and an increased need to create neologisms, EU texts are marked by some unnatural word combination, including untypical collocations and collocational distortions.[74] This is evidenced for example in two compilations prepared by the EU institutions themselves: *EU jargon in English and some possible alternatives*[75] and *Misused English words and expressions in EU publications*,[76] whereby the meaning of some EU English terms is explained to native speakers of English. The consequence of using neologisms and coining new patterns in EU English is that they are semantically opaque—they do not connote any specific meaning to native speakers of English or they have meanings other than those intended. Some English phrases show a strong influence of French, either as literal borrowings (calques), e.g. *social dialogue* in the meaning of industrial relations, i.e. consultations between employers and employees, or as false friends, e.g. *enlargement* from French *élargissement,* a concept better known in English as *expansion*.[77] In the context of Competition Law, it is worth noting that such lists of misused words include, for example, the following terms which show traces of French influence:

- *State aid(s)*
  Derived from French *aide d'état,* meaning (*unfair*) *government support*, which, as the guide notes, is unclear to the general public and misleading since *aid* implies financial help as part of development and disaster relief while the concept of 'State aid' would be better represented by *support* which is not only financial.[78]
- *enterprise*
  For example, *SME — small and medium-sized enterprise*, derived from French *entreprise*, used in the meaning of what is referred to in UK English as businesses, companies and firms.[79]
- *anti-*
  Overuse of the prefix which is usually dropped in UK English,[80] e.g. *anti-competitive, anti-trust.*

Competition Law terminology also shows some German influences: most notably, one of its fundamental terms—an *undertaking*,[81] derived from the German *Unternehmen*, allows for a neutralised widest possible construal of its sense covering legal and natural persons who are engaged in economic activity.[82]

[74]Gardner (2017), p. 161.

[75]European Commission (n.d.).

[76]European Court of Auditors (2016).

[77]European Commission (n.d.).

[78]European Commission (n.d.).

[79]European Court of Auditors (2016), p. 30.

[80]European Court of Auditors (2016), p. 30.

[81]Interestingly, Wikipedia refers to an *undertaking* as "[T]his uncomfortable English word" (https://en.wikipedia.org/wiki/European_Union_competition_law, emphasis added).

[82]Woods et al. (2017), p. 639.

It should be noted though that the etymology of terminological units is sometimes difficult to trace. This is due to the complex origin of EU Competition Law, with the initial impact of US antitrust law,[83] one of the earliest competition laws, especially through Germany after the Second World War[84] as well as through French influences.[85] Thus, some concepts migrated from US antitrust law to German law and were recontextualised in French within the European Communities, and later on again in English and into other EU official languages.[86] It creates a linguistically complex situation.

The ensuing analysis is intended to investigate key collocational patterns and trends in EU English, using the EU Competition Corpus.

4 Material and Method

The study is based on the corpus of EU Competition Legislation and Case Law ('EU Competition Corpus') compiled as part of the project *Training action for legal practitioners: Linguistic skills and translation in EU Competition Law* by an interdisciplinary team composed of legal scholars and linguists. First, the legal scholars compiled a list of key EU Competition legislation, judgments and some related soft law documents under the heading "praxis"; next the documents were downloaded by the linguists in their English versions from the Eur-Lex[87] and Curia[88] websites in the period from May to August 2017. The files were converted into the text format (UTF-8 encoding) and uploaded into the Sketch Engine[89] corpus management and query system, where they were processed with the corpus compilation software, including part-of-speech tagging, sketch grammar and term definition for term extraction. WordSmith Tools 7.0[90] was also used. The corpus design is shown in Table 1.

The corpus comprises three sub-sections: Legislation, Case Law and Praxis:

- EU Legislation comprises 21 legal acts, including Rules on Competition from the Treaty on the Functioning of the European Union[91] (Articles 101-109) and

[83] Leucht and Marquis (2013).

[84] Maher (2000), p. 155.

[85] See Jones and Sufrin on the impact of French and German delegations on the initial shape of EEC Competition Law, with some of the provisions of the ECSC Treaty being drafted by the Harvard law professor Robert Bowie at the request of Jean Monnet; Jones and Sufrin (2016), pp. 36–37 and p. 36, fn 162 and Elhauge and Geradin (2011), p. 49.

[86] See e.g. Kolasiński (2012), Kępiński (2014) on the foreign impact on Polish Competition Law.

[87] http://eur-lex.europa.eu/homepage.html.

[88] https://curia.europa.eu.

[89] Kilgarriff et al. (2014).

[90] Scott (2017).

[91] Consolidated version of the Treaty on the Functioning of the European Union (OJ C 326, 26.10.2012, p. 47).

Table 1 The EU Competition corpus design

	Number of files	Tokens	%
EU Legislation	21	192,762	12.94
EU Case Law	60	1,049,747	70.48
EU Praxis	18	246,824	16.57
Total:	*99*	*1,489,333*	*100%*

20 secondary legislative instruments—directives and regulations, e.g. Directive 2014/104/EU.[92] The Competition legislation constitutes 13% of the corpus and has 192,762 words (tokens).

- EU Case Law comprises 60 judgments related to competition, e.g. Case *Courage Ltd v Crehan* (2001).[93] The case law constitutes 70% of the corpus with 1,049,747 tokens.
- EU Praxis comprises 18 documents, mainly soft law instruments,[94] of which 5 Commission/Council decisions on State aid, 8 Commission notices, 3 communications from the Commission, 1 information and 1 Commission recommendation, most of which lay down guidelines and rules on Competition Law, e.g. Guidelines on Vertical Restraints[95] or Commission Notice Guidelines on the application of Article 81 of the EC Treaty to technology transfer agreements.[96]

Overall, the total corpus comprises 99 files with the number of tokens at 1,489,333 (~1.5 m) and the number of types, that is its lexicon size, is 23,763 words. The time span of the corpus ranges from 1973 to 2016, with the majority of documents coming from the last 15 years. The skewedness of the corpus towards case law is intentional to cater for the needs of project participants, that is national judges from non-English speaking countries (Croatia, Greece, Italy, Poland, Spain), who deal with EU Competition Law in their professional practice.

[92]Directive 2014/104/EU of the European Parliament and of the Council of 26 November 2014 on certain rules governing actions for damages under national law for infringements of the competition law provisions of the Member States and of the European Union (OJ L 349, 5.12.2014, p. 1).

[93]Case C-453/99, *Courage and Crehan* [2001] ECR I-6297, ECLI:EU:C:2001:465.

[94]See Elhauge and Geradin (2011), pp. 51–52 on the growing importance of these instruments in shaping the EU's Competition policy by clarifying the approach behind enactments.

[95]OJ C 130, 19.5.2010, p. 1.

[96]OJ C 101, 27.4.2004, p. 2.

5 Term Extraction and Identification

The first step of our study was to identify nodes, in our case key competition terms, which would then be subject to collocational analysis. For this purpose we used a combination of automatic and manual methods. Using Sketch Engine, we first extracted a few sets of the Keywords/Terms lists against the following reference corpora: EUR-Lex 2/2016 Corpus, DGT Eng, EUR-Lex Judgments English 12/2016, The British National Corpus. The lists were analysed and sorted manually. The list of single-word and multi-word terms (nodes) was next verified against the Wordlist created for the EU Competition Corpus in Sketch Engine. Next, we further excluded terminology related to procedural aspects (e.g. *judgment, plea, defence, limb*), the subject of regulation or proceedings (*e.g. kettle, lignite, decoder, licence, loan*), as well as general business terms (e.g. *turnover*) which were covered under other nodes. The list of nodes was reduced to nouns (lemmas), with key adjectives being accounted for as part of nodes. As a final verification of nodes, we compared them against a reference corpus of EU Competition Law textbooks to add those nodes which may rank lower in judgments (e.g. *prohibition, control, behaviour, coordination*). This procedure produced the following list of 103 term candidates for collocational nodes (in alphabetical order).

abuse, access, action, agreement, aid, allocation, annulment, antitrust, application, appreciability, arrangements, authorities, ban, barrier, behaviour, benefit, bidding, block, brand, cap, cartel, ceiling, circumstances, collusion, compensation, competition, competitor, concentration, concertation, conduct, continuity, contract, control, coordination, cost, damage, damages, discount, discrimination, dispute, distribution, effect, enforcement, exclusivity, exemption, fine, fixing, foreclosure, harm, immunity, influence, information, infringement, insolvency, investigation, judicature, leniency, limitation, loss, mark, market, measures, merger, monopoly, objections, obligation, oligopoly, operator, overcharge, payment, penalty, position, practice, pressure, price, principle, prohibition, protection, purchaser, rebate, recovery, redress, remedy, restraint, restriction, rules, sales, secret, sector, service, share, specialisation, squeeze, subsidiaries, system, tariff, test, threshold, trade, treatment, tying, undertaking, unit

The terms were next subject to the analysis of collocations, concordances and word sketches to identify their key collocational patterns for the glossary presented in next Chap.

6 Analysis of Term-Nodes and Their Collocations

The above list of term-nodes includes both terms which are extremely frequent in the corpus, e.g. *market*, with the frequency of 6823 occurrences in the corpus (NF 4581 pmw[97]), and those which are rare, e.g. *oligopoly* of 18 occurrences (NF 12) or *overcharge* of 20 occurrences (NF 13). The most frequent terms, the frequency of which is above 2000 occurrences, are: *market, undertaking, aid, agreement, competition, price, infringement, product, effect* and *information*. The high frequency is indicative of their cognitive salience (importance); thus, these nodes may be regarded as key concepts which form the conceptual foundations and "aboutness" of Competition Law as represented in our corpus. It should be borne in mind, though, that 70% of the corpus content is judgments, which in general deal with infringements of Competition Law; hence, an increased frequency of negative *infringement,* and seemingly neutral *effect* and *price*, which—quite understandably—demonstrate strong negative semantic prosody[98] through their collocates in the sub-corpus of this genre:

- *anti-competitive effect, deterrent effect, adverse effect, negative effect, exclusionary effect;*
- *price fixing, price collusion, price war, price competition, price cartel.*

Negative prosodies are also prompted by the general nature of Competition Law which is intended to prevent distortions of competition and ensure interventions to deal with market failures[99] and "market imperfections arising in a free market economy".[100] The remaining key terms, in particular *aid, undertaking, market, competition, product* and *information* are also top high-frequency words in the sub-corpus of EU Competition legislation, plus *cost,* which ranks lower in EU Competition judgments. Interestingly, these fundamental terms are shared with the top terms of our reference corpus of EU Competition Law textbooks, with the exception of *aid*, which ranks much lower in academic textbooks. Terms which are significantly much more frequent in the latter against our main corpus are: *merger*, *control*, *prohibition*, *behaviour* and *cartel.*

[97]Figures in brackets provide a normalised frequency (NF) per 1 million words (pmw), as opposed to a raw frequency (RF), that is a frequency in the entire corpus.

[98]Semantic prosody is "a consistent aura of meaning with which a form is imbued by its collocates" (Louw (1993), p. 157).

[99]Rodger and MacCulloch (2015), p. 2.

[100]Jones and Townley (2017), pp. 510, 512.

6.1 Collocational Ranges and Combinatory Potential

The centrality of these frequent terms is also confirmed by their large collocational ranges, that is a potential (and need) to form collocational patterns with other nodes (combinatory potential). Large ranges were observed in particular for *competition*, *aid*, *infringement*, *market* and *agreement*. For example, *aid* has over 15 adjectival premodifiers: e.g. *State aid*, *de minimis aid*, *public aid*, *horizontal aid*, *transparent aid*. Collocational patterns are typically formed with adjectives to assign attributes to nodes and to restrict them to a certain subset (the so-called qualifiers) (*dominant undertaking*, *public undertaking*), with verbs to enable action and interaction with other terms (*to grant aid to undertakings*), as well as, above all, with nouns: premodifying nouns (*cartel infringement*, *competition law infringement*), postmodifying nouns (*infringement proceedings*, *infringement decision*) and complex noun/prepositional phrases (*immunity under a leniency programme*). In particular, noun phrases are typical of specialised communication[101] and may express a broad range of meaning relations, e.g. composition, purpose, identity, content, source, object/subject of the process, location, time, partitive and specialisation.[102] The high combinatory potential of key term-nodes evidences a property of legal language whereby it blurs a boundary between a term and a collocate[103] since a term with its collocate usually forms other multi-word terms, e.g. a *position* collocates with the adjective *dominant* to form a *dominant position*, which forms another term—*an abuse of a dominant position (on the market)*. While key terms and terms which are more general in meaning tend to have broad collocational ranges, some terms have very restrictive ranges, e.g. *leniency*, *recipient*, *dispute*, *coordination*, and collocate with a limited set of words. It is also worth noting that polysemous terms—that is terms which have more than one sense (e.g. *action*, *effect*, *enforcement*)—tend to have a distinct set of collocates for each sense.[104] For example, *action* in the meaning of conduct and activity collocates with adjectives *concerted*, *unilateral* and *anti-competitive action* and with the verb *to undertake action* while action in the sense of proceedings collocates with adjectives *legal*, *representative*, *administrative*, *civil* and *collective action* and verbs *to bring*, *take*, *hear*, *dismiss* and *withdraw an action*.

6.2 Derivational Productivity

Another aspect of keyness is the derivational productivity of nodes. The majority of term-nodes show a propensity for derivability, which is one of the term formation

[101]Jopek-Bosiacka (2010), pp. 114–115, for further discussion.

[102]Biber et al. (1999), pp. 590–591.

[103]Kjær (2007), p. 506, Biel (2012), p. 227.

[104]This is consistent with Hoey's priming hypothesis concerning polysemous words ((2005), p. 13).

principles propagated by Unesco's *Guidelines for Terminology Policies*.[105] One of such productive terms is *competition*, which has the largest number of derivatives based on the lemma *compet**:

- a verb: *to compete, non-compete*
- adjectives: *competing, competitive, anti-competitive/anticompetitive, pro-competitive, uncompetitive, non-competing, competing, supra-competitive*
- nouns: *competition, competitor, non-competitor, competitiveness, pro-competitiveness*
- adverbs: *competitively, anticompetitively.*

Some of the derivatives form very frequent nodes themselves. This applies in particular to the noun *competitor* (RF 934/NF 627) and the adjective *anti-competitive* with its all spelling variants (RF 604/NF 394). Derivatives are not always easy to predict for non-native speakers as they may be irregular or follow some arbitrary patterns. See for example a relation between the following adjectives with the same suffix *–ive* and related nouns with varied suffixes: *abusive – abuse; collusive – collusion; restrictive – restriction* while nouns with the same suffix *–tion* may be connected with varied adjective formation patterns: *compensation – compensatory, competition – competitive, continuation – continuous, concertation – concerted.*

6.3 International Prefixes

Another easily observed feature of EU competition terminology and phraseology is a high productivity of international prefixes of mainly Greek and Latin origin, to form the so-called neo-classical compounds.[106] This is a long-standing tradition in specialised discourse intended to ensure its transparency.[107] Due to technical limitations, the list below contains only compounds which are separated graphically with a hyphen and frequencies exclude spelling variants without hyphens (e.g. *anticompetitive*). The list is arranged according to the frequency of use.

- non-* (RF 830/NF 557): *non-compete, non-confidential, non-discriminatory, non-competitor, non-aseptic, non-payment, non-reciprocal, non-discrimination, non-compliance, non-hardcore, non-exclusive, non-economic, non-dominant, non-disclosure, non-imposition, non-essential, non-settling, non-authorised, non-existent, non-use, non-restrictive, non-conformity, non-challenge, non-appointed, non-participation, non-dominated, non-dairy, non-severable, non-performance, non-patented, non-member, non-exemption, non-entry, non-branded, non-binding, non-assertion, non-specific, non-profit, non-price,*

[105] Infoterm (2005), p. 10.
[106] Bowker and Hawkins (2006), p. 85.
[107] Gotti (2005), pp. 37–40.

non-implementation, non-full, non-existence, non-delivery, non-competing, non-agricultural, non-notified, non-existent, non-transparent, non-tied, non-refundable, non-recovery, non-marketing, non-linear, non-exempted, non-coordinated, non-contestation, non-application, non-accessible, non-Member, non-European, non-Community, non-participation, non-application, non-renewal, etc.

- anti-* (RF 601/NF 403): *anti-competitive, anti-competitively, anti-theft, anti-discrimination, anti-trust*
- intra-* (RF 162/NF 109): *intra-brand, intra-Community, intra-technology, intra-group*
- re-* (RF 123/NF 83): *re-use, re-examined, re-allocation, re-exporting, re-establish, re-imported, re-importation, re-implement, re-establishing, re-utilisation, re-import, re-allocated, re-offend, re-export, re-branding, re-submit, re-examination, re-enter, re-create, re-stated, re-selling, re-sale, re-opening, re-evaluation, re-entry*
- co-* (RF 100/NF 67): *co-infringer, co-sourcing, co-branding, co-operation, co-shipping, co-ordination, co-loading, co-defendant, co-investing, co-production, co-ordinating, co-operate, co-financed*
- sub-* (RF 85/NF 57): *sub-leasing, sub-lease, sub-optimal, sub-part, sub-family, sub-sector, sub-optimally, sub-agent, sub-national, sub-market, sub-contractor*
- inter-* (RF 83/NF 56): *inter-brand, inter-technology, inter-state, inter-group*
- pre-* (RF 79/NF 53): *pre-existing, pre-sales, pre-trial, pre-production, pre-notification, pre-litigation, pre-announced, pre-condition, pre-tax, pre-standard, pre-dated, pre-completed, pre-arranged*
- cross-* (RF 78/NF 52): *cross-border, cross-appeal, cross-supply, cross-licensing, cross-holding, cross-licence, cross-appealed, cross-frontier*
- pan-* (RF 64/NF 46): *pan-European*
- pro-* (RF 52/NF 35): *pro-competitive, pro-competitiveness*
- quasi-* (RF 41/NF 27): *quasi-equity, quasi-delict, quasi-monopoly, quasi-monopolistic, quasi-legislative, quasi-capital*
- self-* (RF 18/NF 12): *self-incriminating, self-restraining, self-limitation, self-employed*
- post-* (RF 14/NF 9): *post-term, post-patent, post-dated, post-suspension, post-licencing*
- ex-* (RF 13/NF 9): *ex-officio, ex-ante*
- micro-* (RF 6/NF 4): *micro-enterprise, micro-finance.*

Most of these prefixes have an average or low frequency, except for two prefixes which connote negation: *non-* (RF 830/NF 557) and *anti-* (RF 601/NF 403). When these negation-marking prefixes combine with words with negative connotations, they in fact neutralise negativity, e.g. *anti-discrimination, non-exclusive, non-discriminatory, non-imposition*. While the use of *anti-* is limited to a few combinations, most notably *anti-competitive*, *non-* combines with over 100 verbs, participles, nouns and adjectives. Some of such compounds are common (e.g. *non-compete obligation,* RF 107/NF 72), while quite a few seem to be introduced idiosyncratically as one-off variants of more standardised forms of negation. Compared to the British Law Report Corpus, available on the Sketch Engine, both prefixes are considerably overrepresented in the EU Competition Corpus, with *non-** being 2.5 times more frequent and *anti-** — 10 times more frequent in EU English than in British English. It is worth noting that *non-* compounds are used alongside the structure *failure to*, e.g. *systematic non-payment* and *systematic failure to pay*.

6.4 Latinisms

Despite the popularity of neo-classical compounds, Latinisms are used relatively rarely to form or premodify terms. Apart from the well-visible example of *de minimis* (e.g. *de minimis aid, rule, threshold*), other Latinisms are used very occasionally, mostly as premodifiers rather than nodes, e.g. *ad hoc aid, de facto monopoly, ex officio investigations, ex post decision, ex ante scrutiny of aid measures, ex nunc effect, ex parte proceedings, the principle of audi alteram partem, bona fide estimate*.

6.5 Premodification by Participles

The next productive group of collocational patterns comprises compounds with premodification by participles: *-ing* and *–ed* participles. This type of premodification is generally regarded as relatively rare in English compared to premodification with adjectives and nouns.[108] The gerund (*-ing*) pattern may have three basic forms, with the first one being most productive and frequent:

- *-ing* noun + node
  the restructuring aid, tying product/market, switching costs, offending conduct, pricing policy, mitigating/attenuating/aggravating circumstances, countervailing benefits, voting rights, contracting parties, blocking position, co-sourcing arrangement;
- Noun + *-ing* noun + node (with or without a hyphen)
  price-fixing agreement, market-sharing cartel, decision-making powers, fact-finding measures, price-cutting distributor, efficiency-enhancing effects, risk-sharing instruments
- Adjective + *-ing* noun + node
  single-branding type arrangement, free-standing exchange of information, dual-pricing system.

[108]Biber et al. (1999), p. 589.

In some cases, gerunds function independently as stand-alone terms: *tying, quantity forcing, bid-rigging, market sharing, time-barring, profit-sharing, free-riding, hiving-off.* See for example:

> The assessment of quantity forcing will depend on the degree of foreclosure of other buyers on the upstream market. (...) Tying exists when the supplier makes the sale of one product conditional upon the purchase of another distinct product from the supplier or someone designated by the latter.[109]

or

> Tying is the practice of a supplier of one product, the tying product, requiring a buyer also to buy a second product, the tied product.[110]

This frequent use of the *-ing* participial modifier in collocational patterns is in line with the expansion of the *–ing* form, observed as one of the distinctive features of EU English.[111]

The premodification with *–ed* participles, which function as deverbal adjectives, is even more frequent, partly due to the context of court proceedings in the major part of the corpus: *a contested decision, alleged cartel, presumed perpetrator, suspected infringement, disputed sale, claimed violation of rights, impugned undertaking, reasoned opinion, accumulated losses.* In most cases, such premodifiers function as linguistic hedges—protective devices which tone done the discourse and are typical of the judicial language. Another group of deverbal premodifiers contains terms typical of Competition Law: *a concerted practice, protected service, tied market, notified concentration, foreclosed manufacturer, dominated market, connected undertakings, sunk costs, coordinated course of action, prohibited agreement, block exempted agreement, differentiated prices, notified concentration, unauthorised place of establishment.* Both *–ing* and *-ed* participial premodifiers are less frequent in the British Law Report Corpus (based on the patterns: *the *ed, a/an *ed, the *ing, a/an *ed* and gerund/participle tags), so this feature is likely to have been transferred from other languages. For example, one of the key terms of Competition Law, *concerted practices*, is a calque of the French *pratique concertée.*[112]

6.6 Adjectives with Negative Connotations

As for the premodification with adjectives, there is a significant range of adjectives which connote negative meanings. They refer to:

- breach of law
  anti-competitive (RF 635/NF 425), *unlawful* (RF 269/NF 181), *illegal* (RF 58/NF 39), *abusive* (RF 87/NF 58), *collusive* (RF 62/NF 42), *incompatible* (RF 167/NF 112)

[109] An example from the corpus: *Guidelines on Vertical Restraint* (OJ C 130, 19.5.2010, p. 1).
[110] Whish and Bailey (2015), p. 729.
[111] cf. Modiano (2017), p. 322.
[112] http://www.eucomplaw.com/the-case/concerted-practice (Accessed 19 Jan 2018).

- restrictive, discriminatory or unilateral treatment or conditions:
  exclusive (RF 756/NF 507), *restrictive* (RF 208/NF 140), *selective* (RF 235/NF 158), *exclusionary* (RF 21/NF 14), *discriminatory* (RF 35/NF 23), *unfair* (RF 84/NF 56), *disproportionate* (RF 82/NF 55), *unilateral* (RF 52/NF 35), *non-reciprocal* (RF 36/NF 24), *dissimilar* (RF 29/NF 19)
- preferential treatment or conditions
  preferential (RF 83/NF 56), *favourable* (RF 73/NF 49), *privileged* (RF 24/NF 16), *favoured* (RF 10/NF 7), *beneficial* (RF 10/NF 7), *advantageous* (RF 20/NF 13)
- other negative conditions
  predatory (RF 23/NF 15), *negative* (RF 197/NF 132), *harmful* (RF 41/NF 27), *serious* (RF 360/NF 241), *adverse* (RF 31/NF 21), *severe* (RF 31/NF 279), *dissimilar* (RF 29/NF 19).

Some of these adjectives are converted into adverbs to collocate with verbs or other adjectives, e.g. *to impose unilaterally, tacitly renewable non-compete obligations, exclusively allocated territories, unlawfully granted aid.* Such negatively marked adjectives and adverbs tend to collocate with neutral nouns (*effect, price, practice, behaviour*) but also with some nouns with positive connotations, e.g. *aid*, to give them negative connotational colouring and shift their semantic prosodies into negative ones (*unlawful aid, predatory prices, anti-competitive behaviour*).[113] While some adjectives have an explicit negative meaning (*abusive, discriminatory, predatory*), those which refer to preferential treatment or conditions typically trigger positive meanings in everyday language. Yet, in the context of Competition Law, and in particular in the genre of judgments, which often assumes the perspective of competition authorities or the injured party, such adjectives acquire negative meaning since the infringer's *privileged access* or *preferential rate* distort competition on the market.

6.7 Deverbal and Deadjectival Nouns

Another collocational trend is a frequent use of deverbal nouns, the so-called "buried" verbs which are derived from verbs with suffixes *–ment, -tion, -ance,* etc. This trend is not unique to EU English but is in general typical of formal registers and administrative language. As nouns, they allow for a conceptual reification of a process denoted by the verb,[114] which facilitates its qualification and use in argumentation,[115] and thematisation of verbal action for emphasis. Nouns may also ensure greater textual conciseness at the expense of conceptual clarity.[116] Such deverbal nouns are often frequent terms themselves: *infringement* (RF 2859/NF 1920), *restriction* (RF 853/NF

---

[113]As an aside, in some cases, prosodies may be stretched to the limit, e.g. the use of *to merit* which should collocate with positive objects: *the applicant's limited or passive participation in the PG Paperboard did not merit a fine or, at most, merited only a small fine.*

[114]Langacker (2008), p. 105.

[115]Jopek-Bosiacka (2010), p. 115.

[116]Gotti (2005), pp. 78–80.

573), *commitment* (RF 612/NF 411), *limitation* (RF 318/NF 213), *annulment* (RF 294/NF 197), *settlement* (RF 171/NF 115), *compliance* (RF 151/NF 101), *distortion* (RF 121/NF 81), *enforcement* (RF 126/NF 85). There is also a broad range of less frequent deverbal nouns which function either as terms, e.g. *performance, procurement, surveillance*, or collocates of terms: *restoration, arrangements, equalization, attainment, readjustment, apportionment, recoupment, adjustment, continuance, observance, maintenance, withdrawal, treatment, establishment*. A related trend is a group of nouns derived from adjectives with the *-ity* and *-ness* suffixes: *(un)lawfulness, soundness, effectiveness, compatibility, proportionality, confidentiality, indispensability, equality, substitutability, appreciability, abusiveness, gravity, validity*. This trend confirms the excessive nominalisation of EU English.[117]

6.8 Other Grammatical Features of Terminological Nouns

Some terminological nouns which are typically used as uncountable nouns show a tendency to be used in a plural form: *aids* (*aids granted by States, regional aids*), *intensities* (*maximum aid intensities*), *abuses, infringements, prohibitions, efficiencies, losses, concentrations*. Some inanimate nouns occasionally take elliptic genitives ('s Saxon Genitive): *the agreement's existence, the agreement's continuance; consequences of the aid's unlawfulness, concentration's effects on competition, scheme's entry into force, technology's share of the market, property's value*. This feature is typical of animate nouns.[118] There are some occasional incorrect forms, for example, the plural *undertakings's participation* or the use of plural *damages* in the meaning of the singular *damage* (*the damages suffered by the beneficiary*).

6.9 Variation

Last but not least, one of the most distinctive features of EU English terminology as studied in the Competition Corpus is its high variation at various levels, mostly due to interlinguistic causes, induced by contacts between languages,[119] and the high intensity of mediation. Following the classification proposed by Bowker and Hawkins,[120] variants have been classified into:

- graphical variants
  anti-competitive versus *anticompetitive* v *anti competitive, cooperation* v *co-operation, coordination* v *co-ordination, quasi-monopoly* v *quasimonopoly, price*

[117]As observed e.g. by Gardner (2017).
[118]Biber et al. (1999), p. 307.
[119]Freixa (2006), p. 63.
[120]Bowker and Hawkins (2006), p. 81.

fixing v *price-fixing, trade mark* v *trademark, import and export trade* v *import-export trade, wholly-owned subsidiary* v *wholly owned subsidiary, hardcore* v *hard core* v *hard-core*. It is quite a frequent type of variation which usually concerns the hyphenation of prefixes and spacing between constituents within a noun phrase. In most cases one form is dominant while the other is introduced idiosyncratically as a result of lower standardisation, e.g. *trade mark* appears 350 times in the corpus while *trademark* only 23 times. Variants usually appear in the same collocational patterns, which suggests they are synonymous, e.g. *anticompetitive foreclosure* v *anti-competitive foreclosure*.

- orthographic variants
  specialise/specialisation v *specialize/specialization*, *recognise* v *recognize, authorise* v *authorize, penalise* v *penalize*, with the *–ise* spelling being dominant; *pan-European* v *Pan-European*
- morphological variants
  continuance of infringement v *continuation of infringement* (another morphological variant, *continuity*, has different collocates and meaning *financial continuity*); *exemptable* v *exemptible, investigatory* v *investigative* (e.g. *investigatory powers, investigative powers/measures*)
- inflectional variants
  passing-on v *pass-on, buying cartel* v *buyers' cartel*
- permutation
  action for damages v *damages action, market share* v *share of the market, leniency application* v *application for leniency.*

From the perspective of collocations, it is also important to account for synonymous collocational variants, e.g. *to grant an aid, to award an aid*; *to conclude an agreement, to enter into an agreement*; *to form a cartel, to establish a cartel, to conclude a cartel.*

Finally, and most importantly, while the above listed types of variation are rather easy to spot, what is more problematic is variation at the level of terminology where the same concept has different denominations ("lexicalised forms")—denominative variation,[121] which go beyond minor modifications but result in different lemmas. It applies for example to *restrictions of competition*, which, as argued by Walter, is synonymous with *impairment of competition.*[122] In most cases, again, one variant—usually a neutral one—is dominant and the other is introduced occasionally under the influence of other languages or is more typically British English. This can be well illustrated with one of the most frequent terms in the corpus the *undertaking* (RF 4139/NF 2779). As already observed, it is of German origin and evidences attempts to neutralise EU English terminology. A more typical corresponding term of UK English, a *company*, is also common (RF 1382/NF 929), but three times less frequent than *an undertaking*. Another synonym, an *enterprise* of French origin, is

[121]Freixa (2006), p. 51.

[122]Walter (2016), p. 58, fn 318.

used far less frequently with the frequency of 372 (NF 250). A similar frequency of use has been observed for a related but broader concept (a conceptual variant) of an *economic operator* (RF 307/NF 206), which is a collocational neologism introduced "in the interest of simplification" to cover contractors, suppliers and service providers, including public entities, in the context of awards of public contracts (Directive 2004/18/EC[123]). A more generic *entity* has a frequency of 277 hits (NF 185). An *entrepreneur*, another synonymous term of French origin, appears once but in a regulation.[124] As can be seen in this example, despite the hypothesis that translators over-standardise and limit variation,[125] EU terminology shows a larger tolerance of synonyms and semi-synonyms, where variants have more national/supranational (neutralised) origin or show foreign influences. Another example is a *merger* (RF 92/NF 62), which is a neutral EU term replacing the former English term *amalgamation* (0 hits in the corpus). The corpus has four examples of the synonym *fusion*, e.g. *the sale or fusion of an entire economic entity*, which is of French origin (*fusion d'entreprises*), all coming from one judgment. Some degree of authors' and translators' idiosyncrasy is unavoidable even in such highly controlled genres and institutionalised settings.

7 Conclusions

To sum up, the analysis of the collocational environment of key terms in EU Competition Law has identified a number of features typical of terminological collocations in this area. These include: a tendency of neutral terms to combine with collocations which give them negative semantic prosodies, frequent use of adjectives with negative connotations, propensity of terms for derivability, high productivity of international prefixes (neo-classical compounds), frequent premodification by *–ing* and *–ed* participles, increased use (overrepresentation) of deverbal and deadjectival nouns, and occasional use of grammatically incorrect forms. Last but not least, the chapter has drawn attention to the high variation of terminology and phraseology at various levels (graphical, orthographic, morphological, inflectional variants and permutation), as well as denominative variation, which is an undesirable phenomenon in legal language. These features attest to the impact of the EU's constitutive languages and cultures and the resulting hybridity of EU English. The practical applications of this analysis are presented in next Chap. in the form of a glossary of terminological collocations in EU Competition Law.

---

[123]Directive 2004/18/EC of the European Parliament and of the Council of 31 March 2004 on the coordination of procedures for the award of public works contracts, public supply contracts and public service contracts (OJ L 134, 30.4.2004, p. 114).

[124]Commission Regulation (EU) No 651/2014 of 17 June 2014 declaring certain categories of aid compatible with the internal market in application of Articles 107 and 108 of the Treaty (OJ L 187, 26.6.2014, p. 1).

[125]cf. Bowker and Hawkins (2006), p. 80.

References

Alcaraz E, Hughes B (2002) Legal translation explained. St. Jerome, Manchester

Bajčić M (2017) New insights into the semantics of legal concepts and the legal dictionary. Benjamins, Amsterdam

Baker M (1992) In other words. A coursebook on translation. Routledge, London

Bhatia VK, Langton NM, Lung J (2004) Legal discourse: opportunities and threats for corpus linguistics. In: Connor U, Upton TA (eds) Discourse in the professions. Perspectives from corpus linguistics. Benjamins, Amsterdam, pp 203–231

Biber D, Johansson S, Leech G, Conrad S, Finegan E (1999) Longman grammar of spoken and written English. Longman, Harlow

Biel Ł (2012) Areas of similarity and difference in legal phraseology: collocations of key terms in UK and Polish company law. In: Pamies A, Pazos Bretaña JM, Nadal LL (eds) Phraseology and discourse: cross-linguistic and corpus-based approaches. Schneider Verlag, Baltmannsweiler, pp 225–233

Biel Ł (2014) Lost in the Eurofog: the textual fit of translated law. Peter Lang, Frankfurt am Main

Biel Ł (2017) Quality in institutional EU translation: parameters, policies and practices. In: Svoboda T, Biel Ł, Łoboda K (eds) Quality aspects in institutional translation. Language Science Press, Berlin, pp 31–57. https://doi.org/10.5281/zenodo.1048183

Bowker L, Hawkins S (2006) Variation in the organization of medical terms. Exploring some motivations for term choice. Terminology 12(1):79–110

Caliendo G (2004) EU language in cross-boundary communication. Textus 17:159–178

Catenaccio P (2008) Implementing Council Directive 1993/13/EEU on Unfair Terms in Consumer Contracts in Great Britain: a case for intra-linguistic translation? In: Bhatia VK, Candlin CN, Allori PE (eds) Language, culture and the law. The formulation of legal concepts across systems and cultures. Peter Lang, Bern, pp 259–280

Crystal D (2003) English as a global language, 2nd edn. Cambridge University Press, Cambridge

Derlén M (2015) A single text or a single meaning: multilingual interpretation of EU legislation and CJEU case law in national courts. In: Šarčević S (ed) Language and culture in EU law. Multidisciplinary perspectives. Ashgate, Farnham, pp 53–72

Doczekalska A (2009) Drafting and interpretation of EU law — paradoxes of legal multilingualism. In: Grewendorf G, Rathert M (eds) Formal linguistics and law. Walter de Gruyter, Berlin, pp 339–370

Elhauge E, Geradin D (2011) Global competition law and economics, 2nd edn. Hart, Oxford

European Commission (2014) Translation and multilingualism. https://publications.europa.eu/en/publication-detail/-/publication/e0770e72-afa1-4971-8824-6190512537dc/language-en. Accessed 1 Jan 2018

European Commission (2016) Strategic plan 2016-2020. DG Translation. Ref. Ares(2016)1329034 - 16/03/201. https://ec.europa.eu/info/sites/info/files/strategic-plan-2016-2020-dg-t_march2016_en.pdf. Accessed 1 Jan 2018

European Commission (n.d.) EU jargon in English and some possible alternatives. http://ec.europa.eu/ipg/content/tips/words-style/jargon-alternatives_en.htm. Accessed 1 Jan 2018

European Court of Auditors, Secretariat General of Translation Directorate (2016) Misused English words and expressions in EU publications. https://www.eca.europa.eu/Other%20publications/EN_TERMINOLOGY_PUBLICATION/EN_TERMINOLOGY_PUBLICATION.pdf. Accessed 1 Jan 2018

Firth JR (1957) Papers in linguistics 1934–1951. Oxford University Press, Oxford

Freixa J (2006) Causes of denominative variation in terminology. A typology proposal. Terminology 12(1):51–77

Gardner J (2017) Errors in EU-English. Altre Modernità 04/2017:149–164. https://doi.org/10.13130/2035-7680/8308

Glanert S (2008) Speaking language to law: the case of Europe. Legal Stud 28(2):161–171

Gotti M (2005) Investigating specialized discourse. Peter Lang, Bern

Hanzl J, Beaven J (2017) Quality assurance at the Council of the EU's translation service. In: Svoboda T, Biel Ł, Łoboda K (eds) Quality aspects in institutional translation. Language Science Press, Berlin, pp 139–153. https://doi.org/10.5281/zenodo.1048196
Hatim B, Munday J (2004) Translation. An advanced resource book. Routledge, London
Heid U (1994) On ways words work together — topics in lexical combinatorics. In: Martin W, Meijs W, Moerland M, ten Pas E, van Sterkenburg P, Vossen P (eds) Euralex 1994: Proceedings. International Congress on Lexicography, Amsterdam, pp 226–257
Hoey M (2005) Lexical priming. A new theory of words and language. Routledge, London
Howarth P (1998) Phraseology and second language proficiency. Appl Linguist 19(1):24–44
Infoterm (2005) Guidelines for terminology policies. Formulating and implementing terminology policy in language communities. Unesco, Paris
Jones A, Sufrin B (2016) EU Competition Law. Text, cases, and materials, 6th edn. Oxford University Press, Oxford
Jones A, Townley C (2017) Competition law. In: Barnard C, Peers S (eds) European Union law, 2nd edn. Oxford University Press, Oxford, pp 509–542
Jopek-Bosiacka A (2010) Legal communication: a cross-cultural perspective. Warsaw University Press, Warsaw
Jopek-Bosiacka A (2011) Defining law terms: a cross-cultural perspective. Res Lang 9(1):9–29
Kępiński M (ed) (2014) Prawo konkurencji, vol 15. C.H.Beck, Warszawa
Kilgarriff A, Baisa V, Bušta J, Jakubíček M, Kovvář V, Michelfeit J, Rychlý P, Suchomel V (2014) The Sketch Engine: ten years on. Lexicography 1:7–36
Kjær AL (2007) Phrasemes in legal texts. In: Burger H, Dobrovol'skij D, Kühn P, Norrick NR (eds) Phraseologie/Phraseology: Ein internationales Handbuch der zeitgenössischen Forschung/An international handbook of contemporary research, vol 1. Walter de Gruyter, Berlin, pp 506–516
Kolasiński MK (2012) Zarys prawa antymonopolowego Unii Europejskiej na tle prawa Stanów Zjednoczonych i Polski. Wydawnictwo Dom Organizatora, Toruń
Koskinen K (2008) Translating institutions. An ethnographic study of EU translation. St. Jerome, Manchester
Koskinen K (2013) Social media and the institutional illusions of EU communication. Int J Appl Linguist 23(1):80–92
Krzyżanowski M, Wodak R (2011) Political strategies and language policies: the European Union Lisbon Strategy and its implications for the EU's language and multilingualism policy. Lang Policy 10:115–136. https://doi.org/10.1007/s10993-011-9196-5
L'Homme MC (2000) Understanding specialized lexical combinations. Terminology 6(1):89–110
Langacker RW (2008) Cognitive grammar: a basic introduction. Oxford University Press, Oxford
Larson ML (1998[1984]) Meaning-based translation: a guide to cross-language equivalence. University Press of America, Lanham
Leucht B, Marquis M (2013) American Influences on EEC Competition Law: two paths, how much dependence? In: Patel KK, Schweitzer H (eds) The historical foundations of EU Competition Law. Oxford University Press, Oxford, pp 125–161
Louw B (1993) Irony in the text or insincerity in the writer? The diagnostic potential of semantic prosodies. In: Baker M, Francis G, Tognini-Bonelli E (eds) Text and technology: in honour of John Sinclair. Benjamins, Amsterdam, pp 157–176
Maher I (2000) Re-imaging the story of European Competition Law. Oxf J Legal Stud 20(1): 155–166. https://doi.org/10.1093/ojls/20.1.155
Mattila HES (2013) Comparative legal linguistics, 2nd edn (trans: Goddard C). Ashgate, Aldershot
Mauranen A (2000) Strange strings in translated language: A study on corpora. In: Olohan M (ed) Intercultural faultlines. Research models in translation studies I. Textual and cognitive aspects. St. Jerome, Manchester, pp 119–141
McAuliffe K (2017) Behind the scenes at the Court of Justice. Drafting EU law stories. In: Nicola F, Davies B (eds) EU law stories. Contextual and critical histories of European jurisprudence. Cambridge University Press, Cambridge, pp 35–57

Meyer I, Mackintosh K (1994) Phraseme analysis and concept analysis: exploring a symbiotic relationship in the specialized lexicon. In: Martin W et al (eds) Euralex 1994: Proceedings. International Congress on Lexicography, Amsterdam, pp 339–348. http://www.euralex.org/elx_proceedings/Euralex1994/. Accessed 1 Jun 2012

Modiano M (2017) English in a post-Brexit European Union. World Engl 36(3):313–327. https://doi.org/10.1111/weng.12264

Nesselhauf N (2005) Collocations in a learner corpus. Benjamins, Amsterdam

Newmark P (1981) Approaches to translation. Prentice Hall, London/New York

Partington A (1998) Patterns and meanings. Using corpora for English language research and teaching. Benjamins, Amsterdam

Pozzo B (2012a) English as a legal lingua franca in the EU multilingual context. In: Baaij CJW (ed) The role of legal translation in legal harmonization. Wolters Kluwer, Alphen aan den Rijn, pp 183–202

Pozzo B (2012b) Multilingualism and the harmonization of European private law: problems and perspectives. Eur Rev Priv Law 20:1185–1198

Robertson C (2010) LSP and EU legal language. In: Heine C, Engberg J (eds) Reconceptualizing LSP. Online proceedings of the XVII European LSP Symposium 2009. http://bcom.au.dk/fileadmin/www.asb.dk/isek/robertson.pdf. Accessed 20 Mar 2018

Robertson C (2012) EU legal English: common law, civil law, or a new genre. Eur Rev Priv Law 20:1215–1240

Robinson W (2017) EU legislation. In: Karpen U, Xanthaki H (eds) Legislation in Europe. A comprehensive guide for scholars and practitioners. Hart, Oxford, pp 229–256

Rodger BJ, MacCulloch A (2015) Competition law and policy in the EU and UK, 5th edn. Routledge, London

Salmi-Tolonen T (1994) The linguistic manifestations of primary and secondary functions of law in the national and supranational contexts. Int J Semiot Law 7(19):13–39

Šarčević S (2001) Preserving multilingualism in an enlarged European Union. Terminologie et Traduction 2:34–50

Šarčević S (2007) Making multilingualism work in the enlarged European Union. In: Kredens K, Goźdź-Roszkowski S (eds) Language and the law: international outlooks. Peter Lang, Frankfurt am Main, pp 35–56

Šarčević S (2010) Creating a pan-European legal language. In: Gotti M, Williams C (eds) Legal discourse across languages and cultures. Peter Lang, Frankfurt am Main, pp 23–50

Šarčević S (2018) Challenges to legal translators in institutional settings. In: Prieto Ramos F (ed) Institutional translation for international governance. Enhancing quality in multilingual legal communication. Bloomsbury, London, pp 9–24

Schäffner C (2000) Introduction: globalisation, communication, translation. In: Schäffner C (ed) Translation in the global village. Multilingual Matters, Clevedon, pp 1–10

Scott M (2017) WordSmith Tools version 7. Stroud, Lexical Analysis Software

Seidlhofer B (2010) Lingua franca English - the European context. In: Kirkpatrick A (ed) The Routledge handbook of world Englishes. Routledge, Abingdon, pp 355–371

Sinclair JM (1991) Corpus, concordance, collocation. Oxford University Press, Oxford

Stubbs M (2004) Language corpora. In: Davies A, Elder C (eds) Handbook of applied linguistics. Blackwell, Oxford, pp 106–132

Teubert W (2010) Our brave new world? Int J Corpus Linguist 15(3):354–358

Tosi A (2002) The Europeanization of the Italian language by the European Union. In: Lepschy AL, Tosi A (eds) Multilingualism in Italy past and present. Legenda, Oxford, pp 170–194

van Els TJM (2001) The European Union, its institutions and its languages: some language political observations. Curr Issues Lang Plann 2(4):311–360

Wagner E, Bech S, Martínez JM (2002) Translating for the European Union institutions. Translation practices explained. St. Jerome, Manchester

Walter F (2016) Handbook of EU Competition Law. Springer, Berlin

Whish R, Bailey D (2015) Competition law, 8th edn. Oxford University Press, Oxford

Whittaker S (2006) The terminologies of civil protection: rights, remedies and procedures. In: Pozzo B, Jacometti V (eds) Multilingualism and the harmonisation of European law. Kluwer Law International, Alphen aan den Rijn, pp 45–60
Woods L, Watson P, Costa M (2017) Steiner & Woods EU law, 13th edn. Oxford University Press, Oxford
Wray A (2002) Formulaic language and the lexicon. Cambridge University Press, Cambridge

Łucja Biel is Associate Professor of Translation Studies and Linguistics at the Institute of Applied Linguistics, secretary general of the European Society for Translation Studies and deputy editor of the Journal of Specialised Translation.

Agnieszka Biernacka is Assistant Professor at the Institute of Applied Linguistics and Head of the Interdisciplinary Postgraduate Studies in Translation and Interpreting at the University of Warsaw, a court interpreting researcher, legal translator and court interpreter trainer.

Anna Jopek-Bosiacka is Senior Lecturer at the Institute of Applied Linguistics of the University of Warsaw, a sworn translator and counsellor-at-law.

The Glossary of EU English Competition Collocations and Terms

Łucja Biel, Agnieszka Biernacka, and Anna Jopek-Bosiacka

Abstract This chapter presents the glossary of collocations of key terms identified in the EU English Competition Corpus for the purposes of the analysis presented in previous chapter. The aim of compiling a glossary of collocations and other phrasemes was to assist legal practitioners and other professionals who are non-native speakers of English in the reception and production of legal texts on Competition Law. Each entry consists of a key term-node in the nominal form, followed by its pronunciation, frequency of use and derivatives. The core of an entry comprises three types of collocational patterns of terms: adjectival patterns, nominal/prepositional patterns and verbal patterns.

1 Introduction

The objective of this chapter is to present the glossary of collocations of key terms identified in the EU English Competition Corpus comprised of key EU legislation, case law and "praxis" documents, as discussed in detail in Sect. 4 of the preceding chapter. To ensure that the glossary is compiled in an exhaustive, systematic and accurate fashion, we used corpus methods and tools: the Sketch Engine[1] and WordSmith Tools 7.0,[2] firstly, to extract and identify key terms of EU Competition Law (see Sect. 5 of the previous chapter for a detailed discussion of the procedure) and, secondly, to identify the collocational patterns of 103 terms extracted through this procedure. The collocational patterns were established through the analysis of concordances and word sketches. The aim of compiling a glossary of collocations and other phrasemes was to assist legal practitioners and other professionals who are non-native speakers of English in the reception of legal texts on Competition Law.

[1]Kilgarriff et al. (2014).

[2]Scott (2017).

Ł. Biel (✉) · A. Biernacka · A. Jopek-Bosiacka
University of Warsaw, Institute of Applied Linguistics, Warsaw, Poland
e-mail: l.biel@uw.edu.pl; a.biernacka@uw.edu.pl; a.jopek-bosiacka@uw.edu.pl

S. Marino et al. (eds.), *Language and Law*,
https://doi.org/10.1007/978-3-319-90905-9_15

The glossary may be used as a writing aid to help express ideas in a natural way which is typical of EU Competition Law. It may also be a learning resource to expand specialised vocabulary in this area.

2 The Structure of an Entry

Each entry consists of a key term-node in the nominal form, which is presented in bold capitals, e.g. **ABUSE**. The line below each term-node shows its broad pronunciation in slashes /əˈbjuːs/ and information on the frequency of a given term in the EU Competition Law corpus, e.g. (RF 382/NF 257), where RF stands for a raw frequency, that is an actual frequency in the corpus, while the NF stands for a normalised frequency (NF) per 1 million words. This is followed by derivatives[3] of the term-node, for example verb forms (v.), adjectives (adj.), adverbs and other more complex nominal forms (n.). Take for example derivative forms of the noun *abuse*:

DERIVATIVES: to **abuse** /əˈbjuːz/, **abusive** /əˈbjuːsɪv/ (~ *conduct, practices*), **abusively** /əˈbjuːsɪvli/, **abusiveness** /əˈbjuːsɪvnəs/ (~ *of a pricing practice*)

Derivatives are accompanied by the pronunciation and, where applicable, by brackets with italicised examples of how they are used in the context (~ *conduct, practices*). For want of space, in accordance with the lexicographical tradition, examples of use contain a tilde symbol (~) in places where the word in question was omitted in the entry; hence, **abusive** (~ *conduct, practices*) should be read as (*abusive conduct, abusive practices*).

The next level of an entry shows three types of collocational patterns where the term-node combines with adjectives, nouns and prepositional phrases, and verbs. Adjectives and participles premodifying the term-node are marked as ADJECTIVE + TERM. Various types of noun phrases and prepositional phrases with the term-node as a premodifier, postmodifier or the head are introduced by the heading NOUN PHRASE. Verbal collocates are marked as VERB + TERM or TERM + VERB. All the levels specify typical collocations illustrated in some cases with examples of use. The main part of an entry looks as follows:

ADJECTIVE + ABUSE:

- **exclusionary** abuse (*abuse that raises barriers to entry or eliminates competitors*), **exploitative** abuse (*abuse whereby the dominant undertaking exploits*

[3] For the sake of simplicity and functionality of a glossary, what we refer to as derivatives are in fact basic forms from which nominal term-nodes are derived, e.g. the term-node *leniency* derives from the adjective *lenient*, and not vice versa.

its economic power for instance by charging excessive or discriminatory prices)

NOUN PHRASE:

- an abuse of a **dominant position on the market**, abuse of **procedures**
- **existence**, **absence** of abuse

VERB + ABUSE:

- to **commit** an abuse
- to **prohibit** an abuse

To increase the training potential of a glossary and its usefulness, we provided the pronunciation of term-nodes, derivatives and a few selected units which may be problematic to non-native speakers of English. For example, some terms may have an identical orthographic form but different pronunciation. e.g. as a noun, *an abuse* is pronounced as /ə'bjuːs/ and as a verb *to abuse* — /ə'bjuːz/. Similarly, *a discount* /'dɪskaʊnt/ versus *to discoun*t /dɪs'kaʊnt/; *a contract* /'kɒntrækt/ versus *to contract* /kən'trækt/, *a conduct* /'kɒndʌkt/ versus *to conduct* /kən'dʌkt/, as well as *in concert* /'kɒnsət/versus *to concert* /kən'səːt/. This is not always predictable; for example *control* as a noun is pronounced in the same way as when it functions as a verb — /kən'trəʊl/. Some terms may be difficult to pronounce for non-native speakers of English because of their Latin origin: *bona fide* /ˌbəʊnə 'faɪdi/, *quantum* /'kwɒntəm/ *of damages*, *de minimis* /ˌdeɪ 'mɪnɪmiːs/ or French origin: *cartel* /kɑː'tel/, *tranche* /trɑːnʃ/. Because of the EU context, the British pronunciation was selected for entries. The primary source of pronunciation was ***Oxford Advanced Learner's Dictionary*** [4] and, if the pronunciation was not available, *Oxford English Dictionary*[5] was used. The reason for choosing a learner's dictionary is that it has a type of transcription[6] which is familiar to learners of British English throughout Europe.

Abbreviations used in the Glossary:
n. = noun
v. = verb
adj. = adjective
RF = raw frequency
NF = normalised frequency per one million words

[4]Deuter et al. (2015) available at https://www.oxfordlearnersdictionaries.com. This is one of the most popular advanced-level dictionaries for learners of English.

[5]OED Online (2018).

[6]The explanation of transcription symbols and the Pronunciation Guide may be found at https://www.oxfordlearnersdictionaries.com/about/pronunciation_english.html.

3 The Glossary of EU English Competition Collocations and Terms

ABUSE
/əˈbjuːs/ (RF 382/NF 257)

DERIVATIVES: to **abuse** /əˈbjuːz/, **abusive** /əˈbjuːsɪv/ (~ *conduct, practices*), **abusively** /əˈbjuːsɪvli/, **abusiveness** /əˈbjuːsɪvnəs/ (~ *of a pricing practice*)

ADJECTIVE + ABUSE:

- **exclusionary** abuse (*abuse that raises barriers to entry or eliminates competitors*), **exploitative** abuse (*abuse whereby the dominant undertaking exploits its economic power for instance by charging excessive or discriminatory prices*)

NOUN PHRASE:

- an abuse of a **dominant position on the market**, abuse of **procedures**
- **existence**, **absence** of abuse

VERB + ABUSE:

- to **commit** an abuse
- to **prohibit** an abuse

ACCESS
/ˈækses/ (RF 608/NF 408)

DERIVATIVES: to **access** /ˈækses/ (~ *market, file*), **accessible** /əkˈsesəbl/, **accessibility** /əkˌsesəˈbɪləti/

ADJECTIVE + ACCESS:

- **privileged**, **preferential** (*to grant preferential ~ under more favourable conditions*), **virtually exclusive** access

NOUN PHRASE:

- **market** access (*a barrier to market ~*)
- **right**, **ease**, **difficulty** of access to
- access **to** the **market**, **files** (*applications for ~ to investigation files held by national competition authorities*), **service**, **finance**, **information**

VERB + ACCESS:

- to **limit**, **restrict**, **prevent** (*preventing or restricting ~ to new competitors*), **impede**, **deny** access; **bar** x from access (*to bar competitors from ~ to the market*), **foreclose** x from access
- to **grant**, **give**, **provide**, **allow** (*allow ~ free of charge to the protected service*), **obtain**, **facilitate** access

- to **have** access
- to **enjoy**, **benefit** from (privileged) access

ACTION
/ˈækʃn/ (RF 964/NF 647)

1. conduct, activity

ADJECTIVE + ACTION:

- **concerted**, **unilateral**, **anti-competitive** actions *(~ against competitors)*

NOUN PHRASE:

- **freedom** of action (~ *to impinge, limit, restrict freedom of ~ in the market*)

VERB + ACTION:

- to **undertake** actions
- to **take part in** concerted action

2. a suit, proceedings

ADJECTIVE + ACTION:

- **legal, civil** action
- **representative** action
- **administrative** action

NOUN PHRASE:

- **collective redress**, **damages** action
- **follow-on** action
- **course**, **subject-matter** of action
- **admissibility/inadmissibility** of an action
- action **against** X (*the applicant has withdrawn its action against the sole co-defendant*)
- action **for** damages, compensation, annulment

VERB + ACTION:

- to **bring** an action, **take** action against (*they took legal ~ against infringers*)
- to **hear** an action
- to **dismiss**, **withdraw** an action

ACTION + VERB:

- action **pends** (*the ~ pending before the national court)*

AGREEMENT
/əˈgriːmənt/ (RF 3710/NF 2491)

DERIVATIVES: to **agree** /əˈgriː/ (~ *prices were agreed by the companies*)

ADJECTIVE + AGREEMENT:

- **vertical**, **horizontal** agreement (*horizontal cooperation ~*)
- **restrictive**, **non-competitive**, **non-reciprocal/reciprocal** (*reciprocal specialisation ~*), **unilateral**, **parallel**, **exclusive** agreement (*exclusive distribution ~*)
- **individual** agreement

NOUN PHRASE:

- **competition**, **cooperation/**co-operation, **price-fixing**, **price**, **market-sharing**, **specialisation** (*specialisation ~ means a unilateral specialisation agreement, a reciprocal specialisation agreement or a joint production agreement*), **joint production**, **cartel**, **subcontracting** agreement
- **licence/**licencing, **technology transfer, distribution, research and development**, **agency**, **supply** agreement
- **object**, **purpose**, **nature**, **categories**, **terms**, **duration** of the agreement
- **existence**, **conclusion**, **implementation** of the agreement
- **effects**, **impact** of the agreement on
- **assessment**, **prohibition** of agreements
- a **network**, a **complex** of agreements
- an agreement **on** . . . (*prices*)
- the **parties to** the agreement, agreement **between** competitors, **members of** the agreement

VERB + AGREEMENT:

- to **conclude**, **enter into** (*vertical ~ entered into by non-competing undertakings*), **adopt** (*the members of the cartel adopted price ~ during the meeting*), **implement** an agreement
- to **reach** (*companies reached an ~ on tariffs*), **achieve** agreement **on**
- to **prohibit**, **exempt** an agreement
- to **notify** an agreement (*to notify an ~ for an exemption*)

AGREEMENT + VERB:

- an agreement **contains** (*~ contains restrictions of competition*), **covers**, **concerns**, **provides for**, **creates**, **leads to**, **causes**, **entails** (*an ~ entails to take place clandestinely*), **imposes** (*an ~ imposes territorial restraints on licensees*)
- an agreement **affects** (*markets adversely affected by the ~*)
- an agreement **restricts** (*the ~ restricts competition*), **prohibits** (*a distribution agreement prohibiting exports*)

AID
/eɪd/ (RF 3918/NF 2631)

DERIVATIVES: to **aid** /eɪd/, **aided** /ˈeɪdɪd/ (*the ~ project or activity*)

ADJECTIVE + AID:

- **state**, **de minimis** /ˌdeɪ ˈmɪnɪmiːs/, **public**, **individual** aid

- **rescue**, **restructuring**, **operating** aid (*operating ~ may be granted for the operation of innovation clusters*)
- **direct/indirect**, **horizontal** aid
- **ad hoc** aid
- **lawful/unlawful**, **illegal**, **incompatible** aid
- **transparent** aid
- **payable** (*~ payable in several instalments*)
- **eligible for** aid

NOUN PHRASE:

- **investment**, **finance**, **urban development**, **innovation** aid
- aid **intensity** (*maximum intensity of public ~ fixed by Article*), **amount**, **tranche** /trɑːnʃ/, **element** (*there was a State ~ element in an agreement for the sale of land by public authorities*), **package**; **categories** of aid
- aid **instrument** (*certain specific ~ instruments, such as loans, guarantees, tax measures, and, in particular, repayable advances may be considered transparent*)
- aid **scheme**, **system**; **regional** aid **map**
- **award** of aid, aid award (*individual ~ award exceeding EUR 500 000*), **application for** aid
- aid **recipient**, **beneficiary**
- **recovery** (*full recovery of unlawful ~*), **repayment** of aid
- aid **rules, policy**
- aid's **unlawfulness**, **misuse** of aid, aid **compatibility**
- aid **for** infrastructure, research, culture
- aid **to** SMEs, shipbuilding
- aid **in the form of** (*State ~ in the form of guarantees*), aid **in favour of** X (*~ in favour of an undertaking*)

VERB + AID:

- to **grant** (*~ granted to natural persons or SMEs*), **award**, **pay** (*the amount of ~ paid in the form of a capital injection*), **put** aid **into effect**, **implement** aid
- to **receive**, **cumulate** aid (*de minimis aid shall not be cumulated with State ~ in relation to the same eligible costs*), **benefit** from aid
- to **authorise**, **approve** (*a decision approving the ~*), **exempt** aid, **declare** aid (*to be*) illegal/compatible/incompatible *with the common market*, **abolish** (unlawful) aid
- to **notify** aid
- to **recover** (*recover unlawful ~ from the economic operator*); **repay** aid
- to **monitor** aid
- to **comprise** aid (*~ comprised in grants, guarantees, interest rate subsidies*)

AID + VERB:

- aid **strengthens** (*the ~ strengthens the financial position of the recipient firms*)
- aid **fulfils** (*the ~ fulfils the conditions of Article 25(1)*)

- aid **affects** (*the ~ no longer affects competition*)

ALLOCATION
/ˌæləˈkeɪʃn/ (RF 155/NF 104)

Derivatives: to **allocate** /ˈæləkeɪt/ (~ *exclusively, proportionately*)

Adjective + allocation:

- **exclusive** (*exclusive customer ~*), **tentative** allocation (*tentative ~ of quotas*)

Noun phrase:

- **customer** (*customer ~ between suppliers*), **quota**, **revenue** allocation
- allocation **period**
- allocation **system**, **agreement**, **discussions** (*quota ~ discussions*)

Verb + allocation:

- to **approve** an allocation

APPLICATION
/ˌæplɪˈkeɪʃn/ (RF 1687/NF 1132)

Derivatives: **applicant** /ˈæplɪkənt/ (*leniency, immunity ~*)

Adjective + application:

- **final** application

Noun phrase:

- **leniency** application
- **immunity** application

Verb + application:

- to **submit**, **lodge** an application
- to **dismiss, reject** an application

APPRECIABILITY
/əˌpriːʃəˈbɪləti/ (RF 22/NF 15)

Derivatives: **appreciable** /əˈpriːʃəbl/ (RF 143/NF 96) (~ *anti-competitive effects, effect on trade, restriction of competition*), **appreciably** /əˈpriːʃəbli/ *(~ restricts competition, ~ affects trade)*

Noun phrase:

- **assessment** of appreciability, **quantification** of appreciability
- appreciability **threshold**

ARRANGEMENT(S)
/əˈreɪndʒmənt/ (RF 256/NF 172)

DERIVATIVES: to **arrange** /əˈreɪndʒ/ (*the participants ~ to align their conduct*), to **pre-arrange** /ˌpriːəˈreɪndʒ/

ADJECTIVE + ARRANGEMENT:

- **collusive**, **anti-competitive**, **non-compete**, **horizontal** arrangements
- **exclusive**, **bilateral** arrangements
- **pan-European**, **European**, **worldwide** arrangements

NOUN PHRASE:

- **price-fixing**, **cartel**, **market-sharing**, **risk-reward sharing**, **single-branding** type, **set-off** arrangements
- **bona fide** /ˌbəʊnə ˈfaɪdi/ licensing arrangement
- **co-sourcing**, **co-loading**, **licensing**, **distribution** arrangements
- **implementation**, **existence** of arrangements; parallel **networks** of arrangements

VERB + ARRANGEMENT:

- to **participate** in, **be involved** in, **enter** into, **make** arrangements; **conclude** an arrangement (*the parties concluded a horizontal price-fixing ~*), **implement** arrangements

AUTHORITY

/ɔːˈθɒrəti/ (RF 1439/NF 966)

ADJECTIVE + AUTHORITIES:

- **competent** authorities
- **public**, **national**, **state**, **local** authorities
- **administrative**, **regulatory** authorities

NOUN PHRASE:

- **competition**, **tax** authority
- (*arbitrary/disproportionate*) **intervention** by public authorities
- **access** to the file of a competition authority
- **procedure/proceedings/claim before** the judicial/competition authorities

VERB + AUTHORITY:

- to **cooperate** with the authorities

AUTHORITY + VERB :

- authorities **grant** (~ *de minimis aid, benefit*)

BAN

/bæn/ (RF 78/NF 52)

ADJECTIVE + BAN:

- post-term ban

NOUN PHRASE:

- (general) **export**, **marketing**, **re-entry**, **sales** ban
- **expiry**, **termination**, **enforcement** of ban
- **duration**, **scope** of ban

VERB + BAN:

- to **impose**, **terminate**, **lift**, **apply** a ban

BARRIER(S)
/ˈbæriə(r)/ (RF 121/NF 81)

ADJECTIVE + BARRIERS:

- **low/high**, **significant/substantial** barriers
- **state**, **private**, **international** barriers
- **regulatory**, **legal** barriers

NOUN PHRASE:

- **entry** barriers, barriers **to entry**
- **existence**, **absence** of barriers
- barriers **to** (~ *to the free movement of products*), **for** a manufacturer

VERB + BARRIERS:

- to **create**, **recreate**, **establish**, **raise** barriers
- to **face** barriers
- to **overcome**, **remove**, **eliminate**, **identify**, **examine**, **measure** barriers

BEHAVIOUR
/bɪˈheɪvjə(r)/ (RF 138/NF 93)

ADJECTIVE + BEHAVIOUR:

- **anti-competitive, collusive, abusive, non-coordinated, aggressive, illegal** behaviour

NOUN PHRASE:

- **cartel, oligopoly** behaviour
- **coordination/co-ordination** of behaviour

VERB + BEHAVIOUR:

- to **coordinate** behaviour on the market

BENEFIT
/ˈbenɪfɪt/ (RF 302/NF 203)

DERIVATIVES: to **benefit** /ˈbenɪfɪt/ (~ *consumers; ~ from*), **beneficial** /ˌbenɪˈfɪʃl/ (~ *effects*), **beneficiary** /ˌbenɪˈfɪʃəri/ (*aid ~*)

ADJECTIVE + BENEFIT:

- **objective** benefit
- **economic**, **financial, tax** benefit
- **exclusive, pro-competitive** benefit
- **countervailing** /ˈkaʊntəveɪlɪŋ/ benefit

NOUN PHRASE:

- benefit of the **block exemption**

VERB + BENEFIT:

- to **generate, confer, create, produce, bring, grant** benefit
- to **withdraw** a benefit
- to **claim** a benefit

BID, BIDDING
/bɪd/, /ˈbɪdɪŋ/ (RF 56/NF 37)

DERIVATIVES: to **bid** /bɪd/ (~ *for contracts, products*), **bidder** /ˈbɪdə(r)/ (~ *wins*)

ADJECTIVE + BID:

- **collusive** bid
- **public** bid

NOUN PHRASE:

- bid-**rigging**
- **announcement** of the bid
- **competitive** bidding **process, unconditional** bidding **procedure**
- bid **for** contracts

VERB + BID:

- to **submit** a bid

BRAND, BRANDING
/brænd/, /ˈbrændɪŋ/ (RF 362/NF 243)

DERIVATIVES: to **brand** /brænd/ (~ *conduct, practices*), **single branding** /ˈsɪŋgl ˈbrændɪŋ/ (*under the heading of "single branding" come those agreements which have as their main element that the buyer is induced to concentrate his orders for a particular type of product with one supplier*) (~ *obligations, type arrangements*), **co-branding** /ˈkəʊ brændɪŋ/ (*to switch from ~ to its own trade mark*)**,** **re-branding** /ˌriːˈbrændɪŋ/, **branded** /ˈbrændɪd/ (adj.) (~ *products*), **non-branded** /ˌnɒn ˈbrændɪd/ (~ *goods*)

ADJECTIVE + BRAND:

- **strong**, **well-known**, **premium**, **dominant**, **leading**, **inferior**, **cheap** brand
- **rival**, **competing** brand
- **own** brand

NOUN PHRASE:

- **portfolio**, **array**, **range** of brands
- brand **name, image**, **loyalty**
- brand **competition,** competition **between** brands
- brand **leader**
- **divestiture** /dʌɪˈvɛstɪtʃə/, **purchaser** of brands

VERB + BRAND:

- to **sell**, **purchase** a brand
- to **launch**, **reintroduce** a brand to the market
- to **develop** a brand

CAP
/kæp/ (RF 40/NF 27)

DERIVATIVES: to **cap** /kæp/ (~ *supplies*)

ADJECTIVE + CAP:

- **national** cap

NOUN PHRASE:

- **ceiling** and national cap

VERB + CAP:

- to **exceed** a cap
- to **increase** a cap
- to **set** (out), **provide for** a cap

CARTEL
/kɑːˈtel/ (RF 1102/NF 740)

ADJECTIVE + CARTEL:

- **secret**, **unlawful**, **horizontal** cartel
- **overall** cartel (*the applicant participated in an overall ~*)
- **worldwide**, **cross-border**, **pan-European** cartel
- **alleged**, **presumed** cartel
- **price** cartel**, price-fixing**, **market-sharing** cartel
- **buying/buyers'** cartel

NOUN PHRASE:

- cartel **meeting**, **agreement**, **arrangements**, **behaviour**, cartel **activity**
- cartel **member**, **participation/participant in** a cartel, **perpetrators** of a cartel

VERB + CARTEL:

- to **participate in**, **join** (in) (*they joined in a price ~*), **form**, **conclude**, **establish** a cartel

- to **prohibit** a cartel
- to **sanction** a cartel (*the ~ sanctioned in Article 1*)

CEILING
/ˈsiːlɪŋ/ (RF 162/NF 109)

ADJECTIVE + CEILING:

- **financial** ceiling
- **permissible** ceiling

NOUN PHRASE:

- **de minimis**, **aid** ceiling, 10%-of-**turnover** ceiling, 10% ceiling
- **rules on** ceilings

VERB + CEILING:

- to **provide for/lay down/set out** a ceiling in Article
- to **respect** the ceiling
- to **exceed** the ceiling
- to **maintain** the ceiling

CIRCUMSTANCES
/ˈsɜːkəmstənsɪz/ (RF 839/NF 563)

ADJECTIVE + CIRCUMSTANCES:

- **mitigating** /ˈmɪtɪgeɪtɪŋ/, **attenuating** /əˈtenjueɪtɪŋ/, **aggravating** /ˈægrəveɪtɪŋ/ circumstances
- **exceptional**, **unforeseeable** circumstances
- **factual** circumstances

NOUN PHRASE:

- the **facts** and circumstances
- circumstances of the **infringement**
- the circumstances of the **case**

VERB + CIRCUMSTANCES:

- to **consider** circumstances, **take** circumstances into account/consideration

COLLUSION
/kəˈluːʒn/ (RF 226/NF 151)

DERIVATIVES: to **collude** /kəˈluːd/ (~ *tacitly; with the competitor*), **collusive** /kəˈluːsɪv/ (~ *contacts, arrangements, behaviour, practices, equilibrium*)

ADJECTIVE + COLLUSION:

- **tacit**, **explicit**, **horizontal** (*horizontal ~ to exclude particular brands*), **bilateral** /ˌbaɪˈlætərəl/ collusion

NOUN PHRASE:

- **price** collusion
- **participation** in collusion; **existence**, **occurrence** of collusion
- **scheme** /skiːm/, **system** of collusion
- **risk** of collusion
- collusion **between** (~ *between manufacturers*), collusion **on** (~ *on prices*)

VERB + COLLUSION:

- to **facilitate** collusion between; **avoid**, **prevent** collusion
- to **participate** in collusion
- to **conceal** the collusion

COMPENSATION
/ˌkɒmpenˈseɪʃn/ (RF 273/NF 183)

DERIVATIVES: to **compensate** /ˈkɒmpenseɪt/ (~ *for disadvantages, deficits*), **compensatory** /ˌkɒmpenˈseɪtəri/ (~ *collective redress, payment, relief*), **overcompensation** /əʊvəˌkɒmpenˈseɪʃn/

ADJECTIVE + COMPENSATION:

- **reasonable**, **full** compensation
- **monetary**, **financial**, **pecuniary** /pɪˈkjuːniəri/ compensation

NOUN PHRASE:

- **claim**, **action** for compensation
- **payment** of compensation, compensation **amount**
- compensation **for** loss, harm, service, damage, costs

VERB + COMPENSATION:

- to **grant**, **pay** compensation to X
- to **obtain** compensation
- to **claim**, **seek** compensation
- to **calculate** compensation

COMPETITION
/ˌkɒmpəˈtɪʃn/ (RF 3650/NF 2451)

DERIVATIVES: to **compete** /kəmˈpiːt/ (~ *effectively, fiercely, aggressively*), **competing** /kəmˈpiːtɪŋ/ (~ *brands, suppliers, undertakings, products*), **competitive** /kəmˈpetətɪv/ (~ *advantage, constraint, pressure, position; on equal ~ footing*), **competitively** /kəmˈpetətɪvli/ (~ *advantageous situation*), **competitiveness** /kəm ˈpetətɪvnəs/ (*to reduce ~; the ~ of the Union industry*), **anti-competitive/anticompetitive** /ˌæntikəmˈpetətɪv/ (~ *effects, object, conduct, discussion, practice, nature, contacts, agreement, behaviour, arrangements; manifestly, severely, highly ~*), **anticompetitively** /ˌæntikəmˈpetətɪvli/ (*to behave/act ~*), **pro-competitive** (~ *effects, efficiency, benefits*), **pro-competitiveness** /ˌprəʊkəmˈpetətɪv/,

uncompetitive /ˌʌnkəmˈpetətɪv/ (*the closure of ~ coal mines*), **supra-competitive** /ˌsuːprə kəmˈpetətɪv/ (*~ prices*), **non-compete** /ˌnɒn kəmˈpiːt/ (*~ obligation, arrangement, agreement; ~ type restraint*), **competitor** /kəmˈpetɪtə(r)/, **non-competitor** /ˌnɒn kəmˈpetɪtə(r)/

ADJECTIVE + COMPETITION:

- **unfair**, **distorted/undistorted** competition (*system of undistorted ~*),
- **free**, **normal** competition,
- **effective**, **direct**, **hidden**, **active**, **strong** competition
- **inter-brand/intra-brand** interbrand/intrabrand competition (*loss of inter-brand ~*), **in-store** inter-brand competition, **intra-technology** competition

NOUN PHRASE:

- competition **law**, **rules**, **policy**
- competition **authorities**, **DG** Competition/Directorate General for Competition, competition **network**
- competition **proceedings, investigation, decision**
- competition **agreement**
- competition **risks**, **conditions**, **situation**
- **degree**, **scope**, **parameters** of competition
- **restriction**, **distortion**, **loss**, **reduction**, **elimination**, **protection**, **maintenance** of competition
- **absence** of competition
- **harm**, **damage** to competition (*risk of serious and irreparable damage to ~*)
- **price/non-price** competition
- competition **in** a market, products, services, **within** the common market, **between** undertakings

VERB + COMPETITION:

- to **be in competition with**
- to **distort**, **affect**, **restrict**, **eliminate**, **reduce**, **impede**, **impair** competition (*~ substantially, considerably*)
- to **maintain** competition
- to **soften** competition (*recommended prices may soften ~*)
- to **restore**, **protect**, **re-establish**, **promote, foster** competition
- to **avoid** unfair competition

COMPETITOR

/kəmˈpetɪtə(r)/ (RF 934/NF 627)

DERIVATIVES: **non-competitor** /ˌnɒn kəmˈpetɪtə(r)/

ADJECTIVE + COMPETITOR:

- **actual**, **potential** competitor
- **main**, **principal**, **nearest**, **direct** competitor
- **strong** competitor

- **effective**, **equally efficient** competitor

NOUN PHRASE:

- **market position** of competitors, competitors' **access** to the market, **conduct** of competitors
- **elimination**, **foreclosure**, **margin squeeze** of competitors
- **action** against competitors
- **between** competitors: **agreement**, **exchange of information, licensing, contacts, meeting ~**
- competitor **with a large/smaller market share**

VERB + COMPETITOR:

- to **be**, **become** competitors
- to **eliminate**, **prevent** a competitor from (*this agreement prevents new ~ from entering the market*), **exclude** a competitor

CONCENTRATION

/ˌkɒnsnˈtreɪʃn/ (RF 649/NF 436)

DERIVATIVES: to **concentrate** /ˈkɒnsntreɪt/ (*the buyer is induced to ~ its orders for a product with one supplier*), **concentrated** /ˈkɒnsntreɪtɪd/ (adj.) (*a highly ~ market*)

ADJECTIVE + CONCENTRATION:

- **high** concentration

NOUN PHRASE:

- a concentration **with a Community dimension**, **compatibility** of the concentration with the common market
- **implementation**, **completion** of the concentration
- **control**, **supervision** of concentrations
- **suspension, dissolution**, **approval**, **notification** of the concentration
- **effects**, **assessment**, **appraisal** of concentrations
- concentrations **between** undertakings, **parties to** the concentration

VERB + CONCENTRATION:

- to **notify** a concentration
- to **effect**, **implement** a concentration
- to **authorise**, **approve** a concentration
- to **oppose**, **dissolve**, **suspend** a concentration
- to **examine**, **appraise**, **review** a concentration

CONCERTATION

/ˌkɒnsəˈteɪʃn/ (RF 37/NF 25)

DERIVATIVES: to **concert** /kənˈsəːt/ (*the undertakings successfully concerted with each other; to ~ together, to ~ on prices*), **concerted** /kənˈsɜːtɪd/ (adj. RF 411/NF

276) (~ *practices, action, price increase*), **in concert with** /ˈkɒnsət/ (*act/decide in ~ with the undertaking)*

ADJECTIVE + CONCERTATION:

- **alleged** /əˈledʒd/ concertation

NOUN PHRASE:

- **existence** of concertation
- concertation **on** prices, concertation **between**

CONCERTATION + VERB:

- concertation **takes place**

CONDUCT
/ˈkɒndʌkt/ (RF 963/NF 647)

DERIVATIVES: to **conduct** /kənˈdʌkt/ (~ *inspection, business, investigation, interview, proceedings*)

ADJECTIVE + CONDUCT:

- **unlawful**, **abusive**, **illegal**, **infringing** conduct
- **anti-competitive**, **unilateral**, **collusive**, **offending** conduct
- **autonomous** conduct (*the principle of autonomous ~*)
- **continuous** conduct
- **alleged**, **impugned** /ɪmˈpjuːnd/, **attempted** conduct

NOUN PHRASE:

- **market** conduct (*market ~ of undertakings)*
- **liable for** the unlawful conduct
- **illegality** /ˌɪliˈgæləti/ of conduct
- **competitors'** conduct (*the existing and anticipated ~ of the competitors*), conduct **of** competitors, subsidiary, undertaking
- the conduct of **proceedings, investigation**

VERB + CONDUCT:

- to **engage in** conduct (*the parties engaged in collusive ~*), **adopt** conduct (*adopt competitive ~*)
- to **influence** (*on the market),* **impose** conduct (~ *was unilaterally imposed upon them)*
- to **penalise**, **prohibit**, **sanction** conduct

CONTINUITY
/ˌkɒntɪˈnjuːəti/ (RF 48/NF 32)

DERIVATIVES: to **continue** /kənˈtɪnjuː/, **continuous** /kənˈtɪnjuəs/ (~ *infringement, conduct*), **continual** /kənˈtɪnjuəl/, **continuance** /kənˈtɪnjuəns/ (~ *of infringement*),

continuation /kənˌtɪnjuˈeɪʃn/ (~ *of infringement*), **continuously** /kənˈtɪnjuəsli/, **continually** /kənˈtɪnjuəli/

ADJECTIVE + CONTINUITY:

- **financial** (*there was a financial ~ between x and y)*, **economic** continuity
- **alleged** continuity

NOUN PHRASE:

- continuity **between two companies**

CONTRACT

/ˈkɒntrækt/ (RF 727/NF 488)

DERIVATIVES: to **contract** /kənˈtrækt/ (~ *loans, services*), **contracting** /kən ˈtræktɪŋ/ (~ *parties*), **contractor** /kənˈtræktə(r)/, **contractual** /kənˈtræktʃuəl/ (~ *obligations, relationship, relations*), **contractually** /kənˈtræktʃuəli/

ADJECTIVE + CONTRACT:

- **long-term**, **multi-year** contract
- **public** contract (*public service/works ~*)
- **exclusive** contract

NOUN PHRASE:

- **leasing**, **supply**, **management**, **cultivation**, **privatisation**, **sales**, **service**, **employment**, **agency** contract
- **conclusion**, **performance**, **breach** of the contract
- **terms**, **clauses**, **subject**, **wording**, **copy** of the contract
- **party to** a contract, contract **for** (*supply*)

VERB + CONTRACT:

- to **conclude**, **enter into**, **sign**, **ratify** a contract
- to **award** a contract
- to **negotiate** a contract
- to **terminate** a contract

CONTROL

/kənˈtrəʊl/ (RF 175/NF 117)

DERIVATIVES: to **control** /kənˈtrəʊl/, **controller** /kənˈtrəʊlə(r)/, **controlling** /kən ˈtrəʊlɪŋ/ (~ *interest*)

ADJECTIVE + CONTROL:

- **joint**, **sole**, **mutual**, **full** control
- **indirect** control

NOUN PHRASE:

- control of **concentrations, monopoly, mergers**, **merger** control (~ *laws, system, proceedings*)

VERB + CONTROL:

- to **exert, exercise, hold** control
- to **tighten** control
- to **acquire** control

COORDINATION, CO-ORDINATION
/kəʊˌɔːdɪˈneɪʃn/ (RF 101/NF 68)

DERIVATIVES: to **coordinate** /kəʊˈɔːdɪneɪt/ (~ *competitive behaviour*), **coordinated** /kəʊˈɔːdɪneɪtɪd/ (*a ~ course of action*), **non-coordinated** /ˌnɒn kəʊ ˈɔːdɪneɪtɪd/, **coordinator** /kəʊˈɔːdɪneɪtə(r)/

NOUN PHRASE:

- coordination of **behaviour, prices, strategy, conduct, policy; price** coordination
- coordination **between** undertakings

VERB + COORDINATION:

- to **facilitate, enhance** coordination
- to **engage in** coordination

COST
/kɒst/ (RF 1738/NF 1167)

DERIVATIVES: to **cost** /kɒst/, **costly** /ˈkɒstli/

ADJECTIVE + COST:

- **eligible** costs
- **variable** costs
- **net**, **additional**, **marginal** costs
- **identifiable** costs
- **sunk** costs

NOUN PHRASE:

- cost of **investment, project, proceeding, treatment, production**
- cost **savings, efficiency**
- **recovery** of costs

VERB + COST:

- to **pay, bear, incur, cover** costs
- to **reimburse** /ˌriːɪmˈbɜːs/ costs

DAMAGE
/ˈdæmɪdʒ/ (RF 147/NF 98)

Derivatives: to **damage** /ˈdæmɪdʒ/

Adjective + damage:

- **irreparable** damage
- **material** (*material ~ to assets*), **significant**, **considerable** damage
- **environmental**, **economic**, **commercial** damage

Noun phrase:

- **legal redress** for damage (*to seek legal redress for ~ resulting from alleged infringements*), **compensation** for damage (*claim for compensation in respect of ~*)
- **liability** for damage

Verb + damage:

- to **cause** damage (*to consumers*)
- to **repair** damage
- to **suffer**, **sustain**, **incur** damage

DAMAGES
/ˈdæmɪdʒɪz/ (RF 228/NF 152)

Adjective + damages:

- **punitive** /ˈpjuːnətɪv/ damages
- **pecuniary** damages
- **multiple** damages
- **moral** damages

Noun phrase:

- damages **action**; **action**, **proceedings** for damages
- **right to** damages
- **claim** for damages (*to bring a claim for ~ before a court*), damages claim, claimant for damages
- **amount**, **quantum** /ˈkwɒntəm/ of damages
- **payment** of damages

Verb + damages:

- to **claim** damages for (*loss*), **obtain** damages
- to **award**, **pay**, **grant** damages

DISCOUNT
/ˈdɪskaʊnt/ (RF 168/NF 112)

Derivatives: to **discount** /dɪsˈkaʊnt/ (*~ conduct, practices*), **discounted** /dɪs ˈkaʊntɪd/ (adj. *~ value*), **discounter** /ˈdɪskaʊntə(r)/ (*price ~*), **discounting** /dɪs ˈkaʊntɪŋ/ (*for ~ purposes*)

ADJECTIVE + DISCOUNT:

- **annual** discount
- **variable**, **fixed** discount

NOUN PHRASE:

- **group**, **quantity**, **loyalty**, **cash** discount
- discount **rate, system**; **policy** of discounts
- discounts and **rebates**, **bonuses** or discounts
- discount **on** sales

VERB + DISCOUNT:

- to **grant** discounts

DISCRIMINATION
/dɪˌskrɪmɪˈneɪʃn/ (RF 79/NF 53)

DERIVATIVES: to **discriminate** /dɪˈskrɪmɪneɪt/ (*to price discriminate amongst customers, to ~ in favour of*), **discriminatory** /dɪˈskrɪmɪnətəri/ (~ *pricing, rebate*), **non-discrimination** /ˌnɒndɪˌskrɪmɪˈneɪʃn/ (*the principle of* ~), **non-discriminatory** /ˌnɒndɪˈskrɪmɪnətəri/ (~ *criteria, call, basis*)

ADJECTIVE + DISCRIMINATION:

- **prohibitive**, **unjustified** discrimination
- **alleged** discrimination

NOUN PHRASE:

- **price** discrimination
- **negative effect** of discrimination
- **without** discrimination (*aid should be granted without* ~)
- discrimination **between** (~ domestic customers)

VERB + DISCRIMINATION:

- to **apply** discrimination
- to **suffer** discrimination
- to **facilitate** discrimination
- to **avoid**, **prevent** discrimination

DISPUTE
/dɪˈspjuːt/ (RF 220/NF 148)

DERIVATIVES: to **dispute** /dɪˈspjuːt/, **disputed** /dɪˈspjuːtɪd/ (adj.) (~ *merger*)

NOUN PHRASE:

- **consensual** /kənˈsenʃuəl/ dispute **resolution**

VERB + DISPUTE:

- to **resolve** a dispute

DISTRIBUTION
/ˌdɪstrɪˈbjuːʃn/ (RF 748/NF 502)

Derivatives: to **distribute** /dɪˈstrɪbjuːt/, **distributor** /dɪˈstrɪbjətə(r)/ (*exclusive, wholesale, unauthorised, non-appointed, independent, price-cutting ~*), **redistribution** /ˌriːdɪstrɪˈbjuːʃn/

Adjective + distribution:

- **quantitative/qualitative selective**, **exclusive**, **limited** distribution
- **dual**, **joint** distribution

Noun phrase:

- **supermarket** distribution
- distribution **of goods, products, medicines**
- distribution **network, system, channel, chain, outlet**
- distribution **agreement, arrangements**

Verb + distribution:

- to **practise**, **use**, **apply** selective distribution
- to **limit** distribution

EFFECT(S)
/ɪˈfekt/ (RF 2214/NF 1487)

Adjective + effects:

- **anti-competitive**, **negative**, **deterrent**, **restrictive**, **adverse**, **exclusionary** effect
- **positive**, **incentive** /ɪnˈsentɪv/, **pro-competitive** effect
- **cumulative** effect
- **appreciable**, **significant** effect
- **direct** effects
- **net** effect
- **possible**, **likely** effect

Noun phrase:

- **foreclosure**, **range**, **portfolio** effect
- effects **of** agreement, concentration, parallel network, practices
- effect **on** trade, competition, the market, prices, consumers (*negative effects on competition*)
- **assessment**, **examination**, **analysis** of the effects

Verb + effects:

- to **have**, **produce** effects
- to **outweigh** effects (*to outweigh the anti-competitive ~ produced by the arrangements*)

- to **examine**, **assess** effects
- to **take** effect, **put/come into** effect (*conduct put into effect*)

ENFORCEMENT
/ɪnˈfɔːsmənt/ (RF 126/NF 85)

DERIVATIVES: to **enforce** /ɪnˈfɔːs/ (~ *a judgment, payment, decision*), **enforceable** /ɪnˈfɔːsəbl/ (~ *judgment*), **enforceability** /ɪnˌfɔːsəˈbɪləti/, **public enforcer** /ˈpʌblɪk ɪnˈfɔːsə(r)/

ADJECTIVE + ENFORCEMENT:

- **public**, **private** enforcement
- **effective** enforcement (~ *of EU competition law*)

NOUN PHRASE:

- enforcement **of competition law/rules, prohibition** (~ *cartel agreements*), **penalties**, **payment**, **export ban**, **judgment**
- enforcement **policy**

VERB + ENFORCEMENT:

- to **seek** enforcement

EXCLUSIVITY
/ˌeksкluːˈsɪvəti/ (RF 56/NF 38)

DERIVATIVES: **exclusive** /ɪkˈskluːsɪv/ (adj.) (RF 751/NF 504) (~ *right, distributor, distribution, licence, supply, territory, customer allocation, competence, purchasing, dealership, licensing, agent, retailer*)

ADJECTIVE + EXCLUSIVITY:

- (absolute) **territorial** exclusivity
- **reciprocal** exclusivity

NOUN PHRASE:

- **period** of exclusivity

EXEMPTION
/ɪgˈzempʃn/ (RF 734/NF 493)

DERIVATIVES: to **exempt** /ɪgˈzempt/ (~ *agreements*), be **exempt** from /ɪgˈzempt/ (~ *the notification requirement*), **block exempted** /blɒk ɪgˈzemptɪd/ (~ *agreement*; *licensing is block exempted up to the market share threshold of 20%*), **exemptable** /ɪgˈzemptəbl/, **exemptible** /ɪgˈzemptəbl/ (~ *obligation*)

NOUN PHRASE:

- **block** exemption (*the Block Exemption Regulation*)
- **tax** exemption, exemption of **agreements**
- **request**, **application** for an exemption

- **withdrawal** of the block exemption
- **benefit** of the block exemption
- **the scope** of exemption, **conditions** for exemption

VERB + EXEMPTION:

- to **provide** for the exemption
- to **establish**, **grant** an exemption
- to **justify** the exemption
- to **qualify** for exemption

FINE
/faɪn/ (RF 1578/NF 1059)

DERIVATIVES: to **fine** for /faɪn/ (*X was fined 1 million EUR per meeting*)

ADJECTIVE + FINE:

- a **symbolic** fine
- an **administrative** fine

NOUN PHRASE:

- **amount**, **level** of fines
- **reduction**, **calculation**, **payment**, **imposition**, **increase**, **annulment** of fines
- **immunity** from fines
- a fine **from** X **to** Y EUR, **ranging from** X **to** Y EUR, **not exceeding** 1% of the aggregate turnover

VERB + FINE:

- to **impose** a fine on
- to **set**, **calculate**, **assess**, **determine**, **fix** a fine
- to **pay** a fine
- to **increase**, **reduce** the fine
- to **annul** a fine

FIXING
/ˈfɪksɪŋ/ (RF 269/NF 180)

DERIVATIVES: to **fix** /fɪks/ (~ *tariffs, prices*)

ADJECTIVE + FIXING:

- **administrative** fixing of tariffs

NOUN PHRASE:

- **price**-fixing (*price-fixing agreement, cartel; horizontal price fixing*); fixing of **prices**, **tariff**-fixing/fixing of **tariffs**; fixing of **fees**, **quota** fixing
- tariff-fixing / rate-fixing **policy**

FORECLOSURE

/fɔːˈkləʊʒə(r)/ (RF 192/NF 129)

Derivatives: to **foreclose** /fɔːˈkləʊz/ (*the market is foreclosed to potential entrants*), **foreclosed** /fɔːˈkləʊzd/ (adj.) (~ *share, manufacturer*), **foreclosing** /fɔːˈkləʊzɪŋ/ (~ *buyer, competitor, effect*)

Adjective + foreclosure:

- **anticompetitive/anti-competitive** foreclosure
- **cumulative** foreclosure
- **significant, serious**, **appreciable** foreclosure
- **real**, **possible** foreclosure

Noun phrase:

- foreclosure **of** distributors, suppliers, competitors
- foreclosure of **the market**
- foreclosure **effect**
- **risk**, **degree** of foreclosure

Verb + foreclosure:

- to **lead to** foreclosure (*licence agreements may lead to ~ of third parties)*

HARM

/hɑːm/ (RF 174/NF 117)

Derivatives: to **harm** /hɑːm/ (*it would irreversibly ~ their interests*), **harmful** /ˈhɑːmfl/ (~ *event, restrictions of competition*)

Adjective + harm:

- **serious** harm
- **personal**, **economic**, **competitive**, **antitrust** harm
- **irreversible** harm

Noun phrase:

- **overcharge** harm
- **quantification** of harm
- **amount**, **degree** of harm
- **mass harm situation** (*'mass harm situation' means a situation where two or more natural or legal persons claim to have suffered harm causing damage resulting from the same illegal activity of one or more natural or legal persons)*
- **compensation**, **responsibility, joint and several liability** for harm
- harm **to** competition, reputation

Verb + harm:

- to **cause** harm to

- to **suffer** harm
- to **quantify** harm
- to **mitigate**, **repair, compensate** for harm

IMMUNITY
/ɪˈmjuːnəti/ (RF 196/NF 132)

Derivatives: **immune** /ɪˈmjuːn/ (~ *to competition*)

Adjective + immunity:

- **conditional** immunity
- **total**, **absolute** immunity (*to benefit from absolute ~ from fines*)
- **eligible for** immunity

Noun phrase:

- immunity **from fines**, immunity **under a leniency programme**
- **application for** immunity, **grant** of immunity
- **threshold for** immunity

Verb + immunity:

- to **apply** for immunity, **seek** immunity
- to **grant** (*X has been granted ~ from fines by a competition authority*), **receive**, **obtain** immunity
- to **qualify** for immunity

INFLUENCE
/ˈɪnfluəns/ (RF 168/NF 113)

Derivatives: to **influence** /ˈɪnfluəns/ (~ *the conduct of its subsidiary*)

Adjective + influence:

- **decisive** influence
- **undue** influence
- **dominant**, **controlling** influence

Noun phrase:

- **exercise** of influence (*the de facto exercise of influence*)
- influence **on/over** the conduct, policy, subsidiary

Verb + influence:

- to **exercise/exert** /ɪɡˈzɜːt/ influence over, **have** influence on

INFORMATION
/ˌɪnfəˈmeɪʃn/ (RF 2085/NF 1340)

Derivatives: to **inform** of/about /ɪnˈfɔːm/ (~ *to inform the Commission of the existence of a cartel*)

ADJECTIVE + INFORMATION:

- **confidential**, **commercially sensitive** information
- **incorrect**, **misleading** information
- **pre-existing** information (*'pre-existing information' means evidence that exists irrespective of the proceedings of a competition authority, whether or not such information is in the file of a competition authority*)

NOUN PHRASE:

- **exchange** of information, information **exchange system**, **exchange agreement**
- information **injunction** /ɪnˈdʒʌŋkʃn/ (*if a Member State does not provide the information requested within the period prescribed by the Commission, the Commission shall by decision require the information to be provided (information injunction)*)
- **request** for information
- **disclosure**, **publication**, **confidentiality** of information
- information **asymmetry**

VERB + INFORMATION:

- to **exchange** information
- to **request** information
- to **provide**, **supply**, **submit**, **disclose**, **communicate**, **give** information
- to **obtain**, **receive**, **gather**, **collect**, **acquire** information
- to **use** information
- to **disseminate** information

INFRINGEMENT

/ɪnˈfrɪndʒmənt/ (RF 2859/NF 1919)

DERIVATIVES: to **infringe** /ɪnˈfrɪndʒ/ (*~ the principle of non-discrimination, competition law; allegedly ~*), **infringer** /ɪnˈfrɪndʒə/, **co-infringer** /ˌkəʊɪnˈfrɪndʒə/

ADJECTIVE + INFRINGEMENT:

- **single**, **continuous**, **repeated** infringement
- **alleged**, **suspected**, **presumed** infringement
- **serious**, **complex**, **minor** infringement
- **vertical** infringement

NOUN PHRASE:

- **cartel** infringement, **competition law** infringement
- infringement of **rules** (*~ of the competition rules*), **article**, **competition law** (*~ of Union/national competition law*), **principle**, **rights**, **provisions** of article, **obligations**
- infringement **proceedings**, **claims**; (final) infringement **decision**

- infringement **period**; **duration**, **gravity**, **seriousness**, **nature**, **scope**, **extent**, **effects** of infringement
- **continuation**, **existence** of infringement
- infringement **of short/medium/long duration**
- **participation** (*renunciation to dispute participation in an ~*), **role**, **involvement** in the infringement; **weight** of X in the infringement (*weight of each undertaking in the ~*); **acknowledgement** of participation in an infringement
- **liability/liable** for (*the imputation of liability for the ~ to the company*) **responsibility/responsible**, **fine**, **damages for** the infringement (*action for damages for ~ of national competition law*)
- **instigator**, **leader** of the infringement, **participant** in the infringement

VERB + INFRINGEMENT:

- to **participate**, **be involved** in, **continue** an infringement
- to **commit** an infringement (*liability for the ~ committed by the company's subsidiaries*)
- to **bring** an infringement **to an end**, **terminate** an infringement
- to **allege**, **prove** an infringement
- to **penalise**, **sanction**, **expose, curb, detect, assess** an infringement

INFRINGEMENT + VERB:

- an infringement **takes place, occurs**
- an infringement **starts**, **continues** (*uninterruptedly*), **lasts**, **ceases**
- an infringement **causes** (*harm caused by ~*), **affects** (*adversely*)
- **injured by** infringement

INFRINGER, CO-INFRINGER

/ɪnˈfrɪndʒə/, /ˌkəʊɪnˈfrɪndʒə/ (RF 74/NF 49)

ADJECTIVE + INFRINGER:

- **settling/non-settling** infringer

NOUN PHRASE:

- **liability** of infringer, co-infringer's **share** of the harm
- **legal action** against infringers

INVESTIGATION

/ɪnˌvestɪˈgeɪʃn/ (RF 736/NF 494)

DERIVATIVES: to **investigate** /ɪnˈvestɪgeɪt/ (~ *thoroughly, carefully*), **investigative** /ɪnˈvestɪgətɪv/ (~ *measures, powers, authority, stage of the case*), **investigatory** /ɪnˈvestɪgətəri/ (~ *powers*)

ADJECTIVE + INVESTIGATION:

- **on-the-spot**, **unannounced**, **preliminary**, **complex** investigation
- **national** investigation

NOUN PHRASE:

- **competition**, **competition law** investigation
- a **tax** investigation
- investigation **file**, **procedure** (*to initiate the formal ~ procedure*), **authorisation**, **decision**
- investigation **stage** (*during the preliminary ~ stage*), **phase**
- the **course**, **purpose**, **subject-matter**, **subject**, **scope** of investigations
- investigation **site**
- **lawfulness**, **effectiveness**, **utility** of investigations
- the proper/normal **conduct** of the investigation
- **cooperation** in the investigation (*active / voluntary cooperation in the ~*)
- **the Commission's** investigation, the Commission's **powers** of investigation
- investigations **into** (~ *into the sectors of the economy, the alleged infringement, the conditions prevailing in the market)*

VERB + INVESTIGATION:

- to **conduct**, **carry out**, **undertake**, **pursue** investigation
- to **open**, **begin**, **initiate** an investigation
- to **order** (*a decision ordering an ~*), **warrant** the investigation (*to set out the reasons warranting the ~ in this case*)
- to **oppose** an investigation (*the undertaking opposes an ~*)
- to **cooperate** in the investigation

INSOLVENCY

/ɪnˈsɒlvənsi/ (RF 23/NF 15)

DERIVATIVES: **insolvent** /ɪnˈsɒlvənt/ (~ liquidation)

NOUN PHRASE:

- **collective** insolvency **proceedings** (*is placed in/is subject to collective ~ proceedings*), insolvency **procedures**

INTERVENTION

/ˌɪntəˈvenʃn/ (RF 105/NF 70)

DERIVATIVES: to **intervene** /ˌɪntəˈviːn/ (*apply for leave to intervene*), **intervener** /ˌɪntəˈviːnə/

ADJECTIVE + INTERVENTION:

- **disproportionate** /ˌdɪsprəˈpɔːʃənət/ intervention
- **arbitrary** intervention

NOUN PHRASE:

- intervention by **public authorities**, **state** intervention

VERB + INTERVENTION:

- to **provoke**, **trigger** an intervention

LENIENCY
/ˈliːniənsi/ (RF 318/NF 213)

DERIVATIVES: **lenient** /ˈliːniənt/ (~ *treatment*), **leniently** /ˈliːniəntli/

NOUN PHRASE:

- leniency **programme** (*to benefit from the ~ programme*), **statement** (*self-incriminating ~ statements*), **notice**, **policy**
- leniency **application / application for** leniency (*to submit the ~ application*), leniency **applicant**

VERB + LENIENCY:

- to **seek** leniency

LIMITATION
/ˌlɪmɪˈteɪʃn/ (RF 318/NF 213)

DERIVATIVES: to **limit** /ˈlɪmɪt/ (~ *parallel trade*)

ADJECTIVE + LIMITATION:

- **annual** limitation
- **contractual** limitation (*breach of contractual ~*)
- **quantitative**, **territorial** limitation

NOUN PHRASE:

- **capacity**, **production**, **quantity**, **market share** limitation
- **non-compliance** with the limitation
- **limitation** period (~ *begins to run, is suspended, interrupted, elapses, expires*) *for bringing actions for damages*

VERB + LIMITATION:

- to **exceed** the limitation
- to **respect** the limitation
- to **impose**, **set** the limitation

LOSS
/lɒs/ (RF 360/NF 242)

DERIVATIVES: to **lose** /luːz/ (~ *sales*), **lost** /lɒst/ (adj.) (~ *profit, revenue*), **losing** /ˈluːzɪŋ/ (~ *party, defendant*), **loser** /ˈluːzə(r)/ (*loser pays principle*)

ADJECTIVE + LOSS:

- **actual**, **indirect, accumulated** loss
- **significant, substantial** loss

- **expected / unexpected** loss

NOUN PHRASE:

- loss **adjuster**
- loss of intra-brand/in-store **competition**
- loss of **profits**, **opportunity**, **revenue**, **efficiency**, **income**, **stocks**
- **recoupment** /rɪˈkuːpm(ə)nt/, **coverage** of losses
- **compensation**, **damages** for loss

VERB + LOSS:

- to **suffer**, **sustain**, **incur**, **bear** loss
- to **cause**, **inflict** loss
- to **recoup** /rɪˈkuːp/ losses, **compensate for** losses
- to **reduce** loss
- to **pass on** loss on purchasers

MARKET
/ˈmɑːkɪt/ (RF 6739/NF 4525)

DERIVATIVES: to **market** /ˈmɑːkɪt/ (~ *products; if the authorised product is no longer marketed in the Member State*), **marketable** /ˈmɑːkɪtəbl/

ADJECTIVE + MARKET:

- **common**, **internal**, **national**, **geographic**, **neighbouring** market
- **downstream**, **upstream** market
- **distinct** market
- **wholesale**, **retail** market
- **dominated** market

NOUN PHRASE:

- **product**, **technology**, **electricity** market
- market **share/share** of the market, market **sharing**, market **share threshold**; market **position**, **leader**, **segment, power**
- market **price**, **value**
- market **conduct**
- market **trends**, **information, structure**, **definition**, **conditions, equilibrium** /ˌiːkwɪˈlɪbriəm/
- **functioning**, **operation**, **value** of the market
- **size**, **maturity**, **transparency** of the market; **foreclosure** of the market
- **organisation**, **partition**, **allocation** of the market
- competition, competitor, position, conduct, effects, concentration **on** the market; competition **in** the market
- access, entry, entrant **to** the market
- market **for** products

VERB + MARKET:

- to **enter**, **cover**, **penetrate**, **supply** a market, **operate** in a market; **exit**, **leave** a market, **withdraw** from the market
- to **define** the market
- to **dominate**, **distort**, **tie** a market
- to **partition**, **divide**, **share** markets

MARKET + VERB:

- the market **liberalises** /ˈlɪbrəlaɪzɪz/

MEASURES
/ˈmeʒəz/ (RF 1259/NF 845)

ADJECTIVE + MEASURES:

- **interim**, **provisional** measures
- **appropriate** measures
- **protective**, **precautionary** /prɪˈkɔːʃənəri/ measures
- **coercive** measures
- **investigative** measures, **fact-finding** measures

NOUN PHRASE:

- **aid** measures (*~ for sport infrastructure; ~ exceeding the de minimis ceiling*), **risk finance** measures
- **state** measures
- **implementation**, **adoption** of measures
- **proportionality**, **legality**, **effect** of measures

VERB + MEASURES:

- to **adopt**, **take**, **implement** measures
- to **grant** measures
- to **notify** measures

MERGER
/ˈmɜːdʒə(r)/ (RF 92/NF 62)

DERIVATIVES: to **merge** /mɜːdʒ/, **merging** /ˈmɜːdʒɪŋ/ (adj.) (*~ undertakings*), **merged** /mɜːdʒd/ (adj.) (*the position of the ~ entity in relation to its competitors)*

NOUN PHRASE:

- merger by **absorption** /əbˈsɔːpʃn/
- mergers and **acquisitions** /ˌækwɪˈzɪʃnz/
- merger **control**
- merger **proceedings, law, Merger Regulation**
- **dissolution** /ˌdɪsəˈluːʃn/ of merger

VERB + MERGER:

- to **form** through a merger

MONOPOLY

/məˈnɒpəli/ (RF 96/NF 64)

DERIVATIVES: to **monopolise** /məˈnɒpəlaɪz/, **monopolistic** /məˌnɒpəˈlɪstɪk/ (~ *undertaking*), **quasi-monopolistic** /ˈkweɪzaɪ/ (~ *rights*)

ADJECTIVE + MONOPOLY:

- **statutory**, **de facto** /ˌdeɪ ˈfæktəʊ/, **legal**, **state**, **public**, **national**, **administrative** monopoly
- **temporary**, **general** monopoly
- **postal** monopoly
- **revenue-producing** monopoly
- **quasi**-monopoly (*an undertaking enjoys a ~ on certain markets*)

NOUN PHRASE:

- **electricity** monopoly
- a monopoly **system**
- **control** of monopolies
- monopolies and **oligopolies**
- monopoly **on the market**

VERB + MONOPOLY:

- to **have** (*to have a de facto ~ in the market*), **enjoy** a monopoly
- to **confer** (*a patent confers a temporary ~ on its holder*), **grant**, **establish** a monopoly
- to **control**, **eliminate** monopolies

OBLIGATION

/ˌɒblɪˈgeɪʃn/ (RF 1233/NF 828)

DERIVATIVES: to **oblige** /əˈblaɪdʒ/, to be **obliged** to /əˈblaɪdʒd/

ADJECTIVE + OBLIGATION:

- **contractual**, **regulatory**, **procedural**, **legal** obligation
- **indirect** obligation

NOUN PHRASE:

- **non-compete** obligation
- **public service**, **recovery**, **publication**, **exclusive supply**, **single branding** obligation
- **failure to fulfil** obligations; **discharge**, **breach**, **infringement**, **apportionment** /əˈpɔːʃnmənt/ of obligation
- **scope**, **duration**, **purpose** of obligation
- obligation **to** the licensee, franchisee

VERB + OBLIGATION:

- to **discharge** obligations
- to **fulfil**, **satisfy**, **meet** obligations
- to **impose** obligations
- to **terminate** obligations
- to **evade**, **infringe** obligations

OLIGOPOLY
/ˌɒlɪˈɡɒp(ə)li/ (RF 18/NF 12)

DERIVATIVES: **oligopolistic** /ˌɒlɪɡɒp(ə)ˈlɪstɪk/ (~ *market*)

ADJECTIVE + OLIGOPOLY:

- **narrow**, **wide**, **tight**, **closed** oligopoly

NOUN PHRASE:

- **members** of oligopoly
- **control** of oligopolies

OPERATOR
/ˈɒpəreɪtə(r)/ (RF 307/NF 206)

ADJECTIVE + OPERATOR:

- **economic** operator, **commercial** operator

NOUN PHRASE:

- **inequality of opportunity** between economic operators

OVERCHARGE
/ˌəʊvəˈtʃɑːdʒ/ (RF 20/NF 13)

NOUN PHRASE:

- **passing-on / pass-on** of overcharges
- overcharge **harm**
- **share** of the overcharge (*to estimate the share of the ~ passed on to indirect purchasers*)

VERB + OVERCHARGE:

- to **pay an** overcharge
- to **pass on** an overcharge (*to pass on the whole or part of the ~*)

PASS-ON, PASSING-ON
/ˌpɑːsˈɒn/, /ˌpɑːsɪŋˈɒn/ (RF 39/NF 26)

DERIVATIVES: to **pass on** (~ *an overcharge; price increases down the supply chain*) **to** (*consumers, suppliers*)

ADJECTIVE + PASS-ON:

- **full / partial** pass-on

NOUN PHRASE:

- passing-on / pass-on of **overcharges**, **actual loss**, **benefits**, **efficiency gains**
- passing-on **defence** (*the infringer invokes the ~ defence*)
- the **quantification** of passing-on, **analysis** of pass-on, **extent** of pass-on
- pass-on **rate**
- **consumer** pass-on
- passing on **to** (~ *to an indirect purchaser, consumer*)

PASS-ON + VERB:

- the pass-on **occurs**

PAYMENT
/ˈpeɪmənt/ (RF 434/NF 291)

DERIVATIVES: to **pay** /peɪ/ (~ *costs, price, compensation*), **payable** /ˈpeɪəbl/ (*royalty ~, aid ~ in several instalments*), **payer** /ˈpeɪə(r)/

ADJECTIVE + PAYMENT:

- **early**, **late** payment
- **upfront**, **advance** payment
- **compensatory** /ˌkɒmpenˈseɪtəri/ payment

NOUN PHRASE:

- **periodic penalty** payment
- **lump sum** payment, **cash** payment
- **access**, **redundancy**, **transfer** payment
- payment **rescheduling** /ˌriːˈʃedjuːlɪŋ/
- payment **of** compensation, debt, remuneration, fine, instalment, fee, charge, penalty
- **imposition**, **suspension** of payment
- **proof**, **date** of payment
- **security** for payment

VERB + PAYMENT:

- to **make** payments
- to **receive** payments
- to **suspend** payments
- to **impose**, **enforce** payments
- to **avoid** payments

PENALTY
/ˈpenəlti/ (RF 238/NF 160)

DERIVATIVES: to **penalise** /ˈpiːnəlaɪz/ (~ *a cartel, anti-competitive conduct*), **penalisation** /piːn(ə)lʌɪˈzeɪʃ(ə)n/, **penal** /ˈpiːnl/ (~ *sanctions*)

ADJECTIVE + PENALTY:

- **financial**, **pecuniary** penalty
- **warning**, **deterrent** /dɪˈterənt/ penalty
- **heavy**, **high**, **disproportionate** penalty
- **periodic** penalty
- **criminal** penalty

NOUN PHRASE:

- penalty **payment**
- **proportionality** of penalty, **lawfulness** of penalty
- **enforcement** of penalty

VERB + PENALTY:

- to **impose**, **enforce** a penalty
- to **assess**, **calculate**, **determine**, **fix** a penalty
- to **pay** a penalty

POSITION
/pəˈzɪʃn/ (RF 1417/NF 951)

ADJECTIVE + POSITION:

- **dominant** position (*abuse of a dominant ~*); **strong**, **significant**, **favourable**, **privileged**, **leading** position
- **competitive** position
- **legal**, **financial** position
- **one-way/two-way blocking** position

NOUN PHRASE:

- **market** position

VERB + POSITION:

- to **hold**, **occupy** a position
- to **strengthen**, **reinforce** a position
- to **abuse** a position
- to **adopt** a position

PRACTICE
/ˈpræktɪs/ (RF 1076/NF 722)

DERIVATIVES: **to practise** /ˈpræktɪs/ (*~ predatory pricing*)

ADJECTIVE + PRACTICE:

- **concerted**, **anti-competitive**, **abusive**, **restrictive**, **collusive**, **unlawful**, **illegal, exclusionary** practice
- **administrative** practice, **commercial** practice
- **tying** practice

NOUN PHRASE:

- pricing **practice**
- **existence**, **effect** of practice

VERB + PRACTICE:

- to **prohibit** a practice
- to **apply**, **implement**, **be engaged** in a practice

PRESSURE
/ˈpreʃə(r)/ (RF 99/NF 66)

ADJECTIVE + PRESSURE:

- **competitive** pressure
- **irresistible** pressure
- **undue** pressure, **improper** pressure
- **downward** pressure

NOUN PHRASE:

- the **exercise** of pressure (*imposed through the exercise of irresistible pressure*)
- pressure **on** sales/prices/margin, competitors

VERB + PRESSURE:

- to **exert** pressure
- to **reduce** pressure

PRICE
/praɪs/ (RF 2882/NF 1935)

DERIVATIVES: **pricing** /ˈpraɪsɪŋ/ (*predatory, excessive ~; ~ policy, practice*), **price leader** /ˈpraɪs ˈliːdə(r)/

ADJECTIVE + PRICE:

- **low**, **high**, **minimum**, **maximum**, **average** price
- **selling** price
- **preferential** price
- **recommended** price
- **differentiated** prices

NOUN PHRASE:

- **sale, resale, purchase**, **production** price
- **market**, **consumer** price; **wholesale**, **retail** price
- **quotation** price
- price **list**, **policy**, **system**, **information**, **strategy**, **level, differentials** /ˌdɪfəˈrenʃlz/
- **index** of prices
- price **increase, change**, **readjustment**
- price **war**, **discrimination**, **competition**, **collusion**, **agreement**, **fixing**

- **coordination**, **setting** of prices
- **collusion, agreement, discussion, information, impact on** prices

VERB + PRICE:

- to **charge**, **apply**, **pay** charges
- to **fix**, **align**, **agree** prices
- to **increase**, **raise**, **reduce** prices
- to **set**, **determine**, **establish** prices
- to **offer** prices

PRINCIPLE
/ˈprɪnsəpl/ (RF 947/NF 636)

ADJECTIVE + PRINCIPLE:

- **general** principle
- **fundamental** principle

NOUN PHRASE:

- principle of: **proportionality, equal treatment, protection of legitimate expectations, legal certainty, non-discrimination, good/sound/proper administration, subsidiarity, effectiveness, procedural economy, an open market economy, equality of arms, legality, no double jeopardy /ˈdʒepədi/, international comity, audi alteram partem, non bis in idem, equivalence, the presumption of innocence, sincere/genuine cooperation, the non-disclosure of business secrets, equity, protection against (arbitrary) intervention**
- general principles of **law**
- **breach, infringement** of the principle
- **exception to** the principle

VERB + PRINCIPLE:

- to **breach**, **infringe**, **disregard** a principle
- to **observe**, **respect**, **accept**, **implement** a principle
- to **set out**, **lay down**, **establish** a principle

PROHIBITION
/ˌprəʊɪˈbɪʃn/ (RF 244/NF 164)

DERIVATIVES: to **prohibit** /prəˈhɪbɪt/, **prohibitive** /prəˈhɪbətɪv/ (~ *discrimination*), **prohibitively** /prəˈhɪbətɪvli/ (~ *expensive*)

ADJECTIVE + PROHIBITION:

- **absolute** prohibition
- **contractual**, **regulatory**, **formal** prohibition
- **anti-competitive** prohibition

NOUN PHRASE:

- prohibition of **derogation** from, of **arbitrariness**
- prohibition **of** resale, exports, agreement; prohibition **on** resale, import, re-export
- **enforcement** of prohibition
- **compliance** with prohibition

VERB + PROHIBITION:

- to **impose** prohibition
- to **contravene** /ˌkɒntrəˈviːn/, **preclude, infringe** prohibition
- to **escape** prohibition

PROTECTION
/prəˈtekʃn/ (RF 385/NF 258)

DERIVATIVES: to **protect** /prəˈtekt/ (~ *competition, interests*)

ADJECTIVE + PROTECTION:

- **absolute territorial** protection
- **effective judicial**, **legal** protection
- **downside** protection

NOUN PHRASE:

- protection of **competition, rights**
- **consumer** protection
- protection **against** (~ *arbitrary intervention by the public authorities*)

VERB + PROTECTION:

- to **enjoy** protection
- to **warrant**, **ensure**, **guarantee**, **confer**, **provide** protection

PURCHASER
/ˈpɜːtʃəsə(r)/ (RF 137/NF 92)

DERIVATIVES: to **purchase**/ˈpɜːtʃəs/, to **repurchase** /riːˈpɜːtʃɪs/, **purchase** /ˈpɜːtʃəs/ (n.) (~ *of goods*), **purchasing** /ˈpɜːtʃəsɪŋ/ (*exclusive* ~)

ADJECTIVE + PURCHASER:

- **indirect/direct** purchaser

REBATE
/ˈriːbeɪt/ (RF 49/NF 33)

ADJECTIVE + REBATE:

- **discriminatory** rebate
- **introductory** rebate

Noun phrase:

- **loyalty**, **fidelity** rebate
- **price**, **sales** rebate
- **tonnage** rebate, **quantity/quantitative** rebates
- **distributor** rebate
- a **grant** of rebate
- rebate **system** (*exclusionary ~ system*), rebate **scheme**
- **discounts** and rebates, **reductions** and rebates

Verb + rebate:

- to **grant**, **offer** rebates to X

RECIPIENT
/rɪˈsɪpiənt/ (RF 159/NF 107)

Derivatives: to **receive** (~ *aid*)

Adjective + RECIPIENT:

- **effective** recipient of aid

Noun phrase:

- **immunity** recipient
- **aid** recipient

REDRESS
/rɪˈdres/ (RF 64/NF 43)

Derivatives: to **redress** /rɪˈdres/ (*bias cannot be redressed*)

Adjective + redress:

- **collective** redress (*antitrust-specific, injunctive, judicial, compensatory, out-of-court collective ~*), **legal** redress

Noun phrase:

- **claims** for collective redress, collective redress **action**, redress **mechanisms**
- **avenues** of redress (*alternative avenues for ~, such as consensual dispute resolution*)
- **redress for**(*~ for damage resulting from the infringement*)

Verb + redress:

- to **seek** (*the action seeks legal ~*), **obtain** redress
- to **fund** redress

REMEDY
/ˈremədi/ (RF 76/NF 51)

Derivatives: to **remedy** /ˈremədi/ (*~ competition problems*)

ADJECTIVE + REMEDY:

- **effective** remedy
- **behavioural**, **structural** remedy
- **legal**, **procedural** remedies
- **domestic**, **national** remedies

NOUN PHRASE:

- **efficiency**, **viability** of remedies

VERB + REMEDY:

- to **impose** remedies

RESTRAINT
/rɪˈstreɪnt/ (RF 283/NF 190)

DERIVATIVES: to **restrain** from

ADJECTIVE + RESTRAINT:

- **vertical**, **horizontal** restraints
- **non-hardcore**, **severely anti-competitive**, **non-compete type** restraints
- **ancillary** /ænˈsɪləri/, **additional** restraints
- **implicit**, **harmful** restraints
- **contractual**, **territorial** restraints, **individual** restraints

NOUN PHRASE:

- the **assessment** of restraints
- restraints **on** (*~ on the purchase, sale of goods*)

VERB + RESTRAINT:

- to **agree** (*the vertical ~ agreed between the supplier and buyer*), **use** restraints
- to **reinforce** restraints
- to **prohibit** restraints

RESTRICTION
/rɪˈstrɪkʃn/ (RF 853/NF 572)

DERIVATIVES: to **restrict** /rɪˈstrɪkt/ (*~ competition*), **restrictive** /rɪˈstrɪktɪv/ (*~ agreement, effect, alternative*), **restrictively** /rɪˈstrɪktɪvli/ (*apply ~*)

ADJECTIVE + RESTRICTION:

- **hardcore**, **harmful**, **appreciable**, **severe**, **serious** restrictions
- **territorial** restrictions
- **contractual** restrictions
- **horizontal** restrictions

NOUN PHRASE:

- **use** restriction (*captive ~*; *field of use restrictions*), **sales/resale** restrictions, **output** restrictions, **threshold** restrictions, **bid-rigging** restrictions

- restriction of **competition**, restriction of **cross-supplies**, restrictions of **import**, restrictions of **capacity**
- restriction **on** (~ *the freedom to provide services, on active sales, on competition*)
- **exception to** restriction

VERB + RESTRICTION:

- to **impose**, **set** restrictions
- to **contain** restrictions
- to **exclude**, **prohibit** restrictions
- to **effect** restrictions

RULE
/ruːl/ (RF 1210/NF 812)

ADJECTIVE + RULE:

- **procedural**, **legal** rules
- **national**, **state**, **EU/Union/Community** rules

NOUN PHRASE:

- **competition**, **de minimis** rules
- **infringement**, **breach**, **implementation**, **application**, **enforcement** of rules, **compliance** with rules
- rule **on** competition, State aid

VERB + RULE:

- to **apply**, **observe**, **comply** with rules
- to **infringe**, **disregard** rules
- to **lay down**, **establish**, **adopt** rules

SALES
/ˈseɪlz/ (RF 1352/NF 908)

DERIVATIVES: to **sell** /sel/, **seller** /ˈselə(r)/, **resale** /ˌriːˈsel/ (~ *of products, goods*)

ADJECTIVE + SALES:

- **passive**, **active** sales
- **direct** sales
- **aggregate** sales
- **retail** sales
- **captive** sale

NOUN PHRASE:

- sales **conditions**, **volumes**, **price**, **quota**, **figure**, **value**, **territory**
- sales **agent, manager, personnel, representative, network**
- sales **agreement, procedure, policy**

- sales **restrictions**
- tax, restrictions **on** sales

VERB + SALES:

- to **make**, **undertake** sales
- to **limit**, **reduce**, **exclude**, **tie**, **prohibit**, **restrict**, **prevent** sales

SECRETS
/ˈsiːkrəts/ (RF 102/NF 68)

DERIVATIVES: **secret** /ˈsiːkrət/ (adj.) (*a ~ cartel*)

ADJECTIVE + SECRETS:

- **military** secrets

NOUN PHRASE:

- **business** secrets (*business ~ or other confidential information*), **production** secrets
- **protection** of business secrets, **deletion** of secrets

VERB + SECRETS:

- to **protect** secrets
- to **contain** secrets

SECRETS + VERB:

- secrets **enjoy** (*business ~ enjoy confidential treatment)*

SERVICE(S)
/ˈsɜːvɪs/ (RF 1672/NF 1223)

DERIVATIVES: to **service** /ˈsɜːvɪs/

ADJECTIVE + SERVICE:

- **public** service
- **protected** service
- **regional** service
- **postal** service

NOUN PHRASE:

- **transport**, **delivery, offer**, **operate**, **perform** service
- service **provider, provider** of services, service **provision**
- **operation** of services

VERB + SERVICE:

- to **provide**, **supply**, **offer** services
- to **protect** services

SETTLEMENT
/ˈsetlmənt/ (RF 171/NF 115)

DERIVATIVES: to **settle** /ˈsetl/ (~ *a dispute, claims*), **settling/non-settling** /ˈsetlɪŋ/ / ˌnɒn ˈsetlɪŋ/ (*a* ~ *infringer*)

ADJECTIVE + SETTLEMENT:

- **extrajudicial** /ˌekstrədʒuˈdɪʃl/ settlement, **out-of-court** settlement
- **consensual** settlement
- **collective** settlement

NOUN PHRASE:

- settlement of **claims**
- settlement **submission**, settlement **procedure**

VERB + SETTLEMENT:

- to **ratify** a settlement
- to **reach** a settlement

SHARE
/ʃeə(r)/ (RF 1036/NF 696)

DERIVATIVES: to **share** /ʃeə(r)/, **sharing** /ˈʃeərɪŋ/ (n.) (*market-, profit-, risk-reward, customer-sharing*)

ADJECTIVE + SHARE:

- a **fair** share
- **combined**, **aggregate** /ˈæɡrɪɡət/ market share

NOUN PHRASE:

- **market** share, market share **threshold**

VERB + SHARE:

- to **hold, have, maintain, gain, increase** a market share

SQUEEZE (MARGIN SQUEEZE)
/skwiːz/ /ˈmɑːdʒɪn skwiːz/ (RF 26/NF 17)

DERIVATIVES: to **squeeze** margins

ADJECTIVE + SQUEEZE:

- **abusive** margin squeeze

NOUN PHRASE:

- **margin** squeeze
- squeeze **on** competitors

VERB + SQUEEZE:

- to **cause**, **apply** a margin squeeze

SPECIALISATION
/ˌspeʃəlaɪˈzeɪʃn/ (RF 60/NF 40)

DERIVATIVES: to **specialise** /ˈspeʃəlaɪz/, **specialised** /ˈspeʃəlaɪzd/ (adj.) (*specialised chains*)

ADJECTIVE + SPECIALISATION:

- **reciprocal**, **unilateral** specialisation

NOUN PHRASE:

- **specialisation** agreement, **specialisation** product (*a ~ product means a product which is produced under a specialisation agreement*)
- specialisation **in** (*agreements on ~ in production / in the preparation of services*)

SUBSIDIARY
/səbˈsɪdiəri/ (RF 230/NF 154)

DERIVATIVES: **subsidiary** /səbˈsɪdiəri/ (adj.) (*~ relationship*)

ADJECTIVE + SUBSIDIARY:

- **wholly-owned** subsidiary
- **intermediary** subsidiary
- **national** subsidiary

NOUN PHRASE:

- the **parent** and its subsidiaries, parent/subsidiary **relationship**
- **board of directors**, **management**, **ownership** of a subsidiary; **capital** of a subsidiary
- **control** of a subsidiary (*the parent company has sole control of the ~*), commercial **autonomy** /ɔːˈtɒnəmi/ of the subsidiary
- **conduct** of a subsidiary (*to attribute the unlawful conduct of a ~ to a parent company*)
- **influence over** a subsidiary

VERB + SUBSIDIARY:

- to **form**, **incorporate** a subsidiary

SYSTEM
/ˈsɪstəm/ (RF 693/NF 465)

DERIVATIVES: **systematic** /ˌsɪstəˈmætɪk/ (*~ non-payment of taxes*)

ADJECTIVE + SYSTEM:

- **exclusive** system (*exclusive distribution/customer allocation ~*)

NOUN PHRASE:

- **information exchange** system
- **selective distribution** system
- **discount** system, **price** system
- **legal** system
- **health insurance** system

VERB + SYSTEM:

- to **establish**, **create**, **implement**, **operate**, **apply** a system

TARIFF
/ˈtærɪf/ (RF 517/NF 347)

ADJECTIVE + TARIFF:

- **uniform** tariffs
- **mandatory** tariffs
- **common** tariffs (*X joined a cartel to fix common tariffs)*

NOUN PHRASE:

- tariff **policy**, tariff **rates**, **tariff** agreement
- the **table** of tariffs
- **import** tariffs, **customs** tariff
- tariff **adjustment/readjustment**, tariff **equalization** /ˌiːkwəlaɪˈzeɪʃn/, **fixing** of tariffs, **ratification** of tariffs, tariff **increase**

VERB + TARIFF:

- to **set**, **establish** tariffs
- to **fix**, **adjust/readjust** tariffs
- to **publish** tariffs
- to **increase** tariffs

TEST
/test/ (RF 137/NF 92)

DERIVATIVES: to **test** /test/ (*~ a new product*)

NOUN PHRASE:

- **private investor**, **private operator**, **private creditor** test
- **indispensability** test
- **ancillary restraints** test
- **application** of private investor test, **outcome** of the test

VERB + TEST:

- to **apply** a test

- to **satisfy**, **fail** a test

THRESHOLD
/ˈθreʃhəʊld/ (RF 227/NF 152)

ADJECTIVE + THRESHOLD:

- **financial** threshold
- **minimum**, **total** threshold

NOUN PHRASE:

- **market share/market-share** threshold (*the 40% market share ~*), **dominance** threshold, **turnover** threshold, **SME** threshold, **de minimis** threshold, threshold of **market penetration**
- the **notification** threshold
- threshold **restrictions** (*above the market share threshold ~ on active and passive sales*)
- **application** of the threshold
- the threshold of x%, above the threshold (*any aid granted above the ~ is subject to notification*)

VERB + THRESHOLD:

- to **attain**, **reach**, **meet**, **apply** the threshold
- to **set** (out) (*to set the ~ for the preferential rate at...*), **fix** the threshold
- to **exceed** the threshold

TRADE
/treɪd/ (RF 1385/NF 930)

DERIVATIVES: to **trade** /treɪd/ (*~ products*), **trader** /ˈtreɪdə(r)/ (*independent / parallel ~; unlawful contact between ~*), **tradable** /ˈtreɪdəbl/ (*~ products*)

ADJECTIVE + TRADE:

- **parallel** trade
- **intra-Community**, **cross-border**, **domestic** trade

NOUN PHRASE:

- **trade** mark, trade mark **licence**, trade **name**
- **import and export** trade, **import-export** trade
- **barriers to** trade, **effect on** trade, **impact** of trade on (*the ambiguous impact of parallel ~ on the welfare of final consumers*)
- trade **flows** (*restrictions on ~ flows*), **pattern** of trade, **level** of trade
- trade **association**, trade **fair**
- trade **between** (*~ between Member States*)

VERB + TRADE:

- to **affect**, **impede**, **limit**, **hinder**, **restrict**, **eliminate**, **prevent** trade

- to **promote**, **facilitate**, **encourage** trade
- to **engage in** trade
- to **compete in** trade (*undertakings competing in intra-Community trade*), **keep** trade **competitive**

TRADE MARK / TRADEMARK
/ˈtreɪdmɑːk/ (RF 364/NF 244)

ADJECTIVE + TRADE MARK:

- **own** trade mark
- **reputable**, **well-known** trade mark

NOUN PHRASE:

- **licensee** of trade mark, **proprietor** of trade mark
- trade mark **license** (*to grant ~*), **products under** a trade mark, trade mark **rights**, products **bearing** the X trade mark
- **reputation** of trade mark
- **portfolio** of trade marks

VERB + TRADE MARK:

- to **use**, **acquire** a trade mark
- to **compete with** a trade mark

TREATMENT
/ˈtriːtmənt/ (RF 285/NF 191)

DERIVATIVES: to **treat** /triːt/ (*to be treated unfairly, differently from X*)

ADJECTIVE + TREATMENT:

- **equal/unequal**, **differential**, **favourable** treatment (*a programme gives favourable ~ to some undertakings*), **beneficial**, **arbitrary**, **non-discriminatory**, **different** (*justified different ~ with regard to fines*), **differentiated**, **lenient** treatment
- **confidential** treatment (*a request/application for confidential ~*)

NOUN PHRASE:

- the **principle of equal** treatment
- **priority** treatment
- **difference** in treatment

VERB + TREATMENT:

- to **obtain** treatment (*to obtain favourable/comparable ~ for x*)
- to **justify** treatment

TYING
/ˈtaɪɪŋ/ (RF 126/NF 85)

DERIVATIVES: to **tie** /taɪ/ (*a purchaser*), **tied** /taɪd/ (adj.) (*~ market share, product, sales*)

NOUN PHRASE:

- tying **practice**, **obligation**, **product**
- **assessment** of tying
- tying and **bundling**

UNDERTAKING
/ˌʌndəˈteɪkɪŋ/ (RF 4139/NF 2779)

DERIVATIVES: to **undertake** /ˌʌndəˈteɪk/ (*~ an investigation, examination, review; ~ to market products*)

ADJECTIVE + UNDERTAKING:

- **dominant** undertaking
- **public**, **private** undertaking
- **small**, **large**, **medium-sized** undertaking
- **connected** undertakings, **single** undertaking (*to form ~*)
- **recipient** undertaking
- **eligible** undertaking
- **competing** undertaking

NOUN PHRASE:

- **association** of undertakings
- **turnover**, **size**, **interest**, **position**, **sales**, **market share**, **business premises**, **situation** of an undertaking
- an undertaking **in a dominant position**
- agreement, competition, concentration **between** undertakings

VERB + UNDERTAKING:

- to **form**, **establish** an undertaking
- to **represent** an undertaking

UNIT
/ˈjuːnɪt/ (RF 139/NF 93)

ADJECTIVE + UNIT:

- **economic** unit, **single** economic unit (*the parent and its subsidiary are considered to form a single economic unit*), single **legal** and economic unit

VERB + UNIT:

- to **establish**, **form** an economic unit

References

Deuter M, Bradbery J, Turnbull J (2015) Oxford Advanced Learner's Dictionary, 9th edn. Oxford University Press. www.oed.com. Accessed 20 Mar 2018

Kilgarriff A, Baisa V, Bušta J, Jakubíček M, Kovvář V, Michelfeit J, Rychlý P, Suchomel V (2014) The Sketch Engine: ten years on. Lexicography 1:7–36

OED Online (2018) Oxford University Press. http://www.oed.com.oed.han.buw.uw.edu.pl/view/Entry/43039? Accessed 20 Mar 2018

Scott M (2017) WordSmith Tools version 7. Stroud, Lexical Analysis Software

Łucja Biel is Associate Professor of Translation Studies and Linguistics at the Institute of Applied Linguistics, secretary general of the European Society for Translation Studies and deputy editor of the Journal of Specialised Translation.

Agnieszka Biernacka is Assistant Professor at the Institute of Applied Linguistics and Head of the Interdisciplinary Postgraduate Studies in Translation and Interpreting at the University of Warsaw, a court interpreting researcher, legal translator and court interpreter trainer.

Anna Jopek-Bosiacka is Senior Lecturer at the Institute of Applied Linguistics of the University of Warsaw, a sworn translator and counsellor-at-law.

Phraseological Profile of Judgments: Complex Prepositions in EU Competition Law Judgments

Dariusz Koźbiał

Abstract The chapter is aimed to raise legal practitioners' and translators' awareness of natural language patterns in judgments relating to Competition Law so that they are better equipped to both understand judgments with ease and to stay close to the established conventions when producing their own texts. Complex prepositions contribute largely to the phraseological profile of legal genres, thus requiring a careful examination. In particular, the chapter discusses the distribution and discourse functions of simple, marginal, compound, and, most importantly, complex prepositions in judgments of the Court of Justice of the European Union (CJEU) relating to Competition Law. In addition, the chapter draws comparisons with the language of judgments relating to all types of subject matter under the authority of the CJEU, the language of UK judicial decisions, and general English. The results point to the marked overrepresentation of certain complex prepositions (e.g. *in accordance with*, *according to*, *relating to*, *in order to*) in the genre of EU judgments as compared to UK judicial decisions (and vice versa) and general English. Therefore, it may be claimed that the high overall distribution of complex prepositions is a distinctive feature of the genre of CJEU judgments.

1 Introduction

Prepositions (e.g. *on*, *of*, *to*, etc.), as well as determiners (*a*, *every*, *the*, *this*, etc.), pronouns (*I*, *you*, *myself*, *mine*, etc.), auxiliary verbs (*be*, *have*, *do*, *must*, *will*, *should*, *shall*, etc.), adverbial particles (e.g. *about*, *after*, *since*, *over*, etc.), coordinators (e.g. *but*, *nor*, *yet*, *for*, etc.) and subordinators (e.g. *although*, *because*, *whereas*, etc.), form a separate class of function words.[1] As opposed to, for instance, auxiliary verbs, prepositions are non-inflectional. Being linking words, their syntactic

[1]Biber et al. (2002), p. 26.

D. Koźbiał (✉)
Faculty of Applied Linguistics, University of Warsaw, Warsaw, Poland
e-mail: d.kozbial@uw.edu.pl

S. Marino et al. (eds.), *Language and Law*,
https://doi.org/10.1007/978-3-319-90905-9_16

function consists of introducing prepositional phrases, that is expressing a relationship between the prepositional complement and the other parts of the sentence.[2] The prepositional complement is usually a noun phrase, a nominal *wh*-clause or a nominal *–ing* clause.[3] Consider the following prepositional phrases (prepositions are italicised; prepositional complements are not italicised):

- *on* the substance
- *from* that viewpoint
- *by* bringing an appeal
- *in addition to* the evidence provided by that Member State

In general, prepositions may be divided into two groups, namely simple and complex prepositions.[4] Simple prepositions consist of one word and, due to varying stress patterns, are either monosyllabic, e.g. *at*, *of*, *on*, *to*, or polysyllabic, e.g. *about*, *before*, *under*.[5] Apart from simple prepositions as such, there are also the so-called marginal prepositions, that is words which function as prepositions despite the fact that they resemble other classes of words, such as adjectives or verbs (e.g. *considering*, *given*, *including*, etc.). The second main group, that is complex prepositions, is composed of either two- or three-word sequences, the meaning of which cannot be derived from the meaning of individual words.[6] In the case of two-word complex prepositions, the second word is a simple preposition, whereas the first word is a noun, adjective or adverb, for instance, *according to*, *apart from*, *because of*, *owing to* (ibid.). Three-word complex prepositions usually have the following structure: preposition + noun + preposition, e.g. *as part of*, *by way of*, *in addition to*.[7] They also include sequences where the noun is preceded by a definite or indefinite article, e.g. *as a consequence of*, *for the sake of*, *in the light of*.[8] Owing to the fact that the boundary between complex prepositions and prepositional phrases is unclear, for the purposes of this analysis complex prepositions are regarded as fixed expressions with a special meaning, whereas prepositional phrases are perceived as ad-hoc combinations of words with a meaning that can be derived from individual words and are not analysed in this chapter.

[2] Quirk et al. (1985), p. 657.

[3] ibid.

[4] Quirk et al. (1985), p. 665.

[5] ibid.

[6] See Quirk et al. (1985), p. 669 and Biber et al. (2002), p. 29.

[7] Biber et al. (2002), p. 29.

[8] Quirk et al. (1985), p. 670.

2 Research Objectives

The study at hand verifies the hypothesis put forward in Biel,[9] according to which a large proportion of non-terminological word combinations in legislation is built around complex prepositions, with the difference being that this study aims to either confirm or negate this hypothesis with regard to the genre of EU judgments by investigating the phraseological profile of judicial language in terms of the distribution of complex prepositions. Considering the fact that complex prepositions contribute largely to the phraseological profile of legal genres, they require a careful examination of distribution and functions in the genre of judgments.[10] The study discusses the distribution and functions of complex prepositions in Competition judgments which were passed by the Court of Justice of the European Union (CJEU), against the corpora of judgments relating to all types of subject matter under the authority of the CJEU, UK judicial decisions (BLRC), and general English (BNC).

As rightly observed by Pontrandolfo,[11] judgments constitute language products of the judicial discourse community. However, due to the fact that it is a community which deals with all types of subject matter under the authority of the court, be it matters relating to civil or criminal law, it is particularly beneficial that this study considers primarily one type of judgments, namely those relating to Competition Law. The main research question is as follows:

- How the phraseological profile of CJEU judgments relating to Competition Law differ from that of CJEU judgments relating to all types of subject matter as well as UK judicial decisions and general English?

Furthermore, the aim of this study is to raise awareness among translators and legal practitioners of language patterns natural in the language of Competition judgments so that they are better equipped to properly understand English-language versions of the said judgments and to stay close to the established conventions when producing their own texts relating to the area of Competition Law. The emphasis has been placed on judgments relating to Competition Law, as this is the field which was thematised during the training session for judges and other legal practitioners from five EU Member States (Poland, Spain, Croatia, Greece and Italy), *Legal English: Lingua Franca and Translation in EU Competition Law,* which took place on December 1, 2017, at the Institute of Applied Linguistics, University of Warsaw.

---

[9]Biel (2015).

[10]See Biel (2015) and Pontrandolfo (2015).

[11]Pontrandolfo (2015), p. 140.

Table 1 Corpus design

Name of the corpus	No. of texts	Time depth	Tokens (words)
Court of Justice judgments relating to Competition Law (CJEU—COMPETITION)	162	2011–2015	1,302,653
Court of Justice judgments relating to all types of subject matter (CJEU—ALL)	897	2011–2015	5,463,176
British Law Report Corpus (BLRC)	1228	2008–2010	8,850,000
British National Corpus (BNC)	4049	1960s–1990s	96,134,547

3 Corpus Design

The main corpus used in this study is the corpus of judgments of the CJEU relating to Competition Law, which comprises 162 judgments translated into English and published in the period of 2011–2015. The three remaining corpora are used for reference purposes, that is to verify the results obtained in the process of analysing the corpus of Competition judgments. The first reference corpus is a corpus of CJEU judgments being analysed within the framework of the Eurolect project.[12] It comprises all judgments relating to all types of subject matter published in the on-line repository of CJEU judgments which were available at the time of the compilation of the corpus, that is in December 2015.[13] The second reference corpus is a corpus of 1228 UK judicial decisions issued between 2008 and 2010 by British courts and tribunals (British Law Report Corpus),[14] whereas the third reference corpus is a corpus of non-judicial, general English (The British National Corpus 2007). Both the BLRC and the BNC were searched via the corpus manager and analysis software Sketch Engine,[15] whereas the CJEU corpora were analysed using Wordsmith Tools 7.0.[16] Exact quantitative data concerning the individual corpora can be verified in Table 1.

Owing to the fact that each of the corpora has a different number of tokens, the results will be normalised to one million words in order to guarantee comparability.

---

[12]For more information, check the website of the Eurolect project: https://eurolekt.ils.uw.edu.pl/; cf. Biel (2016).

[13]See https://curia.europa.eu/jcms/jcms/j_6/en/.

[14]The sampling frames of the BLRC corpus and the corpora of EU judgments are not identical, thus being a limitation of the study.

[15]Kilgarriff et al. (2014).

[16]Scott (2017). The main corpus software used in the analysis was Wordsmith Tools 7.0. Sketch Engine, as an on-line corpus tool, was used to search the BLRC and the BNC due to the fact that the query systems available on the websites of the respective corpora do not allow for sufficiently advanced queries and the generation of long results lists.

4 Methodology

Owing to the extensive nature of the research material and the utilised methodology, it has not been possible to analyse the context of occurrence of all simple and marginal prepositions; therefore, the obtained results are an approximation, especially with regard to the discussion on the functions of complex prepositions in CJEU Competition judgments. The following sentences taken from Foley and Hall aptly illustrate this issue[17]:

1. Did you ever travel *before* the war, Dad?
2. I have a strange feeling that I've been here *before*.

In the first sentence, *before* functions as a preposition, since it has an object. In the second sentence, *before* does not have an object and hence acts as an adverb. Even though the corpus methodology enables us to study a vast textual material, it proves insufficient when it comes to spotting and eliminating such unwanted occurrences of the same lexical unit which may function as different word classes if we do not use grammatically annotated corpora.[18]

Considering the fact that complex prepositions are a vast group with many different types which very often border on prepositional phrases, for the purposes of this analysis complex prepositions were identified based on a review of literature[19] and later supplemented by the results of a manual analysis of a sample of 10 random CJEU judgments.

5 Investigation Into the Phraseological Profile of CJEU Judgments at the Microstructural Level: The Case of Simple, Compound and Complex Prepositions

5.1 Simple and Marginal Prepositions

Before we focus on compound and complex prepositions we should focus our attention on other types of prepositions, namely simple and marginal prepositions. Firstly, let us examine the distribution of simple prepositions across the corpora of judicial discourse (CJEU, BLRC) and general English (BNC). Table 2 presents quantitative data concerning the frequency of the top 18 simple prepositions found in the top 200 words from the wordlist generated for the corpus of CJEU judgments relating to Competition Law in all of the corpora. All of the data relating to

---

[17]Foley and Hall (2004), p. 280.

[18]For the purposes of future analysis, it might be advisable to use annotation tools, such as the one available in the Sketchengine suite of corpus tools.

[19]See Quirk et al. (1985), Klégr (1997), Biel (2015), Pontrandolfo (2013, 2015).

Table 2 Frequency of simple prepositions;[a] simple prepositions are ordered in a descending order in the corpus of CJEU Competition judgments (frequencies normalised to one million occurrences)[b]

Simple prepositions	CJEU—COMPETITION			CJEU—ALL	BLRC	BNC
	Wordlist # (Top 200)	CJEU—COMPETITION A (occurrences of simple prepositions within complex prepositions included)	CJEU—COMPETITION B (occurrences of simple prepositions within complex prepositions excluded)			
of	3	*53,313*	*46,034*	*56,751*	39,563	31,721
to	4	29,941	23,819	30,206	*33,906*	27,040
in	5	*28,423*	22,470	*28,235*	24,525	20,239
by	9	*11,045*	*10,422*	*10,688*	7895	5341
on	12	*8918*	7425	8762	8858	7607
for	14	8416	6955	*10,138*	9398	9162
at	28	4197	2339	3398	4744	*5452*
with	30	4110	2503	4377	5290	*6865*
from	32	4011	3804	4069	3606	*4431*
under	33	*3994*	*3985*	*3339*	2242	635
out	71	1453	1411	1461	1566	*2055*
before	73	*1429*	*1429*	1260	1310	885
within	77	*1382*	681	*1689*	865	476
between	85	*1280*	*1280*	*1124*	1020	943
into	96	1162	1162	1102	1014	*1642*
after	169	703	702	783	759	*1186*
down	178	659	659	955	213	*967*
without	182	*644*	579	*666*	610	466
Total		*165,081*	137,660	*169,002*	147,384	127,112

[a]Italicised figures indicate overrepresentation as compared to the other corpora

[b]Both columns in the CJEU—COMPETITION section of Table 2, i.e. CJEU—COMPETITION A and CJEU—COMPETITION B, present data obtained with the help of the same corpus, with the only difference being that CJEU—COMPETITION B column includes quantitative data concerning the distribution of simple prepositions which exclude occurrences of simple prepositions within complex prepositions. Therefore, column B provides a more accurate view of the distribution of simple prepositions in Competition judgments

frequencies reflect all occurrences of simple prepositions within the texts, that is both as simple prepositions and as part of complex prepositions, except for the corpus of CJEU Competition judgments, in the case of which the quantitative data also include frequencies reflecting occurrences of simple prepositions which do not form complex prepositions analysed in Sect. 5.3. These data provide a closer approximation of the distribution of simple prepositions in EU Competition judgments. However, due to the time-consuming nature of the process of extracting only those simple prepositions which do not form complex prepositional patterns, it has been decided to carry out the procedure only on the smaller CJEU corpus in order to better present the ratio of simple to complex prepositions (see Table 2).

The bigger CJEU corpus has been found to contain ca. 15% more simple prepositions than the BLRC and ca. 33% more than the BNC. The overrepresentation of simple prepositions in EU judgments may be due to their highly analytical nature requiring a great degree of precision. Compared to the BLRC, the following simple prepositions are overrepresented in EU judgments: *of*, *in*, *by*, *for*, *from*, *under*, *within*, *between*, *into*, *after*, *down*, and *without*. Particularly striking is the overrepresentation of the preposition *of*, which, in the bigger CJEU corpus, is 43% more frequent than in the BLRC and 79% more frequent than in the BNC. This considerable overrepresentation is partially due to *of* being present in numerous inter- and intra-textual references, e.g. *Article 1(1)(a)(i) of Directive 2010/13/EU of the European Parliament and of the Council of 10 March 2010*, *in paragraph 299 of the judgment under appeal*, *Statute of the Court of Justice of the European Union*. In addition, in the bigger CJEU corpus, *of* is ca. 88% more frequent than the next top simple preposition, whereas in the case of the BLRC and the BNC, it is only ca. 17% more frequent than *to*. The high distribution of the preposition *of* may also result from increased nominalisation, e.g. *method of determining the amount of a fine*, *misreading of the judgment under appeal*, or *review of the lawfulness of the penalty*. The overrepresentation of the remaining simple prepositions may be due to either the overrepresentation of certain complex prepositions (cf. Sect. 5.3), e.g. *in the context of*, *for the benefit of*, *on the basis of*, *by means of*, *on the part of*, or *for the purposes of*. Prepositions *at*, *with*, *to*, *on*, *out*, *before* are underrepresented in the bigger CJEU corpus. What is visible is the marked underrepresentation of *at* (44%) and *with* (21%).

Since Table 2 is not easy to read, a more easily readable version of this table will be presented. The table below (Table 3) presents simple prepositions in each of the corpora listed according to their frequency. What can be noted at first glance is that the first three simple prepositions are shared between all the corpora, namely *of*, *to*, and *in*. As for the prepositions in the fourth and fifth position, there are fewer similarities between the EU corpora, the BLRC, and the BNC—at the fourth position, the EU corpora prioritise *by*, whereas the BLRC and the BNC *on*; at the fifth position, CJEU judgments relating to Competition Law, the BLRC and the BNC prioritise *on*, whereas CJEU judgments relating to all types of subject matter prioritise *for*.

Table 4 presents quantitative data concerning the distribution of selected marginal prepositions in the corpora.

Table 3 Simple prepositions listed according to their frequency

CJEU—COMPETITION	CJEU—COMPETITION[a]	CJEU—ALL	BLRC	BNC
of	*of*	*of*	*of*	*of*
to	*to*	*to*	*to*	*to*
in	*in*	*in*	*in*	*in*
by	*by*	*by*	*for*	*for*
on	*on*	*for*	*on*	*on*
for	*for*	*on*	*by*	*with*
at	*under*	*with*	*with*	*at*
with	*from*	*from*	*at*	*by*
from	*with*	*at*	*from*	*from*
under	*at*	*under*	*under*	*out*
out	*before*	*within*	*out*	*into*
before	*out*	*out*	*before*	*after*
within	*between*	*before*	*between*	*down*
between	*into*	*between*	*into*	*between*
into	*after*	*into*	*within*	*before*
after	*within*	*down*	*after*	*under*
down	*down*	*after*	*without*	*within*
without	*without*	*without*	*down*	*without*

[a]This column shows the order of those simple prepositions (listed according to their frequency) which were not part of complex prepositions in the corpus of CJEU Competition judgments

Table 4 Frequency of marginal prepositions (frequencies normalised to one million occurrences)

Marginal prepositions	CJEU—COMPETITION	CJEU—ALL	BLRC	BNC
concerning	724	695	85	35
granted	414	258	*157*	*32*
given	378	373	*454*	*193*
including	269	397	362	250
following	229	233	*212*	*83*
regarding	131	124	78	25
considering	53	39	*85*	22
excluding	33	42	23	11
pending	24	163	*16*	*7*
barring	2	1	1	2
Total	2258	2326	*1472*	*660*

Marginal prepositions are ordered in a descending order in the corpus of CJEU Competition judgments. Italicised figures concern results obtained using unreliable search tools which do not allow for the efficient separation of unwanted results

The Eurolect has been found to have a stronger preference for marginal prepositions than UK law reports, since there are ca. 56% more occurrences of such prepositions in both CJEU corpora. However, it cannot be said that the use of marginal prepositions is a unique feature of EU judgments, since this type of prepositions is overrepresented not only in EU judgments but also the BLRC as compared to the BNC. The most marked difference between the CJEU and BLRC corpora concerns the significant overrepresentation of *concerning* in the CJEU corpora, which is very rare in the BLRC. The Eurolect uses *concerning* mostly to introduce further specification/particularisation; however, it is also used in the names of various legislative acts, e.g. *Directive 2006/114/EC of the European Parliament and of the Council of 12 December 2006 concerning misleading and comparative advertising*, thus contributing to the high overall frequency of this marginal preposition.

5.2 Compound Prepositions

A repetitive use of compound prepositions is another distinctive feature of legal language. Compound prepositions consist of adverbial words and connected prepositions, e.g. *hereby*, *thereof*, etc.[20] They make legal language more formal and stale, thus making it almost impervious to lay persons.[21] Despite this fact, lawyers have a strong preference for compound prepositions thanks to their main function, which consists of providing exact references, and thus adding precision to texts. They are also known as prepositional adverbs and are classified as semi-archaisms (see Table 5).[22]

As compound prepositions based around *here-* and *there-* are a feature of legal English, they do not have a significant frequency in general English.[23] The results show that adverbial prepositions are indeed very infrequent in general English (cf. Table 5). The occurrences of compound prepositions noted in the corpus of general English come predominantly from one text type, i.e. written books and periodicals. Although their distribution in the BLRC is approximately four times higher than in the BNC, compound prepositions are still less frequent in UK judicial decisions than in EU judgments. The high frequency of compound prepositions in EU judgments is mainly due to the high salience of three prepositions, namely *hereby*, *thereof* and *thereby*,[24] which contribute disproportionately to the overall high distribution of adverbial prepositions in the Eurolect. *Hereby* is very frequent due to its application in the operative part of each judgment[25]:

---

[20]Crystal and Davy (1969), pp. 207–208.

[21]Mattila (2006), p. 244 and Riera (2015), p. 155.

[22]cf. *inter alia* Riera (2015), p. 155.

[23]cf. Biel (2015), p. 146 and Haigh (2009), p. 35.

[24]*Hereby* and *thereof* have also been found to be very frequent in EU regulations and directives, thus also contributing to the overall salience of compound prepositions in EU legislation as opposed to UK legislation (cf. Biel (2015), p. 146).

[25]The performative hereby has also been found to be used very frequently in the amending clauses of EU regulations and directives (cf. Biel (2015), p. 146).

Table 5 Frequency of compound prepositions (frequencies normalised to one million occurrences)[a]

	Translated EU judgments		Reference corpora	
Compound prepositions	CJEU—COMPETITION	CJEU—ALL	BLRC	BNC
hereby	*129*	*174*	15	3
hereinafter	*25*	*17*	10	1
herein	2	2	*7*	1
herewith	1	0	1	0
hereafter	1	3	*6*	1
hereto	0	1	*5*	1
Total	157	197	43	7
thereof	*207*	*310*	31	5
thereby	*117*	*83*	50	27
thereto	*46*	*85*	9	2
therein	*31*	*44*	15	4
thereafter	14	12	*87*	15
thereon	7	7	*10*	1
therewith	*4*	*5*	2	0
thereupon	2	3	*4*	1
therefor	1	2	2	0
thereunder	0	4	*4*	0
Total	429	554	214	56

[a]Italicised figures indicate overrepresentation as compared to the other corpora

On those grounds, the Court (Fifth Chamber) hereby:

Dismisses the appeal;

[...]

Thereof is even more frequent than *hereby*; however, it does not appear in any specific part of the judgments, but rather functions as a referential device which points to various legislative acts:

Article 8(1)(c) of Directive 2004/48 and Article 8(3)(e) thereof, read together, require that various rights be complied with.

The third salient compound preposition, *thereby*, also appears throughout all parts of the EU judgments, e.g.:

It must be stated that Decision 2011/199 amends a provision of Part Three of the FEU Treaty, namely Article 136 TFEU, and thereby formally satisfies the condition stated in the first and second subparagraphs of Article 48(6) TEU that the simplified revision procedure may concern solely provisions of that Part Three.

or

On those grounds, the Court (Second Chamber) hereby:

[...]

> 3. Annuls the decision of the Commission of 30 May 2011 in so far as the European Commission thereby refused to give to Client Earth full access to the studies referred to in point 1 of the operative part of this judgment;

The remaining compound prepositions, that is *herein*, *herewith*, *hereafter*, *hereto*, appear very infrequently in EU judgments and are more frequent in the BLRC rather than in the EU corpora. When it comes to the less frequent adverbial prepositions, *thereto*, *therein*, and *therewith* are less frequent in EU judgments, whereas *thereafter*, *thereon*, *thereupon*, *therefor*, *thereunder* are overrepresented in the BLRC. Overall, the Eurolect contains twice as many compound prepositions based around *there-* as compound prepositions based around *here-*. Furthermore, CJEU Competition judgments do not rely as heavily on compound prepositions as CJEU judgments relating to all types of subject matter, especially in the case of *there-* compound prepositions.

5.3 Complex Prepositions

This section focuses on the frequency data concerning the distribution of complex prepositions in the corpora as well as on their functions in judgments.

5.3.1 Frequency of Complex Prepositions

Table 6 presents qualitative data on the distribution of two- and three-word complex prepositions in CJEU and UK judgments, and in general English (BNC). It lists complex prepositions in a descending order in terms of their normalised frequency. The only compound prepositions included in this table were those which have at least five occurrences per million words in any of the corpora.

In terms of total numbers of occurrences of complex prepositions appearing at least five times per million words in either EU judgments or UK judicial decisions, or general English (BNC), the corpus of CJEU judgments relating to all types of subject matter has the highest level of distribution of complex prepositions (13,499 per million words). This tells us that CJEU judgments, in general, rely on repeated complex prepositions more heavily than CJEU judgments relating specifically to Competition Law (12,444 per million words), which may suggest that they are even more analytical and precise in nature. However, the number of types of complex prepositions in the corpus of Competition judgments (111) is lower from that in the general CJEU corpus (114) by only three types. This observation suggests that the profiles of both corpora as regards complex prepositions are quite similar to each other, while being substantially different from the BLRC, which has 133 types, and even more so from general English (BNC), which has 101 types. The total number of complex prepositions with at least five occurrences per million words in the BNC is 3549 per million words, which is ca. 3.5 times less than in the corpus of CJEU

Table 6 Frequency of complex prepositions (normalised to one million words)

CJEU—COMPETITION		CJEU—ALL		BLRC		BNC	
according to	892	*in accordance with*	927	*as to*	829	*out of*	496
relating to	818	*according to*	819	*in relation to*	649	*up to*	300
in order to	791	*relating to*	810	*in respect of*	520	*because of*	184
in accordance with	656	*in order to*	767	*for the purpose(s) of*	387	*according to*	162
for the purpose(s) of	639	*for the purpose(s) of*	726	*subject to*	377	*in order to*	126
within the meaning of	559	*within the meaning of*	642	*on behalf of*	299	*due to*	110
on the basis of	530	*subject to*	583	*out of*	274	*in terms of*	105
as to	506	*on the basis of*	569	*in order to*	252	*as to*	103
in the light of	499	*in the light of*	462	*in accordance with*	247	*at the end of*	98
pursuant to	409	*in respect of*	462	*relating to*	237	*instead of*	73
with regard to	374	*pursuant to*	434	*in the case of*	187	*subject to*	68
in respect of	365	*as to*	422	*because of*	179	*apart from*	67
contrary to	323	*in relation to*	320	*in the light of*	172	*in front of*	64
in relation to	317	*with regard to*	297	*on (the) ground(s) of*	164	*together with*	61
subject to	313	*in the context of*	274	*as a result of*	153	*as far as*	59
in support of	304	*contrary to*	244	*pursuant to*	150	*as a result of*	54
in the context of	293	*on behalf of*	209	*on the basis of*	147	*along with*	52
in the case of	134	*in support of*	201	*by way of*	137	*as part of*	50
as a result of	133	*in the case of*	191	*in the course of*	137	*in the case of*	50
by means of	113	*within the scope of*	151	*in the context of*	131	*in relation to*	49
prior to	111	*in conjunction with*	134	*due to*	129	*related to*	47
within the scope of	110	*by means of*	125	*prior to*	127	*in favour of*	37
by virtue of	108	*by virtue of*	122	*contrary to*	125	*in addition to*	36
in the absence of	102	*as a result of*	121	*according to*	114	*relating to*	33
on behalf of	100	*on (the) ground(s) of*	115	*in terms of*	114	*prior to*	32
in view of	95	*in the territory of*	113	*by reference to*	110	*in respect of*	31

with respect to	91	*in the absence of*	112	*at the time of*	110	*on the basis of*	31
because of	89	*prior to*	108	*up to*	105	*in the middle of*	30
related to	88	*with a view to*	107	*related to*	97	*at the time of*	29
by reference to	88	*without prejudice to*	104	*together with*	96	*on behalf of*	28
with a view to	88	*in the course of*	103	*within the meaning of*	95	*in spite of*	28
in the course of	86	*in the event of*	100	*by virtue of*	94	*ahead of*	26
on the part of	83	*in view of*	100	*on the part of*	90	*on top of*	26
at the time of	82	*at the time of*	99	*in the absence of*	86	*depending on*	24
by way of	79	*because of*	96	*in connection with*	82	*thanks to*	23
in conjunction with	79	*by way of*	95	*in consequence of*	82	*in accordance with*	21
in addition to	76	*with respect to*	90	*in favour of*	80	*in response to*	21
on account of	74	*by reference to*	80	*as part of*	78	*in the context of*	20
in the form of	67	*by reason of*	77	*at the end of*	73	*for the purpose(s) of*	20
by reason of	66	*related to*	75	*by reason of*	71	*in the light of*	20
in favour of	65	*irrespective of*	74	*in support of*	70	*except for*	20
without prejudice to	64	*in addition to*	73	*with regard to*	65	*in the course of*	20
in the field of	61	*on the part of*	69	*apart from*	63	*in the form of*	19
irrespective of	60	*in connection with*	68	*in the interest(s) of*	49	*with regard to*	18
up to	60	*up to*	63	*in view of*	46	*as opposed to*	17
in connection with	56	*exempt from*	58	*with a view to*	45	*in charge of*	17
due to	50	*together with*	58	*in addition to*	45	*by means of*	17
as from	47	*in the field of*	57	*in response to*	41	*in connection with*	16
in the event of	46	*due to*	57	*with respect to*	37	*at the top of*	16
as part of	45	*out of*	56	*as far as*	35	*in the absence of*	16
in response to	43	*on account of*	55	*as opposed to*	34	*on the part of*	16
on (the) ground(s) of	43	*in favour of*	49	*in the event of*	34	*in view of*	16
exempt from	42	*in the form of*	48	*in the form of*	33	*in the face of*	15
out of	39	*as part of*	45	*within the scope of*	31	*on (the) ground(s) of*	15

(continued)

Table 6 (continued)

CJEU—COMPETITION		CJEU—ALL		BLRC		BNC	
at the end of	38	*as from*	44	*as of*	30	*by way of*	15
in terms of	37	*at the end of*	43	*in the hands of*	29	*regardless of*	15
in the territory of	36	*depending on*	40	*on account of*	27	*with respect to*	14
together with	34	*in terms of*	39	*for the benefit of*	25	*contrary to*	14
depending on	33	*with effect from*	36	*in excess of*	25	*in conjunction with*	13
regardless of	33	*in conformity with*	36	*irrespective of*	25	*in line with*	13
from the date of	32	*regardless of*	34	*with effect from*	25	*on the edge of*	12
during the period from	31	*for a period of*	33	*for a period of*	25	*at the back of*	12
in the area of	31	*in response to*	33	*on the issue of*	25	*at the expense of*	11
with the exception of	31	*on a point of*	33	*depending on*	23	*in support of*	11
in the amount of	30	*with the exception of*	32	*regardless of*	22	*in the event of*	11
as far as	28	*within the framework of*	31	*instead of*	22	*in the hands of*	11
with effect from	27	*from the date of*	30	*on the question of*	21	*at the bottom of*	11
for a period of	25	*as far as*	30	*from the date of*	21	*in search of*	10
to the amount of	25	*for the benefit of*	28	*by means of*	21	*by virtue of*	10
for the sake of	24	*at the request of*	27	*without prejudice to*	19	*in the interest(s) of*	10
at odds with	24	*in the interest(s) of*	27	*to the extent of*	17	*as of*	10
outside the scope of	22	*owing to*	27	*along with*	17	*in return for*	10
in return for	21	*devoid of*	26	*in pursuance of*	16	*in the way of*	9
instead of	21	*in return for*	26	*in agreement with*	15	*for the sake of*	9
for the benefit of	21	*in the area of*	25	*in conjunction with*	15	*irrespective of*	9
at the request of	20	*in compliance with*	24	*in the name of*	15	*with the help of*	9
in the interest(s) of	20	*in the amount of*	22	*within the ambit of*	15	*with a view to*	9
to the detriment of	20	*outside the scope of*	19	*as from*	14	*in excess of*	9
within the framework of	19	*instead of*	19	*in front of*	13	*in the direction of*	9
apart from	18	*apart from*	17	*in line with*	13	*in the presence of*	8

owing to	18	*as of*	15	*in advance of*	13	*owing to*	8
as of	17	*to the amount of*	15	*at the conclusion of*	13	*for the benefit of*	8
in compliance with	16	*in excess of*	14	*in the territory of*	13	*with the exception of*	8
by comparison with	16	*to the detriment of*	14	*as a consequence of*	13	*in the name of*	8
until the date of	14	*for reasons of*	13	*in the face of*	12	*in common with*	8
on the principle of	14	*during the period of*	13	*with reference to*	12	*in the wake of*	8
subsequent to	14	*during the period from*	10	*in the nature of*	12	*in the field of*	8
during the period of	12	*with the aim of*	12	*by the time of*	11	*in the area of*	7
in conformity with	11	*in line with*	12	*during the period of*	11	*by reference to*	7
on a point of	11	*subsequent to*	11	*in lieu of*	11	*in a state of*	7
except for	11	*except for*	10	*in return for*	11	*in the shape of*	6
in comparison with	11	*in lieu of*	10	*subsequent to*	11	*on the subject of*	5
in exchange for	11	*on the principle of*	9	*at the request of*	10	*at the head of*	5
in pursuit of	10	*at odds with*	9	*in the field of*	10	*on account of*	5
with the aim of	9	*for the sake of*	9	*with the intention of*	10	*in advance of*	5
as a consequence of	8	*in consequence of*	8	*in common with*	10	*in the heart of*	5
at the expense of	8	*as opposed to*	8	*outside the scope of*	9	*as from*	5
with reference to	8	*as a consequence of*	8	*beginning with*	9	*in the midst of*	5
to the extent of	7	*to the exclusion of*	8	*owing to*	9	*in comparison with*	5
to the exclusion of	7	*in the name of*	8	*except for*	9	*in contact with*	5
for reasons of	6	*to the extent of*	8	*without reference to*	9	*in keeping with*	5
in line with	6	*with reference to*	7	*on a point of*	9		
at the head of	6	*in the sphere of*	7	*with the exception of*	8		
on the question of	6	*in spite of*	6	*exempt from*	8		
as opposed to	5	*in comparison with*	6	*in the region of*	8		
in charge of	5	*in the hands of*	6	*to the amount of*	8		
in excess of	5	*for the duration of*	6	*against the background of*	8		
devoid of	5	*by comparison with*	6	*in the presence of*	8		

(continued)

Table 6 (continued)

CJEU—COMPETITION		CJEU—ALL		BLRC		BNC	
in the way of	5	*until the date of*	6	*with the assistance of*	8		
with the intention of	5	*in keeping with*	6	*for the sake of*	8		
in the eyes of	5	*under the supervision of*	6	*in the vicinity of*	7		
		on the occasion of	6	*in the matter of*	7		
		at the expense of	5	*on the day of*	7		
		within the ambit of	5	*in exchange for*	7		
				in the way of	7		
				in charge of	7		
				in the area of	7		
				in compliance with	6		
				for reasons of	6		
				at the expense of	6		
				without regard to	6		
				in spite of	6		
				in the amount of	6		
				in default of	6		
				in conformity with	5		
				on top of	5		
				to the detriment of	5		
				in the middle of	5		
				at the instance of	5		
				to the exclusion of	5		
				in consideration of	5		
				in conflict with	5		
				in the eyes of	5		
Total	12,444	Total	13,499	Total	9186	Total	3549

Competition judgments, ca. 3.8 times less than in the corpus of CJEU judgments relating to all types of subject matter, and only ca. 2.6 times less than in the BLRC. Therefore, in terms of the overall frequency, BLRC is the closest to the profile of general English (BNC). However, these results alone do not suffice to say with all confidence that EU and UK corpora differ substantially from each other, as there are significant differences in the frequencies of different types of complex prepositions in individual corpora. In order to do so, we need to first take a closer look at the frequency of individual types in both EU corpora, and then to compare their profiles in terms of the distribution of complex prepositions to the profile of UK law reports.

What is most telling about the phraseological profiles of both EU judgments and UK judicial decisions as well as general English, are the divergences in the frequency of the top complex prepositions. Across the corpora, the top 10 types of complex prepositions account for roughly 50%, 47%, 44% and 49%, respectively, of the total number of complex prepositions occurring at least five times and differ substantially in terms of frequency, thus contributing to the overall profiles of the texts incorporated in the corpora (see Table 7).

Both the corpora of CJEU judgments share a total of eight out of ten most-frequent complex prepositions, except for *as to* and *pursuant to*, which are present in the smaller CJEU corpus. Seven out of eight co-occurring complex prepositions have similar distribution in both corpora, whereas one of them, i.e. *in accordance with*, is markedly underrepresented in judgments relating to Competition Law (by ca. 29%). In both CJEU corpora, *in accordance with* is used in the same types of contexts, thus, it may be assumed that in Competition judgments there is a lesser need to specify conformity with the law, e.g.:

Table 7 Top 10 complex prepositions

CJEU—COMPETITION		CJEU—ALL		BLRC		BNC	
according to	892	*in accordance with*	927	*as to*	829	*out of*	496
relating to	818	*according to*	819	*in relation to*	649	*up to*	300
in order to	791	*relating to*	810	*in respect of*	520	*because of*	184
in accordance with	656	*in order to*	767	*for the purpose (s) of*	387	*according to*	162
for the purpose (s) of	639	*for the purpose (s) of*	726	*subject to*	377	*in order to*	126
within the meaning of	559	*within the meaning of*	642	*on behalf of*	299	*due to*	110
on the basis of	530	*subject to*	583	*out of*	274	*in terms of*	105
as to	506	*on the basis of*	569	*in order to*	252	*as to*	103
in the light of	499	*in the light of*	462	*in accordance with*	247	*at the end of*	98
pursuant to	409	*in respect of*	462	*relating to*	237	*instead of*	73

It should be noted, that, in accordance with the system established by the Treaties under Articles 281 EC and 184 EAEC, the Communities alone – and not their institutions – were vested with legal personality as legal persons governed by public law. That remains true now, in accordance with Article 47 TEU, as regards the European Union.

Nevertheless, the lower frequency of *in accordance with* in the smaller CJEU corpus may also be explained by the higher distribution of *according to*, which is used not only to specify conformity with the law, but also to introduce information and restate other entities' statements, e.g.:

According to settled case-law, the definition of aid is more general than that of a subsidy.

According to the General Court, since the measure is aimed at the undertakings which are the biggest polluters, that objective criterion is furthermore in conformity with the goal of the measure [...].

In general, *according to* has a similar distribution in both CJEU corpora, however, it is the most-frequent complex preposition in the case of Competition judgments; in the case of the bigger CJEU corpus *in accordance with* is the most often occurring complex preposition.

As for the BLRC, the top 10 complex prepositions occurring in this corpus were compared with the ones from the corpus of CJEU judgments relating to all types of subject matter, which represents the Eurolect, since the bigger CJEU corpus is more congruent with the BLRC in terms of the total number of tokens in the corpora. UK judicial discourse prioritises a similar but slightly different set of complex prepositions, which has a ca. 40% lower overall frequency. The most frequent complex preposition in the BLRC is *as to* as opposed to *in accordance with* in the case of the bigger CJEU corpus. As for the BLRC corpus, *in accordance with* occupies the ninth position, which suggests that there are fewer references to the (case) law. On the other hand, *as to* is not present in the top 10 list of complex prepositions identified for the bigger CJEU corpus, however, it occupies the eight position in the list generated for the corpus of Competition judgments. In general, there are six complex prepositions present in both the CJEU and BLRC lists, namely *as to*, *in relation to*, *on behalf of* and *out of*. Most of the complex prepositions, i.e. *for the purpose(s) of*, *subject to*, *in order to*, *in accordance with*, and *relating to*, are noticeably more salient in the CJEU corpus, except for *in respect of*, which is slightly underrepresented in the Eurolect.

As for the two most frequent complex prepositions in the BLRC, that is *as to* and *in relation to*, their main function is to introduce new topics, e.g.:

- *As to the remainder, this ground of appeal is unfounded.*

or specifying subject matter:

- *The Court is to make a decision as to costs.*

It needs to be noted that *relating to*, which is present in the 10th position, is used to express similar functions as *as to* and *in relation to*. These are illustrated by the following examples taken from the corpus of Competition judgments:

> [...], it should be borne in mind that, in an action on a decision relating to a competition matter, it is for the applicant to formulate his pleas in law [...].

> As regards the first issue relating to inadmissibility referred to by the Commission, which is based on the fact that interpretation of Regulation No 1206/2001 does not appear to be necessary for the resolution of the dispute in the main proceedings, it must be recalled that [...].

The quantitative data show that CJEU judgments prefer *relating to* as opposed to *as to* or *in relation to*, which are more frequent in the BLRC.

When it comes to the frequency of top ten complex prepositions in general English (BNC), it can be said that they are about 57% less frequent than in the BLRC and about 75% less frequent than in the bigger CJEU corpus. The corpus of general English contains eight complex prepositions which are not shared with the CJEU corpus, i.e. *out of*, *up to*, *because of*, *due to*, *in terms of*, *as to*, *at the end of*, and *instead of*; the two shared complex prepositions are *according to* and *in order to*, which are still ca. 5.5 and 6.3 times less frequent in general English. If we compare the list of top 10 complex prepositions generated for the BNC and compare it with the list generated for the BLRC, we will notice that only three prepositions are shared between both corpora, namely *out of*, *in order to* and *as to*, of which only *out of* has a higher frequency in general English.

5.3.2 Prepositional Patterns

What facilitates a quantitative analysis of complex prepositions is the fact that they can be divided into separate patterns, such as *as (a)* * *of*, *for (a/the)* * *of*, or *in (the)* * *of*.[26] Quantitative data concerning the total number of patterns and types of two- and three-word complex prepositions might contribute to making further generalisations as to the behavior of complex prepositions in the judicial genre and the way it compares to non-judicial language. Table 8 presents data on the distribution of all two-word patterns identified in the process of the analysis and their variety (no. of types).

The most frequently occurring pattern in all the corpora is the pattern * *to* (e.g. *according to*, *relating to*, *as to*, etc.), which is overrepresented in the BLRC as compared to the CJEU corpora. The following patterns are also overrepresented in the BLRC corpus: * *of* (e.g. *because of*, *irrespective of*, etc.) and * *with*. Therefore, only half of the two-word patterns is overrepresented in the Eurolect, namely * *from*, * *on*, * *for*. If we also consider the BNC, we will notice that **to*, * *from* and * *on* are underrepresented in general English as compared to EU and UK legal English.

All of the corpora are similar in terms of the variety of two-word complex prepositional patterns; however, it must be observed that the Eurolect is slightly more diverse in this regard. The types of the most frequent two-word complex prepositions which occur in the corpora are presented below.

[26] Pontrandolfo (2015), pp. 145–146.

Table 8 Two-word prepositional patterns (min. 5 occurrences)

	CJEU—COMPETITION		CJEU—ALL		BLRC		BNC	
	Total no. of patterns	Total no. of types of a given pattern	Total no. of patterns	Total no. of types of a pattern	Total no. of patterns	Total no. of types of a pattern	Total no. of patterns	Total no. of types of a pattern
Two-word prepositional patterns (min. 5 occurrences)								
* *to*	3604	12	3652	12	4565	12	900	11
* *of*	263	7	320	7	552	6	817	7
* *from*	107	3	98	3	85	3	72	2
* *with*	34	1	58	1	122	3	112	2
* *on*	33	1	40	1	23	1	24	1
* *for*	11	1	10	1	9	1	20	1
Total	4051	25	4178	25	5356	26	1944	24

The Pattern * *to*

- EN CJEU judgments – Competition (162): *according to, relating to, as to, pursuant to, contrary to, subject to, prior to, related to, up to, due to, owing to, subsequent to*
- EN CJEU judgments (897): *according to, relating to, subject to, as to, pursuant to, contrary to, prior to, related to, up to, due to, owing to, subsequent to*
- EN British Law Report Corpus: *as to, subject to, relating to, pursuant to, due to, prior to, contrary to, according to, up to, related to, subsequent to, owing to*
- EN British National Corpus (BNC): *up to, according to, due to, as to, subject to, related to, relating to, prior to, thanks to, contrary to, owing to*

The Pattern * *of*

- EN CJEU judgments – Competition (162): *because of, irrespective of, out of, regardless of, instead of, as of, devoid of*
- EN CJEU judgments (897): *because of, irrespective of, out of, regardless of, devoid of, instead of, as of*
- EN British Law Report Corpus: *out of, because of, as of, irrespective of, regardless of, instead of*
- EN British National Corpus (BNC): *out of, because of, instead of, ahead of, regardless of, as of, irrespective of*

Table 9 presents the distribution of all three-word patterns with at least five occurrences identified in the analysis and their variety (no. of types). As can be observed, three-word prepositional patterns are much more varied than two-word

Table 9 Three-word prepositional patterns (min. 5 occurrences) (frequencies normalised to one million words)

	CJEU—COMPETITION		CJEU—ALL		BLRC		BNC	
	Total no. of patterns	Total no. of types of a pattern	Total no. of patterns	Total no. of types of a pattern	Total no. of patterns	Total no. of types of a pattern	Total no. of patterns	Total no. of types of a pattern
*in (the) * of*	2296	22	2419	24	1964	38	644	34
*in * to*	1228	4	1193	4	986	4	231	4
*on (a/the) * of*	862	8	1065	8	792	10	140	8
*in * with*	834	7	1213	8	398	9	86	8
*for (a/the) * of*	715	5	815	6	451	5	38	3
*within (the) * of*	688	3	829	4	127	2	0	0
*with (a) * to*	560	4	501	4	159	4	41	3
*by (the) * of*	365	4	419	4	334	5	42	3
*as (a) * of*	187	3	174	3	244	3	104	2
*at (the) * of*	154	5	175	4	217	6	183	7
*by * to*	88	1	80	1	110	1	7	1
*without * to*	64	1	104	1	34	3	0	0
*to (the) * of*	59	4	44	4	35	4	0	0
*with (the) * of*	45	3	44	2	41	4	17	2
*from (the) * of*	32	1	30	1	21	1	0	0
*in * for*	32	2	26	1	18	2	10	1
*during (the) * from*	31	1	10	1	0	0	0	0
*as * as*	28	1	30	1	35	1	59	1
*with * from*	27	1	7	1	25	1	0	0
*at * with*	24	1	9	1	0	0	0	0
*outside (the) * of*	22	1	19	1	9	1	0	0
*by * with*	16	1	6	1	0	0	0	0
*until (the) * of*	14	1	6	1	0	0	0	0
*during (the) * of*	12	1	13	1	11	1	0	0
*as * to*	5	1	8	1	34	1	17	1
*under (the) * of*	0	0	6	1	0	0	0	0
Total 3-word complex prepositions	8388	86	9245	89	6045	106	1618	78
Total 2- + 3-word complex prepositions	12,439	111	13,423	114	11,401	132	3562	102

patterns, as there is a total of 26 three-word complex prepositional patterns as compared to six two-word patterns.

Nearly all three-word complex prepositional patterns are overrepresented in EU and UK judicial discourse as compared to the general English (BNC), except for the *as * as* pattern which is more frequent in general English. This confirms the often made observation that complex prepositions, e.g. *as a result of, in case of, in lieu of, in respect of, in pursuance of*, are a distinctive feature of English legal language.[27] If we compare the distribution of the three-word patterns in the bigger CJEU corpus and the BLRC, we will discover that as many as twenty prepositional patterns are overrepresented in the Eurolect: *in (the) * of, in * to, on (a/the) * of, in * with, for (a/the) * of, within (the) * of, with (a) * to, by (the) * of, without * to, to (the) * of, with (the) * of, from (the) * of, in * for, during (the) * from, at * with, outside (the) * of, by * with, until (the) * of, during (the) * of, under (the) * of*, while six are underrepresented (*as (a) * of, at (the) * of, by * to, as * as, with * from, as * to*).

Similar to two-word prepositional patterns (cf. Table 8), where ** to* had a disproportionately high frequency as compared to the remaining patterns, in the case of three-word patterns, in the CJEU corpora and the BLRC, the most frequent pattern *in (the) * of* is around two times more frequent than the second top pattern *in * to*. In terms of the total number of types of a given preposition in each of the corpora, the BLRC has the highest amount of types of patterns, i.e. 106, whereas the bigger CJEU corpus has 89 types, and the BNC has the lowest number of types, i.e. 78. This suggests that the BNC is less repetitive in terms of the distribution of three-word complex prepositions, as it has a lower number of occurrences of all the patterns than the CJEU corpus, while having a higher number of types of patterns than the Eurolect. Therefore, we might draw the conclusion that the Eurolect is more repetitive in regard to three-word complex prepositions.

The types of three-word complex prepositions which occur in the corpora most often are listed below.

The Pattern *in (the) * of*

- EN CJEU judgments – Competition (162): *in the light of, in respect of, in support of, in the context of, in the case of, in the absence of, in view of, in the course of, in the form of, in favour of, in the field of, in the event of, in terms of, in the territory of, in the area of, in the amount of, in the interest(s) of, in pursuit of, in charge of, in excess of, in the way of, in the eyes of*
- EN CJEU judgments (897): *in the light of, in respect of, in the context of, in support of, in the case of, in the territory of, in the absence of, in the course of, in the event of, in view of, in the field of, in favour of, in the form of, in terms of, in the interest(s) of, in the area of, in the amount of, in excess of, in lieu of, in consequence of, in the name of, in the sphere of, in spite of, in the hands of*
- EN British Law Report Corpus: *in respect of, in the case of, in the light of, in the course of, in the context of, in terms of, in the absence of, in consequence of, in*

[27] cf. Quirk et al. (1985), p. 672, Biel (2015), and Pontrandolfo (2015), pp. 145–146.

favour of, in support of, in the interest(s) of, in view of, in the event of, in the form of, in the hands of, in excess of, in pursuance of, in the name of, in front of, in advance of, in the territory of, in the face of, in the nature of, in lieu of, in the field of, in the region of, in the presence of, in the vicinity of, in the matter of, in the way of, in charge of, in the area of, in spite of, in the amount of, in default of, in the middle of, in consideration of, in the eyes of

- EN British National Corpus (BNC): *in terms of, in front of, in the case of, in favour of, in respect of, in the middle of, in spite of, in the context of, in the light of, in the course of, in the form of, in charge of, in the absence of, in view of, in the face of, in support of, in the event of, in the hands of, in search of, in the interest (s) of, in return for, in the way of, in excess of, in the direction of, in the presence of, in the name of, in the wake of, in the field of, in the area of, in a state of, in the shape of, in advance of, in the heart of, in the midst of*

The Pattern *in * to*

- EN CJEU judgments – Competition (162): *in order to, in relation to, in addition to, in response to*
- EN CJEU judgments (897): *in order to, in relation to, in addition to, in response to*
- EN British Law Report Corpus: *in relation to, in order to, in addition to, in response to*
- EN British National Corpus (BNC): *in order to, in relation to, in addition to, in response to*

The Pattern *on (a/the) * of*

- EN CJEU judgments – Competition (162): *on the basis of, on behalf of, on the part of, on account of, on (the) ground(s) of, on the principle of, on a point of, on the question of*
- EN CJEU judgments (897): *on the basis of, on behalf of, on (the) ground(s) of, on the part of, on account of, on a point of, on the principle of, on the occasion of*
- EN British Law Report Corpus: *on behalf of, on (the) ground(s) of, on the basis of, on the part of, on account of, on the issue of, on the question of, on a point of, on the day of, on top of*
- EN British National Corpus (BNC): *on the basis of, on behalf of, on top of, on the part of, on (the) ground(s) of, on the edge of, on the subject of, on account of*

6 Functions of Complex Prepositions in Competition Law Judgments

Owing to the multi-faceted nature of complex prepositions and their meanings, their functions in the CJEU judgments were decoded based on the analysis of concordances, i.e. the context in which they appear, which were generated by Wordsmith Tools 7.0, as some meanings may be only deciphered when examining a complex preposition within a clause.[28] Despite the effort, the presentation below draws only a cursory picture of the most widely used meanings in the corpus of CJEU Competition judgments, and does not attempt to be exhaustive. Table 10 presents the major functions of complex prepositions in Competition judgments.

Table 10 Complex prepositions: total number of patterns and types according to functions (the total number of types of complex prepositions normalised to one million words)

CJEU—COMPETITION		
	Total number of individual types of complex prepositional patterns fulfilling different functions in judgments	Total number of occurrences of types of complex prepositions fulfilling different functions in judgments
Anchoring, particularisation	32	4227
Referencing (text deixis)	17	3977
Purpose, goal	6	1542
Time deixis	13	538
Cause, effect	10	533
Disagreement, contrast	6	384
Conditionals and hypothetical patterns	5	306
Means, instrument	3	299
Inclusion and exclusion	7	294
Participative patterns	4	208
Benefit, detriment	8	186

[28]Quirk et al. (1985), p. 673.

6.1 Anchoring, Particularisation

Complex prepositions acting as anchoring and particularisation devices[29] represent the most frequently used prepositions in CJEU Competition judgments. They have the highest total number of patterns out of all the function groups, i.e. 32 patterns with a normalised frequency of 4227 occurrences in the corpus of CJEU Competition judgments:

- *in respect of, relating to, with regard to, in view of, in the light of, in relation to, related to, in terms of, with respect to, as to, in the amount of, on a point of, on the question of, in the eyes of, in support of, in the absence of, in the field of, up to, in the territory of, in the area of, as far as, out of, to the amount of, for the sake of, in return for, instead of, in exchange for, in excess of, at the head of, to the extent of, in the case of, in the form of*

The following examples illustrate the context of use of selected nearly synonymous complex prepositions, i.e. *relating to*, *with regard to*, *in relation to*, and *as to*:

#2 relating to

- *[...], it should be borne in mind that, in an action on a decision relating to a competition matter, it is for the applicant to formulate his pleas in law [...].* (=on, related to)
- *As regards the first issue relating to inadmissibility referred to by the Commission, which is based on the fact that interpretation of Regulation No 1206/2001 does not appear to be necessary for the resolution of the dispute in the main proceedings, it must be recalled that [...].* (=regarding)

#11 with regard to (incorrect form: **with regards to*)

- *With regard to the penalties for infringements of competition law, the second subparagraph of Article 15(2) of Regulation No 17 provides that in fixing the amount of the fine, regard is to be had both to the gravity and to the duration of the infringement. The same wording appears in Article 23(3) of Regulation No 1/2003.*
- Function in text: introducing a topic (=in reference to, in regard to)

In the following two examples, we can observe a redundant use of *with regard to*, which could be substituted with the simple prepositions *to* and *into*, respectively, thus contributing to less wordiness.

- *Those considerations apply particularly with regard to a tax system which, as in the present case, instead of laying down general rules [...].*

---

[29] cf. Biel (2015), pp. 157–158.

– *The third plea alleges breach of essential procedural requirements in the context of the Commission's investigation with regard to offshore companies.*

Similarly, i*n relation to* is also used to specify subject matter and may be substituted by, e.g. *regarding* and *with regard to*. It also tends to be overused:

#14 in relation to

– *Those parties argue, first, that the Kingdom of Sweden has not challenged the statement of the General Court, contained in paragraph 49 of the judgment under appeal, that the public interest in obtaining communication of a document does not have the same weight in relation to a document falling within an administrative procedure concerning, for example, competition law, as it does in relation to a document concerning a legislative procedure.*

As to is the last often used complex preposition functioning as an anchoring and particularisation device synonymous to the complex prepositions mentioned above. It is used to both introduce new topics as well as specify subject matter and may be substituted by, e.g. *with regard to*.

#8 as to

– *As to the remainder, this ground of appeal is unfounded.*
– *The Court is to make a decision as to costs.*

6.2 Referencing (Text Deixis)

Complex prepositions used to express text deixis are the second most widely used group which numbers 17 different types of complex prepositions and 3977 occurrences:

– *in accordance with, pursuant to, subject to, on the basis of, without prejudice to, in connection with, in compliance with, in conformity with, in line with, within the meaning of, according to, in the context of, within the scope of, with reference to, outside the scope of, on the principle of, within the framework of*

The following example sentences demonstrate the context of use of several nearly synonymous complex prepositions, namely *according to*, *in accordance to* and *pursuant to*, as well as two complex prepositions, the meaning of which is peculiar to legal English, that is *subject to* and *pursuant to*:

#1 according to:

– *According to the General Court, since the measure is aimed at the undertakings which are the biggest polluters, that objective criterion is furthermore in conformity with the goal of the measure [...].*
– Function in text: restating statements (=as stated/reported by)

- *According to settled case-law, the definition of aid is more general than that of a subsidy.*
- Function in text: introducing information (=under)
- *According to the Commission, [...], the selective advantages enjoyed by offshore companies cannot be justified by the nature of the proposed tax reform.*
- Function in text: restating statements / unsubstantiated information (=as stated/ reported by)

#4 in accordance with

- *In accordance with this Directive, Member States shall protect the fundamental rights and freedoms of natural persons, and in particular their right to privacy with respect to the processing of personal data.*
- Function in text: stating conformity with the law (=under)
- *It should be noted, that, in accordance with the system established by the Treaties under Articles 281 EC and 184 EAEC, the Communities alone – and not their institutions – were vested with legal personality as legal persons governed by public law. That remains true now, in accordance with Article 47 TEU, as regards the European Union.*
- Function in text: stating conformity with the law (=under)

#10 pursuant to (=under, in accordance with)

- *The aid to be recovered pursuant to a recovery decision includes, in accordance with Article 14(2) of that regulation, interest.*
- Function in text: stating conformity with the law (=under)
- *The employer's obligations pursuant to those provisions must be carried out by the management of the establishment in question.*
- Function in text: stating conformity with the law (=under)

The following two sentences illustrate the use of *subject to* and *without prejudice to*. The first one introduces a condition which is to be adhered to, whereas the second one informs the recipient that the earlier clause should not be contradictory to what follows after *without prejudice to*:

#15 subject to

- *The Court has held, in competition law cases, that the application of this principle is subject to the threefold condition that in the two cases the facts must be the same, the offender the same and the legal interest protected the same [...].*

#64 without prejudice to

- *The requirement that the confidentiality of the proceedings of public authorities must be provided for by law applies without prejudice to the other obligations imposed by Article 4 of Directive 2003/4 [...].*

6.3 Purpose, Goal

Complex prepositions expressing purposive functions are not overly varied, as there are only six types of complex prepositional patterns with 1542 occurrences. Purposive functions in the EU case law are connected with the interpretation of legal acts, previous judgments and the actions of the parties to the proceedings.

– *for the purpose(s) of, in order to, with a view to, with the intention of, with the aim of, in pursuit of*
  - *It is apparent from the case-law that the actual conduct which an undertaking claims to have adopted is irrelevant for the purposes of evaluating a cartel's effect on the market, since account must only be taken of effects resulting from the infringement taken as a whole [. . .].*

6.4 Time Deixis

Time deictic expressions are ca. three times less frequent, but ca. two times more varied than complex prepositions in the previous group. They are used to specify duration and consecutive actions or events.

– *for a period of, during the period from, during the period of, from the date of, until the date of, at the end of, prior to, at the time of, subsequent to, in the course of, as from, with effect from, as of*
  - *As regards the applicant undertakings in IMI and Others v Commission, it is clear from paragraph 96 of the judgment in that case that the General Court regarded the infringement as having been interrupted for a period of a little more than 16 months.*

6.5 Cause, Effect

Complex prepositions used to express cause and effect relations are slightly less varied and frequent than time deictic expressions. Their function is self-explanatory, as they are used to provide detailed explanations, which form the overall argumentation of the Court.

– *due to, as a result of, by reason of, because of, owing to, on (the) ground(s) of, on account of, in response to, as a consequence of, for reasons of*
  - *Consequently, due to the use of [such] undefined terms, the General Court did not provide an adequate statement of reasons in support of its judgment.*

6.6 Disagreement, Contrast

The function of expressing disagreement and contrast is performed by six complex prepositions:

– *by comparison with, in comparison with, as opposed to, at odds with, in the way of, contrary to*

  • *[...] the specifications in the call for tender had failed to ensure effective competition and that the financial compensation had not been defined by reference to a base cost established in advance or by comparison with the cost structure of other comparable shipping companies.*

6.7 Conditional and Hypothetical Patterns

Implicit conditional and hypothetical patterns are expressed with the help of the following complex prepositions:

– *in the event of, in the case of, regardless of, depending on, irrespective of*

  • *To this effect and in the event of a procedure before national courts, the Member States concerned shall take all necessary steps which are available in their respective legal systems, including provisional measures, without prejudice to Community law.*

6.8 Means, Instrument

The following complex prepositions are used to specify (legal) tools necessary for the performance of various actions.

– *by means of, by way of, by virtue of*

  • *In view of the extent of the discretion enjoyed by the Council in this case, the contested decision cannot be regarded as breaching the principle of proportionality only because it would have been possible for the Republic of Poland to pursue the objective referred to in paragraph 131 above by means of another type of aid scheme.*

6.9 Inclusion and Exclusion

The next function performed by complex prepositions concerns the including and excluding patterns.

– *with the exception of, except for, apart from, together with, in conjunction with, as part of, in addition to*

  - *With the exception of pleas involving matters of public policy which the Courts are required to raise of their own motion, such as the failure to state reasons for a contested decision, it is for the applicant to raise pleas in law against that decision and to adduce evidence in support of those pleas.*

6.10 Participative Patterns

The penultimate group performs the function of introducing individuals or entities either directly or indirectly involved in the Court's process of coming to a binding decision.

– *on behalf of, in charge of, on the part of, at the request of*

  - *THE COURT (First Chamber),*
  - *[. . .]*
  - *having regard to the written procedure and further to the hearing on 18 March 2010,*
  - *after considering the observations submitted on behalf of:*
  - *[. . .]*
  - *the Polish Government, by M. Dowgielewicz, acting as Agent, [. . .]*
  - *At the request of the Commission, the acting competition authority shall make available to the Commission other documents it holds which are necessary for the assessment of the case.*

6.11 Benefit, Detriment

The last group of complex prepositions, which is in fact quite varied, is used to express either benefit or detriment affecting individuals or entities.

– *for the benefit of, in the interest(s) of, in favour of, exempt from, to the detriment of, to the exclusion of, at the expense of, devoid of*

  - *In the present case, as is clear from paragraph 46 of the present judgment, the Decree of 2001 provides that it is for the credit institutions to implement that decree and thereby to benefit from the State guarantee. Thus, the measure at issue appears to be exclusively for the benefit of the credit establishments.*

In conclusion, complex prepositions fulfil various important discourse functions in EU judgments. Considering the total number of types of complex prepositional patterns fulfilling different functions and the total number of occurrences of these patterns, five discourse functions appear as particularly frequent, namely: anchoring/particularisation, referencing (text deixis), purpose/goal, time deixis, and cause/effect. The high distribution of complex prepositions with these functions contributes to their high salience in the language of judges.

7 Conclusions

The results yielded by the analysis demonstrate that complex prepositions contribute greatly to the phraseological profile of the genre of EU judgments owing to their overrepresentation as compared to UK judicial decisions (BLRC) and non-legal English (BNC). The overall shape of the phraseological profile of the genre is also shaped by the high distribution of simple prepositions and slightly by marginal and compound prepositions. Excluding the cases where simple prepositions are parts of the complex prepositions, the total number of simple prepositions in the corpus of CJEU Competition judgments is ca. 11 times higher than the total number of complex prepositional patterns, be it two- or three-word sequences. This observation together with the cursory examination of the clausal context of simple and complex prepositions leads us to believe that prepositions in general raise the degree of linguistic precision in the judgments, thus creating an impression of highly analytical nature of the genre.

Furthermore, the results confirm the usefulness of corpus methodology in allowing both translators and legal practitioners to learn about the context of use of crucial language items, which, in turn, might help them to properly understand EU judgments (relating to Competition Law) and to produce texts resembling the established conventions of the genre, as in the case of a specific text type, it is crucial to stay close to its linguistic profile. Both authors of such texts as well as their recipients should have the feeling of "being in a genre".[30] As claimed by Biel,[31] the conventional usage of phraseological patterns contributes to greater readability and lesser processing effort on the part of readers. Although an excessive use of complex prepositions in EU judgments contributes to greater wordiness, while at the same time it makes them less easily comprehensible to non-specialists as viewed by advocates of plain English,[32] it needs to be admitted that it also raises the texts' overall level of precision. Results of studies similar to this one[33] provide tools necessary to all those who are in need of producing texts characterised by a high

[30]cf. Biel (2014), p. 190.

[31]Biel (2015), p. 159.

[32]cf. *inter alia* Schiess (2007), Garner (2013) and Kalinowski (2015).

[33]cf. Biel (2015) and Pontrandolfo (2015).

degree of stylistic congruence to original texts of a given genre, e.g. translators and legal practitioners. They may also be used by legal trainers responsible for educating aspiring (international) lawyers and legal translators (lawyer-linguists) and interpreters. Faithfulness to the phraseological profile of the genre remains particularly important to novice translators who are in dire need of developing their phraseological competence as regards many demanding genres, so that their translations read naturally.

In conclusion, the study at hand has demonstrated that in terms of the distribution of simple, marginal, compound and complex prepositions, the phraseological profile of EU judgments is not congruent with the profiles of UK judicial decisions (BLRC) and general English (BNC). However, it also needs to be borne in mind that complex prepositions are just one factor affecting the overall phraseological profile of a genre and that others include, e.g. collocations (e.g. *to impose a sentence*) and routine formulae.

References

Biber D, Conrad S, Leech G (2002) Longman student grammar of spoken and written English. Longman, London

Biel Ł (2014) Phraseology in legal translation: a corpus-based analysis of textual mapping in EU law. In: Cheng L, Sin KK, Wagner A (eds) The Ashgate handbook of legal translation. Ashgate, Farnham, pp 178–192

Biel Ł (2015) Phraseological profiles of legislative genres: complex prepositions as a special case of legal phrasemes in EU law and national law. Fachsprache 37:139–160

Biel Ł (2016) Mixed corpus design for researching the Eurolect: A genre-based comparable-parallel corpus in the PL EUROLECT project. In: Gruszczyńska E, Leńko-Szymańska A (eds) Polskojęzyczne korpusy równoległe. Polish-language Parallel Corpora. Instytut Lingwistyki Stosowanej WLS UW, Warszawa, pp 197–208

Crystal D, Davy D (1969) Investigating English style. Longman, London

Foley M, Hall D (2004) Longman advanced learners' grammar: a self-study reference & practice book with answers. Longman, London

Garner B (2013) The redbook: a manual on legal style, 3rd edn. West Academic Publishing, St. Paul

Haigh R (2009) Legal English, 2nd edn. Routledge, New York

Kalinowski BA (2015) What's 'of' got to do with it? Lawyers and prepositional phrases. Mich Bar J 94:50–51

Kilgarriff A, Baisa V, Bušta J, Jakubíček M, Kovář V, Michelfeit J, Rychlý P, Suchomel V (2014) The sketch engine: ten years on. Lexicography 1(1):7–36

Klégr A (1997) English complex prepositions of the prepositional phrase type. Acta Universitatis Carolinae – Philologica. Prague Studies in English XXII 5:51–78

Mattila HES (2006) Comparative legal linguistics. Ashgate, Aldershot

Pontrandolfo G (2013) La fraseología como estilema del lenguaje judicial: el caso de las locuciones prepositivas desde una perspectiva contrastiva. Cerlis Series 3:187–215

Pontrandolfo G (2015) Investigating judicial phraseology with COSPE: a contrastive corpus-based study. In: Fantinuoli C, Zanettin F (eds) New directions in corpus-based translation studies. Language Science Press, Berlin, pp 137–160

Quirk R, Greenbaum S, Leech G, Svartvik J (1985) A comprehensive grammar of the English language. Longman, London

Riera C (2015) Plain English in legal language: a comparative study of two UK Acts of Parliament. Alicante J Engl Stud (28):147–163

Schiess W (2007) Mind your prepositions. In: Austin Lawyer 13. Available via SSRN. https://papers.ssrn.com/sol3/papers.cfm?abstract_id=1322086. Accessed 17 Feb 2018

Scott M (2017) WordSmith Tools version 7. Lexical Analysis Software, Stroud

The British National Corpus, version 3 (BNC XML Edition) (2007) Distributed by Oxford University Computing Services on behalf of the BNC Consortium. http://www.natcorp.ox.ac.uk. Accessed 17 Feb 2018

Dariusz Koźbiał is a PhD candidate at the Faculty of Applied Linguistics, University of Warsaw, and an investigator in the research project "The Eurolect: an EU variant of Polish and its impact on administrative Polish" funded by the Polish National Science Centre.

Plain English and the EU: Still Trying to Fight the Fog?

Arianna Grasso

Abstract The plain English movement has now been active for almost 50 years and legalese was one of its first targets worldwide because of the role of English as *lingua franca* in the legal sector. The European Union took up the challenge at the beginning of the 1980s, with proclamations of its intention to turn complex institutional language into clear and effective writing set out in various guidelines and glossaries. Almost 40 years later, has the EU really been able to "fight the fog"? I am going to answer this question by looking at the main EU clear writing hints and by comparing them with the official recommendations by the plain English campaign. After this overview, I will explore the implementation of the plain English guidelines by the European institutions by analysing the main EU Competition Law legislation.

1 The Plain English Movement

Although official criticism of complex institutional and legal language is quite recent, as far back as 1387 Geoffrey Chaucer had the host of his *Clerk's prologue and tale*[1] tell the clerk to:

> Speketh so pleyn at this tyme, we yow preye,
> That we may understonde what ye seye.[2]

Later on, in 1946, his fellow countryman George Orwell,[3] among others, started to challenge English writers' tendency to use complex prose and inflated vocabulary and showed that writing could be clear and elegant at the same time.

[1]Chaucer (2008), p. 322.

[2]In modern English: "We pray you, speak plainly at this time, so we can understand what you're saying".

[3]Orwell (1946), pp. 252–265.

A. Grasso (✉)
Università degli Studi dell'Insubria, Como, Italy
e-mail: info@ariannagrasso.com

S. Marino et al. (eds.), *Language and Law*,
https://doi.org/10.1007/978-3-319-90905-9_17

In 1954, the British civil servant Sir Ernest Gowers published *The complete plain words,*[4] in which he stated that writers should:

1. Know the matter of their writing perfectly and adapt their style to the readers' needs;
2. Write in a clear, simple, and concise manner;
3. Be precise and complete; and
4. Avoid generic words and use familiar ones.

Actually, the first and real plain English movement was born in the United States at the beginning of the 1970s. Initially, the staunchest promoters were banks and insurance companies driven by financial aims: some research had shown that using plain language drastically reduced prospects of litigation with clients, hence legal fees.[5]

In the same years, these general principles started to be seriously considered in the fields of law and government in the United Kingdom as well.

The awareness reached its climax on 26 July 1979, when Martin Cutts, director of the Plain Language Commission, launched the Plain English Campaign in Parliament Square, London. In 2009, when celebrating its thirtieth year since foundation, the Campaign boasted over 12,000 members in 80 countries and its Crystal Mark of approval had appeared on more than 18,300 documents.[6]

Plain English theorists have always included "legalese" in their language revolution because it is too complex, obscure, and over-sophisticated. They have always challenged, among other things, the use of (1) archaic, complex and foreign (including Latin) words and phrases; (2) legal pairs and triplets; (3) redundant and compound words; (4) tautologies; (5) passive voice; (6) nominalisation; and (7) very long sentences with numerous modifying clauses and repetition.

2 Plain Language and the European Union

The European Union's first response to the above recommendations was the Commission's *English style guide* in 1982. The eighth edition, dated 2018, reminds readers that the guide is based on "excellent advice on how to improve writing style" in *The plain English guide* by Martin Cutts, who had launched the Plain English Campaign (see Sect. 1 above), and *Style: toward clarity and grace* by Joseph M. Williams, "all of which encourage the use of good plain English".[7]

---

[4]Gowers (1954), pp. 1–7.

[5]Redish (1985), pp. 125–138.

[6]Plain English Campaign. http://www.plainenglish.co.uk. Accessed 23 Feb 2018.

[7]European Commission (2018), p. 1.

The *English style guide*'s authors admit the difficulty of writing in clear language at the Commission due to the complexity of the subject matter and the fact that more and more is written in English by (and for) non-native speakers but conclude that

> we must nevertheless try to set an example by using language that is as clear, simple and accessible as possible, out of courtesy to our readers and consideration for the image of the Commission.[8]

This proclamation and the milestones of the plain English campaign quoted in the Preface might mislead readers into believing that the Commission would take the same strong positions on the subject in the rest of the guide.

On the contrary, the Preface itself makes an important exception to the general plain English rule by allowing for the use of legal or bureaucratic language in legislative texts, preparatory drafting, departmental memos or papers for specialist committees. According to the guide, language that might be regarded as "pompous" elsewhere is admitted in those texts. In documents such as departmental memos or papers for specialist committees, in particular, 'Eurospeak' should be considered as acceptable "professional shorthand" and plain English in these documents would "waste time and simply irritate readers".[9]

The guide also states that "accuracy and clarity are of course paramount" in those technical texts, apparently excluding that legislators might reach such a goal by using plain language. However, it points out that "the specialist terms must be embedded in rock-solid, straightforward English syntax",[10] thus opening up to plain English in terms of structure if not lexicon.

By contrast, the guide discourages the use of in-house jargon in documents addressing the general public, such as leaflets or web pages, which must be

> immediately understandable even to those unfamiliar with the workings and vocabulary of the EU.[11]

The guide contains rules about very specific issues such as punctuation, spelling and capitalisation, but deals with only part of the plain English topics listed in Sect. 1 above. It basically suggests using short paragraphs and simple syntax, avoiding Latin as much as possible and *here-/there-* adverbs. Its partial and cautious position towards plain English is also evident in the section devoted to these adverbs, where it "normally" advises against their use but allows for it if readers "feel" they "must use such forms" sometimes.[12]

Fifteen years after its first plain language guidelines, the European Commission started the "Fight the Fog" campaign. The *How to write clearly* guide related to the campaign is regularly updated online like the *English style guide*.

---

[8]European Commission (2018), p. 1.

[9]European Commission (2018), p. 1.

[10]European Commission (2018), p. 1.

[11]European Commission (2018), p. 1.

[12]European Commission (2018), p. 44.

This publication gives warmer recommendations in favour of plain language, possibly as a result of the proliferation and adoption of these principles in the United Kingdom, in the United States and in other English-speaking countries during the 15 years between the first edition of the *English style guide* and the *How to write clearly* publication. As a matter of fact, the general tone and contents of the publication mirror the style and recommendations of the plain English campaign, which are all but soft.[13] Again, the *Oxford guide to plain English* by the Campaign's founder Martin Cutts is quoted as the main source on which the guide draws.[14]

Nevertheless, the guide is prefaced in such a way as to leave no doubts as to the nature of its recommendations as "hints" and not "rules".

Overall, the guide focuses on the following "hints"[15]:

Hint 1: Think before you write
Hint 2: Focus on the reader — be direct and interesting
Hint 3: Get your document into shape
Hint 4: KISS: Keep It Short and Simple
Hint 5: Make sense — structure your sentences
Hint 6: Cut out excess nouns — verb forms are livelier
Hint 7: Be concrete, not abstract
Hint 8: Prefer active verbs to passive — and name the agent
Hint 9: Beware of false friends, jargon and abbreviations
Hint 10: Revise and check

In 2015, the European Parliament, the Council and the Commission issued the second edition of the *Joint practical guide for persons involved in the drafting of European Union legislation*. This guide too is prefaced with the best intentions towards "better law-making by clearer, simpler acts complying with principles of good legislative drafting".[16]

The guide is the result of previous steps by the Council and the Commission to achieve this goal.[17] This goal was later reaffirmed by Declaration No 39 on the quality of the drafting of Community legislation, annexed to the final act of the Amsterdam Treaty and other common guidelines to improve the quality of drafting of Community legislation.

The guide underlines the need for the EU legal acts to be both clear and precise mainly for democratic purposes but also to avoid disputes and restrictive interpretation by the Court of Justice.[18] This seems to be in contrast with the possibility to use

[13]How to write in plain English. http://www.plainenglish.co.uk/files/howto.pdf. Accessed 28 Feb 2018.

[14]European Commission (2011), p. 16.

[15]European Commission (2011), p. 2.

[16]European Union (2015), p. 6.

[17]Council Resolution of 8 June 1993 on the quality of drafting of Community legislation (OJ C 166, 17.06.1993, p. 1).

[18]European Union (2015), p. 10.

"pompous" language in legislative texts allowed by the *English style guide* a year later.

The *Joint practical guide* basically suggests the same plain language options set out in the *How to write clearly* guide but also leaves readers with the same puzzled feeling over the nature of its position that they experienced in reading the above "hints".

In the first pages the modal *must* is used to refer to the necessity of writing in a clear, simple and precise manner.[19] In the rest of the publication *must* is used in sentences suggesting the need to use a specific drafting style depending on the type of act (Regulation, Directive, Decision, Recommendation). In the same paragraphs the modals *shall* and *should* are also used. As we will see in Sect. 3.8, *shall* is used both as positive imperative and future within the European Union, while *should* leaves no doubt as to the soft nature of the recommendation. Again, this creates confusion as to the position taken by the EU with respect to plain language even in its most complex form: legislation.

The 2014 European Commission *Clear English tips for translators* give the same suggestions as the *How to write clearly* guide but expand the topics. The result is a detailed handbook to help translators (especially non-native speakers) write in correct and plain English.

The EU also published useful explanations of Eurojargon and relevant translations into plain language, thus seeking

> to stimulate thinking on which EU terms might constitute jargon and how they could be expressed more clearly.[20]

3 Has the EU Really Been Able to "Fight the Fog"?

Without aiming to be exhaustive, I have analysed the main EU Competition legislation[21] to check whether the Commission, the Parliament and the Council of the European Union have actually implemented the abovementioned hints 35 years after their first proclamation in favour of plain English.

---

[19]European Union (2015), p. 6.

[20]EU jargon in English and some possible alternatives. http://ec.europa.eu/ipg/content/tips/words-style/jargon-alternatives_en.htm. Accessed 2 Mar 2018.

[21]Articles 101–109 of the Treaty on the Functioning of the European Union (OJ C 202, 7.6.2016, p. 88); Commission Regulation (EU) No 651/2014 of 17 June 2014 declaring certain categories of aid compatible with the internal market in application of Articles (OJ L 187, 26.6.2014, p. 1); Commission Directive 2002/77/EC of 16 September 2002 on competition in the markets for electronic communications networks and services (OJ L 249, 17.9.2002, p. 21); Commission Directive 2006/111/EC of 16 November 2006 on the transparency of financial relations between Member States and public undertakings as well as on financial transparency within certain undertakings (OJ L 318, 17.11.2006, p. 17); Commission Directive 2008/63/EC of 20 June 2008 on competition in the markets in telecommunications terminal equipment (OJ L 162, 21.6.2008, p. 20); Directive 2014/104/EU of the European Parliament and of the Council of 26 November 2014 on

The corpus I have chosen for the study includes documents written over an 11-year time frame, which makes it possible to analyse the evolution of the trend towards plain language within the EU.

I have concentrated on the suggestions strictly related to the morpho-syntactic aspects of language, it being impossible to assess the implementation of the hints concerned with planning, shaping and revising the text.

certain rules governing actions for damages under national law for infringements of the competition law provisions of the Member States and of the European Union (OJ L 349, 5.12.2014, p. 1); Council Regulation (EC) No 1/2003 of 16 December 2002 on the implementation of the rules on competition laid down in Articles 81 and 82 of the Treaty (OJ L 1, 4.1.2003, p. 1); Council Regulation (EC) No 139/2004 of 20 January 2004 on the control of concentrations between undertakings (OJ L 24, 29.1.2004, p. 1); Commission Regulation (EC) No 772/2004 of 27 April 2004 on the application of Article 81(3) of the Treaty to categories of technology transfer agreements (OJ L 123, 27.4.2004, p. 11); Commission Regulation (EC) No 773/2004 of 7 April 2004 relating to the conduct of proceedings by the Commission pursuant to Articles 81 and 82 of the EC Treaty (OJ L 123, 27.4.2004, p. 1); Council Regulation (EC) No 1184/2006 of 24 July 2006 applying certain rules of competition to the production of, and trade in, agricultural products (OJ L 214, 4.8.2006, p. 7); Council Regulation (EU) 2015/1588 of 13 July 2015 on the application of Articles 107 and 108 of the Treaty on the Functioning of the European Union to certain categories of horizontal State aid (codification) (OJ L 248, 24.9.2015, p. 1); Council Regulation (EU) 2015/1589 of 13 July 2015 laying down detailed rules for the application of Article 108 of the Treaty on the Functioning of the European Union (codification) (OJ L 248, 24.9.2015, p. 9); Commission Regulation (EU) No 330/2010 of 20 April 2010 on the application of Article 101(3) of the Treaty on the Functioning of the European Union to categories of vertical agreements and concerted practices (OJ L 102, 23.4.2010, p. 1); Commission Regulation (EU) No 360/2012 of 25 April 2012 on the application of Articles 107 and 108 of the Treaty on the Functioning of the European Union to *de minimis* aid granted to undertakings providing services of general economic interest (OJ L 114, 26.4.2012, p. 8); Commission Regulation (EU) No 717/2014 of 27 June 2014 on the application of Articles 107 and 108 of the Treaty on the Functioning of the European Union to *de minimis* aid in the fishery and aquaculture sector (OJ L 190, 28.6.2014, p. 45); Commission Regulation (EU) No 1218/2010 of 14 December 2010 on the application of Article 101(3) of the Treaty on the Functioning of the European Union to certain categories of specialisation agreements (OJ L 335, 18.12.2010, p. 43); Commission Regulation (EU) No 1388/2014 of 16 December 2014 declaring certain categories of aid to undertakings active in the production, processing and marketing of fishery and aquaculture products compatible with the internal market in application of Articles 107 and 108 of the Treaty on the Functioning of the European Union (OJ L 369, 24.12.2014, p. 37); Commission Regulation (EU) No 1407/2013 of 18 December 2013 on the application of Articles 107 and 108 of the Treaty on the Functioning of the European Union to *de minimis* aid (OJ L 352, 24.12.2013, p. 1); Commission Regulation (EU) No 1408/2013 of 18 December 2013 on the application of Articles 107 and 108 of the Treaty on the Functioning of the European Union to *de minimis* aid in the agriculture sector (OJ L 352, 24.12.2013, p. 9); Commission Regulation (EU) No 1217/2010 of 14 December 2010 on the application of Article 101(3) of the Treaty on the Functioning of the European Union to certain categories of research and development agreements (OJ L 335, 18.12.2010, p. 36).

3.1 *Keep It Short and Simple*

The *How to write clearly* guide points out that "the value of a document does not increase the longer it gets".[22] According to this publication and the *Fight the fog* guide, a document should be 15 pages long at most, and a sentence should not contain more than 20 words. This is in line with The *Plain English guide*'s suggestions that the guide's preface specifies as the main source it draws on (see Sect. 2).[23]

Only 11 out of the 20 documents in the corpus comprise less than 15 pages and one of the documents is even 78 pages long.

As to sentence length, the 20 words suggestion is by far the least followed. Most sentences are at least twice as long and some even include more than 90 words.

The following sentence, for instance, is made up of 61 words:

> In all cases where, as a result of the preliminary examination, the Commission cannot find that the aid is compatible with the internal market, the formal investigation procedure should be opened in order to enable the Commission to gather all the information it needs to assess the compatibility of the aid and to allow the interested parties to submit their comments. (Recital 8 of Regulation 2015/1589)

However, it is very easy to split the sentence in two, and have half the number of words while conveying the meaning more clearly:

> The formal investigation procedure should be opened in all cases where, as a result of the preliminary examination, the Commission cannot find that the aid is compatible with the internal market. This would enable the Commission to gather all the information it needs to assess the compatibility of the aid and to allow the interested parties to submit their comments.

As a matter of fact, the 20 words recommendation is maybe too unrealistic given the complexity of the texts it refers to. However, as we saw in the example above, it is possible to save the meaning while making the sentence shorter and therefore easier to understand, as in the following 84-word sentence:

> In addition, Member States can use a methodology to calculate the gross grant equivalent of guarantees which has been notified to the Commission under another Commission Regulation in the State aid area applicable at that time and which has been accepted by the Commission as being in line with the Guarantee Notice, or any successor notice, provided that the accepted methodology explicitly addresses the type of guarantee and the type of underlying transaction at stake in the context of the application of this Regulation. (Recital 8 of Regulation No 1408/2013)

which could be split in two as follows:

> In addition, Member States can use a methodology to calculate the gross grant equivalent of guarantees which has been notified to the Commission under another Commission Regulation in the State aid area applicable at that time and which has been accepted by the Commission as being in line with the Guarantee Notice, or any successor notice. However,

[22] European Commission (2011), p. 6.

[23] Cutts (2013), pp. 26–29.

> this is subject to the accepted methodology explicitly addressing the type of guarantee and the type of underlying transaction at stake in the context of the application of this Regulation.

Sometimes sentence length can be reduced by avoiding redundant phrases such as "the provisions of" in the following sentence:

> Member States shall provide the Commission at the end of each year with a report allowing it to monitor compliance with the provisions of Articles 2, 3, 4, and 6. (Article 7 of Directive 2008/63/EC)

The same applies to the use of *in the event that* (=if) in the following 58 words long sentence:

> any direct or indirect obligation on the licensee not to challenge the validity of intellectual property rights which the licensor holds in the common market, without prejudice to the possibility of providing for termination of the technology transfer agreement in the event that the licensee challenges the validity of one or more of the licensed intellectual property rights. (Article 5(1)(c) of Regulation No 774/2004)

The *How to write clearly* also suggests that simple words should be used "where possible" because "simple language will not make you seem less learned or elegant: it will make you more credible".[24] The guide lists some examples of complex phrases that should be avoided in favour of plainer ones, such as *the majority of (most), pursuant to (under), within the framework of (under), accordingly (so), for the purpose of (to, for), in the event of (if), concerning, regarding, relating to (on) and with regard to (about).*[25] Some of them are also redundant and their replacement with plain English equivalents would definitely favour the brevity of sentences.

All the above phrases are actually used in the corpus. Some of them are used only in a few documents (*the majority of, consequently* and *accordingly*), some are very common (*for the purpose of, in the event of, within the framework of*) and some are used in almost all the documents (*pursuant to, concerning, regarding, relating to* and *with regard to*).

A further analysis confirms that other complex phrases that plain English proponents suggest be replaced with simpler ones[26] are very common in the corpus analysed. There is a frequent use of phrases such as *in accordance with (under), in order to (to), in relation to (about, with, to), in respect of (on, about), on the part of (by), to the extent that (if, when), in pursuance of (under), by virtue of (under), as a consequence of (because), by means of (by).*

[24]European Commission (2011), p. 6.

[25]European Commission (2011), p. 6.

[26]See The A-Z of alternative words. http://www.plainenglish.co.uk/the-a-z-of-alternative-words.html. Accessed 6 Mar 2018, Rylance (2012), pp. 178–189 and Cutts (2013), pp. 36–65.

3.2 *Make Sense: Structure Your Sentences*

Plain English scholars warmly recommend using a Subject-Verb-Object syntax to make the meaning of sentences clearer and easy to grasp.[27]

We find the EU's reply to the plain English call for simple syntax in the *How to write clearly* guide, which suggests ways of "untangling the information so that readers will understand each sentence straight away".[28]

The first of the guide's recommendations on syntax is "naming the agent of each action and putting the actions in the order in which they occur",[29] as in the following sentence and the suggested rephrased version that follows:

> Its decision on allocation of EU assistance will be taken subsequent to receipt of all project application at the Award Committee's meeting.

> When all applicants have submitted their project applications, the Award Committee will meet to decide how much EU aid it will grant to each one.

The corpus analysis showed numerous hypotactic sentences with an unclear order of events, such as the following:

> The effectiveness and consistency of the application of Articles 101 and 102 TFEU by the Commission and the national competition authorities require a common approach across the Union on the disclosure of evidence that is included in the file of a competition authority. (Recital 21 of Directive 2014/104)

However, we can rephrase the sentence as follows to convey a clearer meaning:

> A common approach by Member States on the disclosure of evidence by their competition authorities would allow the Commission and the national competition authorities to apply Articles 101 and 102 TFEU in an effective and consistent manner.

The guide also suggests not burying important information in the middle of the sentence, such as in the following example found in the corpus:

> The right in Union law to compensation for harm resulting from infringements of Union and national competition law requires each Member State to have procedural rules ensuring the effective exercise of that right. (Recital 4 of Directive 2014/104)

which would be easier to read and understand as follows:

> Each Member State is required to have procedural rules ensuring the effective exercise of the right in Union Law to compensation for harm resulting from infringements of Union and national competition law.

---

[27]See in particular Rylance (2012), pp. 31–32.

[28]European Commission (2011), p. 7.

[29]European Commission (2011), p. 7.

3.3 Cut Out Excess Nouns

Plain English activists define nominalisation as "a type of abstract noun",[30] and Martin Cutts describes verbs as being "clear, crisp and lively" and giving writing "power and precision".[31]

The *How to write clearly* guide too recommends using verbs instead of nouns because they are "more direct and less abstract".[32] According to the guide, noun forms such as *by the destruction of, for the maximisation of* and *of the introduction of* would be therefore more concrete and direct in their verb forms *by destroying, of introducing* and *for maximising.*

An overuse of nominalisation is one of the most striking features found in the corpus. The following are examples of nominal forms taken from the corpus with their suggested verb alternatives in square brackets:

(1) **Upon the entry into force of the Treaty of Lisbon** [when the Treaty of Lisbon entered into force] on 1 December 2009, Articles 81 and 82 of the Treaty establishing the European Community became Articles 101 and 102 TFEU, and they remain identical in substance. (Recital 2 of Directive 2014/104, emphasis added)

(2) The Advisory Committee on State aid should be consulted before **publication of** [publishing] a draft regulation. (Recital 28 of Regulation 2015/15884, emphasis added)

(3) In view of the need to ensure coherence with the objectives of the common fisheries policy and the European Maritime and Fisheries Fund, in particular aid for **purchase of** [purchasing] fishing vessels, aid for **the modernisation** [modernising] or **replacement of** [replacing] main or ancillary engines of fishing vessels and aid to any of the ineligible operations under Regulation (EU) No 508/2014 of the European Parliament and the Council should be excluded from the scope of this Regulation. (Recital 7 of Regulation No 717/2014, emphasis added)

(4) In the first noun structure of the following example, the first part is actually a verb but the final effect is nominal. The guide defines these forms as "simply verbs in disguise":

> The Commission should receive from the Member State the necessary information to be able to **carry out the assessment of** [assess] the evaluation plan and request additional information without undue delay allowing the Member State to complete the missing elements for the Commission to **take a decision** [decide]. (Recital 8 of Regulation No 651/2014, emphasis added)

[30] How to write in plain English. http://www.plainenglish.co.uk/free-guides/60-how-to-write-in-plain-english.html. Accessed 9 Mar 2018.

[31] Cutts (2013), p. 90.

[32] European Commission (2011), p. 9.

3.4 Be Concrete, Not Abstract

According to the *How to write clearly* guide

> too much abstract language might even lead your reader to think either that you don't know what you are writing about or that your motives for writing are suspect.[33]

The guide defines abstract language as "vague and off-putting", preventing the message from being "more direct and therefore more powerful".[34]

Long before the EU institutions, George Orwell had identified insincerity as the greatest enemy of clear language, with a very effective simile:

> When there is a gap between one's real and one's declared aims, one turns as it were instinctively to long words and exhausted idioms, like a cuttlefish squirting out ink.[35]

Plain English specialists oppose the use of vague and abstract terms for the same reasons.[36] The examples of abstract nouns given by the guide (such as *eliminate, determine, employment opportunity* and *remunerated employment)* are mostly Latinate derivatives and their preferred *concrete* option *(cut out, set, job* and *paid work*) is Anglo-Saxon in origin. Hence, although it does not state it openly, the guide seems to suggest that formal English is more abstract than standard English.

The following abstract and vague words were found to be very common in the corpus: *basis*, *circumstance*, *concept*, *determine*, *element*, *eliminate*, *material*, *reasonable*, *situation*.

3.5 Beware of Jargon

Martin Cutts reminds us that even Winston Churchill found the time in 1940, amid the falling bombs, to write a memo called *Brevity*, that told his civil servants he wanted shorter, clearer, jargon-free reports.[37]

According to the *Joint practical guide* "Texts peppered with borrowed words, literal translations or jargon which is hard to understand are the source of much of the criticism of Union law, and result in it being regarded as alien".[38]

The *Fight the fog* guide only allows for Eurojargon words or phrases specifically

> coined to describe European Union inventions and concepts which have no exact parallel at national level

[33]European Commission (2011), p. 9.
[34]European Commission (2011), p. 9.
[35]Orwell (1946), p. 262.
[36]Abstract terms "leave an escape route for the unforeseen", Rylance (2012), p. 38.
[37]Cutts (2013), pp. 22–23.
[38]European Union (2015), p. 19.

such as *subsidiarity, codecision, convergence, economic and social cohesion.* This would leave "few real excuses for using Eurospeak".[39]

The *How to write clearly* guide devotes a full chapter to the topic, in which it suggests avoiding jargon unless the documents containing it are only read by "any group of insiders or specialists to communicate with each other".[40]

The guide also suggests explaining the jargon which cannot be avoided when used for the first time or adding a glossary, hyperlink or reference to one of the websites providing explanations for it.[41]

Some of the main jargon expressions quoted by the guide with relevant plain explanations are *acceding country (=country about to join the EU), candidate country (=country still negotiating to join the EU), cohesion (=approach aimed at reducing social and economic disparities within the EU), enlargement (=expansion of the EU to include new members, mainstreaming (=taking into account in all EU policies),* and *subsidiarity (=principle that, wherever possible, decisions must be taken at the level of government closest to citizens).*

Proportionality is found in almost all the corpus legislation. Less frequent but still present are *cohesion, enlargement* and *subsidiarity.*

Other jargon words and phrases used in the corpus are *actor, apply, approximate/approximation, coherent, common, competence, cross- ,border, de minimis aid, derogation, EEA countries, enlargement, enter into force, entrepreneur, ex ante, ex post, fisheries, governance, implement, innovation/innovative, internal market, legislative, liable to, Member State, methodologies, human capital, mission modalities, officials, outermost regions, premium, proportionality, provisions, public procurement, resources, social dialogue, state aid, subsidiarity, transparent, transpose, union.*[42]

Some of the above words and phrases are also challenged because of their French influence (in particular *actor, cohesion, enlargement, premium, social dialogue, state aid)* and some because they are Latin (see next paragraph).

3.6 Avoid *Here-/There-* Adverbs

The 2018 *English style guide*, which is generally more prudent than the other publications on plain language (see Sect. 2), suggests that *here-* and *there-* adverbs should be avoided where possible because of their archaic and extremely formal nature. There is no mention of these adverbs in any other EU official plain English guide.

[39]Directorate-General for Translation (European Commission) (1998), p. 11.

[40]Directorate-General for Translation (European Commission) (2011), p. 11.

[41]European Commission (2011), p. 11.

[42]For their preferred alternatives see http://ec.europa.eu/ipg/content/tips/words-style/jargon-alternativesen.htm.

The only *here-* adverb found in the corpus is *hereby*, used in the following example with a deictic function:

> Pursuant to Article 81(3) of the Treaty and subject to the provisions of this Regulation, it is hereby declared that Article 81(1) of the Treaty shall not apply to technology transfer agreements entered into between two undertakings permitting the production of contract products. (Article 2 of Regulation No 772/2004)

The use of *hereby* in the above sentence has no particular semantic purpose and the whole clause *it is hereby declared that* could therefore be omitted.

There- adverbs are much more common in the corpus, especially *thereof* (used in 20 documents out of 21), but also *thereby, thereafter, therein* and *therefor.*

They are mainly used for extra-textual reference purposes, as shown by the following examples:

(1) Having regard to the Treaty establishing the European Community, and in particular Article 86(3) **thereof**... (Preamble of Directive 2006/111, emphasis added)

(2) The full effectiveness of Articles 101 and 102 TFEU, and in particular the practical effect of the prohibitions laid down **therein**... (Recital 3 of Directive 2014/104, emphasis added)

However, their function is sometimes anaphoric:

(3) In order to qualify for immunity from or reduction of the fine which would otherwise be imposed, undertakings shall provide the Commission with voluntary presentations of their knowledge of a secret cartel and their role **therein** (Article 4*a*(2) of Regulation No 773/2004, emphasis added)

(4) In certain circumstances, however, such as where the parties agree not to carry out other research and development in the same field, **thereby** forgoing the opportunity of gaining competitive advantages over the other parties, such agreements may fall within Article 101(1) of the Treaty and should therefore be included within the scope of this Regulation. (Recital 6 of Regulation No 1217/2010, emphasis added)

Plain English theorists suggest that these adverbs should always be replaced by explicit mention of the intra or extra-textual element they refer to, or other shorter and plainer deictic equivalent, as shown in the following simplified versions of the above sentences:

(1) Having regard to the Treaty establishing the European Community, and in particular Article 86(3)...

(2) The full effectiveness of Articles 101 and 102 TFEU, and in particular the practical effect of the prohibitions **they lay down**...

(3) In order to qualify for immunity from or reduction of the fine which would otherwise be imposed, undertakings shall provide the Commission with voluntary presentations of their knowledge of a secret cartel and their role **in it**...

(4) In certain circumstances, however, such as where the parties agree not to carry out other research and development in the same field, **thus** forgoing the opportunity of gaining competitive advantages over the other parties, such agreements

may fall within Article 101(1) of the Treaty and should therefore be included within the scope of this Regulation.

As pointed out in Sect. 2, the 2018 *English style guide* is once again ambiguous on its position about the use of the above adverbs, allowing for a general, unspecified possibility that the addressees of the guide might find them indispensable. I believe the only case in which the guide might find them appropriate is when they occur in already long sentences, because their simplified equivalent clauses would make the text even longer. However, none of the above examples justifies their use on these grounds.

3.7 Avoid Latin

All the non-EU plain English guidelines quoted in this chapter suggest avoiding Latin in modern legal texts.[43]

According to the *English style guide*, the use of Latin should be limited as much as possible

> as even common phrases are often misused or misunderstood

and

> translators should check whether Latin phrases have the same currency and meaning when used in English.[44]

The guide also quotes examples of preferable English equivalents of Latin expressions such as *per diem*.

The *Joint practical guide* is more cautious in its position towards the use of Latin, limiting itself to discouraging recourse to "certain Latin expressions used in a sense other than their generally accepted legal meaning".[45]

The corpus shows a preference for the following Latin expressions:

(1) *per (=a, an, by or each in plain English),* used in particular in the phrases *per journey, per day, per beneficiary, per Member State, per year;*
(2) *e.g. (=for example);*
(3) *i.e. (=that is);*
(4) *ad hoc (=special, for this specific purpose);*
(5) *inter alia (=among other things);*
(6) *a fortiori (=for a stronger reason, with even greater reason);*
(7) *bona fide (=genuine, in good faith);*
(8) *de facto (=in fact, in reality, in effect, actual);*

[43]Rylance (2012), p. 40, in particular, finds that it "may have historical roots but has no justification in modern practice".

[44]European Commission (2018), p. 42.

[45]European Union (2015), p. 18.

(9) *infra (=below);*
(10) *mutatis mutandis (=with the necessary changes);*
(11) *prima facie (=at first glance, at first sight);*
(12) *via (=by, through, using);*
(13) *de minimis (=minimum);*
(14) *ex ante (=upstream, prior, advance);*
(15) *ex post (=downstream, subsequent).*

3.8 Prefer Active Verbs to Passive

Plain English experts believe that choosing to highlight the object by omitting the subject of a sentence may prevent clear understanding and exclude important information. Therefore, they suggest limiting the use of passive as much as possible, except when it is vital to

(i) avoid being too straightforward
(ii) when the subject of a sentence is understood, unknown, irrelevant or secret
(iii) to have readers focus on the object rather than the subject of a sentence
(iv) any time you wish to underline the result of an action.[46]

Both the *How to write clearly*[47] and the *Fight the fog*[48] guides give basically the same recommendations about the use of passive and its admitted exceptions. They insist on the level of accountability implied in naming the agent, which is also useful for those translators who work with languages that do not admit the same impersonal tone as English.

The *Fight the fog* guide also allows for the use of *I* and *we*, even in technical documents (which would be unacceptable in Italian), or making an inanimate object the agent of a sentence.

Basically, both plain English theorists and the EU guidelines encourage the use of the active form when the agent is known and not implicit and there is no focus on the object rather than the subject.

Therefore, the active form should be preferred in the following sentence and in many other passive constructions found in the corpus, in which *Member States* seems to be the unspecified but easily to be inferred agent:

> Articles 101 and 102 of the Treaty on the Functioning of the European Union (TFEU) are a matter of public policy and **should be applied** effectively throughout the Union (Recital 1 of Directive 2014/104, emphasis added)

The same applies to the next sentences, where the agent *an area* and *the parties* is even easier to identify and there seems to be no focus requirement:

---

[46]Di Renzo Villata et al. (2017), p. 7.

[47]European Commission (2011), p. 10.

[48]Directorate-General for Translation (European Commission) (1998), p. 15.

> In accordance with Article 26(2) TFEU, the internal market comprises an area without internal frontiers in which the free movement of goods, persons, services and capital **is ensured**. (Recital 7 of Directive 2014/104, emphasis added)

> This Regulation should cover only technology transfer agreements between a licensor and a licensee. It should cover such agreements even if **conditions are stipulated** for more than one level of trade, by, for instance, requiring the licensee to set up a particular distribution system and specifying the obligations the licensee must or may impose on resellers of the products produced under the licence. (Recital 19 of Regulation 772/2014, emphasis added)

3.9 *Shall*

The modal verb *shall* is very common in legal texts, especially if drafted in "legalese" style. Its use is frequent in EU acts too and plain English theorists within the EU have never challenged it.

On the contrary, plain English theorists outside the EU have long identified the use of *shall* in legal texts as formal and unfamiliar.

It is possible to identify the following main differences:

(1) ***Shall*** is used as positive imperative in enacting terms (obligation or requirement) in EU legislation[49]:

Member States ***shall*** *ensure that any natural or legal person who has suffered harm caused by an infringement of competition law. . . .*

Plain English prefers ***must*** to ***shall*** for positive imperative functions:

A party to an agreement who makes an application ***must*** *take all reasonable steps to notify all other parties to the agreement of whom he is aware (UK Competition Act 1998).*

(2) ***Shall not*** is used as negative imperative (prohibition) in the EU acts[50]:

Full compensation under this Directive ***shall not*** *lead to overcompensation.*

"Must not" is preferred for prohibition purposes in Plain English.

(3) ***Shall*** is used for future reference in the EU acts[51]:

This Regulation ***shall*** *enter into force on . . .*

Plain English prefers ***will*** to ***shall*** for future reference:

This Act ***will*** *enter into force on . . .*

[49]European Commission (2018), p. 47.

[50]European Commission (2018), p. 47.

[51]European Commission (2018), p. 48.

4 Conclusion

The analysis of the corpus described in this article shows that there is still a gap between the EU's declared aim to simplify its language and the implementation of its official guidelines. One of the reasons may be the older tradition of plain English outside the EU but we cannot deduce that the future trends within the European institutions will be towards plainer language. Brexit, in particular, will deprive the EU of the support of a country where plain English is particularly encouraged.

Another reason for being sceptical about the future implementation of plain English within the EU is the lack of a clear engagement by the European institutions. The cautiously vehement tone of their guidelines explains the partial observance of the same. This hesitation is well reflected in the *English style guide*'s admission of *here-/there-* adverbs with the words "if you feel you must use",[52] which create strong cognitive dissonance in readers.

There are even reasons to contest the legitimacy of these disclaimers: the *English style guide*'s authors' admission of the difficulty of writing in clear language at the Commission due to the complexity of the subject matter should be a reason to write even clearly and not an excuse to do the reverse.

The differences set out in the chapter between the official plain English guidelines and the EU's implementation of the same is another clear indication of the EU's initial and current intentions. The European Union does not challenge the use of *shall* nor does it officially discourage the use of foreign words, including Latin. The overuse of Latinate (or other foreign language) derivatives instead of Anglo-Saxon ones is maybe the legalese characteristic that plain English experts have always most fiercely contested by and there is no mention of this feature in any EU publication.

The Plain English Campaign's Founder-Director, Chrissie Maher's 1998 speech to the European Commission contains both an appreciation of the EU's past efforts in favour of plain language and an acknowledgement of its big challenge ahead:

> My dream is that there will be a jargon-free European community, where every word which flows from the EC will be understood by people like me. . . .When I told one of my friends that I had been invited by you to help 'Fight the FOG', she said 'they might as well have asked you to knit it'. . . .But seriously, I don't share her pessimism. I am heartened by your efforts to tackle the problem. I'm here in good faith to tell you how big I believe the problem is, and what we can do together to fight this man-made mist. . . ..Well, you've got a pretty tough job on your hands really.[53]

Although the efforts are "heartening", the "fog" is still very thick and we can only hope that future EU leaders will find more effective weapons to fight it.

---

[52]European Commission (2018), p. 44.

[53]Chrissie Maher's speech to the European Commission. http://www.plainenglish.co.uk. Accessed 23 Feb 2018.

References

Chaucer G (2008) The Canterbury tales. Oxford University Press, Oxford

Cutts M (2013) The plain English guide. Oxford University Press, Oxford

Di Renzo Villata M, Grasso A, Cadel G, Buzzi R (2017) Legal English. CEDAM, Padova

Directorate-General for Translation (European Commission) (1998) Fight the Fog, How to write clearly. http://www.au.af.mil/au/awc/awcgate/eu/fight_the_fog_en.pdf. Accessed 10 Mar 2018

European Commission (2011) How to write clearly. Publications office of the European Union, Luxembourg. https://publications.europa.eu/en/publication-detail/-/publication/c2dab20c-0414-408d-87b5-dd3c6e5dd9a5/language-en. Accessed 23 Feb 2018

European Commission (2018) English style guide. https://ec.europa.eu/info/sites/info/files/styleguideenglishdgten.pdf. Accessed 10 Mar 2018

European Union (2015) Joint practical guide of the European Parliament, the Council and the Commission for the persons involved in the drafting of the European Union legislation. Publications office of the European Union, Luxembourg. http://eur-lex.europa.eu/content/techleg/EN-legislative-drafting-guide.pdf. Accessed 28 Feb 2018

Gowers E (1954) The complete plain words. Her Majesty's Stationery Office, London

Orwell G (1946) Politics and the English language. Horizon 76:252–265

Redish JC (1985) The plain English movement. In: Greenbaum S (ed) The English Language today. Pergamon Press, New York, pp 125–138

Rylance P (2012) Legal writing & drafting. Oxford University Press, New York

Arianna Grasso is Legal English Professor and Translator in Milan, Italy.

r's authorised representative in the EU is Springer
Service Centre GmbH, Europaplatz 3, 69115 Heidelberg,
ve any concerns regarding our products, please
ty@springernature.com

CPI Group (UK) Ltd, Croydon, CR0 4YY
05/10/2026
2228138-0014